Worksheet Commands

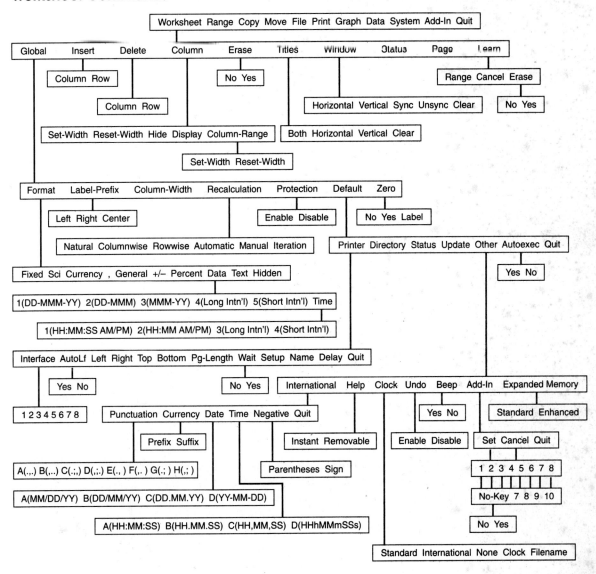

- Worksheet Range Copy Move File Print Graph Data System Add-In Quit
  - Global Insert Delete Column Erase Titles Window Status Page Learn
    - Format Label-Prefix Column-Width Recalculation Protection Default Zero
      - Fixed Sci Currency , General +/– Percent Date Text Hidden
        - 1(DD-MMM-YY) 2(DD-MMM) 3(MMM-YY) 4(Long Intn'l) 5(Short Intn'l) Time
          - 1(HH:MM:SS AM/PM) 2(HH:MM AM/PM) 3(Long Intn'l) 4(Short Intn'l)
      - Left Right Center
      - Natural Columnwise Rowwise Automatic Manual Iteration
      - Enable Disable
      - No Yes Label
      - Printer Directory Status Update Other Autoexec Quit
        - Interface AutoLf Left Right Top Bottom Pg-Length Wait Setup Name Delay Quit
          - 1 2 3 4 5 6 7 8
          - Yes No
          - No Yes
        - Yes No
        - International Help Clock Undo Beep Add-In Expanded Memory
          - Punctuation Currency Date Time Negative Quit
            - A(.,.) B(,..) C(.;,) D(,;.) E(.,) F(,.) G(.;) H(,;)
            - Prefix Suffix
            - A(MM/DD/YY) B(DD/MM/YY) C(DD.MM.YY) D(YY-MM-DD)
            - A(HH:MM:SS) B(HH.MM.SS) C(HH,MM,SS) D(HHhMMmSSs)
            - Parentheses Sign
          - Instant Removable
          - Standard International None Clock Filename
          - Enable Disable
          - Yes No
          - Set Cancel Quit
            - 1 2 3 4 5 6 7 8
              - No-Key 7 8 9 10
                - No Yes
          - Standard Enhanced
    - Column Row
    - Column Row
    - Set-Width Reset-Width Hide Display Column-Range
      - Set-Width Reset-Width
    - No Yes
    - Both Horizontal Vertical Clear
    - Horizontal Vertical Sync Unsync Clear
    - Range Cancel Erase
      - No Yes

DECISION MAKING USING LOTUS 1-2-3

Building Quality Applications

Donald Amoroso
University of Colorado,
Colorado Springs

Mitchell McGRAW-HILL
New York St. Louis San Francisco Auckland Bogotá Caracas
Lisbon London Madrid Mexico Milan Montreal New Delhi Paris
San Juan Singapore Sydney Tokyo Toronto Watsonville

Mitchell **McGRAW-HILL**
Watsonville, CA 95076

DECISION MAKING USING LOTUS 1-2-3
Building Quality Applications

1 2 3 4 5 6 7 8 9 0 DOH DOH 9 0 9 8 7 6 5 4 3

ISBN 0-07-001574-0

Sponsoring editor:	*Erika Berg*
Editorial assistant:	*Jennifer Gilliland*
Technical reviewer:	*Karen Loch*
Director of production:	*Jane Somers*
Production assistant:	*Richard DeVitto*
Project manager:	*Merrill Peterson, Matrix Productions*
Interior designers:	*Michael Rogondino, John Edeen*
Cover designer:	*Michael Rogondino*
Compositor:	*Arizona Publication Service*
Printer and binder:	*R.R. Donnelley & Sons*

Library of Congress Card Catalog No. 91-62259

Brief Contents

Detailed Contents

Preface to the Instructor

Lotus 1-2-3 is the most popular spreadsheet on the market. It has revolutionized the way we conduct business analyses, enabling us to more easily develop worksheets, graph data, conduct what-if analyses, test sensitivities, and build custom menus.

Most Lotus 1-2-3 books focus on teaching keystrokes. However, students need to understand more than which keys to push to achieve each function of Lotus 1-2-3. *Employers expect graduates to also have the what-if analysis skills needed to make informed decisions and solve complex business problems.*

Decision Making Using Lotus 1-2-3: Building Quality Applications prepares students to satisfy this demand. It is designed for use in a spreadsheet course devoted to teaching students how to use Lotus 1-2-3 to enhance decision making, or can be used as a lab supplement in a Management Information Systems course or a Decision Support/Expert Systems course.

Distinguishing Features

The following features differentiate ***Decision Making Using Lotus 1-2-3: Building Quality Applications***.

Decision Support System Methodology

A decision support system (DSS) represents the total integration of data, models, and a user interface. ***Decision Making Using Lotus 1-2-3*** shows how to build a DSS using 1-2-3. *Once students have built the DSS, they learn how to interact with it to analyze and solve a wide range of business problems.* This DSS methodology supports the way students actually learn software: by mastering keystrokes as needed to solve a particular problem.

Balancing Tools with Methods and Techniques

"Finally!" one reviewer said, "a software tutorial that encourages my students to think." Part 1 covers the basics of 1-2-3: commands, formulas, and how to set up a worksheet. Part 2 demonstrates how to develop each component of a DSS. Table 1.1 illustrates how every chapter in the text addresses *why* underlying concepts are important, *what* important features and techniques relate to 1-2-3 concepts, and *how* 1-2-3 can be exploited to enhance decision making. *Balancing the what, why, and how, students learn to focus on the goal of developing each worksheet before lunging for the keys.*

Integrated Case Study

A single case that reflects the goals of an actual business weaves through every chapter in the text. Spreadsheet development methods are illustrated throughout Part 1; DSS development techniques, throughout Part 2. *The integrated case gives students an opportunity to act as active decision makers.* Working within this real world environment students confront and solve a variety of business problems using 1-2-3, problems in accounting, finance, production, and marketing. 1-2-3 screen displays illustrate each of the important steps taken to manage their data and conduct what-if analyses.

Emphasis on Building Quality Applications

Students lacking business experience tend to overlook the potentially devastating consequences of a carelessly conceived spreadsheet. Incorrect data or a dysfunctional spreadsheet design can distort the perceptions of, for example, an organization's profitability and prompt a poor decision. On the other hand, *a well-developed spreadsheet can empower users to react to a problem or opportunity quickly and effectively*. Quality is emphasized throughout the text in three ways:

1. **Hint sections** highlight time-saving techniques for developing effective spreadsheets, and appear in the margins in each chapter.
2. A **Quality Assurance Checklist** concludes each chapter, summarizing the key issues involving quality addressed.
3. **Practicing Good Spreadsheet Hygiene** (Chapter 5), is dedicated to setting up worksheets that can be continually improved as a problem evolves.

Learning Aids

Each chapter contains numerous screen displays to monitor student progress. Concluding each chapter are Review Questions, Skill Building Activities, Hands-On Exercises, and Problem Solving Projects, as described below.

- **Review Questions** are open-ended to stimulate critical thinking and classroom discussion.
- **Skill Building Activities** lead students step by step through the commands and techniques needed to develop a worksheet for the integrated case study. Concepts are reinforced with 1-2-3 screen displays.
- **Hands-On Exercises** give students an opportunity to practice and reinforce their understanding of 1-2-3 keystrokes and functions.

- **Problem Solving Projects** are comprehensive and designed to challenge students' problem solving skills while reinforcing key concepts in the chapter.

Instructor Support

The comprehensive **Instructor's Manual** provides Teaching Tips, Answers to Review Questions, additional Exercises and Projects. The Instructor's Manual comes with a 3 1/2" IBM **Instructor's Solutions on Disk.**

Acknowledgments

Thanks to all of my colleagues at the University of Colorado and students who helped shape this text. Students in my undergraduate and MBA classes over the last four years patiently endured a variety of incomplete manuscripts in order to learn how to build decision support systems using 1-2-3. I especially want to thank my students Michelle Carr, Lisa Jordan, Renee Steeve, and Laura Placido.

A special thanks to the following teachers who reviewed the manuscript and provided invaluable suggestions for improvements:

Gary Armstrong, Shippenburg University

William Bullers, University of New Mexico

Jim Davies, DeAnza College

Mike Harris, Del Mar College

Roger Hayen, Central Michigan University

Thom Luce, Ohio University

Wally Lui, Fresno State University

Elizabeth Magalski, Marquette University

Anne McClanahan, Ohio University

Priscilla McGill, Rogue Community College

Robert McGlinn, Southern Illinois University

John Melrose, University of Wisconsin, Eau Claire

Jeffrey Moore, Stanford University

Marilyn Meyer, Fresno City College

Beverly Oswalt, University of Central Arkansas

Z. Przansnyski, Loyola Marymount University

Jill Smith, University of Denver

James Teng, University of Pittsburgh

Merrill Warkentin, Bryant College

Thank you, Karen Loch, Georgia State University, my technical reviewer, for providing specialized and hard-hitting comments on the manuscript. A special thanks to Erika Berg, Senior Editor, for all her encouragement, insightful suggestions, sense of timing, and especially her patience throughout this project. I also am grateful to Jennifer Gilliland and Denise Nickeson, editorial assistants at Mitchell McGraw-Hill.

Most of all, I want to thank my wife, Mysha, and children Jonathan, Joshua, and Joelle for their support and sense of reality in this much-too-busy world.

Don Amoroso
University of Colorado
Colorado Springs

Decision Making Using Lotus 1-2-3

Building Quality Applications

CHAPTER

What This Book Is All About

We know a thing when we understand it.

—*George Berkeley*

Objectives

- Understand the use of the electronic spreadsheet in business.
- Understand how rapidly the business environment is changing.
- Grasp the nature of decision making and the systems that support it.
- Know the criteria for developing quality spreadsheets.

Electronic Spreadsheets in Business

You make important decisions every day. And for each decision you need to make, you probably have more data than you know what to do with. But do you use that data in such a way that you make *effective* decisions? Spreadsheet software can improve your ability to take a large number of facts and convert them into meaningful comparisons, graphs, and trends. With spreadsheet software, you can use the power of your computer to support your decision-making processes.

Lotus 1-2-3 is one of the most popular spreadsheet packages on the market. With Lotus 1-2-3 you can build computer-based applications, called **decision support systems**, to better understand the problem you want to solve. The role of modeling is critical to creating and evaluating business opportunities. This is a book about learning how to use Lotus 1-2-3 to make more effective decisions.

In a recent Computerworld survey, almost 96 percent of the managers surveyed said they used electronic spreadsheets to conduct some sort of business analysis. The good news is that spreadsheets are easy to use. Spreadsheet packages make a variety of analyses easier to conduct. The bad news, however, is that a lot of users build models and then use them to make important decisions without ever having learned how to distinguish a good model from a bad one.

Maybe you have heard of what-if analysis. When you conduct **what-if analyses**, you examine a number of different scenarios in order to explore the decision environment. What-if scenarios provide a richer look at the overall picture. These scenarios help you to discover trends and to quickly identify problems.

Electronic spreadsheets are equipped with many built-in functions. Graphing and publishing capabilities are embedded into today's electronic spreadsheets so that you can see the changes in your data. A good graph is even more effective than a table if it communicates information in a clear and concise manner.

Another built-in function is the use of formulas that allow you to change values. As soon as you change a value, the formula automatically recalculates the results. This means you can view the problem you are attempting to solve from several perspectives before you develop a creative solution.

The real power of the electronic spreadsheet lies in its capabilities for tailoring your applications to your needs and requirements. It does this with the use of menus and prompts.

This chapter provides you with an overall framework for using Lotus 1-2-3 to enhance your decision making. We will examine (1) the dynamic business environment, (2) the decision-making processes that we all go through, (3) the systems that support our decision-making processes, and (4) the importance of building quality into those systems.

The Dynamic Business Environment

In the business environment, you are inundated with data from all sources, including some data that may be critical to a decision you need to make. Data is not knowledge, and only knowledge contributes to effective decision making. To make effective decisions, you must absorb an ever-increasing body of data and transform it into meaningful information. Your computer can help you make sense of all of that data so that the gap between data and information can be closed. Decision support systems (DSS) give you that capability.

With the computer-based tools of today, your effectiveness in making decisions can be radically improved. Managers reportedly have developed more applications with electronic spreadsheets than with any other DSS tool. These applications have supported strategic initiatives rather than merely crunching more data. Today managers are using spreadsheet applications to change the entire direction of their organizations. These applications are vital to the strategic positioning of the organizations using them.

One example of a strategic spreadsheet application is the development of a pharmaceutical database. At Anequest, one sales manager with a laptop became more effective in the field after he used Lotus 1-2-3 to create a two-dimensional database of all pharmaceutical products. Within a year, the firm implemented a program equipping all salespersons with laptops and an enhanced Lotus application to more effectively and accurately assist them in the field. One manager with the proper DSS tools can change an organization's way of doing business and improve its bottom-line measures.

The Decision-Making Process

As a businessperson, you must make countless decisions every day. Although many of those decisions are routine, they are essential to the smooth and successful operation of the firm. People groping for solutions to problems often do not realize that they will go through a series of steps before deciding on a course of action. Decision support systems must support the decision-making process if they are to be useful to you. **Decision making** is a process that involves collecting information, weighing it, evaluating it, searching for alternatives, and then choosing among the alternatives. Let's look at the decision-making process step by step.

1. **Identify the problem.** You first need to be aware that a problem exists. Often the symptoms of a problem are evident long before their cause is recognized.

2. **Define the problem.** You carefully consider the stated objectives, the variables that impact the decision, the constraints, and the benefit stream that may result from the decision.

3. **Collect and analyze the data.** You collect data to develop a model that takes all of the problems into account. The data can be external as well as internal to the firm. You can analyze the data by using a variety of techniques.

4. **Develop a model.** You use a model to analyze the data and generate alternatives. Often that model is actually in the mind of the decision maker rather than on paper or in a computer. You need to explicitly identify variable relationships and then create model statements or formulas.

5. **Generate alternatives.** You generate a variety of solution alternatives, taking into account several problem characteristics, such as project size, scope, and risk.

6. **Make a decision and implement it.** Finally, you must choose an alternative that meets all or most of your requirements. You may find it helpful to use a weighting or ranking scheme in making your decision.

Figure 1.1 summarizes the decision-making phases. Some feedback loops may extend from some of the phases back to previous phases. For example, after you have collected and analyzed the data, you may decide to redefine the problem and then collect additional data. Your analysis will invariably lead to additional data collection and further analyses.

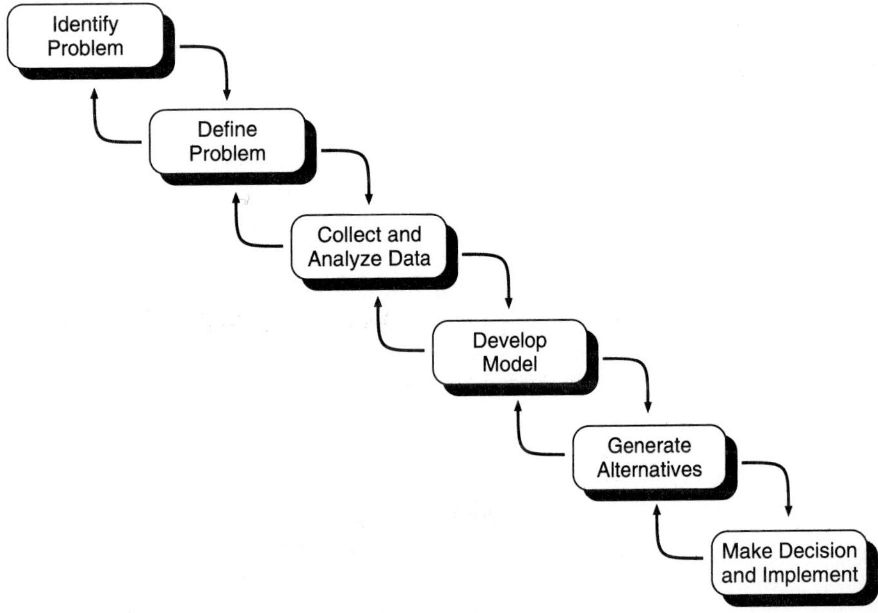

Figure 1.1
Phases in the Decision-Making Process

Systems to Support Decision Making

A decision support system (DSS) supports the phases of the decision-making process. A DSS must be interactive so that you can talk to it, in a sense. Electronic spreadsheets encourage you to make important value judgments based on the relevant data that is modeled within the DSS. Lotus 1-2-3 is a DSS shell—a decision support system program from which any number of useful applications can be built. A **DSS shell** is a flexible tool that supports decision-making. Its capabilities include managing data and displaying graphics.

If we were to examine the decision support systems that have been built in Lotus 1-2-3, we would find three major components: (1) a place to store and manage data (a database), (2) models that describe the relationships of those data (a model base), and (3) menus and commands from which the user interacts with the system (a user interface). Figure 1.2 illustrates the typical decision support system. When linked together for a specific purpose, the three components form a DSS application that can be used for decision making.

Component 1: Database

The **database** is a place where the data are stored. The programs or the part of the spreadsheet program that manages these data is called the **database management system** (DBMS). Usually, spreadsheet programs contain a very simple DBMS. Data that reside in the database will include, first of all, data that are captured at their source, also called transaction data. Examples of business data that reside in a spreadsheet program include income, expenses, payroll, and accounting data. Other internal and external data should also be available for analysis in the decision support system.

Component 2: Model Base

The **model base** is a collection of models developed and stored in the DSS. The model base enables the decision maker to conduct analysis. Models contain formulas that show relationships between and among the data variables. The Lotus 1-2-3 program, a DSS shell, provides many simple model building blocks or functions useful in building formulas. You can build many different types of models by using DSS shells. One example of a model is the cash flow for a company for the past 12 months.

Component 3: User Interface

The **user interface** is the part of the DSS in which you directly interact with the system, usually by the use of menus and commands. The user interface should be powerful and yet flexible enough to provide for a variety of needs. Some users like to pull down menus; others prefer commands. You can write

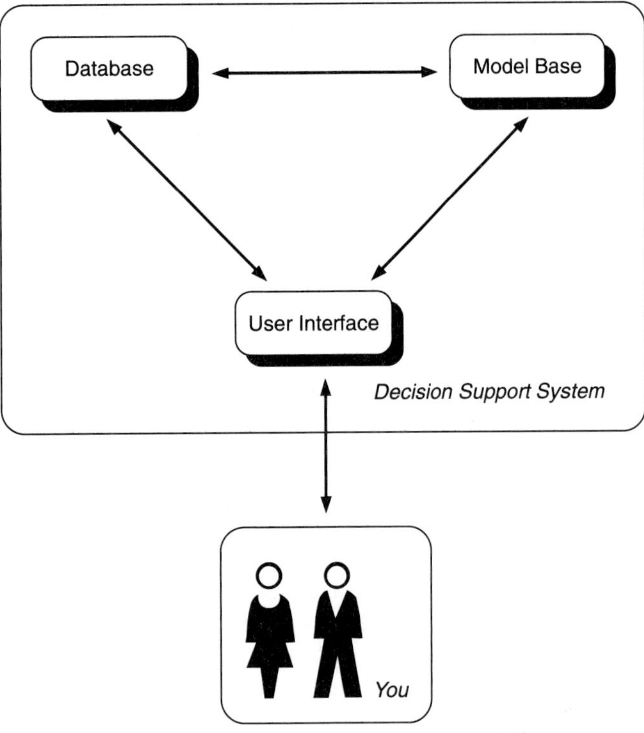

Figure 1.2
Components of a Decision Support System

statements, called macros, which tell the program how to run. Lotus 1-2-3 macros give you a powerful capability for creating a custom user interface.

How the user interface is built will, of course, depend on how well you know how to use Lotus 1-2-3. Unsophisticated Lotus 1-2-3 users can interact with customized Lotus macro menus instead of with the traditional 1-2-3 menus, which require a knowledge of Lotus 1-2-3 commands. Actually, Lotus 1-2-3 commands are easy to learn, even for less sophisticated users. But when a complex problem is being addressed, all types of users find it easier to interact with an interface that has been developed.

Building Quality into an Application

HINT: Worksheet developers should assess the quality of their applications.

Building a "quality" application becomes critical when a decision hinges on its output. In general, **quality** is defined as something of "high grade," superiority, or excellence, or as an accomplishment or the attainment of a goal. Quality must be reflected in the bottom line if you are going to invest your time and effort in developing your own applications. The bottom line is that the spreadsheet application must effectively improve decision making; otherwise the development effort will prove to be a waste of time.

HINT: Making sense of the data is the reason why we are using 1-2-3 to analyze problems.

How can you ensure quality when building a decision support system? You can use the following criteria for evaluating the quality of a spreadsheet application. First, you need a decision support tool that gives you access to all the data that are relevant to the decision in question. When you have a lot of data to analyze, you may often find it difficult to understand the complete picture. Second, once the data are available, you need a decision support tool that will make sense of the data. A spreadsheet application must therefore provide a comprehensive set of analysis techniques. It must give more experienced users the freedom to develop sophisticated applications. To do this, electronic spreadsheets must be able to accommodate the need for commands and menus. Third, a decision support tool should give you the capability of conducting a variety of analyses. In other words, the application must be flexible. Often, the results of one analysis will lead to another analysis. You should be able to query the data with models in the broadest number of ways. Finally, you should find the decision support tool easy to use. Help screens, menus, and English-based commands often enable users to adopt new DSS tools. Lotus 1-2-3 is a good example of a DSS shell that is user-friendly because it gives novice users a quick entry into simple application development.

Now let's look at quality from the opposite perspective. What problems should you avoid? Earlier in this chapter we discussed how electronic spreadsheets can provide users with a great deal of analytical power for decision making. Many businesspeople who use electronic spreadsheets to aid their decision making reportedly have had little experience in using computers. The less experience you have had in using Lotus 1-2-3, the greater your risk of low-quality applications.

You may find some spreadsheets that have unreliable output and some mistakes in logic. Obviously, you would not want to base an important decision on a decision support tool that has faulty data or incorrect formulas. You should examine your spreadsheet applications for three characteristics: (1) reliability, (2) auditability, and (3) modifiability. **Reliability** is the degree to which the spreadsheet generated output is correct. This will, in turn, affect the degree of confidence you place in the model. **Auditability** is the ability to retrace the steps followed in the generation of the spreadsheet results. The question you must answer here is, Can you determine how the key numbers you are using to make a decision got there? **Modifiability** is the ability to change or enhance the spreadsheet to meet dynamic changes in the business environment. Do you know how to change the numbers in your application now that the world has changed?

You must keep these potential problems in mind as you learn a variety of spreadsheet development techniques and keystrokes in Lotus 1-2-3. Errors caused by poor design could be disastrous to effective decision making. To avoid these errors, you must use development techniques that yield quality applications. In summary, you should try to develop a spreadsheet that (1) produces accurate and consistent output, (2) can be audited to determine the validity of the results, and (3) can be modified easily without introducing errors.

What This Book Is All About

In this book we will discuss a variety of techniques that yield quality spreadsheet applications. Your goal is to support and enhance decision making by using Lotus 1-2-3 to develop quality spreadsheet applications. The range of business problems that can be modeled using Lotus 1-2-3 is extensive. We will, however, examine the decisions that one company faces. This is a real firm with real problems. By exploring the key issues, we will learn more about developing and using Lotus 1-2-3 to support decision making.

Throughout this book we will distinguish between methods, techniques, and tools. Table 1.1 concisely summarizes the methods, techniques, and tools that will be emphasized in each chapter. **Methods** are the underlying concepts that enable us to build spreadsheet applications. Methods describe the procedures needed to develop systems that support decision making. Methods also show us *why* underlying concepts are important. **Techniques** are the activities that help us develop a portion of the decision support system, such as the model base, during a particular phase of development. Techniques show us *what* we need to do. **Tools** are the parts of the Lotus 1-2-3 program that we must use to build our applications. Tools show us *how* to carry out the development.

Managerial users are able to conduct analysis because they use:

> A toolkit packed with a variety of spreadsheet functions (tools) and managerial models (techniques), all under the umbrella of good development guidelines (methods).

This book is divided into two sections. Part 1 focuses primarily on worksheet development methods, while Part 2 concentrates on DSS development techniques. In Part 1 you are introduced to the Lotus 1-2-3 worksheet, commands, formulas, and good development methods. If you are unfamiliar with Lotus 1-2-3, you can build your skills by completing the exercises and problems in Part 1. Part 2 is devoted to developing a working, effective decision support system. This material is what we are working toward. By the time you have completed all the exercises and activities in this book, you should find it easy to develop a decision support system that will handle a variety of business problems.

All of the chapters in this book address decision-making issues in a similar way. You are introduced to the critical activities, and then given "Hint" boxes as guidelines throughout each chapter, as well as a quality assurance checklist to assess the work you have performed. You will probably benefit more from this book by working through the case in each chapter.

In summary, this book is about *enhanced capabilities*:

1. For conducting decision analysis in the business environment
2. For supporting decisions with electronic spreadsheet tools
3. For developing models that allow for a variety of analysis

This book is about improving your productivity with computers.

Table 1.1 Decision Making Using Lotus 1-2-3

Chapter	WHY underlying concepts/methods are important	WHAT important features/techniques of Lotus 1-2-3 relate to concepts	HOW can 1-2-3 tools be used to enhance decision-making/ productivity
1 What This Book Is All About	Computer-based tools can be used to provide support for decision making.		
Part 1 - Spreadsheet Development Methods			
2 Working with the Components of a Spreadsheet	Electronic spreadsheets open the door for analysis and critical problem solving.	Worksheet screen	Rows, columns, control panel, status indicators
		The cell and range	Cell pointer, value, label, formulas
		Moving around	Cursor movement keys, function keys
		Important features	Automatic recalculation, worksheet linking, presentation of results/ customization
3 Invoking Spreadsheet Commands	Knowledge of 1-2-3 commands is an important first step in building effective, dynamic models.	Range commands	Formatting, erasing, searching, protecting, naming
		Copy and Move commands	Relative/absolute addressing
		Worksheet commands	Inserting columns/rows, opening a window, changing global settings
		File commands	Default directory, retrieving and saving a file
		Print commands	Setting a range, options, align, and go
		Other 1-2-3 commands	/System, /Add-in, /Graph, / Data, /Quit
4 Developing Formulas: Model Building Blocks	The formula is the fundamental building block of a dynamic model.	Formula structure	Operators, values and cell references, @functions
		Point mode	When to use: cell references versus cell names
		Copying a formula	Types of cell referencing
		Types of @functions	Statistical/database, financial, date/time, mathematical, special, logical, and string functions
5 Practicing Good Spreadsheet Hygiene	Worksheets should be planned to yield accurate, auditable, modifiable, and readable results.	Structuring the worksheet	Mapping worksheet parts (models, data, menus, macros) into quadrants
		Hygiene issues	Inconsistent worksheet organization, lack of limit checking, failure to test model, poor cell addressing, bad cell references, little use of documentation, limited control over user access

Table 1.1 Decision Making Using Lotus 1-2-3 (*cont.*)

Chapter	WHY underlying concepts/methods are important	WHAT important features/techniques of Lotus 1-2-3 relate to concepts	HOW can 1-2-3 tools be used to enhance decision-making/ productivity
Part 2 - DSS Development Techniques			
6 Managing Data Areas	The database is a critical component, central to the dynamic model, in building applications in Lotus 1-2-3.	Importing data	/File Import, /Data Parse
		Sorting the database	/Data Sort, primary and secondary keys
		Querying the database	/Data Query, /Data Extract
		Frequency distributions	/Data Frequency
		What-if scenarios	/Data Table 1, /Data Table 2
		Filling a data range	/Data Fill
		Communications with graphics	Graph commands, PrintGraph, graphs that mislead, effective graphing
7 Building Dynamic Models	Dynamic models allow decision makers to create a variety of scenarios used to conduct what-if analyses.	Understanding model complexity	Descriptive/predictive, probabilistic/deterministic, optimizing/sacrificing
		Activities in dynamic modeling	Making sense of data, building a common platform for analysis, enhancing the user interface, querying the model
		Uncovering between column trends	Simple percent forecasting, moving average, exponential smoothing, linear regression
		Uncovering within column trends	Ratio analysis, correlation analysis
		Conducting what-if analyses	Figuring out what the data are telling us
8 Developing the User Interface with Macros	After the dynamic model has been built, the user interface makes the complex attributes of the spreadsheet transparent to the decision maker by using menus.	Types of macros	Macro commands, placement of macro commands in worksheet
		Development of macros	Planning phase, design phase, implementation phase, testing phase
		Structure charts	Developing hierarchy, creating and linking macro modules
		Creating custom menus	Using the {MENUBRANCH} command, multilevel custom menus
		Using the learn feature to record macros	{LET}, {RECALC}, {PUT}, {CONTENTS} commands
		Macros that support sequence	{IF} and {BRANCH}, {DISPATCH} commands
		Macros that support selection	{FOR}, {IF} and {BRANCH} commands
		Macros that support iteration	Screen control: {PANELOFF} {BORDERSOFF} commands
		Fine tuning the user interface	Initializing a macro block with counters and range names

Review Questions

1. Describe what-if analysis. How can what-if analysis help managers to better understand their decision environment?
2. How have changes in the business environment prompted the use of information technology by managers?
3. Describe each of the six decision-making phases.
4. Discuss the decision support system in terms of its three components.
5. What is a DSS shell, and how does Lotus 1-2-3 fit into this category of software?
6. What is the function of the user interface?
7. How can we build quality into our spreadsheet applications?
8. What are the characteristics we must observe in the development process?

Quality Assurance Checklist

As we conclude our discussion, be sure you have considered the following factors that will contribute to the quality of your worksheet:

✓ The cost of not using information technology can be high; a corporation may be left behind.

✓ Building decision support systems using spreadsheet software enables you to analyze data so that you may make more effective decisions.

✓ The decision-making process should be used when solving a business problem; the steps in the model break down the problem into smaller, workable parts.

✓ The main goal in developing a decision support system is to make sense of the data.

✓ You should assess the quality of your application as soon as it is put into operation so that you can modify it and thus make a more effective decision.

PART

1 Worksheet Development Techniques

CHAPTER

2 Working with the Components of a Spreadsheet

There is no such thing as a primitive language. All are highly complex.

—Jeremy Campbell

Objectives

- Understand the electronic worksheet
- Walk through a brief history of spreadsheet packages
- Understand the worksheet screen
- Move around within the worksheet
- Know the important features of automated spreadsheets

The Electronic Worksheet

This chapter introduces the electronic spreadsheet and Lotus 1-2-3. Key worksheet terms and important features are discussed. We will identify the components of a generic worksheet, and you will have an opportunity to work with Lotus 1-2-3, move around within the worksheet, and enter a few values and labels.

Most Lotus 1-2-3 books hand-hold the novice user through a wide variety of commands and functions, followed by problems that illustrate their use. That learning technique is called **training**. This book, however, attempts to **educate** the user. You will learn not only how to use Lotus 1-2-3, but also how to solve business problems using Lotus 1-2-3. In this way, you will be able to apply the mixture of methods, accompanying techniques, and Lotus 1-2-3 tools to solve new business problems as they arise.

HINT: Training differs from education in that the latter applies 1-2-3 techniques to solve problems.

The **electronic worksheet** is a computer program organized into a matrix of columns and rows overlaid with menu-based commands. Electronic worksheets allow you to enter and store data, build formulas to relate data, make changes to data, and display data in order to solve complex problems. The power of the electronic worksheet lies in its ability to help you manipulate important variables and conduct a variety of analyses. Electronic worksheets can recalculate formulas and then show you the results in an interactive manner.

Spreadsheet Packages: A Brief History

The first spreadsheet package, VisiCalc, was designed and marketed in 1979 for the Apple II microcomputer. The original VisiCalc program provided the user with a workspace of 254 rows and 63 columns. In 1980 Sorcim Corporation released SuperCalc, which was similar to Visicalc in its functions. Subsequent releases of VisiCalc and SuperCalc added important integrated features, such as limited database management capabilities and graphics. Within the next three years new spreadsheet packages were introduced to compete with VisiCalc and SuperCalc, including Multiplan, Framework, Context MBA, and Lotus Symphony.

In 1982 Lotus Corporation released its first version of Lotus 1-2-3. By 1983, 1-2-3 was upgraded with Release 1A, and in 1985 Release 2.0 appeared with an increase in row size from 2,048 to 8,192 and with enhanced memory management capabilities. By 1986 Lotus was the industry leader in the spreadsheet market. Release 2.01 appeared in 1986, adding greater functionality, including a facility to attach additional programs to 1-2-3 and a larger number of macro commands.

Late in 1988 Lotus released its newest versions of 1-2-3—Releases 2.2 and 3.0. Release 2.2 contained significant enhancements over its predecessor, making use of expanded memory managers, bundling Allways (a desktop publishing package), incorporating more sophisticated graphics, and reflecting enhanced macros. Almost simultaneously, Lotus shipped Release 3.0 and later 3.1+ in order to add a WYSIWYG (what-you-see-is-what-you-get) presentation manager, address more memory, and add mouse capabilities.

In 1991 Lotus Corporation shipped Releases 2.3 and 1.0 for Windows. Release 2.3 utilizes the WYSIWYG graphic interface similar to that used in Release 3.1+. With Release 2.3 you can use expanded memory more effectively, print in the background, and make graphs look more professional. Release 2.3 provides mouse support and contains additional macro commands. In 1992, Releases 2.4 and 1.1 for Windows were shipped providing the ability to use SmartIcons to save time, a backsolver to calculate a formula in reverse with a focus on the bottom line, clip art that you can place in a worksheet, and a landscape printing facility.

In this text we will use Release 2.3 to illustrate the development of spreadsheet applications. Release 2.3 worksheets are interchangeable with previous releases, and applications are upwardly compatible. Also, many of the features in the enhanced Release 2.4 (SmartIcons and Backsolver) are add-in packages and do not affect the primary functionality of the spreadsheet package. All screen illustrations in Release 2.3 will have WYSIWYG displayed to enhance the worksheet's appearance. With this in mind, we will also reference the capabilities of both Releases 3.1+ and 1.1 for Windows throughout the text.

Getting to Know the Worksheet Screen

The Worksheet

HINT: A spreadsheet is the 1-2-3 program, whereas the worksheet is a specific DSS application.

Before we go any further, let's get acquainted with some terms. First, we want to distinguish between a spreadsheet and a worksheet. The terms are not the same, although they are often used interchangeably. A **spreadsheet** is the 1-2-3 program, which is comprised of a set of program instructions representing the "shell" in which you enter data, build models, or execute commands. A **worksheet** is a specific spreadsheet application that you create by using the spreadsheet software package. The spreadsheet program may contain one or more worksheets linked together to perform a task or a set of activities. Figure 2.1 illustrates the components of an empty Lotus 1-2-3 worksheet. We will look at one portion of the worksheet screen at a time. When you first bring up the 1-2-3 program, an empty worksheet will appear on the screen. You can decide at that point to either create a new worksheet or retrieve an existing one.

A worksheet, divided into columns represented by letters and rows represented by numbers, is in essence a **matrix**. You can use a worksheet to enter and store data, create tables, develop reports, perform business calculations, and even link to other worksheets or files.

Besides the matrix, the worksheet also contains a **control panel** which displays three lines of information (at top), and a status line which tells you what the program is doing (at bottom). The control panel is located at the top of the screen and gives you the following information:

(Line 1) Address of current cell, other cell data, and mode indicator

(Line 2) Either current cell contents or Main menu commands

(Line 3) Either current cell contents (continued) or menu

The first line contains information on the location of the cell pointer and cell contents. In Figure 2.1, "A1:" shows you the address of the current cell. In the control panel you see that no information is displayed because the cell A1 is empty. Normally you would see a formula, value, or label displayed on line 1 of the control panel.

On the right of the control panel is the **mode indicator**. In Figure 2.1 the mode indicator reads MENU, indicating that the 1-2-3 program is displaying a menu in the control panel. The mode indicator can also display other important information. The most common display is READY, telling you that the system is waiting for a command. Other information includes:

EDIT	You may edit the contents of a cell.
ERROR	An error has occurred. You may press the ESC or the ENTER key to correct it.
FILES	The system is waiting for you to select a file.
FIND	The Data Find feature is in operation.
HELP	The Help screen has been requested.
LABEL	You may enter a label into a cell.
MENU	A Lotus 1-2-3 menu is active.
NAMES	The system is waiting for you to select a range name.
POINT	A range is being pointed to.
STAT	The status of your worksheet has been requested.
VALUE	You may enter a value or formula into a cell.
WAIT	The system is executing a command.

The second and third lines of the control panel will contain either the 1-2-3 menu when you press the / key as highlighted in Figure 2.1 or the contents of a cell that is being edited with the F2 function key. If there is a submenu, it will appear in the third line of the control panel. When you are editing the contents of a cell, the mode indicator reads EDIT. When there are long formulas or labels, the third line is also used to display cell contents for editing.

On the bottom row of the worksheet screen are **status indicators**, which give you additional information on the condition of your worksheet. Note in Figure 2.1 the NUM and CAPS indicators on the bottom line. These indicators tell you that the Num Lock and Caps Lock keys have been turned on. Other status indicators include:

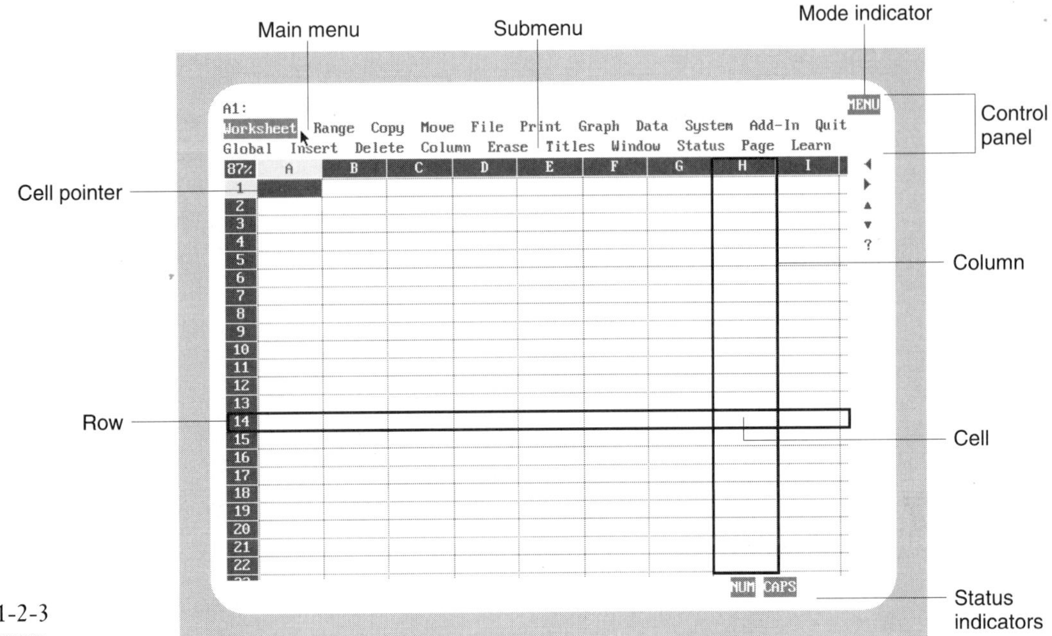

Figure 2.1
The Lotus 1-2-3 Opening Screen

CALC	The worksheet needs to be recalculated.
CIRC	A circular formula reference has been found in the worksheet.
CMD	A macro is being executed by the system.
Date/Clock	Always on except when an error message appears.
END	The (END) key has been pressed.
MEM	There is little memory available for additional data .
OVR	The (INS) key has been pressed, and the system will type characters over existing characters.
SCROLL	The (SCROLL LOCK) key has been pressed.
SST	A keyboard macro is in single-step execution.
STEP	You are stepping through a macro a cell at a time using the (ALT)-(F2) function-key sequence.
UNDO	You may reverse the last recorded action.

The Cell

The **cell**—the intersection of a single column and a row—is the fundamental building block in all worksheets. When building models for decision making, we use cells to enter values or labels. Able to hold up to 240 characters each, cells represent unique locations for storing pieces of data or formulas. Cells are identified by a COLUMN-ROW notation; for example, H14 indicates we are referring to column H, row 14. Lotus 1-2-3 allows you to enter values or labels into more than 2,000,000 cells (256 columns by 8,192 rows).

The **cell pointer** is the highlighted rectangular area that indicates the location of the cursor. The address of the current cell is also displayed in the upper-left corner of the control panel. Lotus cells can contain one of two types of data: values or labels. A **value** is a number or formula containing only the following characters:

```
0 1 2 3 4 5 6 7 8 9 + - . ( @ # $ %
```

When you enter a value into a Lotus cell, the program will accept only one decimal point.

HINT: A formula is considered a value by 1-2-3 for calculations.

A **formula**, considered a value by 1-2-3, is a mathematical expression that contains one or more cell addresses. Let's say we want to add the contents of the cells E8 through E12. One way to enter this formula is:

```
+E8+E9+E10+E11+E12
```

Another way to add the numbers in the 5 cells above is to use a built-in *function*—a specialized formula—that can be identified with the @ sign:

```
@SUM(E8..E12)
```

A **label** is a cell entry that begins with a character other than one of those we just listed. When you enter labels, the first character will be represented by one of the following:

' Left-justified label (this is the default value)
" Right-justified label
^ Center-justified label

Usually you will enter a label by using a letter as the first character. You may, however, want to enter a number (0 through 9) as a label because you may want to add another symbol to it. Beginning the label with a number rather than a letter alerts the Lotus 1-2-3 program that you are entering a value. Therefore you will want to preface your entry with one of the label characters listed above. For example, in Figure 2.2 the cell E6 has the entry `"1 Qtr`, indicating the presence of a right-justified label.

Keep in mind that if you make a mistake and then backspace out of the label, you may not have permanently erased it; you may still have a valid label of blank spaces in the cell. Place your cell pointer on the cell in question, and look at the contents of the cell. If the cell contains a single quote ('), you know you have blank spaces in your cell. To erase them, use the /**R**ange **E**rase command.

Harrison Electronics, Inc.

Throughout this text we will develop a DSS application by using progressive case material from a firm called Harrison Electronics, Inc., located in Colorado Springs. The primary business of Harrison Electronics is the repair of a variety of electronic equipment. They also sell small products, such as hair dryers and toaster ovens. The firm has eleven employees, seven of whom are repairers. Frank Jones is the founder, owner, and general manager. Figure 2.2 shows the three sales categories over four quarters. These data are summarized for purposes of illustration.

The Range

A **range** is a rectangular block of cells that you define for a variety of functions. A range can consist of a single cell or a group of neighboring cells, a column or several columns, and a row or several rows. You name a range by identifying its borders, which usually start with the upper-left cell and extend diagonally to the lower-right cell. Ranges cannot be irregular; that is, they must form a rectangle.

Moving Around within the Worksheet

The size allowed by Lotus 1-2-3 leaves plenty of room for you to develop large worksheets. Usually you cannot see more than 8 columns (A through H) and 20 rows on the screen at any one time. By default, each column is set to a width of 9 characters. Therefore you can view 72 characters times 20 rows on each screen. When the cell pointer reaches the screen's edge, the screen begins to scroll in the direction the cell pointer is moving. In this section you will get acquainted with the keyboard (if you aren't acquainted with it already) and the keys needed to

Other cell data

Label in cell E6

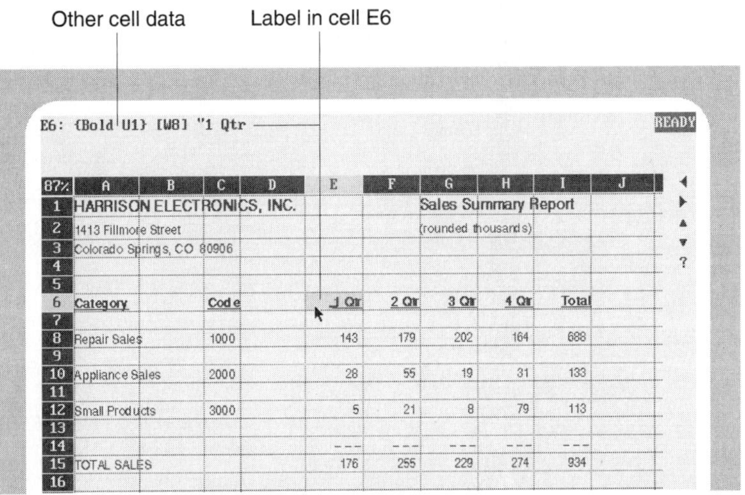

Figure 2.2
Labels

move around within the worksheet. There are two ways to move the cell pointer around within the worksheet: (1) by using the keyboard and function keys and (2) by using the mouse.

Using the Keyboard and Function Keys to Move Around within the Worksheet

The four directional **cursor movement keys** allow you to move one cell at a time within the worksheet in the direction of the key pressed:

↑ ↓ ← →

To move right one screen, use either the CTRL → or the TAB key. To move left one screen, use the CTRL ← or the SHIFT TAB key. Press either the PGDN or the PGUP key to move one page down or up. Pressing the HOME key moves the cursor to the upper-left corner of the worksheet, cell A1. Conversely, pressing the END HOME keys in sequence moves the cell pointer to the lower-right corner of the active worksheet. The END key in combination with the cursor keys serves as a powerful tool for moving around within large worksheets.

HINT: The fastest way to move around a worksheet is by using the GOTO (F5) key.

The fastest way to move to a specific area of your worksheet is to use the GOTO function key, F5. Figure 2.3 illustrates the use of the F5 key to move from one area to another in the worksheet. After pressing the F5 key, you are prompted to type the location you wish to go to—either a cell reference (for example, H14) or a cell name (for example, RATE). To obtain a list of range names, you can press the NAME key, F3, immediately after pressing F5.

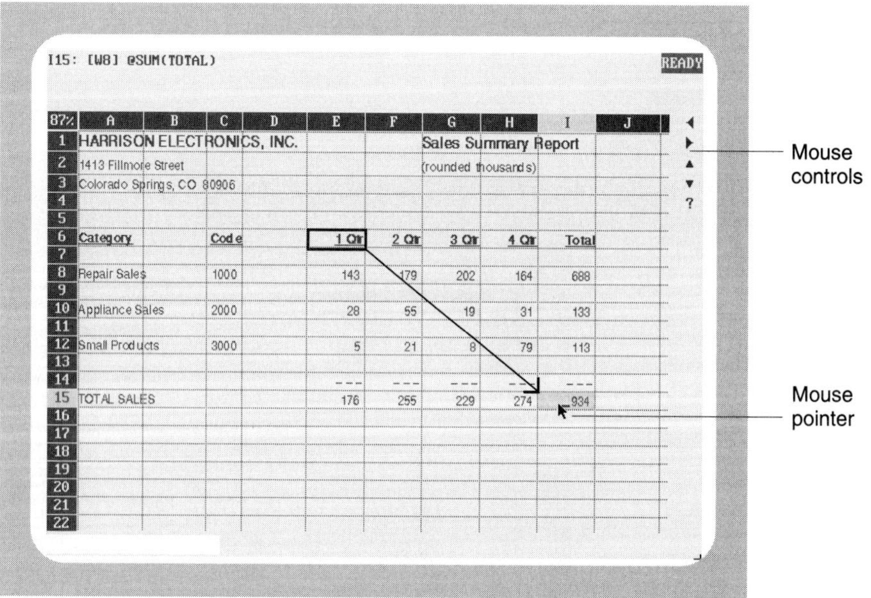

Figure 2.3
Use of the GOTO Key

There are several other keys you will often want to use for moving around within the worksheet:

BACKSPACE	Erases the last character typed, just left of the cell pointer's location.
CTRL	When used with cursor movement keys, moves one page left or right.
DEL	Erases the character at the cursor's location.
ENTER	Tells the program to execute a command or that you have finished entering data.
ESC	Tells the program to go back one step—either (1) to back out of a cell, or (2) if executing a menu command, to go back up to a higher submenu.
SCROLL LOCK	Keeps the cursor from moving off the screen and instead moves the screen while keeping the cursor stationary.
TAB	Used for moving around within the worksheet one page at a time.

Using the Mouse to Move Around within the Worksheet

HINT: Use the mouse whenever possible to move around within the worksheet.

One of the most efficient ways you can move from one area of your worksheet to another is by using the mouse. Releases 2.3, 3.1+, and 1.1 for Windows all support the mouse. In Figure 2.3 you can see the mouse pointer aiming its arrow at cell E6. To move to another location, you simply move the mouse to the new cell and press the button. You can also use the mouse control panel at the upper right of the worksheet screen. The arrow keys move the cell pointer one cell in the direction pressed.

Important Features of Lotus 1-2-3 Releases 2.3(4) and 3.1+

The new releases of Lotus 1-2-3 have four features in common that give spreadsheets tremendous power:

1. automatic recalculation
2. worksheet linking
3. presentation capabilities
4. worksheet customization

As we discuss each of these features in the following sections, we will see their importance to the development of DSS applications.

Automatic Recalculation

HINT: Automatic recalculation allows the development of dynamic models.

One of the most powerful functions of the Lotus 1-2-3 electronic spreadsheet is its ability to automatically recalculate a worksheet when you make changes. **Automatic recalculation** is universal among all spreadsheets and is critical when you are working with decision-making models. **Models** are mathematical representations of the business system in which you are making decisions. You use formulas to represent and describe the relationships between the variables you are considering within those models.

After entering formulas, you may decide to change the values of certain variables so that you can see how those changes affect other variables. This type of analysis would not be possible in complex worksheets without the automatic recalculation feature. With this feature you can create multiple what-if scenarios because the worksheet calculates the effects of a change in one variable on other variables or on the entire worksheet.

You can choose one of two ways to have your worksheet automatically recalculated. One way is to enter new data into the cells that are affected by formulas and are therefore related to other cells. The other way is to copy formulas from one area of your worksheet to another. The program recalculates the worksheet for you.

Worksheet Linking

A very important feature of spreadsheets is **worksheet linking**—a process that allows you to link together different worksheet files. For small amounts of data, you can use **single-sheet files**—files that contain just one worksheet. As software package developers have improved the data management and reporting facilities, worksheets increasingly have been used to store and manipulate large collections of data. Consequently, it is more appropriate to subdivide data by logical areas into two or more worksheets and link them together with a unique key. You link worksheets by referencing another worksheet with a formula.

Another form of worksheet linking involves the development of summary worksheets, which can be used to consolidate data and which results from a variety of worksheets. Nowadays you can have two or more worksheets active simultaneously, and you can move data from one active file to another. This feature lets you conduct advanced analyses, in which you consider risks and other complexities, by comparing and analyzing the relationships among open, active file windows.

Presentation of Worksheet Results

Two areas of worksheet presentation have undergone continual improvement ever since the shipment of Lotus 1-2-3 Release 2.01. The first area is the what-if modeling, using graphics capabilities embedded within modern spreadsheet releases. The graphs change automatically whenever you change the data. Graphs provide information in a different format for visually oriented people who prefer not to look at tables. Graphs within Lotus 1-2-3 are interactively updated with changes in data or in what-if queries. In fact, graphs often suggest areas for additional analysis and aid users in the control of resources.

The second area of worksheet presentation is the bundling of spreadsheet desktop publishing programs. Desktop publishers such as Allways with Release 2.2 and WYSIWYG with Releases 2.3, 2.4, and 3.1+ show evidence of the trend toward professional presentations within worksheets. You can customize your screen display by selecting colors for worksheet backgrounds and foregrounds, cellpointers, and frames. You can usually choose from a variety of fonts, as well as from bold, italics, underlining, shading, outlines, and drop shadows. Grids are standard, giving you more control over page layout. You can embed your graphs within the worksheet and enhance them with colors, text, arrows, and geometric shapes.

HINT: WYSIWYG presents worksheet results with a variety of desktop publishing options.

Worksheet Customization

Advanced macro commands allow you to customize menus so that you can establish user interfaces. A **macro** is a set of instructions for automating a 1-2-3 task, consisting of a sequence of keystrokes and commands that you type into a worksheet as cell labels. Macros constitute the programming language for Lotus 1-2-3. In addition to the availability of the macro language, libraries containing subroutines give you the development tools for further worksheet customization. You can now create dynamic subroutines with "smart" modules that are to some extent self-modifying. In essence, you have the power in the new Lotus 1-2-3 releases to create programs that can modify its instructions with each pass through the loop.

The On-line Help Facility

You can access the **on-line help facility** within Lotus at any point by pressing the HELP function key, (F1), or by clicking on the ? in the mouse control panel. 1-2-3 responds by presenting a Help screen index that lets you choose one of several options. For example, if you need some information on how to enter a formula, you select Formulas from the menu to get more specific help.

You can enter the on-line help facility no matter what the status indicator registers. Let's assume you are editing a formula in your worksheet. When you press (F1) or select the ? from the mouse control panel, the system displays the appropriate Help screen rather than the main Help index screen. Whenever you have questions, this feature can save you a tremendous amount of time.

You have now been introduced to the Lotus 1-2-3 program. In Chapter 3 you will explore 1-2-3 menus and commands from which you will develop DSS applications.

Review Questions

1. What is an electronic spreadsheet?
2. How can electronic spreadsheet packages improve decision-making effectiveness?
3. Describe the evolution of electronic spreadsheet packages in terms of features.
4. Compare a spreadsheet and a worksheet.
5. How do you identify a cell?
6. What is the name for a group of cells?
7. For what are the three lines in the control panel used?
8. What are the differences between a value and a label?
9. Is a formula considered by 1-2-3 to be a value or a label?
10. How many columns and rows are in a worksheet page?
11. What is the most efficient way to move around within a worksheet?
12. Describe the value of automatic recalculation.
13. What are the advantages to linking two or more worksheets together?
14. What features of 1-2-3 allow for the presentation of worksheet results in a pleasing way?
15. What is a macro?
16. How does 1-2-3 provide help to users?
17. How is the online help facility invoked?

Skill-Building Activities: Using Lotus 1-2-3 for the First Time

Activity 1: Load the Lotus 1-2-3 Spreadsheet Software

If you are loading 1-2-3 from the Lotus Access System, select 1-2-3 from the menu. The Lotus Access System also allows you to print graphs you have created in 1-2-3 and translate files from other programs. Otherwise type `123` from the subdirectory in which you have loaded the program. While Lotus 1-2-3 is loading, you should see the 1-2-3 opening screen.

Shortly, a blank worksheet similar to that shown in Figure 2.1 appears. In the set of activities that follows, you will create the Sales Summary Report for Harrison Electronics as shown in Figure 2.2.

NOTE: To help you with this exercise, ***boldface*** *letters indicate a message from the system or the worksheet while the commands in the box tell you to make a specific entry.*

Activity 2: Moving Around within the Worksheet

Your cell pointer should be located in the home position—A1. Whenever you pull up an existing worksheet, the cell pointer will be located wherever you last left it.

Move the cell pointer with the cursor keys: down, right, up. Use the (HOME) key to go back to the A1 cell.

Practice moving one page to the right, using both the (TAB) and the (CTRL) (→) keys. Similarly, use the (PGDN) key to scroll down a couple of pages. Use the (HOME) key to go back to the A1 cell. If you have a mouse, practice moving around the worksheet by clicking on different cells. Use the GOTO key, (F5), to go to a cell inside the current worksheet page. Go to the G17 cell by using the following keystrokes:

1. Press the (F5) function key.
2. Move the cursor to cell G17.
3. Press the (ENTER) key to confirm the move.

Activity 3: Entering Labels

Next, enter the labels for the titles, categories, and quarters.

1. Press the (HOME) key to go to cell A1, and enter `HARRISON ELECTRONICS INC.`
2. Go to cell A2 and enter `1413 Fillmore Street.`
3. Go to cell A3 and enter `Colorado Springs, CO 80906.`
4. Use the (F5) key to go to cell G1, and enter `Sales Summary Report.`
5. Drop to cell G2 and enter `'(rounded thousands).` Note the left-justification symbol.
6. Go to cell A6 to enter the report heading `Category.`
7. In cell C6 enter the report heading `Code.`
8. In cell E6 through H6 enter the report headings `"1 Qtr` and so on.

9. Go to cell I6 and enter the report heading `"Total`.
10. Enter the labels for the sales categories—as follows:

    A8 `Repair Sales`

    A10 `Appliance Sales`

    A12 `Small Products`

    A15 `TOTAL SALES`

11. Go to cell E14 and enter the label `"---`.
12. Copy the label to cells F14 through I14 using the /**C**opy command.

Don't worry if the labels in cells A8 through A15 exceed the default column width of 9. Later you will learn how to change column widths to accommodate larger values and labels. Your worksheet should now look like the one in Figure 2.4.

Activity 4: Entering Values and Simple Formulas

Now it's time to enter values for each of the categories in each quarter. First, you will enter the code numbers in column C. Second, you will enter the data into the quarters by category. Finally, you will calculate the total sales for each quarter. Be sure that you don't enter the total sales values, since you will place a formula in each cell of row 15.

1. Enter the code numbers into column C:

    C8 1000

    C10 2000

    C12 3000

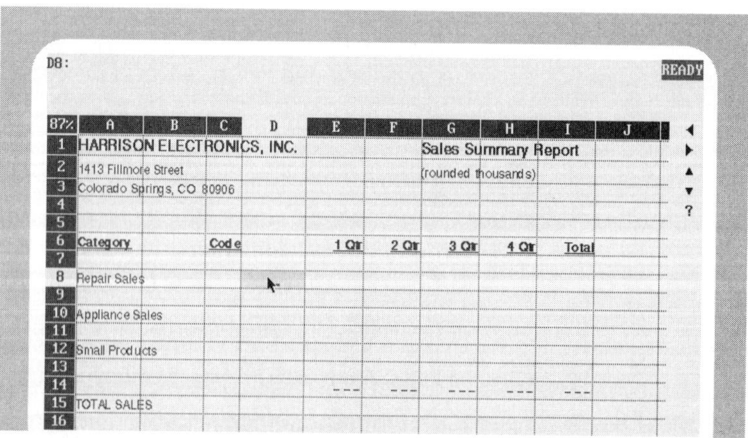

Figure 2.4
Labels for Harrison Electronics

2. Now enter the following values in columns E–H:

	Column			
Row	E	F	G	H
8	143	179	202	164
10	28	55	19	31
12	5	21	8	79

3. To calculate our Total column, go to cell I8 and enter the formula that totals columns E–G: `+E8+F8+G8+H8`.

4. Use the **/C**opy command to copy the same formula into cells I10 and I12.

5. For the quarter subtotals, let's use the @SUM function to total sales. In cell E15 enter `@SUM(E8..E12)`.

6. Now move to cell F15. Let's use the @SUM function for the row, but instead of typing the formula, we will use the cursor or mouse to point to the range to be included. To do this, enter `@SUM(` and move the cell pointer to cell F8. Then press the decimal point `.` to anchor the upper boundary of our range. Move the cell pointer down to cell F12 and enter the right parentheses [`)`] followed by the ENTER key.

Activity 5: Saving the Worksheet

At this point, all values and formulas in your worksheet have been entered. Check your worksheet with Figure 2.5. We have used few if any 1-2-3 menu commands in this development exercise. Now it is time to save the worksheet for future use. Let's call the file HARRIS.

1. Use the 1-2-3 menus to save the file, and press the **/F**ile **S**ave command.

2. Enter `HARRIS` for the filename.

3. Press the ENTER key to confirm the save.

Congratulations! You have completed your first worksheet. You will soon build more sophisticated worksheets based on the experience you have gained so far.

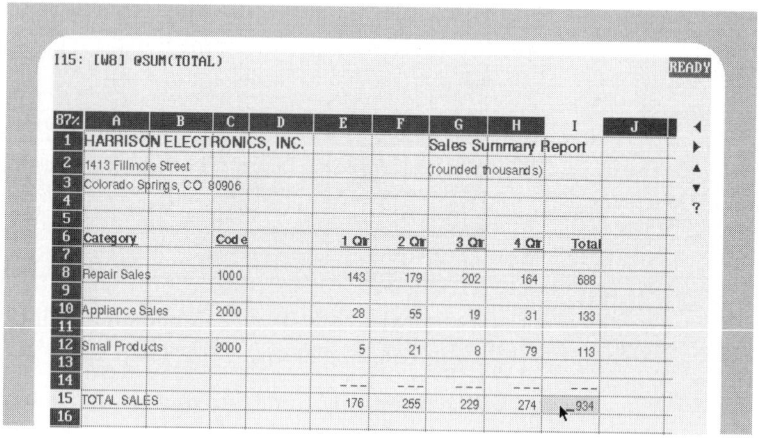

I15: [W8] @SUM(TOTAL) READY

87%	A	B	C	D	E	F	G	H	I	J
1	HARRISON ELECTRONICS, INC.						Sales Summary Report			
2	1413 Fillmore Street						(rounded thousands)			
3	Colorado Springs, CO 80906									
4										
5										
6	Category		Code		1 Qtr	2 Qtr	3 Qtr	4 Qtr	Total	
7										
8	Repair Sales		1000		143	179	202	164	688	
9										
10	Appliance Sales		2000		28	55	19	31	133	
11										
12	Small Products		3000		5	21	8	79	113	
13										
14					---	---	---	---	---	
15	TOTAL SALES				176	255	229	274	934	
16										

Figure 2.5
Values and Formulas for Harrison Electronics

Hands-On Exercises

1. Bring up a blank worksheet in 1-2-3. Identify the following parts:
   a. Control panel
   b. Cell pointer
   c. Mode indicator
   d. Status indicator
   e. Borders
   f. Row
   g. Column
   h. Date/time indicator

2. Practice moving around within the worksheet, noting your location each time.
   a. Press the (TAB) key twice.
   b. Press the (SHIFT)-(TAB) key twice.
   c. Press the (PGDN) key once.
   d. Move the cell pointer to the right three times with the cursor keys.
   e. Press the (HOME) key.
   f. Use the GOTO ((F5)) key to go to cell G6.
   g. Press the (END) key with the right cursor key a few times.
   h. Use the mouse control panel to move from cell A1 to H6.

3. Enter the following labels and values into your worksheet:

Row	A	B	C	D	E	F
4		1988	1989	1990	1991	Total
6	Sales	53	66	43	71	
7	Expenses	23	38	24	47	
9	Income					

4. In cell B9 enter the following formula: `+B6-B7` to calculate the income (sales – expenses). Place this same formula (adjusting for columns) in cells C9, D9, and E9.
5. Use column F to calculate total sales, expenses, and income. In cell F6 enter the following formula: `+B6+C6+D6+E6`. Write the same formula in cell F7.
6. Invoke the online help facility with the (F1) key. Move around and select a topic of interest.
7. Place the formula `@SUM(B9..E9)` in cell F9. Compare this formula with formulas in cells F6 and F7.
8. Change a value in the worksheet and observe the result of the automatic recalculation feature. In cell C6 change the sales figure from 66 to 56 by using the (F2) key to edit the cell.
9. Save the worksheet to a disk as BUDGET by using the /**F**ile **S**ave command. (In this text, bold letters within commands tell you which keys to press.)

Problem-Solving Projects

Create a Lotus 1-2-3 worksheet to develop a database for capturing and managing sales transactions for a local pet store. The owners want to use only a portion of the inventory to set up the system, and have decided to start with the small mammals. The data that need to be captured include stock number, stock name, wholesale price, and retail price. First you need to erase any worksheets on your screen using the /**W**orksheet **E**rase command. Use the following information to set up your worksheet:

Row	A	B	C	D	E
1					
2	Tri-Lakes Pet Store				
3					
4		Stock	Stock	Wholesale	Retail
5	Product	Number	Name	Price	Price
6					
7	Rabbit	1214	RAB4	8.00	12.00
8	Black rat	1235	RAT5	2.50	4.00
9	Persian cat	1238	CAT8	75.00	140.00

Row	A	B	C	D	E
10	Rottweiler	1244	DOG4	95.00	175.00
11	Greenhouse snake	1257	SNA7	12.50	19.50
12	White mouse	1278	MOU8	9.00	11.25
13					
14	AVERAGE				

1. Set up the worksheet with labels in rows 2, 4 and 5.
2. Enter the labels in column A. Make column A wider by using the /**W**orksheet **C**olumn **S**et width command.
3. Enter the right-justified labels into columns B through E for stock number, stock name, wholesale price, and retail price, respectively.
4. Enter the values for columns B through E. Be sure to right-justify the stock name descriptions in column C. To format values with two decimal places, use the /**R**ange **F**ormat **F**ixed 2 command.
5. Add an average formula for columns D and E (adjusting for columns). The formula for cell D14 is: `@AVG(D7..D12)`.
6. Add a new column, F, which calculates the percentage profit for each product. Label the column:

   ```
   Percentage
   Profit
   ```

   Use the formula `+(E7-D7)/E7` and copy it to cells F8 through F12, adjusting for rows. To copy, use the /**C**opy command.
7. Calculate the average profit for the percentage profit in cell F14 using the same formula used in problem 5.
8. Save the worksheet to a disk as PETSHOP by using the /**F**ile **S**ave command.

Quality Assurance Checklist

As we conclude our discussion of spreadsheet components, be sure you have considered the following factors that will contribute to the quality of your worksheet:

✓ It is helpful to approach 1-2-3 with an education emphasis rather than a training emphasis in which you try to solve a problem using 1-2-3 commands.

- ✓ Keeping your eyes on the control panel, which displays three lines of information, will keep you apprised of the condition or status of your program or worksheet.
- ✓ The mode indicator tells you which part of the program is being executed—for example, commands or formulas.
- ✓ A cell can hold up to 240 characters, not what it necessarily displays; in other words, if the default column width is 9 characters, the cell may contain a formula that is much greater than 9 characters.
- ✓ Only values can be used in calculations; a formula is considered a value in 1-2-3, while a label is not.
- ✓ The mouse is the most effective way to move around within the worksheet.
- ✓ Automatic recalculation is one of the most powerful features of 1-2-3 because it allows you to develop dynamic models.
- ✓ WYSIWYG gives you worksheet results with a variety of desktop publishing options such as boldface, italics, underlining, shading, outlines, and drop shadows.
- ✓ Grids in WYSIWYG should be used as often as possible because they give you more control over page layout.
- ✓ You can invoke the online help facility at any time by pressing the (F1) key or by clicking on the ? in the mouse panel.

CHAPTER

3 Invoking Spreadsheet Commands

Learning without thought is useless; thought without learning is dangerous.

—Confucius

Objectives

- Understand Lotus 1-2-3 command menus and submenus.
- Know the detailed operation of /**R**ange and /**W**orksheet commands.
- Understand relative, absolute, and mixed cell addressing when copying and moving.
- Know different file types for retrieving and saving files.
- Use print commands for getting a printout of your worksheet.

Spreadsheet Commands

We will now examine the Lotus 1-2-3 command menu structure. Lotus menus give both novice and advanced users access to much of the power in the spreadsheet package. A **command** is an instruction given to the 1-2-3 program. A **menu** groups the commands into logical choices that appear on the control panel. With Lotus menus, you can manipulate data, generate graphs, and set up the structure of your worksheet. Lotus 1-2-3 menus are easy to use.

HINT: The Add-In command is not on the 3.1+ menu.

After loading 1-2-3 and making sure it is in READY mode, you can choose one of two ways to invoke the menus. The first involves using the slash key (/) located in the lower-right section of the keyboard. The second way is to move the mouse up to the control panel. After you have pressed the slash key or moved the mouse, the indicator displays the MENU mode. The Main menu structure has the following options:

Worksheet Range Copy Move File Print Graph Data System Add-In Quit

You can choose from the menus in one of three ways:

- Move the menu pointer to your choice, and then press ENTER,

or

- Select the first letter of the command,

or

- Move the mouse to your choice, and then press the mouse button.

To back out of a menu, press ESC or choose **Q**uit if it appears on the menu. Save your file by using the command /**F**ile **S**ave.

Most of the commands displayed on the Main menu in Lotus 1-2-3 contain additional commands in lower-level menus called **submenus**. The submenu commands, when available, are displayed in the description line of the control panel. For example, when you move the menu pointer over **W**orksheet, the following submenu command is displayed:

HINT: In 3.1+ you will also find the Hide command.

Global Insert Delete Column Erase Titles Window Status Page Learn

In this chapter we will discuss each of the 11 Lotus 1-2-3 menu commands in order according to most frequent use. For example, we will begin with the range commands, which are the commands reported to be used most often by worksheet developers and users. We will explore the following categories of commands in this chapter:

/RANGE commands

/COPY and /MOVE commands

/WORKSHEET commands

/FILE commands

/PRINT commands

Range Commands

The **Range commands** are available for you to use with a single cell or with groups of cells in 1-2-3. A group of interconnected cells, called a range, may consist of an entire row or an entire column in the worksheet. More commonly, a range is a rectangle or "block" of cells. Figure 3.1 illustrates the **/R**ange command menu, which you invoke by pressing **/R**ange, and gives examples of some spreadsheet ranges. The first range contains two cells: C2..D2. The notation C2..D2 indicates that the first cell of the range (usually the upper left) is C2 and the last cell (usually the lower right) is D2. Another range contains 9 cells from B5 through B13. The range C14..D20 contains 14 cells, 2 columns by 7 rows. Notice that the range is identified by C14, the upper-left cell, to D20, the lower-right cell. The invalid range depicted in Figure 3.1 is called invalid because it does not represent a rectangle of interconnected cells.

There is a difference between range commands and a range. Range commands are usually used to format and manipulate worksheet ranges. Ranges are embedded within a number of other Lotus commands such as copying or moving

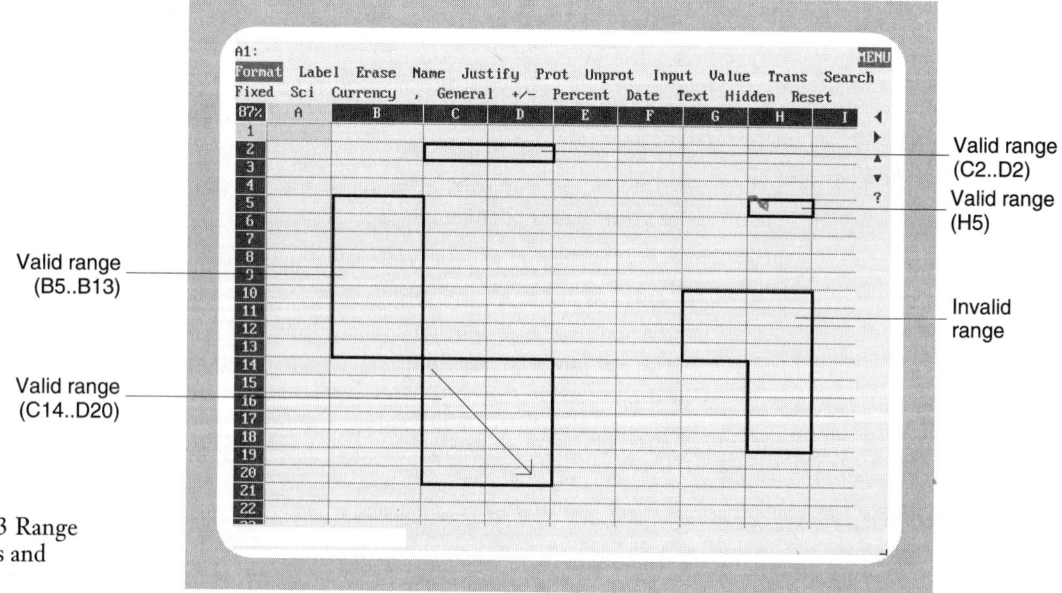

Figure 3.1
Lotus 1-2-3 Range Commands and Examples

a block, formatting a block, naming a block, printing a block, and other more advanced 1-2-3 commands.

Anchoring a Range

Before we discuss specific range commands, it is important to understand the "anchoring" principle as it applies to setting ranges. We will discuss anchoring as a separate topic because it is crucial to many of the 1-2-3 commands that follow, including /**C**opy and /**M**ove. **Anchoring** means to position or set the first of the two cell addresses used to identify a range. In this way the range can be expanded visually to the right and/or down in your worksheet.

When setting ranges in commands, you can choose one of two ways to indicate the boundaries of a range. The first is to type the cell addresses that comprise the range. For example, you can anchor a range by typing `D16.H16` directly into the menu prompt that requests a range. The second is to use the cell pointer to highlight or expand the range down and to the right (usually), or up and to the left, after anchoring. A range is anchored by pressing the (.) (period) key. Backspacing or using the (ESC) key releases the anchor.

Once you have anchored a range, use the cell pointer to expand the highlighted area in the worksheet until you have defined the range, and then press the (ENTER) key to confirm the range. When using a mouse, you anchor a range by moving the mouse to the upper-left cell of the range and clicking with the mouse button. Then you move the mouse to the lower-right cell of the range by holding the mouse button and releasing to set the range.

Formatting a Range

Now let's format a single cell or range of cells. The default condition in 1-2-3 for the cell format of values and labels depends on the general settings made in the /**W**orksheet **G**lobal menu. We will discuss the /Worksheet commands later in this chapter. The default setting that Lotus uses for values is the General format and the Left-alignment format for labels. **Global settings** are worksheet settings that affect the entire worksheet and defaults.

The General format is frequently used where values appear right-justified and have zero decimal places unless the user enters a value with decimal places. The General format displays as many decimal places as those entered for the value within a cell. You may often want to choose the Fixed option, which assigns a specified number of decimal places to the cells in your range. The Comma option inserts commas and a specified number of decimal places in your range. The Currency option is similar to the comma format; however, it adds a dollar symbol before the value displayed. The Percent option divides all entries by 100 and adds a % sign to the end of the cell entry. The Text option converts the entry to a right-aligned label.

You may also change the justification of a label in a cell or range after the label has been entered. Figure 3.2 illustrates the different types of formats. Like

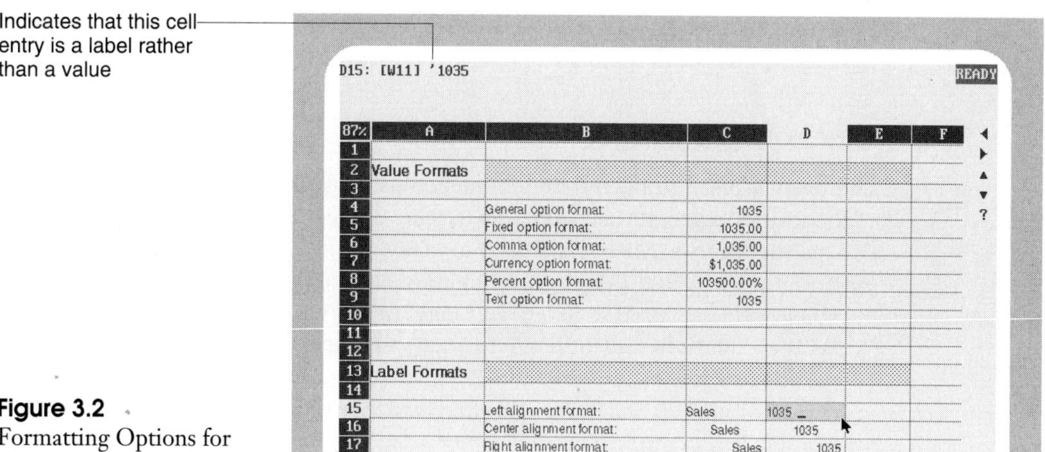

Figure 3.2
Formatting Options for Ranges

the Value format, the label prefix depends on what was entered in the default settings in /**W**orksheet **G**lobal. Labels can be left-, center-, or right-justified. The /**R**ange **F**ormat **R**eset command tells the system to revert the range indicated to the current global format type.

Note that when entering what appears to be values as labels as shown in Figure 3.2, in cells D15 through D17, they cannot be mathematically manipulated. You can identify labels in 1-2-3 with a leading character (', ^, or ") after positioning the cell pointer over the appropriate cell. Remember that 1-2-3 does not consider '1035 to be a value. For example, if you decide later to sum a group of values that includes labels, those labels will not be added to the total.

HINT: Labels cannot be used in calculations.

Naming a Range

Lotus 1-2-3 has a feature that lets you name a range with English-like expressions. A **range name** is a word that represents a cell reference, and it can be substituted for a cell address or range. You can use range names in formulas or to go to a certain location in the worksheet. When cells are named and then moved, the range cell addresses are updated automatically. Range names are easier to remember and use than are cell addresses, and they may be substituted for cell addresses whenever 1-2-3 asks for a range. As you build dynamic models you will want to use range names as often as possible so that the application is easier to modify, thus satisfying one of our quality criteria.

To create a range name, invoke the /**R**ange **N**ame **C**reate submenu. In our case example, you need to create a new range name called TOTAL SALES, which encompasses the cells E15..H15 as illustrated in Figure 3.3. Note that while in the /**R**ange **N**ame **C**reate submenu, you are asked to supply (1) the range name and (2) the range you are naming. The range can be either a single cell or a group of contiguous cells (cells that are adjacent to each other).

Now let's return to the Harrison Electronics case. Since you have named this range, you can now use it to sum up the total sales for each of the four quarters. In cell I15 you have the formula `@SUM(Total Sales)` instead of `@SUM(E15..H15)`. The range name TOTAL SALES easily substitutes for the cell reference and makes the worksheet easier to modify and enhance.

HINT: A cell may have more than one range name.

Once you have created a range name, you can later delete it if you don't need it. Remember that a cell can have more than one range name or it can be used in more than one range. These characteristics are useful if you want to create a name for a single cell and also create another range name to include that cell in a larger range.

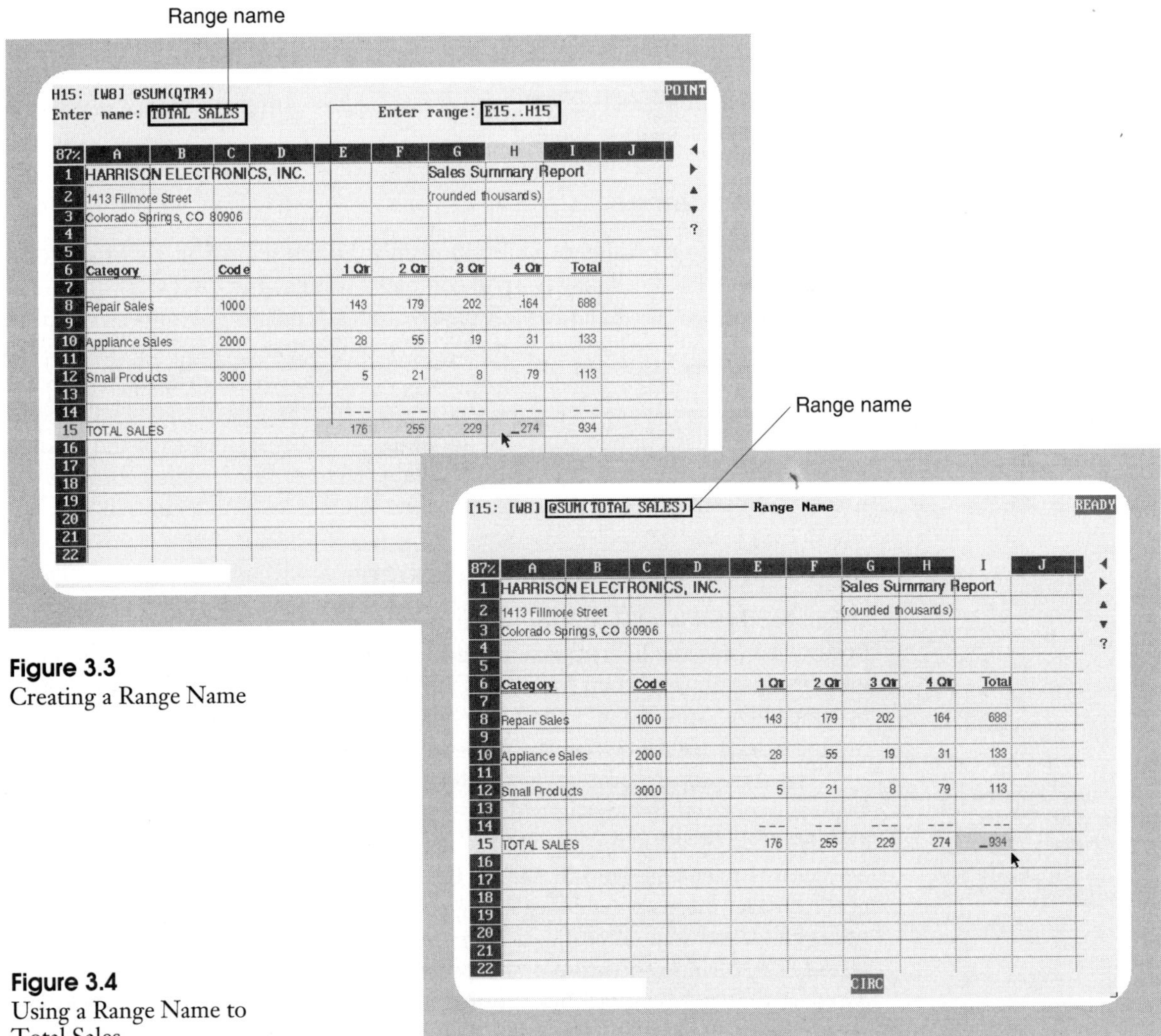

Figure 3.3
Creating a Range Name

Figure 3.4
Using a Range Name to Total Sales

So far, you have created one range name, and you have used it in the formula. But assuming you have created a hundred or more range names, you may want to produce a list for your later reference. To do this, use the /**R**ange **N**ame **T**able command to insert a reference table of ranges and their names in your worksheet.

Notice that the table fits into the columns; their widths were set by the default. The control panel shows TOTAL SALES, even though there appears to be a running together of items in the table. You can either widen the column or move the cell references. Since a column for a range table should not be widened, the logical choice is to move the cell references to column C.

Erasing a Range

HINT: You must use /**R**ange **E**rase to delete cell contents.

You can erase the contents of a cell or range of cells by using the /**R**ange **E**rase command. You must use the /**R**ange **E**rase command to properly delete the cell contents. Note that you cannot edit a cell by backspacing over labels. This approach leaves another label, with no cell display but with the evidence of a single quotation mark (') within the cell.

Searching a Range

Often with large worksheets, you will need to locate a label in a formula or a string. Because each cell may contain complex formulas and each worksheet may hold many cells of formulas, the /**R**ange **S**earch command can be very useful in searching for labels or parts of formulas. Remember that each cell can hold up to 240 characters. Figure 3.5 depicts the range to search, which includes in this case a major part of the worksheet. To learn how the command works, you will search for a formula that contains the @SUM function in Figure 3.6 with the /**R**ange **S**earch @SUM command. You should then be led to cell E15, which contains the first @SUM formula in your range, and then to other cells that contain @SUM.

Protecting and Unprotecting a Range

When you build worksheets for other users, certain formulas, labels, and values need to be protected. **Protection** prevents other users from typing over a cell expression or an important formula. This two-step process allows you to protect or "unprotect" specific cells (by using /**R**ange commands) and then to enable or disable worksheet protection (by using /**W**orksheet commands).

HINT: With large worksheets, use the /**R**ange **U**nprotect command.

The first step in protecting a cell or a range of cells is to use the /**R**ange **U**nprot command to indicate which cells should be unprotected. Protected cells are identified by a PR that appears in the control panel before the cell formula. So that we can change our individual sales amounts and leave the Total Sales data protected, we must unprotect the range incorporating E8 through I12.

The second step, after identifying the range and the specific cells to be protected, is to turn on the protection feature for the entire worksheet by using the command /**W**orksheet **G**lobal **P**rotection **E**nable. You can turn off worksheet protection with a similar command: **D**isable.

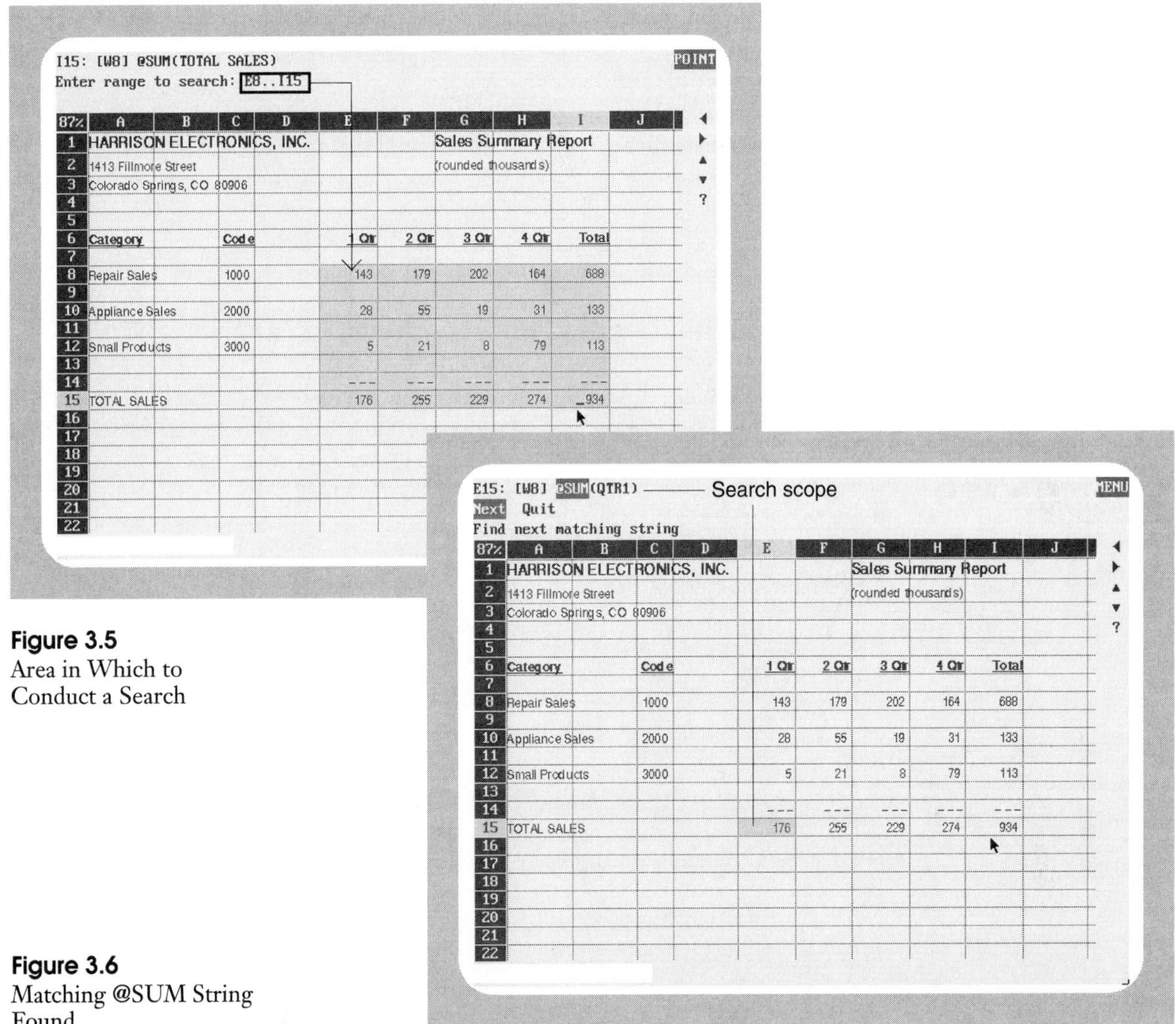

Figure 3.5
Area in Which to Conduct a Search

Figure 3.6
Matching @SUM String Found

Copy and Move Commands

One of the most appreciated features of Lotus 1-2-3 is its ability to recalculate an entire worksheet whenever a cell is changed. Using the /**C**opy command on cell contents is fundamental to worksheet building because it automatically adjusts cell references. You will save an enormous amount of time by copying similar formulas rather than entering them one at a time. Therefore, /**C**opy is one of the most frequently used Lotus 1-2-3 commands, as it allows for the development of modifiable worksheets. The /**M**ove command is similar to the /**C**opy command except that you physically move the original range to a new location.

HINT: For multiple-cell copies and moves, point to the top cell of the *to* range.

There are four types of copying and moving that you can do in 1-2-3. Figure 3.7 reflects the four copy (and move) types based on two dimensions: (1) copying *from* one or multiple cells and (2) copying *to* an identical or multiple number of cells. Understanding which of these copy (and move) types you are going to use is important because of the steps you must take for the copy (and move) From and To ranges. The following matrix delineates the activities needed for each copy (and move) type:

		Copying To	
		Identical Number of Cells	**Multiple Number of Cells**
Copying From	**Multiple Cells**	**Copy Type 1** Identify cell you are copying *from* Identify cell you are copying *to*	**Copy Type 2** Identify cell you are copying *from* Identify range of cells you are copying *to*
	One Cell	**Copy Type 3** Identify range of cells you are copying *from* Identify upper-left cell you are copying *to*	**Copy Type 4** Identify range of cells you are copying *from* Identify upper-left cell (only) of each range you are copying *to*

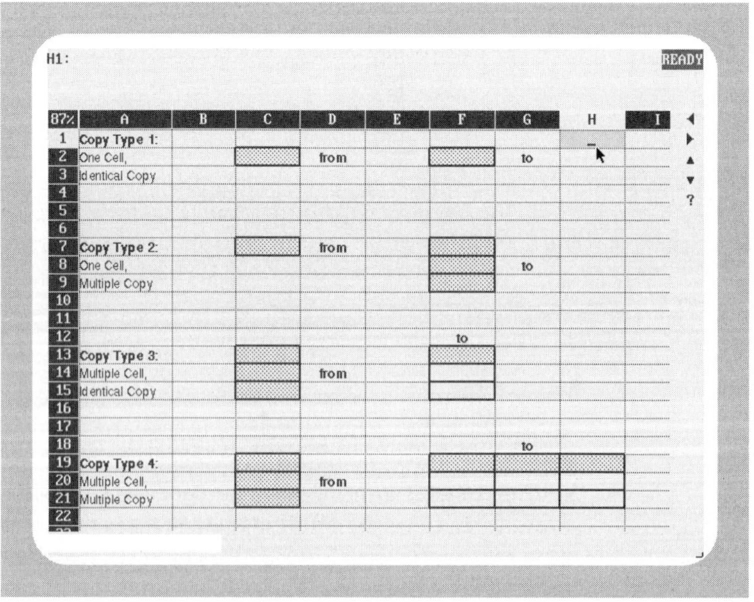

Figure 3.7
Different Copy Types

Copying and moving cell contents involves up to five steps. The actual number of steps depends on whether you are using a mouse or the cell pointer to copy (and move) and what type of copying (and moving) you are doing. Copying (and moving) from multiple cells involves pointing to the top cell of the To range only, not to the entire range. Refer to Figure 3.7 as you follow these steps:

With the cell pointer:

1. Locate the cell pointer in the upper-left cell of the range you are copying *from*.
2. Invoke the command /**C**opy.
3. Move the cell pointer to the end of the Copy From range (if necessary), and press (ENTER).
4. Move the cell pointer to the upper-left cell of the range you are copying *to*.
5. Move the cell pointer to the end of the Copy To range (if necessary), and press (ENTER).

With the mouse:

1. Locate the mouse pointer in the upper-left cell of the range you are copying *from*.
2. Move the mouse to the end of the Copy From range (if necessary).
3. Invoke the command /**C**opy.
4. Move the mouse pointer to the upper-left cell of the range you are copying *to*.
5. Move the mouse pointer to the end of the Copy To range (if necessary).

HINT: Make sure you have enough space in your worksheet *before* you copy or move.

One note about copying and moving cell contents: 1-2-3 is always in the typeover mode; this is different from word processors, which default to the insert mode. Therefore, be sure you are copying or moving to a blank area of the worksheet. If you copy or move a cell or a group of cells to an area of the worksheet that contains entries, those entries will be replaced with the new information that was copied or moved.

Relative versus Absolute Addressing

HINT: Adjustable cell references are the key to flexible formulas.

To be effective at copying, you must learn the ins and outs of cell addressing. Formulas composed of cell references form links in a chain that enables 1-2-3 to establish models that can be changed. Adjustable cell references are what make formulas *flexible*.

When you copy or move a formula within a range, you must know whether the address type is relative or absolute. **Relative addresses** are cell addresses that are adjusted when copied to a different location in the worksheet. **Absolute addresses**, in contrast, are those whose columns and/or rows *do not* change when moved or copied. A hybrid cell addressing, called **mixed cell addressing**, adjusts either the row or the column when a formula is copied. Such a variety of cell addressing allows you to write formulas that are copyable and modifiable, rather than write many different formulas that accomplish essentially the same thing. Ultimately, you will save yourself time by learning how to use all three of these cell referencing techniques.

HINT: The default for copying is relative addressing; for moving, it is absolute addressing.

Note that when you *copy* a formula, the default operation is relative addressing. However, when you *move* a formula, the default operation is absolute addressing; that is, the cell addresses within the formula do not change.

In the Harrison Electronics case, if you copy the formula in cell E15 (`@SUM(E8..E12)`) in Figure 3.8 from the location E15 to E17, then the cell references in the formula will change to reflect its new location (`@SUM(E10..E14)`). Relative addressing is not necessarily desirable in this situation because you require the original formula, with the original cell addresses, in the new location. In the example, you can make either the column or the row absolute by inserting a $ (the dollar sign) into a formula before either the column or the row reference. You can either insert the dollar sign directly into a formula when inputting it into a cell using the ABS ((F4)) key or use the EDIT ((F2)) key after you have entered the formula.

Once you have invoked the editor by using the (F2) key, you must move the cell pointer over to the cell references. Using the Absolute ((F4)) key, you can toggle among four options:

1. Column and row absolute (absolute addressing)
2. Row-only absolute (mixed addressing)

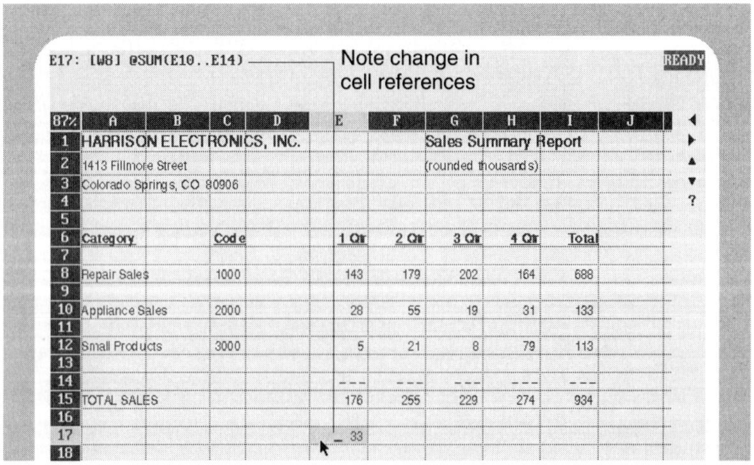

E17: [W8] @SUM(E10..E14) — Note change in cell references — READY

	A	C	E	F	G	H	I
1	HARRISON ELECTRONICS, INC.				Sales Summary Report		
2	1413 Fillmore Street				(rounded thousands)		
3	Colorado Springs, CO 80906						
4							
5							
6	Category	Code	1 Qtr	2 Qtr	3 Qtr	4 Qtr	Total
7							
8	Repair Sales	1000	143	179	202	164	688
9							
10	Appliance Sales	2000	28	55	19	31	133
11							
12	Small Products	3000	5	21	8	79	113
13							
14			---	---	---	---	---
15	TOTAL SALES		176	255	229	274	934
16							
17			33				
18							

Figure 3.8
An Incorrect Copy with Relative Addressing

3. Column-only absolute (mixed addressing)

4. Neither column nor row absolute (relative addressing)

Note that there are two versions of mixed cell addressing: row-only absolute and column-only absolute. In this example, you want to use the row-only absolute (option 2) so that the new formula will change to `@SUM(E$8..E$12)`. If you make the column absolute also, you will not be creating a copyable formula to be used in cells E15 through H15. With the row absolute in the formula, the formula is now copyable to cells F15 through H15. Using the row-only absolute also ensures quality in your overall worksheet. Making both the column and row absolute would have resulted in an error if you had tried to copy the formula into cells F15 through H15, as Figure 3.9 indicates.

HINT: Create copyable formulas by adjusting cell references.

Formulas often contain more than one cell reference. It may be necessary to adjust one of the cell references in the formula, but not all of them. Each cell reference can be adjusted individually for maximum flexibility. For example you have two cell references in your formula where you were referring to a specific row of cells in your worksheet for one of the cell references. If you then copied the formula residing in cell E20 to F20 through H20, the formula may look like this:

Original formula in cell E20:	E8 * B$35
Copied to cell F20 (different column):	F8 * C$35
Copied to cell E21 (different row):	E9 * B$35
Copied to cell F21 (different column and row):	F9 * C$35

Notice that when you copy a formula with a mixed cell address (row absolute) across the row to a different column, the column changes in both the relative address *and* the mixed address. When you copy the same formula down one row in the same column, only the row changes in the relative cell address. However, when you copy the formula to a different column and row, both the column

F15: [W8] @SUM($QTR1) READY

	A	B	C	D	E	F	G	H	I	J
1	HARRISON ELECTRONICS, INC.						Sales Summary Report			
2	1413 Fillmore Street						(rounded thousands)			
3	Colorado Springs, CO 80906									
4										
5										
6	Category		Code		1 Qtr	2 Qtr	3 Qtr	4 Qtr	Total	
7										
8	Repair Sales		1000		143	179	202	164	688	
9										
10	Appliance Sales		2000		28	55	19	31	133	
11										
12	Small Products		3000		5	21	8	79	113	
13										
14					---	---	---	---	---	
15	TOTAL SALES				176	176	176	176	704	
16										
17										

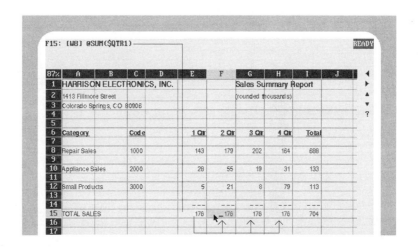

Figure 3.9
An Incorrect Copy with Absolute Addressing

and row change in the relative address *and* the column changes in the mixed address. The mixed cell address, in various combinations, allows you to create a large number of copyable formulas.

Worksheet Commands

Rather than perform operations on certain cells or ranges, **/Worksheet commands** affect the entire worksheet. The /**W**orksheet **S**tatus command shows the amount of conventional and extended memory available for creating worksheets, and the default settings for cell displays are readily available.

Working with Columns and Rows

You will often need to change the width of a specific column or range of columns in order to account for long labels or large numbers. Column widths do not affect the size of the cell—that is, the number of characters allowable per cell. The feature for modifying column widths changes the appearance of the worksheet only. You can also change the width of columns and rows through the WYSIWYG menu. To invoke the WYSIWYG menu, press the : (colon) key and select **W**orksheet and either **C**olumn or **R**ow.

The default column width for Lotus 1-2-3 worksheets is 9. Figure 3.10 shows an adjustment of the width of columns E through I to a size of 10. The command to use is /**W**orksheet **C**olumn **C**olumn-range **S**et-width. After asking for the range of columns to set, you enter the new width for the range of columns. After the column widths have been changed, you will notice that [W10] precedes the cell address in the control panel. If you are using a mouse, highlight the range of columns before you execute the /**W**orksheet command.

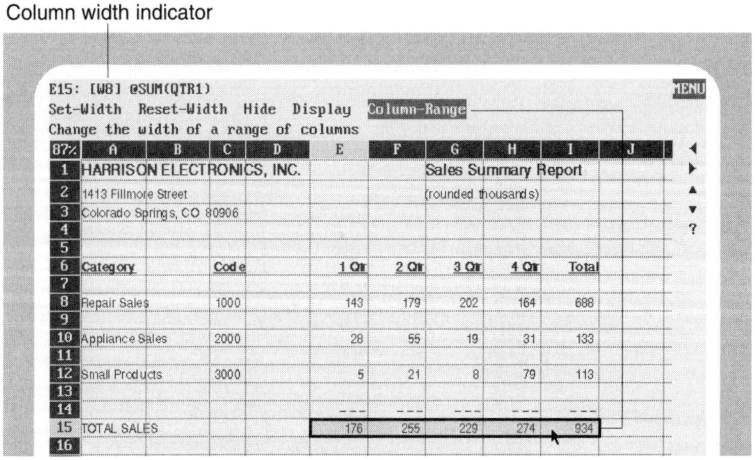

Column width indicator

Figure 3.10
Changing a Range of Column Widths

HINT: You can resize a range of columns by selecting **C**olumn-range prior to **S**et-width.

At this point, you may want to delete column B and change the width of column A to accommodate the larger category descriptions. To do this, use the /**W**orksheet **D**elete **C**olumn command. After you have selected either a column or a row, you are given the choice to delete a single column or range or to delete columns. After deleting column B, you will also need to change the width of column A from 8 to 17.

You may insert a column or row into an existing worksheet in exactly the same way, using the command /**W**orksheet **I**nsert.

Opening a Window

If you are using a large worksheet consisting of many rows and columns that do not fit on one screen and that require you to constantly reference another part of the worksheet, you may want to create a second window on the screen that contains a range of cells from any area of the worksheet. A **window** is a horizontal or vertical division of the worksheet into two screens so that you can see different parts of a large worksheet. This feature lets you see the impact of changes from one area of a worksheet on another area.

You use the /**W**orksheet **W**indow command to keep track of more than one area at a time. Lotus 1-2-3 gives you a choice of creating either a horizontal or a vertical window. To create a window, you move the cell pointer to the place in the worksheet where you want to open the window. Figure 3.11 illustrates the new window immediately after the 1-2-3 command has been executed.

If you change the width of a column in the new window, it will not affect column size in the original window. To delete the new window, use the **C**lear

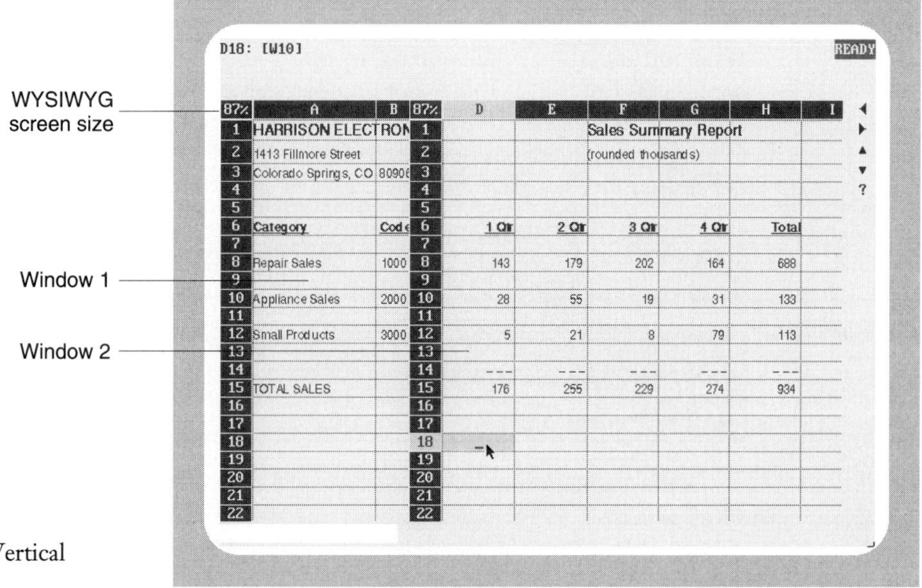

Figure 3.11
Opening a Vertical Window

HINT: Changing the width of a column in Window 2 will not affect the column size in the original window.

sub-command from the **/W**orksheet **W**indows command. The right window (Window 2) will always be deleted when you clear windows. To move from one window to another, use the Window ((F6)) key or click the mouse between windows. The (F6) key acts as a toggle to move the cell pointer from Window 1 to Window 2 and vice versa.

Changing Global Settings

You may want to customize your worksheet by changing some of the settings that affect the entire worksheet and the defaults. Figure 3.12 depicts the **/W**orksheet **G**lobal submenu. Global settings include:

1. Setting the global format for the entry of values
2. Setting the global alignment for the entry of labels
3. Setting the global column width
4. Setting the recalculation mode and process
5. Turning worksheet protection on and off
6. Changing the way cells with a value of zero appear on the screen

The **D**efault Settings submenu is illustrated in Figure 3.13. Default settings deal primarily with the printer, directory, and add-in packages.

File Commands

/File commands are fundamental to saving and retrieving worksheet files from hard disks. Lotus 1-2-3 does not automatically save worksheets, but when you exit from the program it reminds you that the worksheet has not been saved. The following file extensions have been created for files depending on the version of 1-2-3 used:

Version	File Extension
1 or 1a	.WKS
Student 1	.WKE
2, 2.01, 2.2, 2.3, 2.4, Student 2	.WK1
3.0, 3.1+, 1.1 for Windows	.WK3

A **file extension** indicates the type of Lotus 1-2-3 worksheet that has been saved to a disk. We will discuss only the saving and retrieving of files and the listing of .WK? files in the default directory. The **/W**orksheet **G**lobal **D**efault

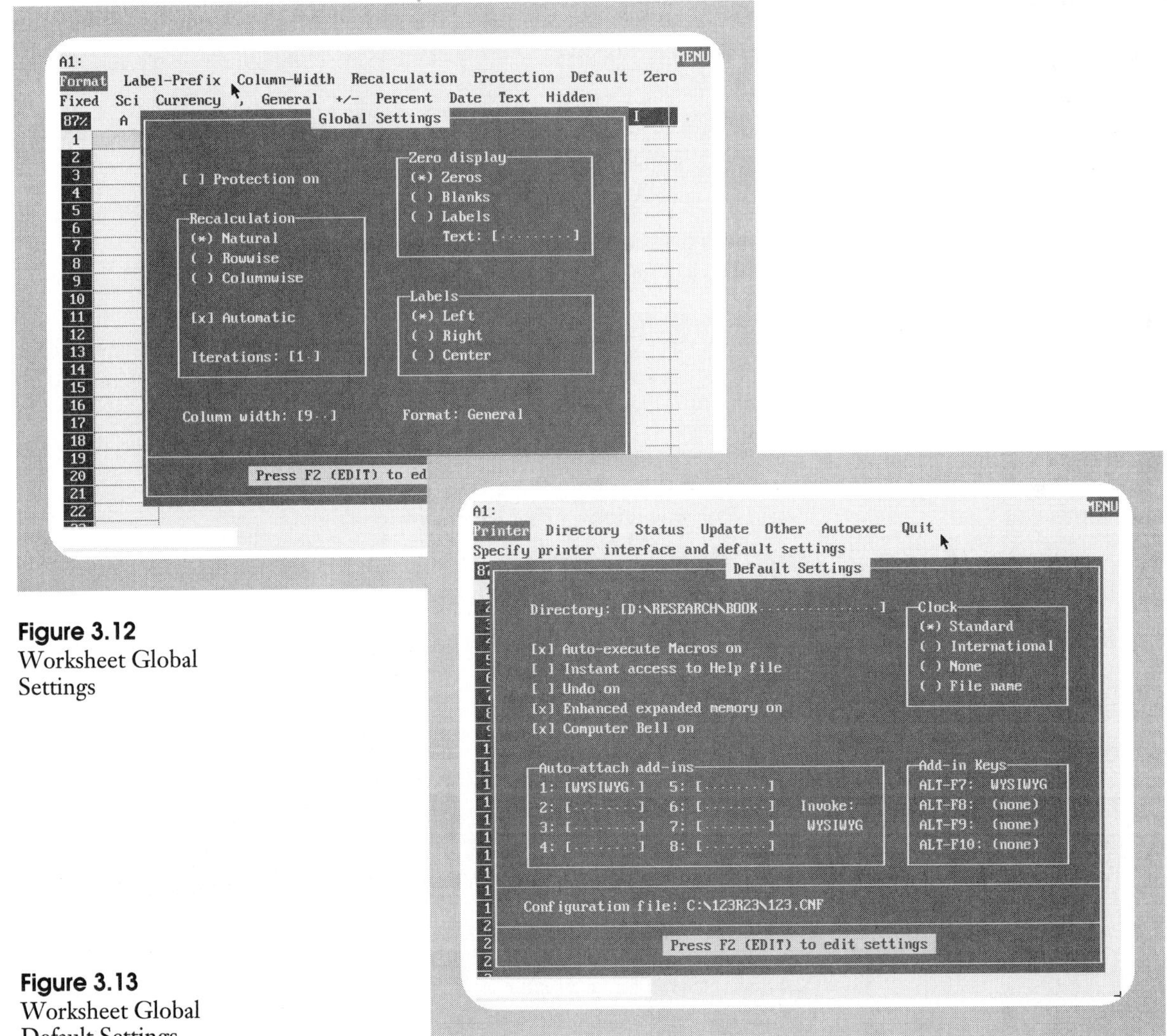

Figure 3.12
Worksheet Global Settings

Figure 3.13
Worksheet Global Default Settings

Directory submenu allows you to set the default directory in which you will save and retrieve files. If you plan to use the same directory repeatedly, you may want to change the default directory; otherwise you can change the directory within the **F**ile menu.

To save a file, you use the /**F**ile **S**ave command. Let's say you had retrieved a file as HARRISON.WK1, an existing 1-2-3 file. The system automatically gives you the same file name again, asking you to confirm. To retrieve a file, you use the /**F**ile **R**etrieve command. First, check the subdirectory that appears on the control line to be sure you are in the right location. There are four ways to modify the subdirectory of worksheet files that appears on the control line:

1. *Press the* ESC *key once* to change the file, correcting from right to left, moving the cell pointer in conjunction with the INS key to make the appropriate changes.
2. *Press the* ESC *key twice* and type the subdirectory information—for example: `C:\123R3\FILES`. Notice the backslash *after* the last locator, as well as before. Lotus automatically searches for all *.WK? files.
3. *Use the* BACKSPACE *key* to move up one subdirectory level on the tree. You can then highlight another set of subdirectory branches to move down the tree, using the ENTER key to confirm.
4. *Use the mouse* to select the file, move up one subdirectory level by selecting the .. symbol, change drives, or list files by pointing at the symbol at the top of the control panel.

Lotus 1-2-3 also handles the following types of file and data transfers, which you can choose from the /File menu:

Combine:	Incorporates all or part of another worksheet into the current one.
Import:	Reads text or numbers from a text file into the current worksheet.
Xtract:	Saves a specific range from the current worksheet into a new one.
Admin:	1. Gets or releases a current file's reservation if sharing the file on a network. 2. Produces a four-column table that lists worksheets, print files, graph files, and linked files. 3. Updates linked files.

Print Commands

HINT: Always save your file *before* printing your worksheet.

/Print commands allow you to print a copy of a worksheet to be used in a report or presentation. It is important to always save your file *before* printing a copy, because printers may jam, causing the print signal to lock up your spreadsheet program. To invoke the printer commands, press /**P**rint and select **P**rinter as the output device. If you are using a mouse, you invoke the same commands. You can also route your output to a file with the /**P**rint **F**ile command, which will be given the .PRN extension automatically by Lotus 1-2-3. You can select the **B**ackground submenu command to print the background while you continue to operate on the worksheet. Figure 3.14 displays the /**P**rint command menu.

By using the WYSIWYG program, built into 1-2-3, you can print a worksheet that includes fonts and formatting for your worksheets. Figure 3.15 shows the WYSIWYG **P**rint menu. The WYSIWYG lets you choose from a variety of fonts, shading, lines, and shadows in the final copy.

The first step in printing a 1-2-3 worksheet is to set the range that you want to print. Use the /**P**rint **P**rinter **R**ange command and highlight the entire worksheet or the area you want to print. To get a printout of the worksheet, first select **A**lign to go to the top of the page, and then choose **G**o to start printing. Figure 3.16 shows a printout of the worksheet; Figure 3.17 displays the same

Figure 3.14
Print Commands

Figure 3.15
WYSIWYG Print Command Menu

HARRISON ELECTRONICS, INC. 1413 Fillmore Street Colorado Springs, CO 80906					Sales Summary Report (rounded thousands)
Category	Code	1 Qtr	2 Qtr	3 Qtr	4 Qtr
Repair Sales	1000	143	179	202	164
Appliance Sales	2000	28	55	19	31
Small Products	3000	5	21	8	79
		---	---	---	---
TOTAL SALES		176	255	229	274

Figure 3.16
A Printout of the Worksheet

HARRISON ELECTRONICS, INC. 1413 Fillmore Street Colorado Springs, CO 80906					**Sales Summary Report** (rounded thousands)
Category	**Code**	**1 Qtr**	**2 Qtr**	**3 Qtr**	**4 Qtr**
Repair Sales	1000	143	179	202	164
Appliance Sales	2000	28	55	19	31
Small Products	3000	5	21	8	79
		---	---	---	---
TOTAL SALES		176	255	229	274

Figure 3.17
The Worksheet Printed from the WYSIWYG Program

worksheet printed from the WYSIWYG program. The **O**ptions submenu contains print options that enhance the appearance of your worksheet. The following commands can be selected from the **P**rint menu:

Header/**F**ooter	Creates a header or footer on your printed output.
Margins	Sets left, right, top, or bottom margins.
Borders	Specifies border columns and/or rows.
Setup	Manipulates the printer's functions.
Pg-length	Specifies the number of lines per page.

Selecting the **O**ther command submenu allows you to print in one of these four formats:

- As displayed
- Cell formulas
- Formatted—with headers, footers, and page breaks
- Unformatted—without headers, footers, and page breaks

Figure 3.18 illustrates the printing of the Harrison Electronics worksheet cell contents: labels, values, and formulas, using the Cell formulas format. Use the **/P**rint **P**age command to advance the paper to the top of the next page.

Figure 3.18
A Printout of the Worksheet Cell Contents

```
A1: [W17] 'HARRISON ELECTRONICS, INC.
F1: [W10] 'Sales Summary Report
A2: [W17] '1413 Fillmore Street
F2: [W10] '(rounded thousands)
A3: [W17] 'Colorado Springs, CO  80906
A6: [W17] 'Category
B6: [W5] "Code
D6: [W10] "1 Qtr
E6: [W10] "2 Qtr
F6: [W10] "3 Qtr
G6: [W10] "4 Qtr
H6: [W10] "Total
A8: [W17] 'Repair Sales
B8: [W5] 1000
D8: [W10] 143
E8: [W10] 179
F8: [W10] 202
G8: [W10] 164
H8: [W10] @SUM(D8..G8)
A10: [W17] 'Appliance Sales
B10: [W5] 2000
D10: [W10] 28
E10: [W10] 55
F10: [W10] 19
G10: [W10] 31
H10: [W10] @SUM(D10..G10)
A12: [W17] 'Small Products
B12: [W5] 3000
D12: [W10] 5
E12: [W10] 21
F12: [W10] 8
G12: [W10] 79
H12: [W10] @SUM(D12..G12)
D14: [W10] "---
E14: [W10] "---
F14: [W10] "---
G14: [W10] "---
H14: [W10] "---
A15: [W17] 'TOTAL SALES
D15: [W10] @SUM(QTR1)
E15: [W10] @SUM(QTR2)
F15: [W10] @SUM(QTR3)
G15: [W10] @SUM(QTR4)
H15: [W10] @SUM(TOTAL SALES)
```

Other Lotus 1-2-3 Commands

The System Command

The **/System command** leaves the Lotus 1-2-3 program temporarily to let you use DOS commands. Here you can execute a number of DOS commands and programs, such as file managers or batch files that control printing, for example. Remember that 1-2-3 resides within conventional memory; therefore, trying to execute programs that are too large may not work. To return to the 1-2-3 program, enter `EXIT` at the DOS command line.

The Add-in Command

The /**A**dd-in and /**W**orksheet **G**lobal **D**efault **O**ther **A**dd-in commands instruct 1-2-3 to attach, detach, or invoke an additional program that was created to run with 1-2-3 commands. These **add-in applications**, such as WYSIWYG, Allways, or Auditor were not necessarily developed by Lotus Corporation, yet they all can be run while you are using 1-2-3. Figure 3.19 shows the attachment of an add-in program. Add-in programs also consume conventional, expanded, and/or extended memory, so you must be careful how many programs you attach. The more programs you attach, the slower 1-2-3 operates.

The Graph Command

One of the most important criteria of any spreadsheet package is its ability to create presentation graphics. **/Graph commands** are a very effective tool for conveying information visually and thereby proving the adage that "a picture is worth a thousand words." The ability to translate tables of data into graphics for presentations is an essential feature of Lotus 1-2-3. Graphs present information in a way that allows you to be more creative as you analyze data. As a result, your decisions will be more effective.

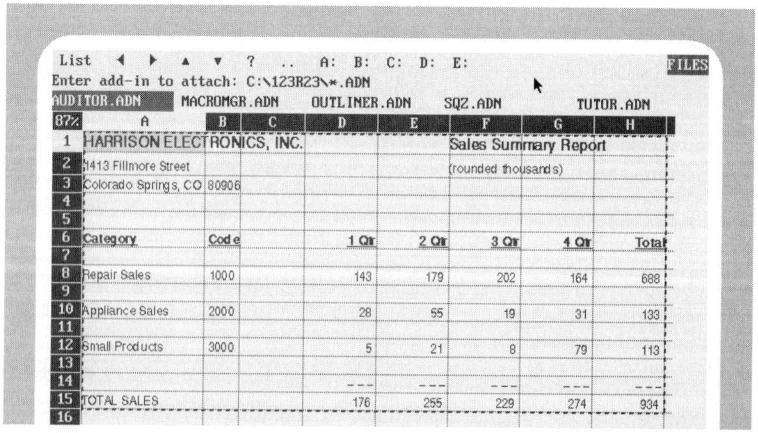

```
List  ◄  ►  ▲  ▼  ?  ..  A:  B:  C:  D:  E:                    FILES
Enter add-in to attach: C:\123R23\*.ADN
AUDITOR.ADN   MACROMGR.ADN   OUTLINER.ADN   SQZ.ADN   TUTOR.ADN
```

87%	A	B	C	D	E	F	G	H
1	HARRISON ELECTRONICS, INC.					Sales Summary Report		
2	1413 Fillmore Street					(rounded thousands)		
3	Colorado Springs, CO	80906						
4								
5								
6	Category	Code		1 Qtr	2 Qtr	3 Qtr	4 Qtr	Total
7								
8	Repair Sales	1000		143	179	202	164	688
9								
10	Appliance Sales	2000		28	55	19	31	133
11								
12	Small Products	3000		5	21	8	79	113
13								
14				---	---	---	---	---
15	TOTAL SALES			176	255	229	274	934
16								

Figure 3.19
Attaching an Add-in Program

The Data Command

Lotus can manage data in a two-dimensional format. Versions 2.3 and 2.4 manage flat files, while Releases 3.1+ and 1.1 for Windows manage relational databases. The 1-2-3 database can be created and accessed with the /**D**ata command. The /**D**ata menu gives you access to a set of widely used commands for manipulating data. With the /**D**ata commands you can sort and query the database, derive descriptive statistics, create a data table, sort data, generate frequencies, and run a multiple regression.

The Quit Command

When you indicate that you want to quit the Lotus 1-2-3 program, you are first asked whether you want to end your 1-2-3 session. If you choose No, you are returned to the Lotus 1-2-3 program. If you have made changes to the worksheet since last saving it, selecting Yes prompts the system to display the message:

```
WORKSHEET CHANGES NOT SAVED! End 1-2-3 Anyway?
```

HINT: Always make a backup of your worksheet using the /**F**ile **S**ave **B**ackup command.

Obviously you have the option to exit the 1-2-3 program without saving your changes. You might choose to do this especially if you have made some changes that you don't want to keep. But remember, you must always save a current copy of your worksheet to a backup file by using the /**F**ile **S**ave command and designating a **B**ackup file.

Review Questions

1. How do you invoke the 1-2-3 menus?
2. What is the difference between /Worksheet and /Range commands?
3. Contrast a worksheet range and /Range commands.
4. What are the steps in anchoring a range?
5. What do *global* and *default* mean in 1-2-3?
6. What is the default format for values and labels?
7. Describe the steps necessary to change the format for a range of values.
8. What is the proper way to erase the contents of a cell?
9. The /Range Search command is most useful for finding what type of cell entry?
10. Describe the two-step process for protecting or unprotecting a range.
11. How do you name a range?

12. How can you use a named range in worksheet formulas?
13. What steps are necessary to create a range name table?
14. In what ways can worksheet windows be used?
15. Detail the steps needed to copy a formula from one location to another.
16. What is the difference between relative and absolute addressing?
17. How do you change a range of column widths?
18. What do file extensions indicate?
19. What are the different types of printed output from 1-2-3 that can be extracted?

Skill-Building Activities: Enhancing a Worksheet

Activity 1: Retrieving a Worksheet

Let's continue to develop the Harrison worksheet. You will use the File **R**etrieve menu to bring up a copy of the file.

NOTE: To help you with this exercise, ***boldface*** *letters indicate a message from the system or the worksheet.*

1. Use the 1-2-3 menus to retrieve the file, and press /**F**ile **R**etrieve.
2. Enter `HARRIS` for the filename.
3. Press the ENTER key to confirm the retrieve.

Your worksheet should now look exactly like the one you left in Chapter 2. Compare your worksheet with the one in Figure 3.20.

Activity 2: Deleting and Resizing Columns

You will now delete the column between the category and code entries (column B) and resize column A so that the category descriptions can fit within it. Your cell pointer should be located somewhere in the B column. If so, do the following:

Select the menu command /**W**orksheet **D**elete **C**olumn.

Press the ENTER key to confirm the delete.

Next, you will enlarge column A and columns D through H (previously E through I). Always position the cursor on the first column you want to resize.

I15: [W8] @SUM(TOTAL) READY

87%	A	B	C	D	E	F	G	H	I	J
1	HARRISON ELECTRONICS, INC.						Sales Summary Report			
2	1413 Fillmore Street						(rounded thousands)			
3	Colorado Springs, CO 80906									
4										
5										
6	Category		Code		1 Qtr	2 Qtr	3 Qtr	4 Qtr	Total	
7										
8	Repair Sales		1000		143	179	202	164	688	
9										
10	Appliance Sales		2000		28	55	19	31	133	
11										
12	Small Products		3000		5	21	8	79	113	
13										
14					---	---	---	---	---	
15	TOTAL SALES				176	255	229	274	934	
16										
17										
18										
19										

Figure 3.20
The Harrison Electronics Worksheet

Position the cell pointer anywhere on column A.

Select the menu commands **/W**orksheet **C**olumn **S**et-width.

Type `17` at the prompt and press the (ENTER) key to confirm.

Move the cell pointer to anywhere on column D.

Select the menu commands **/W**orksheet **C**olumn **C**olumn-range **S**et-width.

Move the cell pointer to column H and press the (ENTER) key to confirm.

Type `10` at the prompt and press the (ENTER) key to confirm.

Figure 3.21 displays your worksheet with the column changes.

Activity 3: Naming a Range

Now you will name the range that comprises the row TOTAL SALES for each quarter (D15..G15).

Position the cell pointer on the first cell (D15) of the range.

Select the menu command **/R**ange **N**ame **C**reate.

Enter the name by typing `TOTAL SALES` (note the space).

Enter the range by moving the cell pointer 4 spaces to the right to column G by using the right cursor key or the mouse.

Press the (ENTER) key to confirm.

D4: [W10] READY

87%	A	B	C	D	E	F	G	H
1	HARRISON ELECTRONICS, INC.					Sales Summary Report		
2	1413 Fillmore Street					(rounded thousands)		
3	Colorado Springs, CO	80906						
4								
5								
6	Category	Code		1 Qtr	2 Qtr	3 Qtr	4 Qtr	Total
7								
8	Repair Sales	1000		143	179	202	164	688
9								
10	Appliance Sales	2000		28	55	19	31	133
11								
12	Small Products	3000		5	21	8	79	113
13								
14				---	---	---	---	---
15	TOTAL SALES			176	255	229	274	934
16								

Figure 3.21
Working with Columns

Activity 4: Erasing the Contents of a Range

Although the newly named range already contains formulas, you will erase the formulas and then recreate them. You will check your results against those in Figure 3.22.

Be sure the cell pointer is still positioned on cell D15.

Select the menu command /**R**ange **E**rase.

Enter the range by highlighting through cell H15.

Press the (ENTER) key.

Activity 5: Entering and Copying a Formula

In cell D15 you will enter a formula that totals the three categories of sales for Quarter 1. You will then copy the formula from D15 to E15 through H15.

Position the cell pointer on cell D15.

Type the formula `@SUM(`.

Move the cell pointer up to cell D8 and

1. anchor the cell pointer by entering a (.), and move the cell pointer down to cell D12, *or*

2. use the mouse to highlight the range D8..D12

Enter a closed parenthesis [)] and press the (ENTER) key to confirm the formula. You should now see the value 176 in cell D15.

Select the menu command /**C**opy.

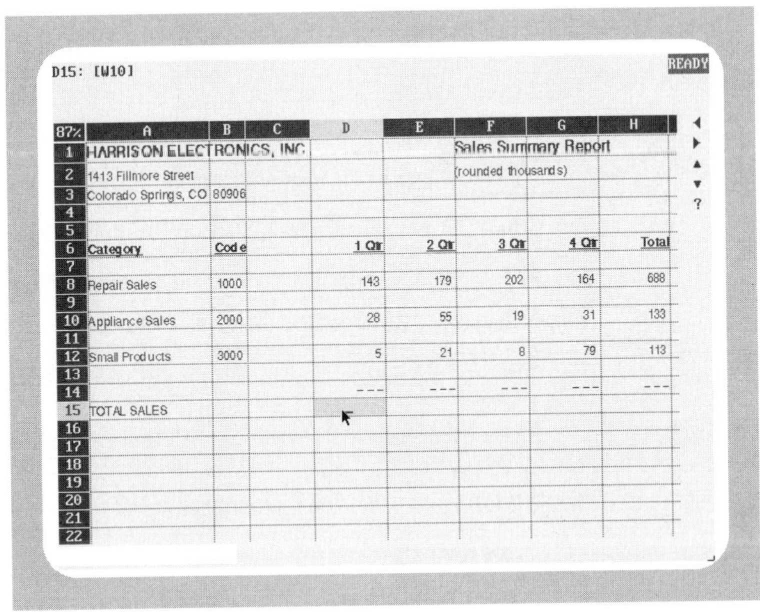

Figure 3.22
Erased Formulas

Press the ENTER key to confirm the From range, which is cell D15.

Move the cursor one cell to the right to cell E15 and

1. anchor the cell pointer by entering a (.), and move the cell pointer over to cell H15, *or*
2. use the mouse to highlight the range E15..H15.
3. press ENTER to confirm the range.

Activity 6: Printing your Worksheet

Your final activity in this chapter is to print a copy of your modified worksheet. Be sure your printer is connected and set up properly and that WYSIWYG is loaded as the add-in. Before printing, it is always wise to save the file first in case of printer error. Save the file as HARRIS and choose Replace to copy over the file you saved from Chapter 2.

You will print your worksheet from both 1-2-3 and WYSIWYG to compare the output. Move the cell pointer home to the A1 cell by using the HOME key.

Select the menu command /**P**rint **P**rinter **R**ange.

Enter the range A1..H15 by using either the cell pointer or the mouse.

Press the ENTER key.

Select the menu subcommand **A**lign **G**o **Q**uit to start the printing process.

Your printer should now be printing a hard copy to compare with the output shown in Figure 3.23. Notice that in Figure 3.23 we are missing column H, Total, due to incorrect margin settings. To deliver a proper output, you must change the margins.

While in the **P**rint menu, select the **O**ptions **M**argins **R**ight subcommand.

Enter 90 to change the margins and press ENTER.

Press the ESC key to move up one menu level.

Select the subcommand **A**lign **G**o **Q**uit to start the printing process.

Figure 3.24 shows the reinstatement of column H and the associated Total Sales data.

To compare the 1-2-3 output with that of the desktop publisher, you will use the WYSIWYG add-in to create a printout. You will use WYSIWYG to shade the titles in your worksheet, change some of the font sizes, and bold the headings.

Press the colon key (:) to bring up the WYSIWYG menu.

You will select one of the formatting options in the WYSIWYG program. Invoke the **F**ormat **S**hade **L**ight command.

Use either the mouse or the cell pointer to highlight the range A6..H6.

Press ENTER to confirm the formatting.

To change the font type for the titles, invoke the **F**ormat **F**ont command from the WYSIWYG menu.

Select the font number that corresponds to the font: Bitstream Swiss 14 Point.

Format the range A1..F1 and press ENTER to confirm.

Now invoke the **F**ormat **B**old **S**et command from the WYSIWYG menu.

Format two ranges: A1..F1 and A6..H6.

Before printing, select **L**ayout **C**ompression **A**utomatic to space the worksheet on the page.

Select **P**review from the **P**rint WYSIWYG menu to see the document.

Select **P**rint **R**ange **S**et WYSIWYG command and set the print range as A1..H15.

Press the **G**o to start printing.

The WYSIWYG program automatically aligns the highlighted range with the top of the page. Figure 3.25 illustrates the preview screen in WYSIWYG. The preview screen is a useful option prior to printing your document. By selecting automatic compression, WYSIWYG makes sure that all of the columns and

```
HARRISON ELECTRONICS, INC.                         Sales Summary Report
1413 Fillmore Street                               (rounded thousands)
Colorado Springs, CO 80906

Category          Code        1 Qtr     2 Qtr     3 Qtr     4 Qtr

Repair Sales      1000          143       179       202       164

Appliance Sales   2000           28        55        19        31

Small Products    3000            5        21         8        79

                                ---       ---       ---       ---
TOTAL SALES                     176       255       229       274
```

Figure 3.23
Worksheet Output with Incorrect Margins

```
HARRISON ELECTRONICS, INC.                         Sales Summary Report
1413 Fillmore Street                               (rounded thousands)
Colorado Springs, CO 80906

Category          Code        1 Qtr     2 Qtr     3 Qtr     4 Qtr     Total

Repair Sales      1000          143       179       202       164       688

Appliance Sales   2000           28        55        19        31       133

Small Products    3000            5        21         8        79       113

                                ---       ---       ---       ---       ---
TOTAL SALES                     176       255       229       274       934
```

Figure 3.24
Worksheet Output with Correct Margins

rows in the range you selected fit on the page without having to adjust your margins as you did earlier when printing from 1-2-3.

Before you quit 1-2-3, you must save your worksheet which should be similar to Figure 3.26. This time, call the Harrison Electronics worksheet HARRIS2 so that you have incremental and auditable documents of your work.

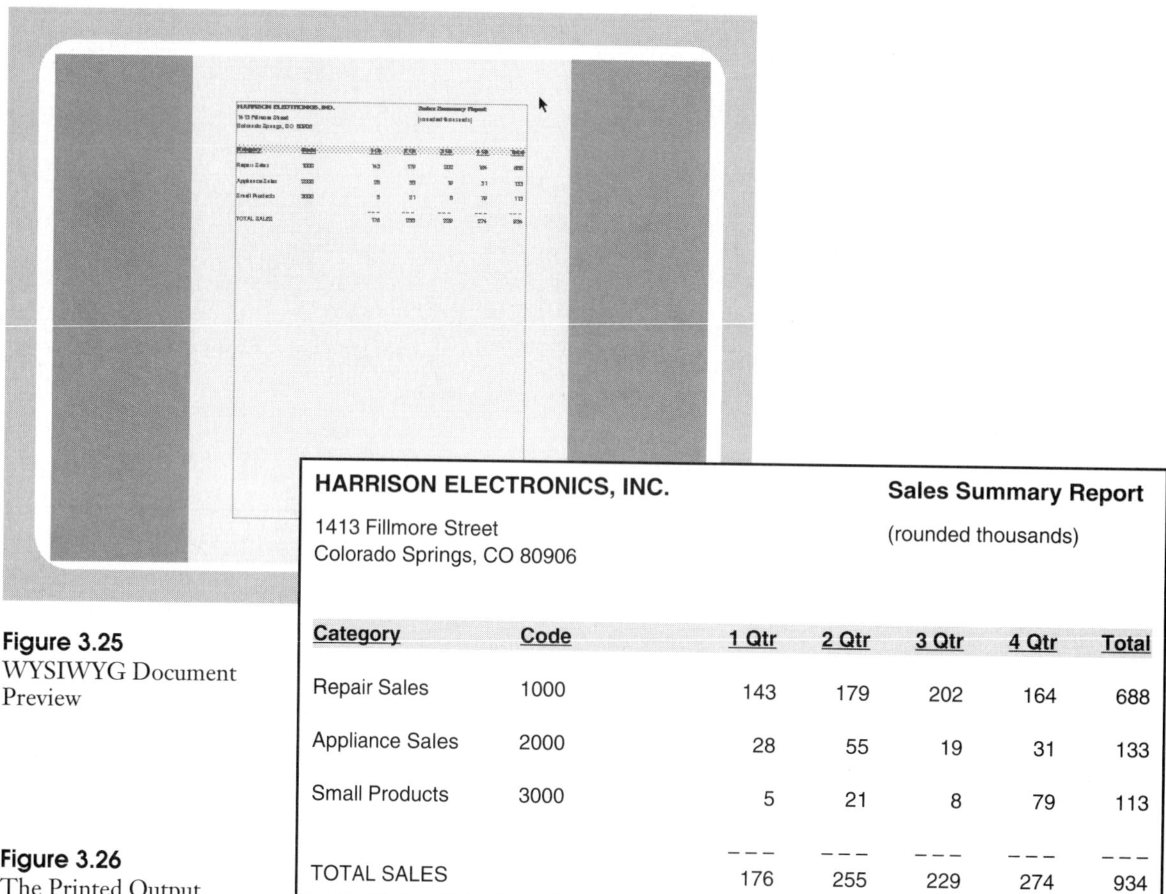

HARRISON ELECTRONICS, INC. — **Sales Summary Report**

1413 Fillmore Street
Colorado Springs, CO 80906

(rounded thousands)

Category	Code	1 Qtr	2 Qtr	3 Qtr	4 Qtr	Total
Repair Sales	1000	143	179	202	164	688
Appliance Sales	2000	28	55	19	31	133
Small Products	3000	5	21	8	79	113
		---	---	---	---	---
TOTAL SALES		176	255	229	274	934

Figure 3.25
WYSIWYG Document Preview

Figure 3.26
The Printed Output

Hands-On Exercises

1. Retrieve the worksheet from the hands-on exercises in Chapter 2 or reenter the following worksheet. It was saved as BUDGET in Chapter 2.

Row	A	B	C	D	E	F
4		1989	1990	1991	1992	Total
6	Sales	53	66	43	71	233
7	Expenses	23	38	24	47	132
9	Income	30	28	19	24	101

Remember that the Income row (Row 9) contains a formula that subtracts expenses from income and that the Total column (Column F) contains formulas that sum the values in the main worksheet. Look at the following formulas:

Row	A	B	C	D	E	F
4						
6						+B6+C6+D6+E6
7						+B7+C7+D7+E7
9		+B6-B7	+C6-C7	+D6-D7	+E6-E7	@SUM(B9..E9)

2. Set the format for rows 6–9 to Fixed with 2 decimal places.
3. Use the /Range Search command to find the label @SUM in the formula contained in cell F9. Set the search range to A1..F9 and search for *both* formulas and labels.
4. Copy the formula in cell F9 to cells F6 and F7 replacing the formulas in those cells.
5. Protect all the cells in column F and row 9 by turning on protected data in the range A6..E9. Try to change the value of any cell in the protected area of the worksheet. The formula should resemble `@SUM(INCOME)` in cell F9.
7. Add a tax rate to the worksheet in cell B14:

	Column	
Row	A	B
14	Tax Rate	15%

8. Label row 10 Taxes and row 12 Profit. In cell B10 calculate the taxes for the budget by multiplying the income by the tax rate. Since you will copy the formula across all the years, you need to make the reference to the tax rate absolute. Enter the following formula in cell B10:

   ```
   +B9*$B$14
   ```
9. Copy the formula across to the other cells in row 10, C10..F10.
10. Print the worksheet and save it to a disk as BUDGET2.

Problem-Solving Projects

1. Retrieve the PETSHOP worksheet from the problem in Chapter 2. Enter the worksheet by hand if you did not complete the exercise in Chapter 2.
2. Format the values for Wholesale Price (Column D) and Retail Price (Column E) as currency with 2 decimal places.
3. Format the values for Percentage Profit (Column F) as percent with 1 decimal place.
4. Change the column width for Product (Column A) to 12, Wholesale Price (Column D) to 11, and Percentage Profit (Column F) to 10.
5. Delete Column B from the worksheet.
6. Right-justify the Stock Name labels now in Column B.
7. Add three new right-justified column headings:

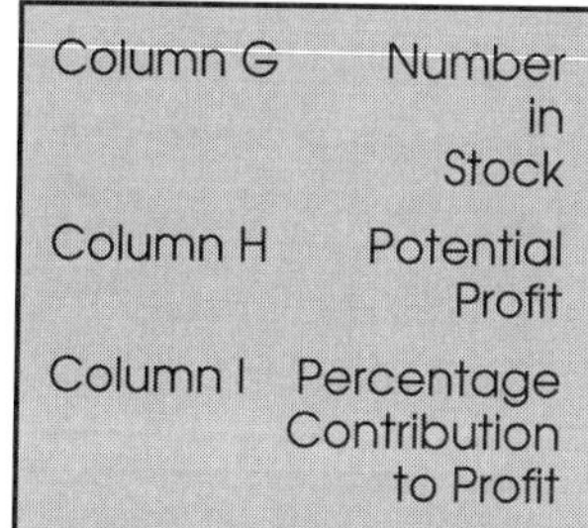

Column G	Number in Stock
Column H	Potential Profit
Column I	Percentage Contribution to Profit

8. Add the following data for the number of animals in stock:

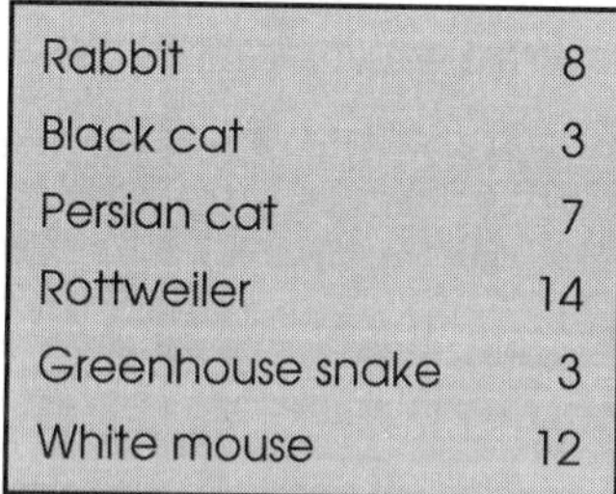

Rabbit	8
Black cat	3
Persian cat	7
Rottweiler	14
Greenhouse snake	3
White mouse	12

   If you see asterisks (***) in a cell, your column width needs to be enlarged. Use the /Worksheet Column Set-width command to resize your column.

9. Calculate the Potential Profit by subtracting the Wholesale Price from the Retail Price and multiplying the result by the Number in Stock.
10. Add a left-justified TOTAL label to cell A16.

11. Total the Potential Profit (Column G) for the Tri-Lakes Pet Store by using the @SUM function.
12. To calculate the Percentage Contribution to Profit, divide the Potential Profit for a product by the total Potential Profit. Be sure to use mixed and absolute addressing where appropriate.
13. Move the cell pointer to Column B and open a vertical window. Switch to Window 2 and move around.
14. Save your worksheet as PETSHOP2.

Quality Assurance Checklist

As we conclude our discussion of spreadsheet commands, be sure you have considered the following factors that will contribute to the quality of your worksheet:

✓ Use a cell pointer or mouse to highlight a range to provide visual feedback.

✓ Use the /**W**orksheet **G**lobal command to set the default format for the worksheet and then to modify individual ranges as needed.

✓ Use range names whenever possible to define (1) areas of the worksheet you may want to move to and (2) cells or areas you may want to use in a worksheet formula.

✓ Remember that a cell may have more than one range name.

✓ Use the /**R**ange **E**rase command to delete cell contents.

✓ Use the /**W**orksheet **G**lobal **P**rotection **E**nable command to turn on the protection feature for a worksheet, and then use the /**R**ange **U**nprotect command to unprotect specific cells or ranges.

✓ Use the /**C**opy and /**M**ove commands only when you have determined that you have enough space or that you have made enough space to move to.

✓ Use adjustable cell references to create copyable and maintainable formulas by using relative, mixed, and absolute addressing.

✓ Use the **C**olumn-range command to resize a range of columns prior to **S**et-width.

✓ Use the /**W**orksheet **C**olumn **S**et-width command in Window 1 only; Window 2 column widths will not be affected in the original window.

✓ Use the /**F**ile **S**ave command before you print your worksheet in case there is a problem with the printer.

✓ Use the WYSIWYG add-in program to format ranges and to change fonts.

CHAPTER

4 Developing Formulas: Model Building Blocks

He has the facts, but not the phosphorescence of learning.

—Emily Dickinson

Objectives

- Understand the importance of the formula as a model building-block.
- Learn the different parts of a formula and how to develop formulas.
- Work with predefined spreadsheet functions.
- Understand the POINT mode for working with formulas.
- Develop complex models with the @IF statement.
- Use the Auditor to analyze and display information about worksheet formulas.

The Building Blocks

In the previous two chapters, you were introduced to the Lotus 1-2-3 spreadsheet program and you created several simple worksheets. We will now discuss the importance of Lotus formulas, and the structure and construction of those formulas. Lotus 1-2-3 contains a number of built-in functions that help you to develop dynamic models more easily and more efficiently. In later chapters, we will discuss in detail the use of formulas for building dynamic models and for creating a model base, a critical part of the decision support system.

The **formula** is the key to building a dynamic model. Remember that a formula is a mathematical statement that represents a specific situation. A **dynamic model** is a collection of formulas that, when interrogated, produces a variety of scenarios for analysis. To conduct what-if analysis and test variable sensitivities, you must develop effective formulas. When you create formulas that are copyable and therefore maintainable, you create a better worksheet. Without effective formulas, you cannot develop such a dynamic model.

The formula is the building block that models are built upon. You can use formulas to conduct analyses, build models, create scenarios, explore what-ifs, and accomplish even more advanced analyses. Figure 4.1 illustrates the importance of formulas as model building-blocks.

Formula Structure

A formula is a directive to perform a calculation using values, cell contents, or other formulas. Since cell contents can be either a value or a label in 1-2-3, it is

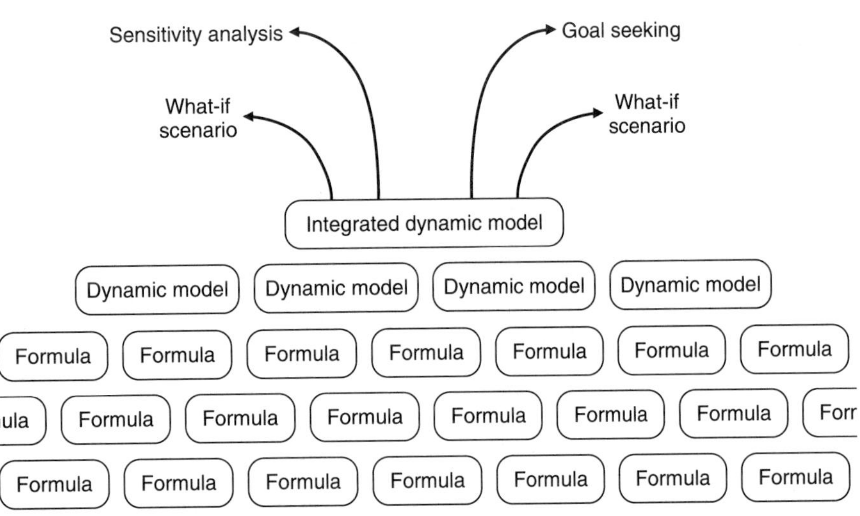

Figure 4.1
The Formula as the Building Block for Models

important to remember that formulas are values rather than labels. Although a formula is *stored* in the cell in which it was entered, the cell *displays* the resulting value of the formula's calculation. Formulas can start with any value, value symbol, or mathematical operator. Values include numbers from 0 to 9, and value symbols include . + - @ # $ (. When the formula starts with a cell address, the first character should be a plus (+) sign, as in `+C4+C5` or `+C4-$A$21`. The basic structure of a formula is as follows:

HINT: A cell stores a formula but it displays its results.

Argument 1 Operator 1 Argument 2 ... (Operator 2 Argument 3...)

Operators

Formulas have four components: operators, cell references, values, and/or functions. Every formula does not have to contain all of these components, but the operator is essential. An **operator** tells the formula which action to take. Because mathematical operators are the heart of the formula, one or more operators must reside within all formulas. Figure 4.2 illustrates the different uses of operators within formulas. The results in column E are in a fixed format with one decimal place. Operators execute in the following order beginning with the most important:

1. Exponentiation (^)
2. Multiplication (*) and division (/)
3. Addition (+) and subtraction (-)

A1: [W39] READY

87%	A	B	C	D	E
1	–	Operators	Formula	Values	Result
2					
3				6.0	
4				2.0	
5					
6	Operators on the same level:	+ –	+D3+D4–4		4.0
7		* /	+D3*D4/4		3.0
8					
9	Operators on different levels:	^ /	+D3^D4/4		9.0
10		/ ^	+D3/D4^4		0.4
11					
12	Operators on different levels with parentheses:	^ /	+D3^(D4/4)		2.4
13		/ ^	(D3/4)^D4		2.3
14					
15	Operators on different levels with nested parentheses:	+ / ^	+D3+D3/D4^4		6.4
16			+D3+(D3/D4)^4		87.0
17			(D3+(D3/D4))^4		6561.0
18			((D3+D3)/D4)^4		1296.0
19			(D3+D3)/(D4^4)		0.8
20					
21					
22					

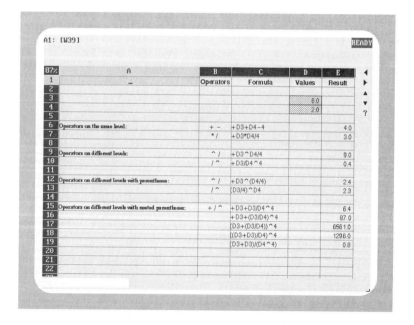

Figure 4.2
The Use of Parentheses with Different Operators

Operators on the same level execute from left to right. Operators on different levels execute according to their order of mathematical importance (such as the formula `+D3/4^D4`, in which 4 is risen to the second power first). In general, the use of values is discouraged in formulas, but for the sake of this example we have included a value. Operators in parentheses are performed from the innermost set of parentheses outward, beginning from the left of the equation.

Arguments

An **argument** can take the form of a value or a cell reference. A **variable** is a row of interrelated cells that explain a phenomenon or capture information, such as Repair Sales or Operating Expenses. The simplest formula to understand is one with values for arguments, for example +5+7. Cell references, rather than values, in formulas allow for expected and unexpected changes, thereby increasing the quality of the dynamic model output. The following table shows the relationship between the Operating Expenses and Total Sales for the first quarter for Harrison Electronics:

HINT: Using cell references in formulas increases the quality of the dynamic model.

Variable	Column D	Related Formula	Column H
TOTAL SALES	176	@sum(D8..D12)	
Operating Expenses	45		
Ratio: OE/Total Sales	25.6%	+D17/D15	22.6%
Average Operating Expenses	40	+D15*$H$19	

Notice that Operating Expenses have been added to the worksheet as an expense in Figure 4.3. We now want to calculate the ratio of Operating Expenses to Total Sales in order to develop a formula that approximates the Operating Expenses variable. In a business sense, we want to better understand how Operating Expenses behaves, given changes in Total Sales. In cell D19 of Figure 4.3, we have entered the formula `+D17/D15` in order to capture the ratio of Operating Expenses to Total Sales.

@Functions

@Functions are formulas that are built into the Lotus 1-2-3 program to save you time and to help you with the program logic. All built-in functions are preceded by the symbol @. Functions can exist within larger formulas, or they can stand alone. A function usually has an argument (cell reference) which is the major component of any function. The arguments in an @function must be enclosed in parentheses. Different arguments are separated by commas. However, some @functions in 1-2-3 do not require an argument. Some functions in 1-2-3 are significantly different from those in other spreadsheet programs, such as Excel and Quattro Pro, and cannot be transferred as formulas.

HINT: @functions differ among spreadsheet programs and are not always transferrable.

D19: (P1) [W10] +D17/D15 READY

87%	A	B	C	D	E	F	G	H
1						Sales Summary Report		
2	1413 Fillmore Street					(rounded thousands)		
3	Colorado Springs, CO	80906						
4								
5								
6	Category	Code		1 Qtr	2 Qtr	3 Qtr	4 Qtr	Total
7								
8	Repair Sales	1000		143	179	202	164	688
9								
10	Appliance Sales	2000		28	55	19	31	133
11								
12	Small Products	3000		5	21	8	79	113
13								
14				---	---	---	---	---
15	TOTAL SALES			176	255	229	274	934
16								
17	Operating Expenses			45	54	44	67	
18								
19	Ratio: OE/Total Sales			25.6%	21.2%	19.2%	24.5%	
20								
21								
22								

Variable

Figure 4.3
Ratio of Operating Expenses to Total Sales

Formulas can consist solely of a single function or several functions. Turning back to the Harrison Electronics case in Figure 4.4, you can substitute a function that averages the four OE/Total Sales ratios. The formula in cell H19, which is a function, averages this variable as follows:

```
@AVG(D19..G19)
```

The @AVG function substitutes for the following formula:

```
+(D19+E19+F19+G19)/4
```

HINT: Always make a reference to a single cell absolute when using it in more than one formula.

To use the value in cell H19 in a copyable formula, we have to make the reference to cell H19 absolute so that the cell reference does not change when the formula is copied. Always make a reference to a single cell absolute when using it in more than one formula. The variable Average Operating Expenses in Figure 4.4 shows what Operating Expenses should have been if Operating Expenses was based upon the average. Comparing average with actual operating expenses gives the decision maker a good handle on costs. Now if we needed to change the average ratio value for any reason the formulas would adjust the values automatically.

HINT: Formulas in dynamic models do not contain values.

We will discuss dynamic modeling in depth in Section 2. However, keep in mind that dynamic models do not contain any values within formulas. We must assume that all values are subject to change in a dynamic model, therefore data is *extracted* either from the related data area or from another dynamic model. Model linking is critical to successful analysis, and successful analysis leads to effective decisions.

D21: (F0) [W10] +D15*$H$19 READY

87%	A	B	C	D	E	F	G	H
1						Sales Summary Report		
2	1413 Fillmore Street					(rounded thousands)		
3	Colorado Springs, CO	80906						
4								
5								
6	Category	Code		1 Qtr	2 Qtr	3 Qtr	4 Qtr	Total
7								
8	Repair Sales	1000		143	179	202	164	688
9								
10	Appliance Sales	2000		28	55	19	31	133
11								
12	Small Products	3000		5	21	8	79	113
13								
14				---	---	---	---	---
15	TOTAL SALES			176	255	229	274	934
16								
17	Operating Expenses			45	54	44	67	
18								
19	Ratio: OE/Total Sales			25.6%	21.2%	19.2%	24.5%	22.6%
20								
21	Average Operating Expenses			40	58	52	62	
22								

Key variable

Figure 4.4
Formula-Driven Variable: Average Operating Expenses

POINT Mode

HINT: Use the cell pointer or mouse to point to range areas unless using named cells.

HINT: Pointing to range names saves time and provides visual feedback.

You can enter formulas into a cell in one of two ways: (1) by typing the formula directly from the keyboard or (2) by pointing to the cell or range with either the cell pointer or the mouse. Both of these methods have their strong points. With the **POINT mode** you use the cell pointer or mouse to highlight a range that you want to include in a formula or a 1-2-3 command. One rule of thumb can guide you in determining which method is the more appropriate: *If you are using cell references in your formula, use the point method.* We will discuss both methods in depth here. Notice that the rule of thumb doesn't say if you are referring to a *cell name*, but rather if you are using a *cell reference*. The distinction is important and will save you time when you enter formulas. If you are referring to a named cell, then the keyboard entry or the selection from the F3 (range names) list is much faster than pointing to the range. Because range names help you to maintain your worksheet, you will want to use them whenever possible.

Generally, though, you will use the POINT mode to reference cells in formulas. When entering or editing a formula, you can use the point method to save yourself time and to get feedback on the accuracy of the range contained in the formula. Let's go through the sequence of steps necessary to enter a formula using the point method.

The POINT mode can be used to highlight a range of cells when totaling sales for the first quarter. The formula originally located in cell D15 was erased so that it can be reentered using the POINT mode. Notice that the cells in

HINT: When creating formulas that sum, average, or count cells, include the cell above and below the desired range.

rows 19 and 21 that depended upon cell D15 for their results now display `ERR` until you enter a formula in cell D15. This illustrates the magic of the dynamic model. You are going to total the range D6 through D14 including the titles (in row 6) and underlines (in row 14). Then if you add new sales categories either before cell D8 or after cell D12 in the future, you will not need to adjust your total formula in cell D15. You can build quality into your worksheets by including cells above and below your desired range at the moment. The formula will look like this:

```
@SUM(D6..D14)
```

You are in the EDIT mode when entering a formula and the POINT mode when pointing to a range either with the cell pointer or mouse. The formula in the control panel (upper-left corner of the spreadsheet screen) reads `@sum(`. Notice that the cell pointer is located in the cell where you want the formula to reside.

The cell pointer must be moved up to cell D6. The mode indicator now tells us that the POINT mode is being used. The formula must be anchored by using the period key or by pressing the left mouse button and holding it down as you move to the end of the range. In Figure 4.5, the end point of the range is shown, as the cell pointer has been moved down nine cells to cell D14. The program has highlighted the range you are using to total sales for the first quarter to provide feedback on the accuracy of the area. To finish up the formula you must enter the closed parenthesis in cell D15. Finally, you press (ENTER) to complete the formula entry.

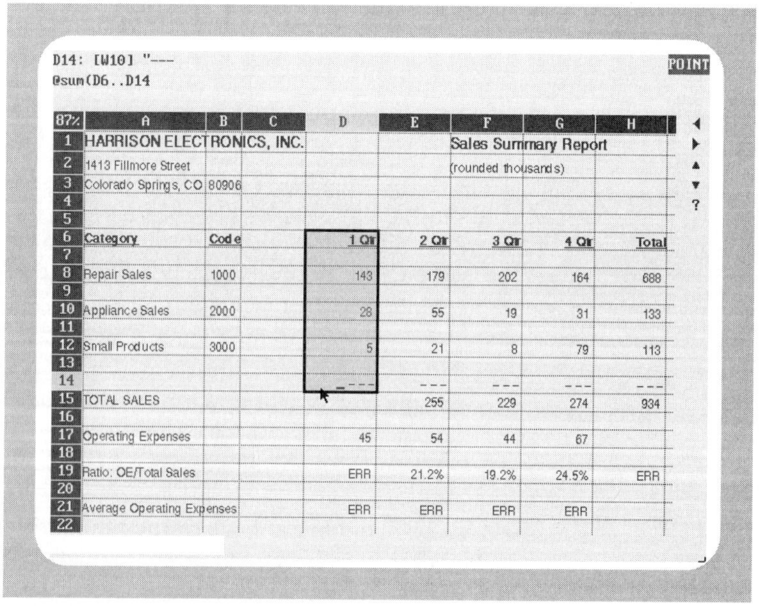

```
D14: [W10] "---                                                    POINT
@sum(D6..D14
```

87%	A	B	C	D	E	F	G	H
1	HARRISON ELECTRONICS, INC.					Sales Summary Report		
2	1413 Fillmore Street					(rounded thousands)		
3	Colorado Springs, CO 80906							
4								
5								
6	Category	Code		1 Qtr	2 Qtr	3 Qtr	4 Qtr	Total
7								
8	Repair Sales	1000		143	179	202	164	688
9								
10	Appliance Sales	2000		28	55	19	31	133
11								
12	Small Products	3000		5	21	8	79	113
13								
14				---	---	---	---	---
15	TOTAL SALES				255	229	274	934
16								
17	Operating Expenses			45	54	44	67	
18								
19	Ratio: OE/Total Sales			ERR	21.2%	19.2%	24.5%	ERR
20								
21	Average Operating Expenses			ERR	ERR	ERR	ERR	
22								

Figure 4.5
Using the POINT Mode to Enter a Formula

Types of @Functions

You can choose from a variety of predefined spreadsheet functions available for formula development. Lotus 1-2-3 Versions 2.3 and 2.4 contain 92 @functions, Version 3.1+ has 104 @functions, and Version 1.1 for Windows includes 107 @functions. These @functions are organized into five general categories for formula development and are discussed in detail in Appendix C. The categories are as follows:

1. Statistical and database @functions
2. Date and time @functions
3. Financial and mathematical @functions
4. Logical and cell @functions
5. String @functions

Function arguments must be separated by commas. Although each function differs in the number of arguments needed, the basic format of an @function formula is:

```
@FUNCTION(argument 1,argument 2,...)
```

HINT: @function arguments that contain values should reside in cells.

The first character of all 1-2-3 functions must be the symbol @. Argument types include numeric values, strings, and ranges. Ranges can be either single cells or a group of contiguous cells, depending on the nature of the function. As with formulas, the values and labels in @function arguments should reside in cells and be referenced with ranges. This is highly recommended, as it reduces the need for formula maintenance later.

Although we will not discuss each @function in detail, we will highlight some of the major @functions needed to create dynamic models. You may find others that are useful for special tasks and for creating valuable formulas within dynamic models. This chapter should serve as a reference for developing worksheets. Screens that explain the purpose and structure of each @function can be called up by selecting the Help facility (F1), the @functions index, and then the function that you want to see. We will begin our discussion with the most widely used @functions.

Statistical and Database Functions

HINT: Arguments for statistical @functions require a range of adjacent cells.

Statistical functions are provided to give you some simple guidelines for evaluating a variable or time-sequenced data. Statistical @functions are the most frequently used @functions because they provide information about a set of data and they describe a distribution of data when individual items alone are not useful for decision analysis. Arguments in all statistical @functions require a range of contiguous cells or a list of values with which to conduct calculations. Only one argument is required.

We have already used the @SUM and @AVG functions to total and average a column or row of data values in a variable. @COUNT counts the number of nonblank values in a range. @MAX and @MIN display the largest and smallest value in a range of values. @STD and @VAR are two functions that calculate the standard deviation and variance of a group of values clustered into a distribution. Statistical functions are invaluable to model builders. There are few models that do not use them at least once.

HINT: To avoid unexpected results when using statistical @functions, denote ranges rather than individual cells.

When using statistical and database functions in 1-2-3 you should follow several guidelines. First, keep in mind that statistical functions ignore blank cells in multiple-cell ranges used as the argument. Statistical functions do not, however, ignore references to blank cells listed individually as part of the argument.

Database functions are identical to their statistical counterparts, except that they are used to perform statistical calculations on Lotus 1-2-3 databases. The only difference in function names is that the database @functions have a D preceding the function; for example, @DAVG, which averages the values in an offset field that match specified criteria. All of the database functions have three arguments: input, offset, and criteria. The *input* range includes the entire database, incorporating the first row of field names. The *offset* is the number of the columns that contain the specified data to be used in the calculation. The *criteria* range consists of a field name and a value (record) with which to select records.

Here is an example of the use of a database function. Let's say you have a large database of customer names, addresses, purchases, purchase dates, and purchase amounts. Using @DSUM, you want to find the total purchase dollars for a customer named T. J. Smith. The input range is the entire database—the amount of area you want to search. The offset is the field labeled Purchase Amount. The criteria is the range containing the selection criteria you have set up; in this case, the field is Last Name and the customer number is 45456. The function then sums up all occurrences of T. J. Smith that match the customer number 45456, for example, and totals the purchase amounts.

For worksheets containing large databases and using complex selection criteria, the database statistical functions are critical for extracting important statistical information. We will talk about managing data and large worksheets in Chapter 6.

Date and Time Functions

Because the computer uses a systems clock to internally store date and time information, Lotus 1-2-3 makes that information available for you to use in a worksheet. The 1-2-3 program treats dates as serial numbers, allowing you to program date arithmetic—adding or subtracting one date from another. Serial numbers are anchored to the dates January 1, 1900, through December 31, 2099. For example, the serial number for the date January 1, 1900 is 1; for the date July 3, 1993, it is 34153. Hours and minutes are represented in fractions of a day which appear as serial decimals.

To format date and time functions you use the /**R**ange **F**ormat **D**ate command and then choose from a variety of arguments. Figure 4.6 illustrates the use of some date and time functions. Five date formats and four time formats are available.

The @NOW function yields the date and time at the moment of calculation. The serial number automatically reflects the date and time of the current system clock. In Figure 4.6, the serial number 34028.88130 was formatted into DD-MMM-YY by using the /**R**ange **N**ame **D**ate command. The @NOW function can also be formatted into the current time, as shown in cell C15 of Figure 4.6.

@TODAY yields the same results as the @NOW command, except that time is not calculated. Notice, therefore, that the serial number does not include any decimals. It is the values after the decimal in the serial number that yield the time. The formula, once it is entered, reflects an embedded function, @INT(@NOW), which rounds off the current time.

HINT: Use the @Date function to calculate the difference between two dates.

The most commonly used function in this category is the @DATE function. The argument for the @DATE function has three parts: the year, the month number, and the day of the month. The year 1992 must be written in the number of years from the base year (1900) as 92. @DATEVALUE is a function that acts similarly to @DATE, except that you enter a label in quotation marks for the date. One of the most important features of the @DATE function is its ability to calculate the number of days from one date to another. For example, how many days are there from March 3, 1991, to June 6, 1994? To answer this question, you subtract one @DATE function from another, as follows:

```
@DATE(94,6,30) – @DATE(91,3,10)
```

C15: (D7) [W15] @NOW READY

87%	A	B	C	D
1	Function	Serial No.	'Formatted	Format Option
2				
3	@NOW	33750.95850	26–May–92	DD–MMM–YY
4				
5	@TODAY	33750	05/26/92	Long Intn'l
6				
7	@DATE(92,12,28)	33966	Dec–92	MMM–YY
8				
9	@DATEVALUE("12/28/92")	33966	28–Dec–92	DD–MMM–YY
10				
11	@TIME(13,14,3)	0.551423611	01:14:03 PM	HH:MM:SS AM/PM
12				
13	@TIMEVALUE("13:14")	0.551388888	13:14:00	Long Intn'l
14				
15	@NOW	33750.95850	_11:00 PM	HH:MM AM/PM
16				
17	@DAY(33966)	28		
18				
19	@MONTH(33966)	12		
20				
21	@YEAR(33966)	92		
22				

Figure 4.6
Date and Time @Functions

This equation returns the value of 1,208 days from March 3, 1991 until June 6, 1994.

The @TIME function result in cell B11 yields a fraction of the serial number. Like the @DATE function, @TIME has three arguments, in this case, hour, minutes, and seconds. @TIMEVALUE in cell B13 behaves much like the @DATEVALUE command. The @DAY, @MONTH, and @YEAR functions separate or partition the serial number into categories and display the current day, month, and year, respectively.

Financial and Mathematical Functions

Financial functions are important in performing calculations relative to the building of financial models, such as investment tracking, stock portfolios, cash-flow statements, depreciation, and projections. Each @function in this category has a different number and type of arguments. The mathematical equations used in these @functions are shown in Appendix C.

Let's now examine @NPV to determine the net present value and internal rate of return for a series of cash flows. Figure 4.7 illustrates the cash flows expected for years 1 through 4 for new repair equipment at Harrison Electronics. In our example, we have inserted an additional row for the cash flow. The equipment requires an investment of $200,000 at the beginning of Year 1 of the investment. We entered the value of the equipment in cell C19 as a negative cash flow. The annual interest rate, in cell C20, is 11.5 percent annually. The firm wants to see a positive payback at the end of Year 4. Before we execute the @NPV formula, it appears that the investment will be useful to Harrison

C21: (F2) [W10] @NPV(C20,D19..G19) READY

87%	A	B	C	D	E	F	G	H
2	1413 Fillmore Street					(rounded thousands)		
3	Colorado Springs, CO	80906						
4								
5								
6	Category	Code		1 Qtr	2 Qtr	3 Qtr	4 Qtr	Total
7								
8	Repair Sales	1000		143	179	202	164	688
9								
10	Appliance Sales	2000		28	55	19	31	133
11								
12	Small Products	3000		5	21	8	79	113
13								
14				---	---	---	---	---
15	TOTAL SALES			176	255	229	274	934
16								
17				Year 1	Year 2	Year 3	Year 4	Total
18								
19	Cash Flows ($000)		−200	40	65	50	80	235
20	Annual Interest Rate		11.5%					
21	Net Present Value		175.99					
22								
23								

Figure 4.7
Net Present Value Analysis

Electronics, since we show a total of $235,000 from the cash flows (in cell H19), and we are making a $200,000 investment. However, we have not yet considered the time value of money.

The @NPV function requires two arguments, as follows:

```
@NPV(interest rate,range of cash flows)
```

If you are uncertain about the arguments needed for an @function, type the @function in a cell and invoke the Help facility, as shown in Figure 4.8. The Help facility goes immediately to the @function you are using, and displays the function's format, the details of the arguments, and the expected results.

The @NPV function assumes that the cash outflows occur at equal time intervals and that the first and subsequent cash outflows occur at the end of the periods. If an initial cash outlay is made immediately, followed by a series of future inflows, factor the initial outflow separately, because it is not affected by the interest. You can do this by adding the initial cash outflow to the result of the @NPV calculation.

HINT: Remember to divide the interest rate by the number of periods.

If you are calculating expected cash flows on a quarterly basis, divide the annual interest rate by 4; similarly, divide it by 12 for monthly cash flows. The result of the calculation, shown in Figure 4.7, yields an NPV of $176,000 *without* factoring in the immediate outlay of $200,000. The result is an adjusted NPV of –$24,000 on our investment over the next four years.

The @IRR function calculates the percentage rate that equates the present value of an expected future series of cash flows to the initial investment. @IRR uses a series of approximations, starting with your expected value, to calculate internal

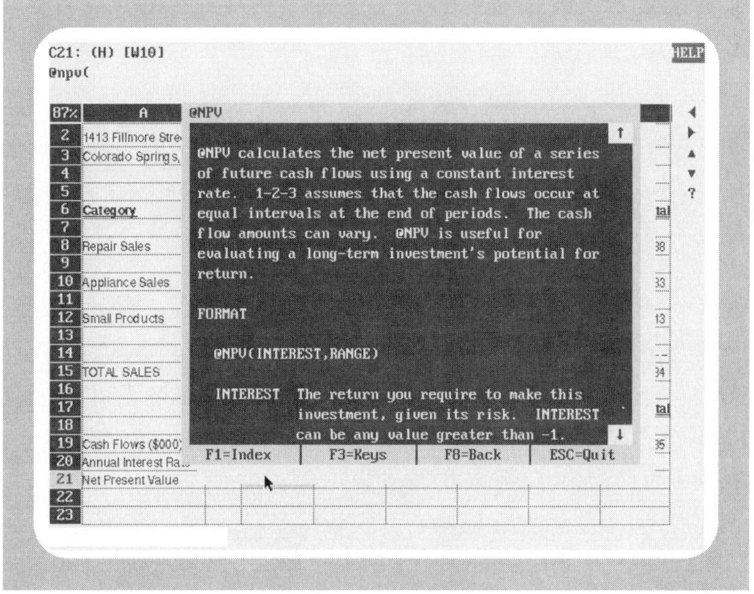

Figure 4.8
Net Present Value Help Screen

rate of return. More than one solution may be feasible, so changing your guess may prove to be worthwhile. The @IRR function requires two arguments, as follows:

```
@IRR(estimated IRR,range of cash flows)
```

HINT: When calculating IRR, include the initial investment.

In Figure 4.9 we set the expected IRR at 12 percent—a little higher than the annual interest or discount rate. Remember that we are hoping to get at least 11.5 percent return on our investment. When calculating internal rate of return, you must include the initial investment of $200,000 (in cell C19) in the range of cash flows.

The IRR turned out to be 6.2 percent for our example. This was far less than the 11.5 percent management desired. Now let's recap the results of this investment analysis. The investment costs $200,000. The total of cash flows in the first year of the investment's life is $235,000. The net present value for the investment is –$24,000 with an internal rate of return of 6.2 percent. At first, the investment looked good; however, when considering the time value of money, it is clear that the project is not worth the investment.

There are seventeen mathematical functions that simplify complex calculations. Two of these functions are widely used: @ROUND and @INT. @ROUND is a function that rounds a value to a specific number of decimal places as set in the argument. It rounds the number up to the specified decimal place if the value is greater than .5 and down if it is less than .5. The function @INT calculates the integer part of a value. The @INT function has only the value as its argument. Another mathematical function, @SQRT, calculates the square root of a number.

C21: (P1) @IRR(C20,C19..G19) READY

87%	A	B	C	D	E	F	G	H
2	1413 Fillmore Street					(rounded thousands)		
3	Colorado Springs, CO	80906						
4								
5								
6	Category	Code		1 Qtr	2 Qtr	3 Qtr	4 Qtr	Total
7								
8	Repair Sales	1000		143	179	202	164	688
9								
10	Appliance Sales	2000		28	55	19	31	133
11								
12	Small Products	3000		5	21	8	79	113
13								
14				---	---	---	---	---
15	TOTAL SALES			176	255	229	274	934
16								
17				5 Qtr	6 Qtr	7 Qtr	8 Qtr	Total
18								
19	Cash Flows ($000)		-200	40	65	50	80	235
20	Estimated IRR		12.0%					
21	Calculated IRR		6.2%					
22								
23								

Figure 4.9
Internal Rate of Return Analysis

The function @RAND calculates a random number between 0 and 1 and can be used to simulate a distribution for applications such as inventory management, product demand, manufacturing output, or an estimate of the queue of a line. Simulations are useful for modeling complex problems and generating a variety of scenarios. Distributions of random numbers that are used to create simulations are called Monte Carlo simulations. @RAND has no arguments.

Logical and Cell Functions

Logical functions produce a value or string, or they branch to another location on the worksheet based on the result of a conditional statement. The most commonly used @function in this category is the @IF function. The @IF function is very useful in simulating real-world situations that involve complex decisions.

HINT: Avoid using values and labels in the @IF function—instead, use cell references.

As with formula development, you will want to avoid using values and labels in your @IF functions so that you can maintain the modifiability of your worksheets. @TRUE and @FALSE are special cases of the @IF function. A number of specialized functions test for errors (@ISERR), numeric values (@ISNUMBER), strings (@ISSTRING), and add-in applications (@ISAPP) and add-in functions (@ISAFF). We will discuss the @IF statement, since it is more comprehensive than the specialized logical functions.

The @IF function tests a condition and then, based on its results, returns one of two results. You can use this function in many different types of applications whenever your processing depends on the result of a test. The @IF function requires three arguments, as follows:

```
@IF(condition exists,true result, false result)
```

The organization of the @IF statement is similar to that of a decision tree. A **decision tree** is a diagram which depicts conditions and outcomes. Decision trees help you visualize how certain conditions affect outcomes.

The arguments in an @IF statement can contain values, labels, cell references, formulas, and other functions. The condition part of the argument nearly always contains a comparative operator and often a logical connector. @IF functions use the following comparative operators and logical connectors:

Comparative Operators		Logical Connectors	
=	equal to	#AND#	logical AND
<	less than	#OR#	logical OR
<=	less than or equal to	#NOT#	logical NOT
>	greater than		
>=	greater than or equal to		
<>	not equal to		

Using the Harrison Electronics case, we want to predict whether the average consumer wants to repair an electric appliance. We will use some historical data to help us with our prediction. We have found that if the cost of repair for an appliance exceeds a certain dollar amount, the customer will less likely authorize the repairs. For example, if the cost of repairing a hair dryer exceeds $5, the customer will probably buy another hair dryer and not repair the existing one.

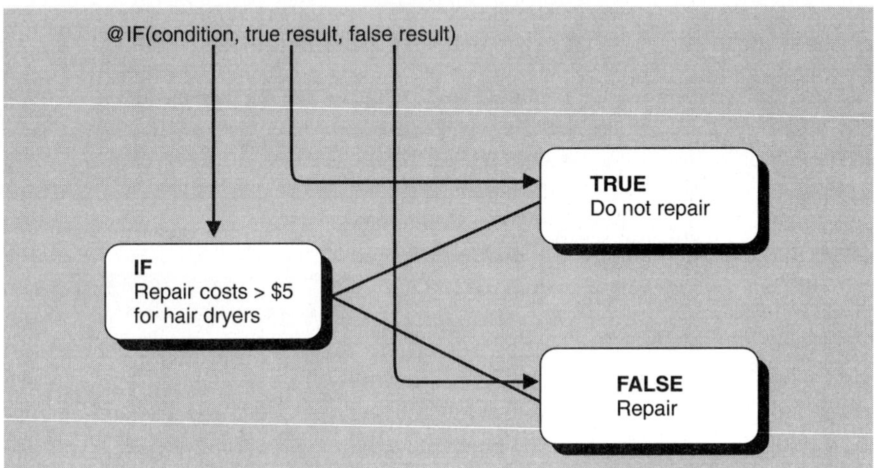

With the @VLOOKUP ("vertical lookup") function, you can look up a value in the table on the lower half of the worksheet in Figure 4.10 based on the Current Quarter and the Item to Be Repaired. Notice that in Figure 4.10 the values for the Current Quarter (a "2" in cell B6) and the Item to Be Repaired (a "Hair Dryer" in cell B7) have been entered. In cell B8, we have used the @VLOOKUP function to look up the repair price on the appliance table. The @VLOOKUP function has the following arguments:

```
@VLOOKUP(value or text,range,column-offset)
```

In Figure 4.10, the @VLOOKUP function found the value of $6.00 in Quarter 2 from the table. The range includes the item name in column A as well as the four quarters. A value of $6.00 is extracted from the table and copied into cell B8.

You can now use the @IF function, displayed in Figure 4.11, to ask whether the Approximate Cost is greater than $5.00. If so, a "No" appears in cell B9; otherwise a "Yes" appears. Given the value of $6.00, the @IF function tells us that the customer will not want to repair their hair dryer.

Let us add an additional condition to the repair decision. If a consumer's decision is affected by both the repair price and the time required to repair the appliance, there may be a different impact. We will examine this decision in binary form, with Yes and No answers to each condition. The number of outcomes (n) in a binary decision tree or table must be n^2 , and since there are now two conditions in our example, the number of outcomes is four. A **decision**

table is a table that lists conditions and outcomes. It appears that if both conditions are true, we can predict that our customer will give the OK to repair the appliance. Our primary @IF statement needs a nested @IF statement on the false side of the outcome.

B8: (C2) [W12] @VLOOKUP(B7,A15..E18,B6) READY

87%	A	B	C	D	E	F	G
1	HARRISON ELECTRONICS, INC.						
2	1413 Fillmore Street						
3	Colorado Springs, CO	80906					
4							
5							
6	Current Quarter	2					
7	Item to be Repaired	Hair dryer					
8	Approximate Cost	$6.00					
9	Repair Approval?	No					
10							
11							
12							
13	Item	1 Quarter	2 Quarter	3 Quarter	4 Quarter		
14							
15	Toaster oven	$14.00	$12.00	$11.00	$16.00		
16	Hair dryer	$4.00	$6.00	$5.50	$4.25		
17	Microwave	$45.00	$68.00	$57.00	$61.00		
18	Food processor	$28.00	$30.00	$26.00	$32.00		
19							
20							
21							
22							

Figure 4.10
Using @VLOOKUP to Determine Cost

B9: [W12] @IF(B8>5,"No","Yes") READY

87%	A	B	C	D	E	F	G
1	HARRISON ELECTRONICS, INC.						
2	1413 Fillmore Street						
3	Colorado Springs, CO	80906					
4							
5							
6	Current Quarter	2					
7	Item to be Repaired	Hair dryer					
8	Approximate Cost	$6.00					
9	Repair Approval?	No					
10							
11							
12							
13	Item	1 Quarter	2 Quarter	3 Quarter	4 Quarter		
14							
15	Toaster oven	$14.00	$12.00	$11.00	$16.00		
16	Hair dryer	$4.00	$6.00	$5.50	$4.25		
17	Microwave	$45.00	$68.00	$57.00	$61.00		
18	Food processor	$28.00	$30.00	$26.00	$32.00		
19							
20							
21							
22							

Figure 4.11
Using @IF to Predict Repair Approval

Condition	Outcome			
	1	2	3	4
Cost for repair < $5	Y	Y	N	N
Repair time < 2 days	Y	N	Y	N
Result				
Repair	X	X	X	
Do not repair				X
@IF Statement	@IF(B8<=5,"Yes",@IF(B9<=3,"Yes","No"))			

In Figure 4.12 we have added the second decision condition in cell B9 to address the number of days it will take to repair an appliance. We have also added a second @IF statement within our original @IF statement to test this condition. Notice in the decision table that since we have three Yes conditions, we have reversed the condition tests—the tests of whether B8<=5 and B9<=3 days. Only one of the two conditions has to exist for the consumer to decide to repair the appliance; therefore we did not need to test both the true and false results.

We can also use the logical connector #OR# to simplify the @IF formula by eliminating nesting. Since we had only one situation in which the result was to not repair, we isolate it in order to use a logical connector. Figure 4.13 illustrates the use of the #OR# connector. We can also use the #AND# connector to

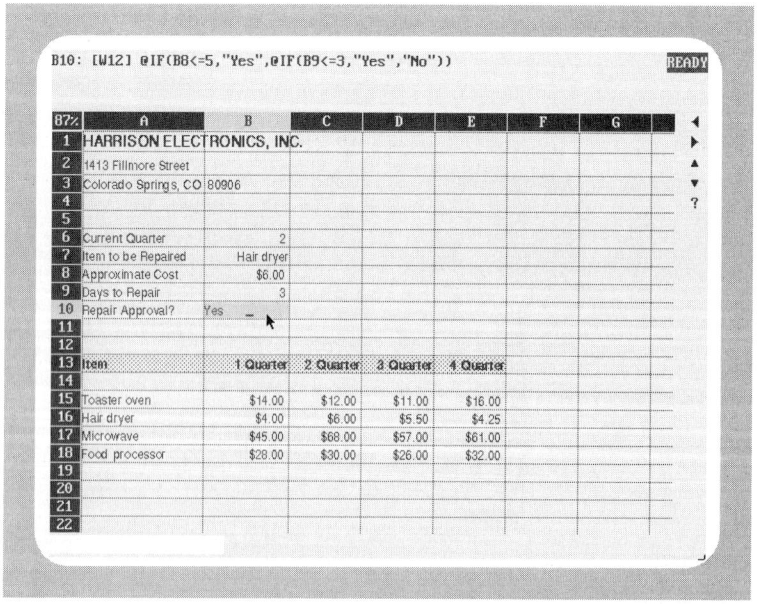

B10: [W12] @IF(B8<=5,"Yes",@IF(B9<=3,"Yes","No")) READY

	A	B	C	D	E	F	G
1	HARRISON ELECTRONICS, INC.						
2	1413 Fillmore Street						
3	Colorado Springs, CO	80906					
4							
5							
6	Current Quarter	2					
7	Item to be Repaired	Hair dryer					
8	Approximate Cost	$6.00					
9	Days to Repair	3					
10	Repair Approval?	Yes					
11							
12							
13	Item	1 Quarter	2 Quarter	3 Quarter	4 Quarter		
14							
15	Toaster oven	$14.00	$12.00	$11.00	$16.00		
16	Hair dryer	$4.00	$6.00	$5.50	$4.25		
17	Microwave	$45.00	$68.00	$57.00	$61.00		
18	Food processor	$28.00	$30.00	$26.00	$32.00		
19							
20							
21							
22							

Figure 4.12
A Nested @IF Statement

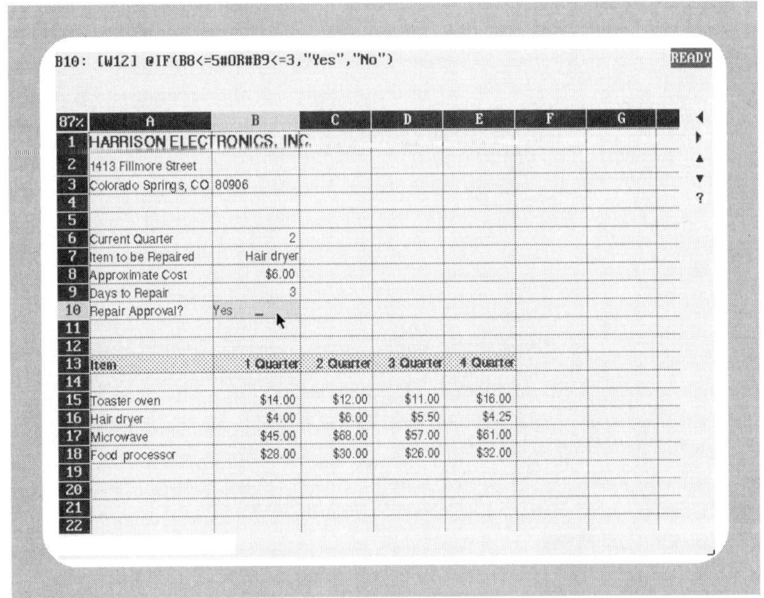

Figure 4.13
An @IF Statement with a Logical Connector

accomplish the same purpose if we reverse the condition tests as well as the outcomes. The @IF statement could be written either of the following ways:

```
@IF(B8<=5#OR#B9<=3,"Yes","No")
@IF(B8>5#AND#B9>3,"No","Yes")
```

HINT: Logical connectors are easier to maintain for large @IF problems.

In general, given the choice between nested @IFs and logical connectors with extremely large and complex problems, logical connectors are easier to modify and maintain. A healthy combination between the two is very effective as a development tool. The @IF function is by far the most powerful function Lotus 1-2-3 has to offer. It is considered the fundamental statement in many procedural languages. Rule-based IF statements are the heart of today's expert systems.

The @CELL function returns information about an attribute that you want to examine in a specified range. @CELL has two arguments: string (labels) and range. @CELLPOINTER is a function similar to @CELL, except that it gives you information about the contents of a specified cell. There is a single argument for @CELLPOINTER: the string. For the string argument in both @CELL and @CELLPOINTER, ten different attributes are available, each yielding a variety of results. Figure 4.14 illustrates some of the attributes you can use with the @CELL function.

Most of the effects from the @CELL function are easy to understand. The "format" attribute returns the value of the first letter in the Range Format command menu. For example, G indicates the general format, while F0 indicates a fixed format with zero decimal places. The "prefix" attribute indicates the justification

A1: {SWISS14 Bold} [W24] 'HARRISON ELECTRONICS, INC. READY

87%	A	B	C	D	E	F	G	H
1	HARRISON ELECTRONICS, INC.					Sales Summary Report		
2	1413 Fillmore Street					(rounded thousands)		
3	Colorado Springs, CO 80906							
4								
5								
6	Category	Code		1 Qtr	2 Qtr	3 Qtr	4 Qtr	
7								
8	Repair Sales	1000		143	179	202	164	
9								
10								
11	@CELL("address",D8)		$D$8					
12	@CELL("col",D8..D8)		4					
13	@CELL("contents",D8)		143					
14	@CELL("filename",D8)		C:\RESEARCH\BOOK\WORKSHEE\CH4-16.WK1					
15	@CELL("format",D8..D8)		G					
16	@CELL("prefix",D6)		"					
17	@CELL("protect",D8)		1					
18	@CELL("row",D8)		8					
19	@CELL("type",D8)		v					
20	@CELL("type",D6)		l					
21	@CELL("width",D8)		10					
22								

Figure 4.14
Cell Attributes

of cell contents that are labels (', ^, or "). The "protect" attribute yields a 1 if the cell is protected and a 0 otherwise. Coupled with the @IF command, the "contents" and "type" attributes are most often used to test for an entry's content or type. A "b" is returned if the cell is blank, a "v" if the cell contains a value or formula, and an "l" if it contains a label.

The @COLS and @ROWS functions each contain a range argument, and they count the number of columns or rows in a range. The @@ function returns the contents of the cell whose cell address is contained in another cell. This function is important for identifying the formulas that create links. All of the formulas in an integrated dynamic model reference values or formulas in other cells. You will find the @@ function useful for problem solving and for modifying existing dynamic models. The functions @ERR and @NA help you discover entry errors within your worksheet. When used with @IF in an adjacent column or row, these functions can help you identify entries that fall outside of reasonable limits. @NA can be input into a data area to indicate that the value is not yet available. There are no arguments associated with these functions.

String Functions

The last function category that we will discuss is comprised of functions that let you manipulate strings or labels. These string functions use the symbol "&" to combine one label with another. If cell B21, for example, contains the label "1981" and B20 the label "Total Sales", and we want to combine the two labels in cell A26, the formula we would enter is as follows:

Cell B20:	Total Sales
Cell B21:	1991
Formula:	+B21&" "&B20
Result:	1991 Total Sales

Notice that in our formula we are really connecting three parts—the label in cell B21, a blank space, and the label in cell B20.

Three functions can extract portions of labels from strings. Figure 4.15 illustrates some of the string functions we will discuss. @LEFT and @RIGHT have two arguments: the string and the number of characters to extract. The string argument should be a cell reference as often as possible for ease of modification. With the @LEFT function, we have asked the program to extract the first five characters from cell A5, yielding the string "Appro". The @MID function is a more powerful extraction command that has three arguments: string, starting point, and the number of characters to extract. In our example, we have extracted seven characters, starting in position 12 and resulting in the string "Applian".

Three functions can help you change character case: @LOWER, @UPPER, and @PROPER. Notice in Figure 4.15 that the only argument for these functions is the cell reference. @PROPER, which returns the proper case, is different from the other two functions in that it begins each new word with a

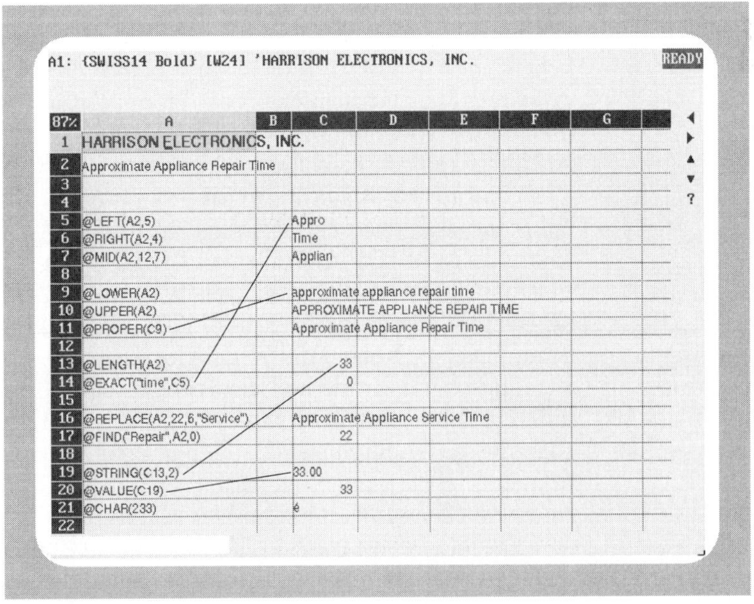

Figure 4.15
@String Functions

HINT: Use the case-sensitive string functions for standardizing user input.

capital letter. @LENGTH, which also requires only the cell reference as its argument, returns the total number of characters in the string residing in cell A2. The @EXACT function compares the contents of two strings. The function's two arguments in this example are a string ("time") and the address of a cell (C5) containing a second string ("Appro"). Since the @EXACT function is case sensitive, the function has returned a value of 0. You will find these string functions especially useful in checking your input before looking up a value in a table.

There are two powerful string functions that find or replace parts of a string. The @REPLACE function searches a string for a predefined label. It consists of four arguments: string, starting point, number of characters to replace, and replacement string. In Figure 4.15 the string "Repair" has been replaced by "Service". The @FIND function was used to locate the number of characters from the starting point. The example illustrates that the string "Repair" appears 22 characters from the beginning of the string in cell A2.

The Auditor

HINT: The Auditor is a useful tool for maintaining worksheets with many formulas.

The **Auditor** is an add-in program that analyzes and displays information about worksheet formulas. The Auditor can analyze formula relationships by identifying precedents of dependents to a worksheet formula. **Precedents** are all cells that provide data for a specified formula cell. In other words, what cells does the cell you are investigating depend upon for its data. In contrast, **dependents** are all cells that refer to a particular cell. Formulas that refer to cells and ranges are dependent on those cells or ranges. The Auditor can also list all formulas in a given range, list formulas in order of recalculation, or identify circular references if any exist. There are three reporting methods in the Auditor: Highlight, List, and Trace cell contents. Figure 4.16 illustrates the Auditor menu.

You can attach add-ins (mini programs to enhance Lotus 1-2-3) by using either the /**A**dd-in **A**ttach command or the ALT-F10 function key. Select Auditor from the list of add-ins available to attach. You are then prompted to select a function key for invoking the add-in. Typically, WYSIWYG is attached to the ALT-F7 key and the Auditor to the ALT-F8 function key. To invoke the Auditor at any time, press the ALT-F8 function key.

The Highlight method displays particular cells in bright intensity or in a different color so that you can examine formula relationships. If you change the contents of a highlighted cell, the highlight remains. However, if you make adjustments to the worksheet, such as by moving cells, or by inserting or deleting rows or columns, all highlighting is removed.

The List report method identifies formulas in a worksheet range that you specify. You need only identify the first cell of the range. The List method has an

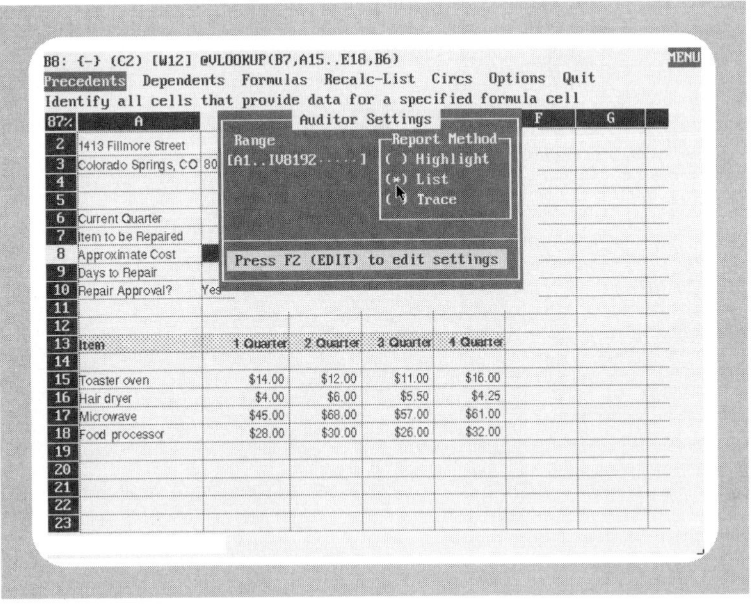

Figure 4.16
Use of the Auditor to Analyze Formulas

advantage over the Highlight method in that it prints out formula precedents, dependents, or a recalc list of a specified formula in a relevant order for analysis.

The Trace method of reporting formulas lets you move the cell pointer forward or backward through the specified cells. The Auditor displays any hidden columns in the Trace mode. The Trace mode is extremely useful when you want to analyze the order of formulas and their execution.

Figure 4.17 illustrates the worksheet we will use to identify the precedents and dependents for the formula in cell B8: @VLOOKUP(B7,A15..E18,B6). The precedents analysis identifies all cells in the audit range that provide data or other formulas needed to calculate a formula result. Only a formula can have precedents. The dependents analysis identifies all formula cells in the specified audit range that refer to a particular cell. The recalc list identifies all worksheet formula cells, except file-linking formula cells, in order of the method of relcalculation for the entire worksheet (natural, columnwise, or rowwise).

Remember that for the formula in the cell we are examining, we used the @VLOOKUP function to identify the cell in the table that contains the value for the current quarter and the item to be repaired. Figure 4.18 displays the results of the Auditor formula analysis. Using the List reporting method, we ran four different types of analysis. The precedents of the @VLOOKUP formula in cell B8 are listed in column A. Each cell listed displays the cell reference as well as its contents. Notice that the formula requires the lookup of each cell in the table, starting with column A and moving down the row until it is completed.

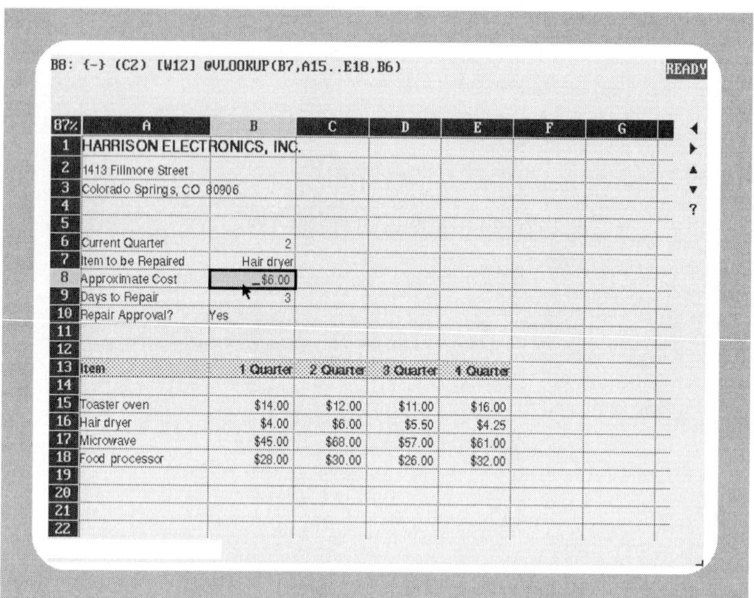

B8: {-} (C2) [W12] @VLOOKUP(B7,A15..E18,B6) READY

	A	B	C	D	E	F	G
1	HARRISON ELECTRONICS, INC.						
2	1413 Fillmore Street						
3	Colorado Springs, CO 80906						
4							
5							
6	Current Quarter	2					
7	Item to be Repaired	Hair dryer					
8	Approximate Cost	$6.00					
9	Days to Repair	3					
10	Repair Approval?	Yes					
11							
12							
13	Item	1 Quarter	2 Quarter	3 Quarter	4 Quarter		
14							
15	Toaster oven	$14.00	$12.00	$11.00	$16.00		
16	Hair dryer	$4.00	$6.00	$5.50	$4.25		
17	Microwave	$45.00	$68.00	$57.00	$61.00		
18	Food processor	$28.00	$30.00	$26.00	$32.00		
19							
20							
21							
22							

Figure 4.17
A Formula to Be Analyzed with the Auditor

B35: [W12] READY

	A	B	C	D	E	F	G
22							
23							
24	Precedents of Cell B8		Dependents of Cell B8				
25	B7: "Hair dryer		B10: @IF(B8<=5#OR#B9<=3,"Yes","No")				
26	A15: 'Toaster oven						
27	A16: 'Hair dryer		Formulas in Audit Range A1..IV8192				
28	A17: 'Microwave		B8: @VLOOKUP(B7,A15..E18,B6)				
29	A18: 'Food processor		B10: @IF(B8<=5#OR#B9<=3,"Yes","No")				
30	B15: 14						
31	B16: 4		Natural Recalculation List				
32	B17: 45		B8: @VLOOKUP(B7,A15..E18,B6)				
33	B18: 28		B10: @IF(B8<=5#OR#B9<=3,"Yes","No")				
34	C15: 12						
35	C16: 6						
36	C17: 68						
37	C18: 30						
38	D15: 11						
39	D16: 5.5						
40	D17: 57						
41	D18: 26						
42	E15: 16						
43	E16: 4.25						

Figure 4.18
Results of the Auditor Formula Analysis

There are only two formulas in this worksheet, as indicated by the formula analysis, and the @IF formula in cell B10 depends on the current formula in B8. The Natural Recalculation List shows us that the formula in B8 is recalculated before the formula in cell B10. Of course, this worksheet is quite small. You will find that the Auditor is a useful tool in maintaining large worksheets with many formulas. The results, when using the Auditor, are worksheets of much higher quality.

Review Questions

1. How can a collection of formulas be used to develop a dynamic model?
2. Describe the basic format of a formula.
3. Why do worksheets with formulas represent a significant improvement over worksheets without formulas?
4. What is a function argument?
5. Do all 1-2-3 functions discussed require arguments? Which functions require arguments and which do not?
6. Can arguments in @functions be listed in any order? Why or why not?
7. How is a variable positioned in the worksheet?
8. What are the advantages of using the POINT mode when entering ranges in a formula?
9. Why should formulas in a dynamic model not contain values? What should they contain instead?
10. Describe the range within a formula that sums, averages, or counts a group of cells.
11. How does @DSUM differ from the @SUM function?
12. What happens when we use individual cells rather than a range as the argument in the @AVG function?
13. What is the difference between @NOW and @TODAY?
14. How is the date serial number used to calculate the difference between two dates?
15. Serial numbers are derived from which starting date?
16. If you are considering an investment, which @functions are the most useful in your analysis?
17. Describe the difference between the @NPV and @IRR functions.
18. How can a decision tree or decision table help you structure a decision?
19. How does @VLOOKUP work?

20. How many attributes does the @CELL function have?
21. What is a logical connector, and how would you use it to develop the @IF function?
22. Describe the different types of functions available for manipulating strings.
23. How does the Auditor add-in work, and what are the benefits of using it?

Skill-Building Activities: Using @Functions and the Auditor

Activity 1: Retrieving a Worksheet

Beginning with this activity, you will continue developing the Harrison Electronics worksheet. Use the **F**ile **R**etrieve menu to bring up a copy of the file used in Chapter 3. Your worksheet should look similar to the one in Figure 4.19.

NOTE: To help you with this exercise, ***boldface*** *letters indicate a message from the system or the worksheet.*

Activity 2: Working with Range Names

In this activity you will create five range names—one for each of the four quarters and one for total sales—to use in the formulas. Remember to name the cell above

A16: {Page} [W17] READY

	A	B	C	D	E	F	G	H
1	HARRISON ELECTRONICS, INC.					Sales Summary Report		
2	1413 Fillmore Street					(rounded thousands)		
3	Colorado Springs, CO	80906						
6	Category	Code		1 Qtr	2 Qtr	3 Qtr	4 Qtr	Total
8	Repair Sales	1000		143	179	202	164	688
10	Appliance Sales	2000		28	55	19	31	133
12	Small Products	3000		5	21	8	79	113
14				---	---	---	---	---
15	TOTAL SALES			176	255	229	274	934

Figure 4.19
The Harrison Electronics Worksheet

and below the desired range in case you want to add rows to the top or bottom of the existing range.

Position the cell pointer on cell D7.

Select the /**R**ange **N**ame **C**reate command.

Enter the range name: `QTR1`

Anchor the cursor by pressing the ⌄ key or by using the mouse to move the cursor down to cell D14. Press the ENTER key to confirm.

Create the other four range names by using the same set of keystrokes and the following table:

`QTR2`	E7..E13
`QTR3`	F7..F13
`QTR4`	G7..G13
`TOTAL`	H7..H13

You will now print a table of range names by positioning the cell pointer on cell A18. Select the /**R**ange **N**ame **T**able command, and press the ENTER key to confirm.

You have now named the five ranges and printed a range name table.

Range names can be used as cell references in formulas and as part of the worksheet's structure. Practice moving around within the worksheet with the GOTO (F5) key. When you GOTO a multiple-cell range, you always move the cell pointer to the upper-left cell of the range.

First, go to another area of the worksheet and press the F5 key.

Type `A44`, and press the ENTER key to confirm.

Now go to QTR1 by using the same set of keystrokes.

Press F5, then type `QTR1` to go to cell D7.

You should see part of the worksheet. Notice that if you are moving to an area of the worksheet where the cell reference is not located in the current screen, the cell you are moving to appears in the upper-left corner. Always go to the upper-left corner of the screen you want to go to first, and then move the range.

Activity 3: Adding Labels for New Formulas

Now you will add some labels in column A to identify the formulas you are going to enter. You will use the statistical @functions to calculate the average sales, minimum sales, maximum sales, and the count for each quarter. You must first erase the range name table.

Move the cell pointer to cell A18 by using the F5 key.

Select the /**R**ange **E**rase command, and highlight the range A18..B22. Press the (ENTER) key to confirm the erase.

Move the cursor to cell A17 by using the (F5) key, type `AVERAGE SALES`, and press the (ENTER) key to continue.

Move the cursor to cell A18 by using the (F5) key, type in `MINIMUM SALES`, and press the (ENTER) key to continue.

Move the cursor to cell A19 by using the (F5) key, type in `MAXIMUM SALES`, and press the (ENTER) key to continue.

Move the cursor to cell A20 by using the (F5) key, type in `COUNT`, and press the (ENTER) key to continue.

Your worksheet should look similar to the one shown in Figure 4.20. You are now ready to enter the statistical @functions into the worksheet.

Activity 4: Using Range Names in the @Function Formula

Now you will enter a series of @function-based formulas by using the range names you just created. Actually, you will enter a formula for the cells in column D only and copy it to the other cells in the row. You may notice that Lotus automatically adjusts for the new range names you have just created.

Move the cell pointer to cell D17 by using the (F5) key.

A20: {Page} [W17] 'COUNT READY

87%	A	B	C	D	E	F	G	H
1	HARRISON ELECTRONICS, INC.					Sales Summary Report		
2	1413 Fillmore Street					(rounded thousands)		
3	Colorado Springs, CO	80906						
4								
5								
6	Category	Code		1 Qtr	2 Qtr	3 Qtr	4 Qtr	Total
7								
8	Repair Sales	1000		143	179	202	164	688
9								
10	Appliance Sales	2000		28	55	19	31	133
11								
12	Small Products	3000		5	21	8	79	113
13								
14				---	---	---	---	---
15	TOTAL SALES			176	255	229	274	934
16								
17	AVERAGE SALES							
18	MINIMUM SALES							
19	MAXIMUM SALES							
20	COUNT							
21								
22								

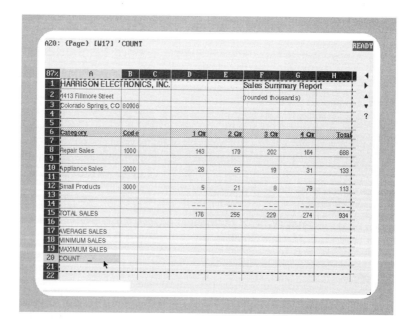

Figure 4.20
Adding Formula Labels

Type the formula `@AVG(QTR1)`, and press the (ENTER) key to confirm.

Copy the formula across the columns to cell H17 by using the **/Copy** command.

Go to cell D18, type the formula `@MIN(QTR1)`, and press the (ENTER) key.

Go to cell D19, type in the formula `@MAX(QTR1)`, and press the (ENTER) key.

Go to cell D20, type in the formula `@COUNT(QTR1)`, and press the (ENTER) key.

Copy the formulas from cells D18 through D20 to cell H17.

Your worksheet should now look similar to that in Figure 4.21. Other functions can be entered and copied in the same way, saving development time and effort.

Activity 5: Using the Auditor

You will now use the Auditor to analyze the formulas and structure of your worksheet. (If you are using Lotus 1-2-3 versions 3.1+ or 1.1 for Windows, skip this activity.) Before you analyze the formulas, you need to restructure the average formula in the total sales column. Be sure you set up the Auditor as an add-in if you have not already done so; use the (ALT)-(F10) key, select Attach, then Auditor.

Use the (F5) key to go to cell H17.

D17: (F1) [W10] @AVG(QTR1) READY

87%	A	B	C	D	E	F	G	H
1	HARRISON ELECTRONICS, INC.					Sales Summary Report		
2	1413 Fillmore Street					(rounded thousands)		
3	Colorado Springs, CO	80906						
4								
5								
6	Category	Code		1 Qtr	2 Qtr	3 Qtr	4 Qtr	Total
7								
8	Repair Sales	1000		143	179	202	164	688
9								
10	Appliance Sales	2000		28	55	19	31	133
11								
12	Small Products	3000		5	21	8	79	113
13								
14				---	---	---	---	---
15	TOTAL SALES			176	255	229	274	934
16								
17	AVERAGE SALES			58.7	85.0	76.3	91.3	311.3
18	MINIMUM SALES			5	21	8	31	113
19	MAXIMUM SALES			143	179	202	164	688
20	COUNT			3	3	3	3	3
21								
22								

Figure 4.21
Statistical @Functions

Enter the formula `@SUM(D17..G17)` in cell H17.

Invoke the Auditor add-in ((ALT)-(F8)).

Using the Highlight report mode, select **P**recedents from the menu.

Select cell H17 as the precedent source cell.

Notice in Figure 4.22, that the highlighted cells supply H17 with data. The cells appear lighter than other cells in the worksheet. The ranges D8..G12 and D17..G17 are highlighted. Now use the List mode to get a report of precedents, worksheet formulas, and a natural recalculation list.

Press the (F2) key to edit the Auditor settings, then select `M` and press `L` for the List reporting method. Press the (ENTER) key to confirm.

Select **P**recedents from the Auditor menu. The source cell is H17, and the range for List is A23.

Select **F**ormulas from the Auditor menu. The range for List is C23.

Select **R**ecalc List from the Auditor menu. The source cell is H17, and the range for List is F23.

Your output from the Auditor should resemble the worksheet in Figure 4.23. You have now completed your worksheet. Save the new worksheet as HARRIS3 so that you have incremental and auditable documents of your work.

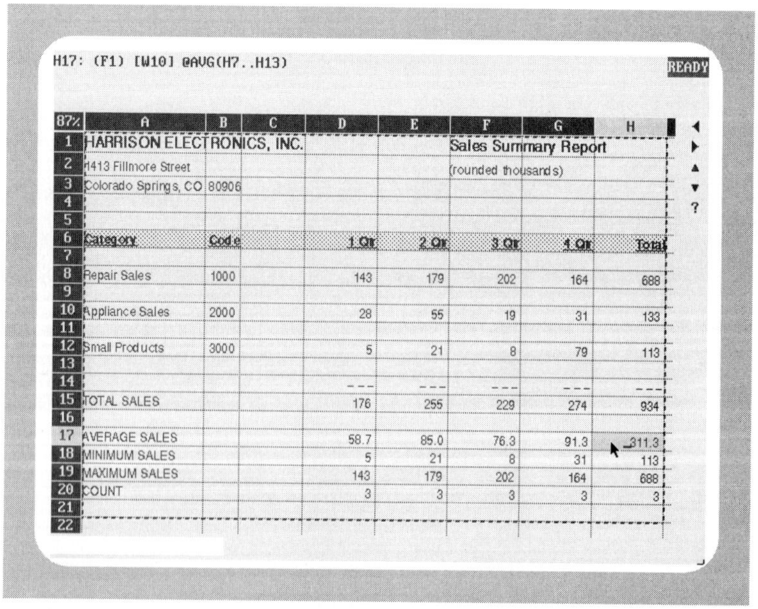

H17: (F1) [W10] @AVG(H7..H13) READY

87%	A	B	C	D	E	F	G	H
1	HARRISON ELECTRONICS, INC.					Sales Summary Report		
2	1413 Fillmore Street					(rounded thousands)		
3	Colorado Springs, CO	80906						
4								
5								
6	Category	Code		1 Qtr	2 Qtr	3 Qtr	4 Qtr	Total
7								
8	Repair Sales	1000		143	179	202	164	688
9								
10	Appliance Sales	2000		28	55	19	31	133
11								
12	Small Products	3000		5	21	8	79	113
13								
14				---	---	---	---	---
15	TOTAL SALES			176	255	229	274	934
16								
17	AVERAGE SALES			58.7	85.0	76.3	91.3	311.3
18	MINIMUM SALES			5	21	8	31	113
19	MAXIMUM SALES			143	179	202	164	688
20	COUNT			3	3	3	3	3
21								
22								

Figure 4.22
Using the Auditor to Check Formula Precedents

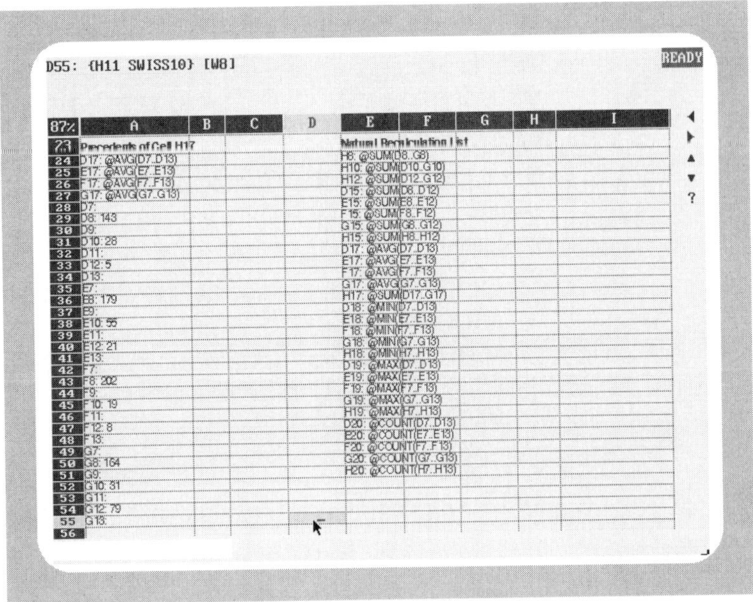

Figure 4.23
The Auditor List Report Format

Hands-On Exercises

1. Create a worksheet for John's Country Woodworking that allows John to categorize pricing information about his three main products: 1) dining room table, 2) dresser, and 3) chest.

Product	Unfinished	Unfinished with hardware	Finished	Finished with hardware
Product code	U	UH	F	FH
Table	885	925	1,150	1,200
Dresser	620	700	745	800
Chest	500	575	625	700

2. Use the @VLOOKUP command to query the table created in exercise 1 as to which price to quote a customer. Your worksheet should have a cell where the user enters a product code (cell B8) and a product name (cell B9). A third cell should be reserved for the output of the lookup (cell B10).

3. Perform the following statistical functions on each row and column of the data table created in exercise 1:

   @SUM, @AVG, @COUNT, @STD, @VAR, @MAX, @MIN

4. Position the cell pointer on the cell that contains the title for your worksheet: "John's Country Woodworking". Use this cell (we will assume it is A1 for these functions) in your calculations for the following string functions:

   @LEFT (A1,10)
   @RIGHT(A1,10)
   @MID(A1,7,9)
   @LENGTH(A1)
   @FIND("Wood",A1,0)

5. Use the @REPLACE function to replace "Woodworking" with "Wood".

6. Use the title cell (A1) for the following cell functions:

   @@(A1)
   @CELL("address",A1)
   @CELL("contents",A1)
   @CELL("format",A1)
   @CELL("type",A1)
   @CELL("width",A1)

Problem-Solving Projects

Mopar Commercial Auto Supplier, Inc., is thinking about investing in new equipment to conduct emissions inspections in Colorado. The equipment will cost $40,000 up front. Each inspection costs $12 for automobiles and $15 for registered trucks. All vehicles, except new vehicles, are required to have an annual inspection. New vehicles get a two-year inspection as they are driven off the lot. Managers anticipate the following number of cars annually:

	1992	1993	1994	1995	1996
Automobiles	300	350	400	450	550
Trucks	200	250	350	350	400
New vehicles	50	50	75	75	75

1. Set up a worksheet with three major sections:

   Number of inspections—enter the table above starting in cells A4 through F7.

Amount of Income—enter the price for inspections in cells A9 through B10.

Cash flow—multiply the number of inspections by the price for each vehicle in cells A12 through F15.

Sections 1 and 2 should be tables that include the price, the five years, and the total. Include the data on automobiles, trucks, and new vehicles.

2. Calculate cash flow with a formula that multiplies the number of inspections with the price per inspection. Since we do not know what the mix of new vehicles will be (automobiles versus trucks), we must estimate the price per inspection by the total mix of automobiles and trucks. Use the following formula to estimate the price per inspection for new vehicles:

$$\begin{array}{c}\text{Difference between}\\ \text{Truck Inspection Price}\\ \text{and Automobile}\\ \text{Inspection Price}\\ (\$15 - \$12)\end{array} \times \frac{\text{Total number of Automobile Inspections}}{\text{Total number of Inspections}} + \begin{array}{c}\text{Automobile}\\ \text{Inspection}\\ \text{Price}\end{array}$$

3. Total each column (year) and each row (type of inspection). Calculate a total figure of totals—the amount of total income that will be produced from inspections.

4. In the cash flow section, the total of each column will be the cash flow used in the net present value and internal rate of return calculations. Add the investment outflow of `($40,000)` to the beginning of the cash flow variable. The cash flow variable will match the total amount of income.

5. Set up three cells: for the interest rate, the NPV, and the IRR. Calculate the net present value by using the @NPV function on the investment. Remember: do not include the initial investment in the cash flow, but subtract the initial investment from the value given.

6. Calculate the internal rate of return of the investment by using the @IRR function. With @IRR, you must have the initial investment of `($40,000)` as the first cash flow of the range. Use the interest rate as your estimated IRR, or guess at an IRR.

7. Based upon the NPV and IRR you calculated, do you recommend that Mopar Commercial Auto Supplier invest in the emissions inspection equipment? Does it appear that Mopar will make a profit in the five-year period? What do you suggest they pay for the equipment if they want to make at least $5,000 over the five-year period?

Quality Assurance Checklist

As we conclude our discussion of spreadsheet commands, be sure you have considered the following factors that will contribute to the quality of your worksheet:

✓ Remember that although a cell stores a formula, it displays the resulting value.

✓ Use cell references in formulas so that they are copyable and maintainable.

✓ Do not use values in your formulas; instead, extract them from cells in a data area.

✓ When creating formulas that sum, average, or count cells, include the cell above and below the desired range.

✓ Remember that @function arguments containing values should reside in cells.

✓ If you are using cell references in your formula, use the POINT method.

✓ Use ranges rather than individual cells with statistical @functions to avoid unexpected results.

✓ Use the date and time serial number to calculate the difference between two dates.

✓ Divide the interest rate by the number of periods when using financial @functions.

✓ Subtract the initial cash outlay of an investment from the NPV value given and include the initial cash outlay in the IRR cash flow range.

✓ For maximum flexibility in changing the dynamic model, use the @VLOOKUP or @HLOOKUP function to pull data from a table.

✓ Use the case-sensitive string functions—@UPPER, @LOWER, or @PROPER—to standardize your input prior to looking up values in a table with @VLOOKUP or @HLOOKUP.

✓ Build decision trees and/or decision tables when tackling complex @IF functions that are nested or that require logical connectors.

✓ For easier maintenance in complex problems, use nested @IF statements rather than @IF statements with logical connectors.

✓ Use the Auditor to maintain worksheets with many formulas.

CHAPTER

5 Practicing Good Spreadsheet Hygiene

It ain't so much the things we don't know that get us in trouble. It's the things we know that ain't so.

—Artemus Ward

Objectives

- Understand the hygiene problem when structuring worksheets.
- Know how to structure a worksheet for maximum efficiency.
- Know how to work with the parts of a worksheet.
- Develop good spreadsheet hygiene by recognizing problem issues.

The Hygiene Problem

You are the developer. In organizing effective worksheets, you must consider other users in your organization. This chapter gives you a way to lay out all worksheets consistently. Consistency will enable you to easily modify your worksheets as the business environment changes.

Spreadsheet packages, like Lotus 1-2-3, have a variety of functions that allow you to tackle a variety of tasks. Because spreadsheet packages are convenient to use, applications come forth like the flow of a river after a dam has been opened. As there are many good applications to help you with decision-making problems, so also there are applications that contain a host of errors. Some of these errors are unknown to the developers who created them. Errors often remain hidden when the time is not taken to check the quality of worksheet formulas and related references. Unfortunately, faulty worksheets will inevitably result in flawed decisions unless you carefully test your worksheets before using them in production.

Besides inadequate testing, a lack of adherence to a rigorous design methodology has helped create this bad situation. Some of the errors frequently found in worksheet applications include:

- mistakes in logic
- incorrect ranges in formulas
- incorrect cell references
- incorrect use of formats and column widths
- accidentally overwritten formulas
- misuse of built-in functions

HINT: Modifiable worksheets are crucial because of changes in the business environment.

Good worksheets meet at least five criteria. First, a worksheet should produce **accurate** results—the degree to which a worksheet generates output that is correct. Accuracy, in turn, impacts on the degree of confidence you place in the model. Second, a worksheet should be capable of being **audited**. You should be able to retrace the steps you took in developing an application. Third, a worksheet should be capable of being **modified** easily without introducing errors. Perhaps this is the most difficult issue because it takes a special type of planning. Fourth, a worksheet should be **readable** and attractive so that you and others who see it can easily understand its organization, content, and formulas. Finally, a worksheet should be **consistent**, producing results that are reliable. That is, if a model is run a number of times, you can expect the same output.

Learning to develop *modifiable* worksheets will produce applications that are usually *reliable* and *auditable*, although the latter must be tested independently.

The key to producing a worksheet that meets all five criteria is to plan appropriately, following some guidelines that will be introduced in this chapter.

Planning for effective worksheets requires you, the developer, to answer a number of questions prior to development. Each of these questions will push you into considering the full range of uncertainties that need to be addressed. The first question is, Who will use the worksheet—a single user, or multiple users? Multiple users require a greater degree of planning for user-friendly interfaces, so that users can interact easily with the worksheet. Even a single user, if that person is not the developer, will add to the complexity to be addressed.

The second question is, How frequently will the worksheet be used? Worksheets that will be used only one time do not have the same degree of complexity, nor do they need to be as readable as those that will be used more than once. However, one-time decisions can be every bit as important as recurring decisions. For example, the capital budgeting decision involving the purchase of new manufacturing equipment and requiring choices from among several options can represent a strategic application for an organization.

HINT: Develop the worksheet to meet the needs of users who have the least amount of experience in using 1-2-3.

The third question you must ask is, What is my own skill level and that of others who will use the worksheet? You must clearly identify your own skill level so that you know how much complexity to filter out. You must also know the skill level of others who will use the worksheet you will develop. The less a user's experience level with using worksheets, the more complex the development effort you must undertake. Often, menus must be created so that users will not have to interact directly with the 1-2-3 package. A problem that must be resolved is how to develop a worksheet for more than one user, each with a different skill level. What should be the rule of thumb in developing a worksheet for multiple users? A worksheet should be developed to the lowest common denominator—the users who have the least amount of experience. The greater the complexity, the greater the need to adhere to the planning guidelines presented in this chapter.

Less Complexity ⟶	More Complexity
Single user	Multiple users
One-time use	Frequent use
Experienced 1-2-3 user	Inexperienced 1-2-3 user

By combining these three factors, we increase the complexity that needs to be dealt with in the development of the worksheet. For example, if a worksheet is being developed for many inexperienced users for frequent use, you must be sure that all of the criteria are carefully adhered to. Worksheets that are not developed carefully in such situations are bound to be riddled with errors. We will now discuss structuring the worksheet, working effectively with parts of a worksheet, and managing large worksheets.

Structuring the Worksheet

Worksheets should be structured consistently from application to application, and from developer to developer. The consistency of structure is important because it enables developers to modify parts of a model, its formulas, and its other important components, regardless of the application. To structure the worksheet, you need to use a standardized worksheet format so that other users will soon be familiar with it. It should also be a layout that is easy to understand and modify. Above all, you should structure your worksheet so that it operates smoothly. Use spreadsheet packages to develop applications that are powerful, user-friendly, and understandable to novice users.

Effective worksheet structures usually contain some sort of block formatting that incorporates models, data, macros, and custom user menus. To provide a "map" to the worksheet structure, it is best to use an area of the worksheet for a description of the worksheet's organization. Each worksheet area should be appropriately named with the use of the /**R**ange **N**ame command. To do this, you break the worksheet into four logical quadrants, each quadrant holding different types of worksheet information. Figure 5.1 illustrates the four logical quadrants, comprising Models and Data in the northwest (NW), Worksheet Identification and Development Map in the southwest (SW), Custom User Menus in the northeast (NE), and Macros in the southeast (SE). Much of our attention will be spent within the Models and Data quadrant.

If you are using releases 3.1+ and 1.1 for Windows, you may decide to place each of these quadrants in a separate worksheet. The three-dimensional capabilities of these packages allows you to link the four worksheets together. The principle of consistent organization remains the same, however.

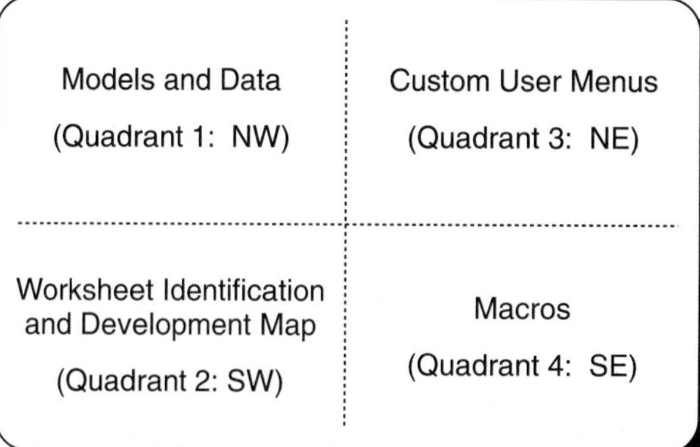

Figure 5.1
The High-Level Organization of a Worksheet

The Models and Data Quadrant

Models and data will reside in the northwest quadrant of the worksheet. You may have many models in your Models and Data quadrant. You can expect to expand a model as you add more variables for analysis. With the expansion of the model area, you can also expect increases in the data from which your model is anchored. The primary model is the integrated dynamic model, the culmination of your analysis. It holds the prominent spot in your worksheet, starting in the A1 or Home cell. Figure 5.2 displays the Models and Data quadrant.

The model areas contain the dynamic models that consist of only pure formulas. The first model in the upper northwest quadrant is the integrated model that puts together all of the analysis results found in other models. For example, in the Harrison Electronics case, you may conduct a set of analyses to discover which variables are related to which other variables and where the trends are. You will then build a number of smaller models to conduct analyses, such as moving average, exponential smoothing, linear regression, ratio analysis, and correlation analysis. Although they are useful, these models alone do not give you enough information to conduct an effective analysis. A dynamic model that integrates the findings of each of these line items is critical to making a decision.

HINT: The models area contains only pure formulas.

You may notice in Figure 5.3 that a Supporting Data and Assumptions area accompanies each model. This data area is critical to developing a dynamic model that consists only of formulas. The Supporting Data area may contain raw data

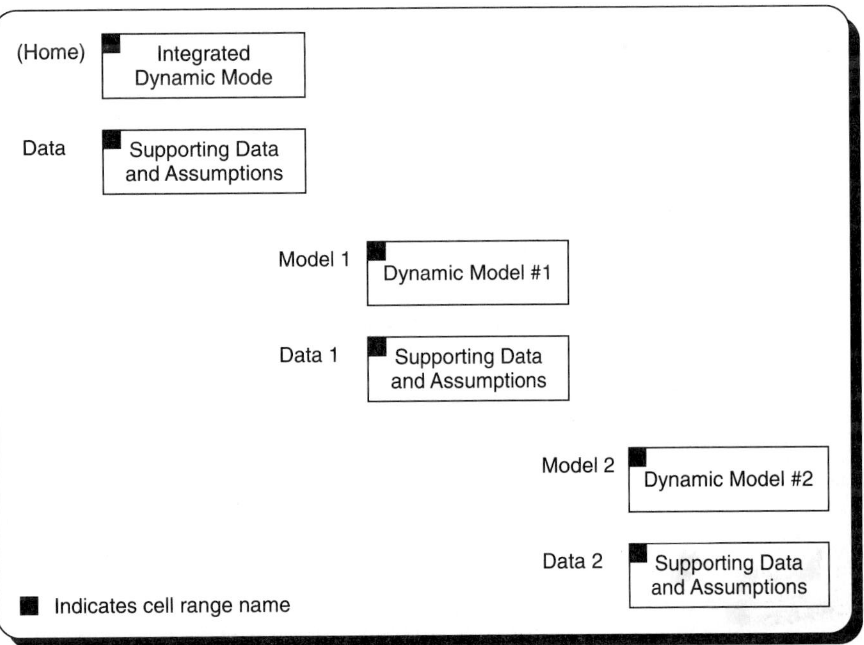

Figure 5.2
The Models and Data Quadrant

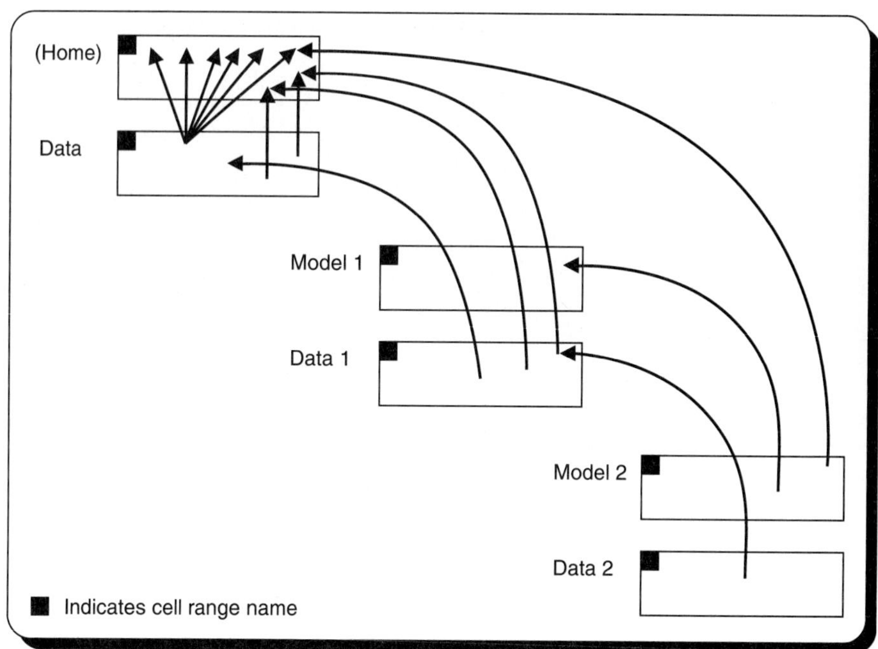

Figure 5.3
Some Links between Models and Data Blocks

keyed in from reports, assumptions (such as growth rates or inflation), starting values for trends, and output areas for commands (regression, for example). Even if a data item is contained in one cell, you do not want to introduce a single value into the model, because that value may need to be changed before you can generate a new scenario. Part of the data area may contain one or more graphs that help you visualize changes in the data. Therefore it is best to create an area close to the model, where you can run a number of what-if situations.

HINT: The data area may contain one or more graphs to illustrate changes in the data.

Notice the references between the integrated model and its data area, between the integrated model and other models, and especially between the main data area and other data areas. Obviously, Figure 5.3 cannot show all of the possible links or calls. Usually, every cell in the integrated model imports data or other references from either its own data area or another model in the worksheet. A well-designed worksheet speeds up the testing process, as we will soon see.

The second important thing to observe in the Models and Data area is the diagonal nature of the model placement. You can expect a degree of expansion in your worksheet, and expansion means inserting and deleting rows and columns. You may have seen some worksheets with models placed directly under or next to each other. The problem with that structure is that when a row or column is inserted into the current model, rows and columns are also inserted into other worksheet models, causing errors. Although such errors are not as critical as the insertion or deletion of a row to or from a macro, which would stop execution, the models are flawed. Deletion is much more of an issue, however. Copying and moving also creates a problem in the models when existing data or model formu-

HINT: Place your models and associated data in a diagonal format.

las are inadvertently overwritten. Placing models in a diagonal line avoids these problems so that you are free to insert or delete rows and columns into your worksheet without concern. Also, you don't need to worry about the setting of column widths for one model interfering with that of another.

Finally, the cells in the upper-left corner of each model and data block are highlighted in Figure 5.3 to indicate the need for range names. You should name each block area so that you can skip around within the worksheet to whatever model you want to use without having to memorize cell references. You use the **/R**ange **N**ame **C**reate command to name each cell. You can then press the GOTO key (F5), followed by the range name, to move directly to another area. You will soon print a table of range names in the Worksheet Identification and Development Map area to depict the set of range names.

The Worksheet Identification and Development Map Quadrant

The Worksheet Identification and Development Map quadrant will contain a number of important items helpful in identifying the developer and understanding the overall layout of the worksheet. Figure 5.4 illustrates the four modules that must be located here.

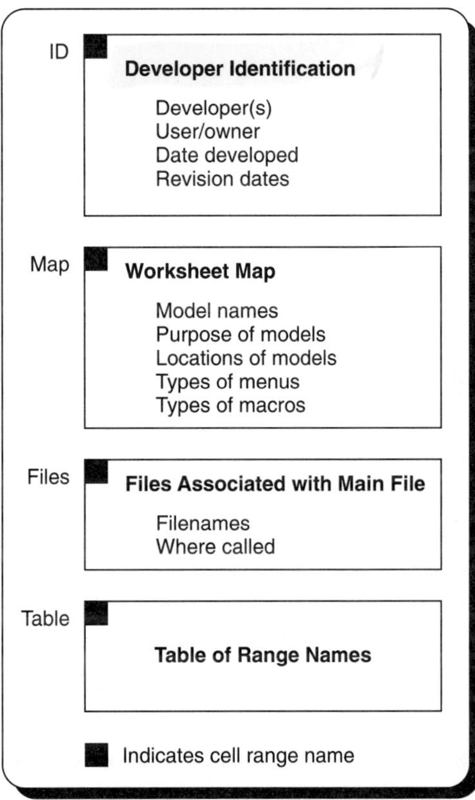

Figure 5.4
The Worksheet Identification and Development Map Quadrant

First is the identification section. The documentation in this section is especially critical because it identifies the developer of the worksheet, who may need to make subsequent changes. The documentation also identifies the user, the date the application was developed, and the dates of any revisions.

The second section is the worksheet map, which gives the user a clear idea of how the worksheet is organized without having to move through it. The worksheet map identifies each model, describes what the models do, and gives their cell addresses in the worksheet.

The third section describes other 1-2-3 files associated with the main worksheet. The filenames are shown, along with where the files are called in the worksheet. With Releases 3.1+ and 1.1 for Windows, some developers place each quadrant in a separate worksheet. Each worksheet must be identified and documented in this section.

HINT: Print a fresh range name table before quitting.

Finally, a table of range names is included in this quadrant. To create this section, you invoke the **/R**ange **N**ames **T**able command, which gives an alphabetical listing of range names along with their cell addresses. You will have a mixture of range names here—those used in formulas and those used for moving around within the worksheet. Notice that each section in this quadrant has been assigned generic range names also, so that the user can get to any of these sections regardless of the worksheet. The range name table is not automatically updated, so you will need to print a fresh range name table before quitting.

The Custom User Menus Quadrant

The third quadrant of the worksheet contains custom user menu screens. Although you can create menus in the upper portion of the screen, so as to make 1-2-3 commands understandable to other users, this section directs users to special areas of the worksheet to customize the worksheet. These menus let the user choose from a number of options that lead the user to another screen, model, or data area. Custom user menus are tied directly to macros, which contain IF statements that test for user responses. We will discuss custom user menus in Chapter 8. Figure 5.5 illustrates the layout for menus in this section.

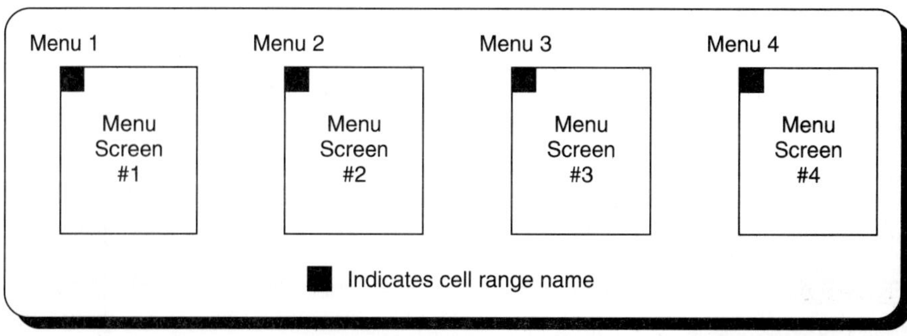

Figure 5.5
The Custom User Menus Quadrant

The Macros Quadrant

The Macros quadrant is the area of the worksheet where you will place your macros. As the rows in this quadrant are shared with the Worksheet Identification and Development Map quadrant, macros must get the priority. The reason for this priority is that *inserting rows* causes macros to stop executing. To solve this problem, you can use the /**M**ove command to relocate the Identification sections so that you create a blank row. Rather than delete rows, you will plan for revisions by leaving blank rows in the Identification quadrant. However, you must be careful not to inadvertently *delete rows* in the Macro quadrant or you may delete important information in the Models and Data quadrant. Figure 5.6 shows the layout of the Macros quadrant.

The Macros quadrant is composed of three sections. Each section will help you create macros that run effectively and that can be later modified.

HINT: The area for naming macros does not reflect the true names of the macros.

The first section is the one in which you name your macros. Macro names are displayed in the first cell (not in the entire range) in which the sequence of macro commands begins. This area does not, however, reflect the true range names for the macros. Macro labels are added only for the development and for later modification so that you understand the macro name. The true macro range names are embedded in the first cell of the macro commands section, as illustrated in Figure 5.6.

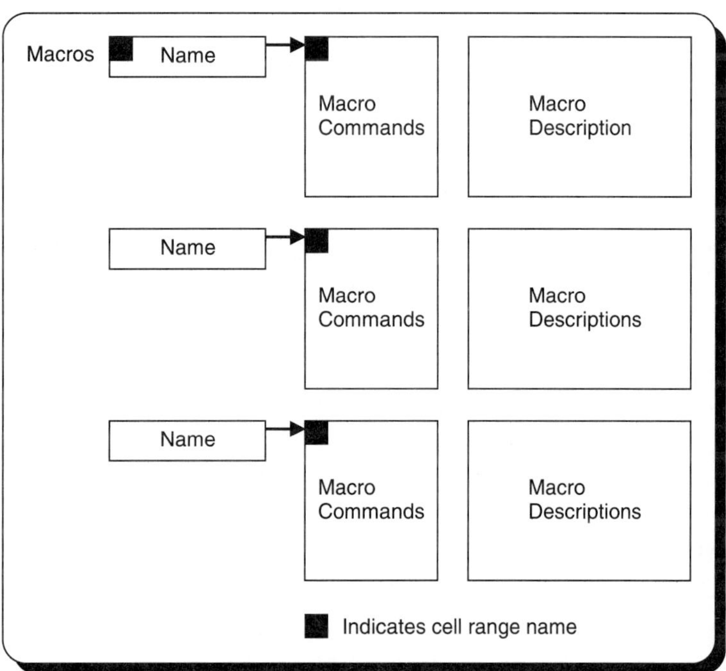

Figure 5.6
The Macros Quadrant

Macro commands comprise the central area in the Macros quadrant. It is here that the macros are named, and created and that the execution takes place. Most of the macros are developed, with the exception of the MENUBRANCH command, in sequential cells from top to bottom. Notice that each set of macro commands is separated by a blank cell, which indicates the end of the macro and its execution. It is here that developers link together custom user menus and create automated what-ifs and optimization routines.

The third section within the Macros quadrant is used for documenting each macro command within a set. Documentation is often overlooked by worksheet developers who have an intimate knowledge of macro commands. This is one of the most important areas for ensuring effective modification of the worksheet.

Hygiene Issues

There are a host of good practices that lead to good spreadsheet hygiene. By **hygiene** we mean the process of building and maintaining spreadsheet applications that are healthy, vibrant, robust, rich, vigorous, and powerful. Your goal as a developer is to build spreadsheets that will contribute to the organization in which you operate. We want to use the power of spreadsheets to not only increase our personal productivity but also the enterprise's competitive position. Good hygiene practices consist primarily of the consistent and effective "trapping" of worksheet errors. In this section we will discuss seven hygiene issues to consider as you develop your worksheets. Each of these issues affects the health of the worksheet and eventually the quality of the decisions that result from its use.

Hygiene Issue #1: Inconsistent Worksheet Organization

Since we just discussed worksheet organization, you probably already understand this hygiene issue. Worksheets that are organized according to the whim of the developer are more difficult to enhance, maintain, and modify. This is true not only for subsequent developers and users, but for the original developer as well. Often we forget the purpose and logic of the models and macro code we ourselves have developed.

HINT: Design your worksheet by using distinct blocks to store models and data.

Remember, when developing your worksheet, to focus on block designs. Earlier in this chapter, we discussed how to organize the Models and Data area of the worksheet into blocks (see Figure 5.2). You will have an integrated model that may reference one or more models and one or more supporting data areas. We referred to individual models and supporting data areas as **blocks**. These blocks are considered **modules** in the field of systems development. Modules call one another and pass data back and forth. Figure 5.3 illustrates some of the links between worksheet modules.

Often, developers set up a string of worksheets, each as a separate module, thus linking files together. This practice is good for large worksheets with multiple models that need to be overlaid in the same worksheet space. Memory limitations can often create situations in which multiple files are necessary—where the hard disk is, in essence, used as extra Lotus memory. Three-dimensional file linking cannot substitute for a single, well-designed worksheet. Worksheet organization is the first thing that both decision makers and model developers see when using the worksheet. The same worksheet organization that we discussed here must apply for single- or multiple-sheet designs.

HINT: Each sheet in an application should be considered a separate block.

Hygiene Issue #2: Lack of Limit Checking

Limit checking involves testing user input to ensure that the data are within predictable limits. What-if analysis allows you to enter a variety of data into a worksheet in order to observe changes in one or more decision variables. You can create scenarios in which to evaluate the impact of these variables. Be aware, however, that it is easy to enter an incorrect value in a cell. You may often have an accurate estimate of the upper and lower limits of a decision variable. Let's return to the Harrison Electronics case. You will use high and low symbols, an error message (@ERR), and graphs to determine appropriate data limits.

First, let's look at the use of high and low symbols. Figure 5.7 shows that the Total Sales column has been deleted and that three new columns have been added: a Forecast for Quarter 4, Error, and Difference. In column I the difference between the forecast and the actual sales amounts for Quarter 4 has been calculated. Notice that the difference has been divided by four and that the column has been formatted with the /**R**ange **F**ormat **+/-** command.

HINT: Use +/- cell formatting to illustrate high and low values.

Obviously, the fourth-quarter sales for small products have been underestimated by a sizable amount. The column in Figure 5.7 does not show the 13 hyphens, since they would exceed the column width. Either the column can be widened or the font in column I can be changed to accommodate more characters. The adjacent worksheet cells tell you whether individual entries or differences are within acceptable limits.

Column widths and range formats give you a level of protection. For example, if values for the Repair Sales variable will not exceed 99 (thousand), the column width should be kept narrow, to 4. Values that exceed three characters are displayed as **** in the worksheet cell. Do not set a column width to fit the variable title, like most worksheet developers, rather set it to fit the values it will contain. You can change title fonts with the WYSIWYG program to fit within suggested widths based on values.

HINT: Column widths should be set to trap values at the high end.

@IF functions can be used in two ways to corroborate values or labels and to detect errors. The first way to use an @IF statement is coupled with the @CELL function to test whether a value is present in a cell. The second way to use an @IF statement is to check whether an entry is within the low and high limits. Figure 5.7 illustrates the use of the @IF and @CELL functions to test for a value. In cell G10 you can see that a label yields an error message in the adjacent cell;

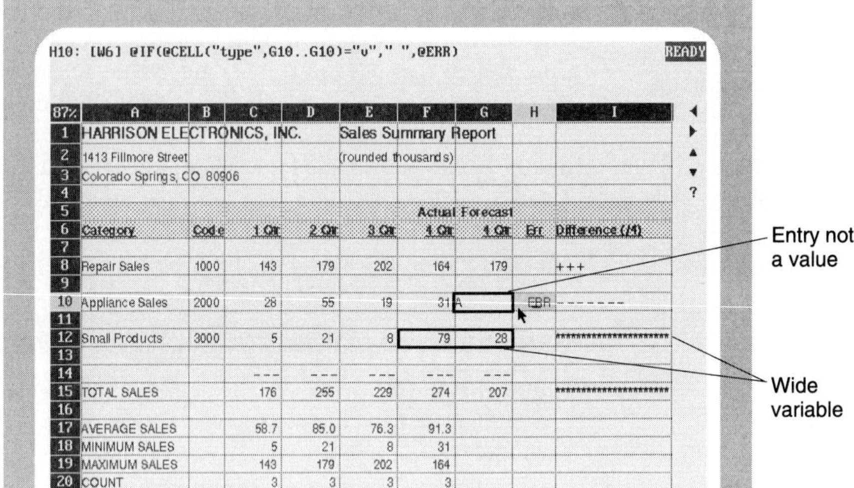

Figure 5.7
Using @IF and @CELL Functions to Check Data Input

otherwise the cell contains a blank. The two uses of the @IF statement in trapping user input errors are:

```
@IF(@CELL("type",G10)="v"," ",@ERR)
@IF(G10<30#AND#>50,@ERR," ")
```

In the first formula, you are testing whether the cell type is a value. If so, blank characters should appear in the current cell; if not, an ERR message should appear in this cell. In the second formula, you are checking the low and high ranges of the budget amount for the fourth quarter. Unless a value between 30 and 50 is entered, an ERR message should appear in the current cell.

Inconsistencies can also be detected with graphs. Often, setting up a graph for the variable under consideration shows values that are not in the range of other relevant values. Once the X and relevant ranges are set and the graph is named, you simply press the GRAPH ((F10)) key to illustrate the variable values. Figure 5.8 is a graph that shows the fourth-quarter sales for actual and forecast data. Notice the wide variance for small products sales. Although it is not always obvious how much of a spread is a wide variance, graphs give decision makers another way to look at data entered by users. If you have looked regularly at the Harrison Electronics data, you may be already aware of this error. As you develop models, consider providing graphs in addition to other limit checking techniques.

Hygiene Issue #3: Failure to Test a Model Prior to Its Use

The implications of making decisions based on an untested model are far-reaching. Therefore this is perhaps one of the most dangerous hygiene issues. One

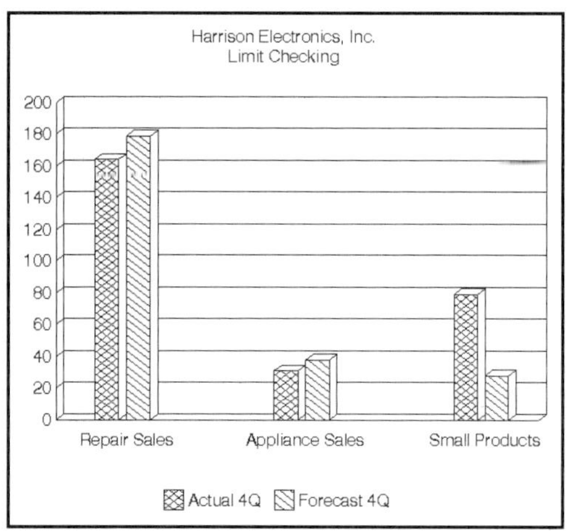

Figure 5.8
Graphing Output to Identify Wide Variances to Data Limits

obvious result of neglecting to test an application is a bad decision. Bad decisions destroy the credibility of the model and maybe even the credibility of the spreadsheet program for building dynamic decision models. Credibility is destroyed not only in the eyes of the developer, but also in the eyes of the people who ultimately evaluate the quality of the decision in question. Well-designed systems have a series of modules or blocks, which we defined earlier as model and data areas. It is important, then, that each of these modules is tested for accuracy and reliability.

There are many horror stories of decisions based upon models containing bad algorithms or inaccurate links that were not checked prior to use. Look at the following story:

Financial Institution in the Southeast

The managers of a financial institution in the southeastern United States developed and used a Lotus 1-2-3 model to help them decide in which area to open up a new branch. After marketing and cost data were collected, a worksheet was developed. It was brought into the boardroom *prior to testing*. The model directed the decision makers to favor a certain location, so a decision was made, and the digging commenced. About a month after construction had begun, someone checked the algorithms of several key variables. The manager found an incorrect formula that had been copied to a range. When corrected, the model led the decision makers to strongly consider another location. Construction was halted immediately, of course, and the decision was re-investigated. Unfortunately, the developer (a marketing analyst) was fired.

Such situations are common and yet are avoidable if proper testing of the model is conducted.

Cell and Module Testing. Worksheet modules should be tested in three phases. First, you should check the limits of each cell independently. Then test the cells of one module together. Finally, test all of the modules in an integrated fashion.

At least two common-sense cell tests should be conducted. One of these should use data that test the extreme points of a model. If good limit checks are in place, you should be able to tell by way of an adjacent cell or graph whether the formula you're investigating is behaving appropriately. This is called **cell testing**. You should also check other figures in the module in which the formula is being tested. This type of testing is referred to as **module testing**. Each module is a function of its cell formulas. It tests the interaction between cell formulas. The Auditor add-in is very helpful in testing modules. To comprehensively test module formulas, you need to examine formula precedents and dependents. Module testing is probably the most time-consuming test of all, because you test the interacting cells of each variable for accuracy. When you have finished, you should have determined that each module works independently.

Integration Testing. You should also observe the behavior of the model by focusing on two or more key variables in the integrated model. This type of testing is called **integration testing**, and it is just as important as cell and module testing. Knowing that each module works appropriately, you must now determine whether the links between modules are functioning well. Remember, you are attempting to develop a healthy, robust worksheet that can be used for decision making. All the modules must work together in harmony or the decision maker will not be able to conduct effective analysis. The most common problem found when conducting integration tests is inaccurate cell address referencing. When you develop variable algorithms, you may often copy a formula across a row or down a column. Within the formula, you may use the wrong type of addressing—in other words, relative addressing (the default) instead of absolute or mixed addressing. Cell addressing is another hygiene issue that we will address next.

Hygiene Issue #4: Poor Cell Addressing in Formulas

Before discussing poor cell addressing, let's review the different types of cell addressing. *Relative* cell addresses are the cell-reference rows and columns that change when a formula is copied. Cell references are then changed automatically after copying. With *absolute* cell addressing, you must fix both the row and the column so that they do not change when the formula is copied. To fix a row or a column, you must precede the cell reference or cell name with a `$`.

HINT: Mixed cell referencing is especially useful when you are copying a formula across either column or row.

One of the problems experienced by novice developers is the tendency to use either relative or absolute cell addressing exclusively. More often, *mixed* cell addressing is the appropriate way to create copyable formulas. Mixed cell addressing fixes either the row or the column, but not both. The cell reference `B$34` is an example of a mixed cell address. Mixed cell addressing is especially useful when you are copying a formula across either a column or row.

HINT: Do not use blank spaces in range names that will use absolute cell addressing.

Creating copyable formulas that accurately use cell addressing is essential to effective development efforts. Copyable formulas save you development time and effort. Developing copyable formulas also ensures the accuracy of your results. It shows a planned effort that enables you to design modules. Coupled with range names, the spreadsheet program provides for a variety of cell addressing. This variety gives you a great deal of power and flexibility. Note that range names can be used in place of cell addresses. You can use absolute addressing with range names by placing a $ sign in front of the range name—for example `$OPER_EXP`. Mixed cell addressing, however, cannot be used with range names. Although cells and ranges can be named with blank spaces (as in `OPER EXP`), they should not be used in cell addressing, and therefore it is recommended that you use an underscore (`OPER_EXP`) to name cells and ranges.

Hygiene Issue #5: Creating Bad Cell References

Bad cell references occur when you refer to a cell that is neither desired nor expected. Bad cell references can occur in two ways, often without your knowledge. The first is by an inappropriate use of the /**M**ove command. The second is by an inappropriate use of the /**C**opy command.

Inappropriate Move. Like the /**C**opy command, /**M**ove transfers the contents of a cell, formula, value, or label to another location. A problem such as a false appearance can result when you move a formula to another location. Consider Figure 5.9, which depicts an inappropriate move of the formula. The sum of Total Sales has been calculated in the Average Sales cell (from G15 to G17). Notice that the formula `@SUM(C15..F15)` still points to the Total Sales row. However, the

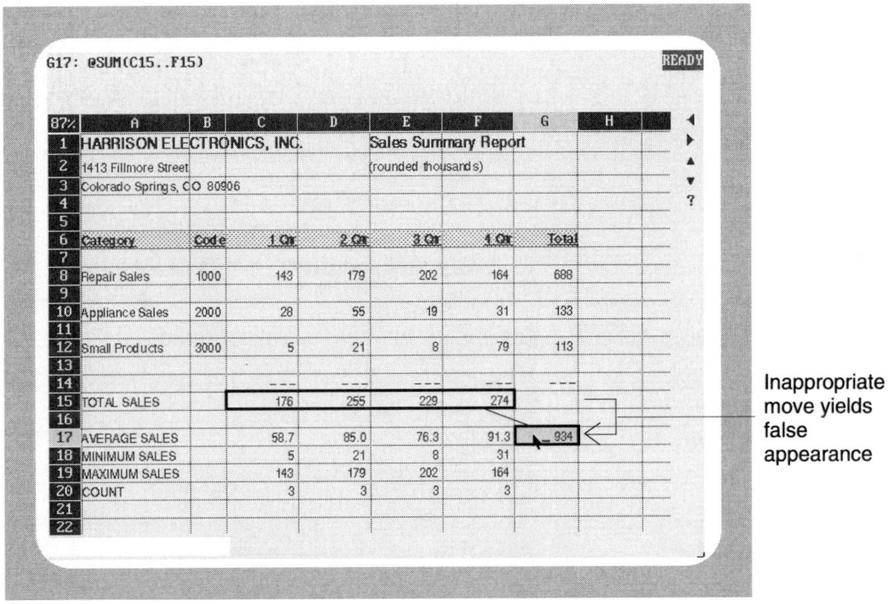

G17: @SUM(C15..F15) READY

87%	A	B	C	D	E	F	G	H
1	HARRISON ELECTRONICS, INC.				Sales Summary Report			
2	1413 Fillmore Street				(rounded thousands)			
3	Colorado Springs, CO 80906							
4								
5								
6	Category	Code	1 Qtr	2 Qtr	3 Qtr	4 Qtr	Total	
7								
8	Repair Sales	1000	143	179	202	164	688	
9								
10	Appliance Sales	2000	28	55	19	31	133	
11								
12	Small Products	3000	5	21	8	79	113	
13								
14			---	---	---	---	---	
15	TOTAL SALES		176	255	229	274		
16								
17	AVERAGE SALES		58.7	85.0	76.3	91.3	934	
18	MINIMUM SALES		5	21	8	31		
19	MAXIMUM SALES		143	179	202	164		
20	COUNT		3	3	3	3		
21								
22								

Inappropriate move yields false appearance

Figure 5.9
A False Appearance Created by Moving a Formula

result, 934, is shown as the sum of Average Sales for the four quarters, which is misleading to the decision maker.

Inappropriate Copy. The second way you can cause a bad cell reference to occur is by copying a formula beyond the physical boundaries of a spreadsheet (not just the worksheet). The result of such a copy is nonsense. In Figure 5.10 the formula that sums Total Sales has been copied from cell G17, where it was inappropriately moved, to D2. Notice the change in formula cell references.

Old Formula: `@SUM(C15..F15)`
New Formula: `@SUM(IV8192..C8192)`

Suddenly the argument range has moved off the scale, out of the worksheet and spreadsheet range. The formula has been adjusted to include the rightmost and lowermost cells in the spreadsheet even though there are no values in this part of the worksheet. The value in cell D2 is meaningless, yielding a result of 0.

The importance of avoiding bad cell references is obvious. A bad cell reference creates errors that are difficult to detect and that introduce inaccuracy into a dynamic model. Be sure to check all statistical functions for bad references (especially the @SUM and @AVG functions). The lesson here is that care must be taken with the /**M**ove and /**C**opy commands that involve formulas.

Hygiene Issue #6: Little Use of Documentation

Most worksheet developers do not spend much time documenting the key areas of the worksheets they create. There may be several reasons for neglecting this important practice. First, cell noting is the best method of documenting specific cells, and yet it is rather time-consuming. Cell noting is supported directly in Releases 3.1+ and 1.1 for Windows but requires an add-in package for Releases

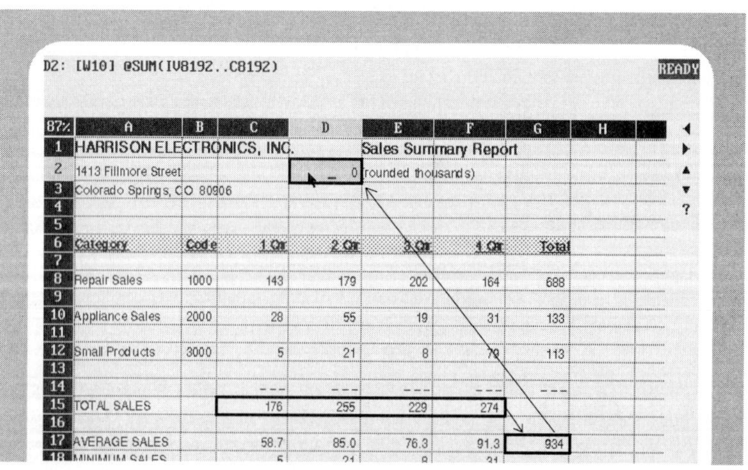

Figure 5.10
An Inappropriate Use of the Copy Command

2.3 and 2.4. Many developers do not have such a program. Second, documenting worksheets takes time. This alone may be the most important reason why worksheets are rarely documented.

HINT: Document "pivotal" cells that contain complex formulas or that link one module to another.

Let's look at the four types of documentation in worksheets. The first is *the Worksheet Identification and Development Map area* as illustrated in Figure 5.3. This area contains documentation, including the identification of persons and dates, a map of the worksheet layout, a description of associated files, and a table of range names. The second type of documentation is *a description of each major block within the worksheet*. This description should encompass the module's purpose and its critical variables. It can be placed at the beginning of each block next to the name. The third type of documentation includes *descriptions that must accompany each line of a macro*. The fourth type is *cell documentation*, which highlights key cells and formulas. Documenting every cell could be extremely time-consuming. You may want to select important "pivotal" cells that contain very complex formulas or that link one module to another. You can write cell notes in an adjacent cell and then hide the note by using the **/R**ange **F**ormat **H**idden command. Each cell can hold up to 240 characters. One last note about cell documentation: it should be standardized within organizations, especially when a worksheet is being created and maintained by two or more developers.

Hygiene Issue #7: Limited Control Over User Access

Our final hygiene problem to consider is the concern over users and decision makers who may inappropriately access a worksheet or inadvertently damage parts of a worksheet. Lotus 1-2-3 allows you to control access by placing password security on a file.

HINT: To set a password, follow the file name with a blank space and a *p* when saving.

You use the **/F**ile **S**ave command to initiate a password. Follow the filename with a blank space and then a *p*. The Lotus program asks you to enter the password twice; the second time is for confirmation. In the future, when you use the **/F**ile **R**etrieve command, the program will ask you for the password that was assigned to the file. Be sure, however, that you don't forget the password; otherwise you will lock yourself out of the worksheet.

Often, worksheet users accidentally erase or change a worksheet's cell contents. Lotus 1-2-3 contains an important feature to prevent unintentional worksheet modification by users or other developers. First, select the cells and/or ranges that you want to protect, and use the **/R**ange **P**rotect and **/R**ange **U**nprotect commands. After selecting the appropriate cells and/or ranges, turn on the global protection feature with the **/W**orksheet **G**lobal **P**rotection **E**nable command. What should be protected? All macros, the integrated dynamic model, and cells that are not subject to frequent changes.

Good worksheet hygiene inevitably improves the quality of the dynamic models that you create for decision making. Effective decisions rely essentially on well-designed worksheets. The guidelines discussed in this chapter will help you develop worksheets that meet all the criteria desirable in dynamic models.

Review Questions

1. What is the essence of the hygiene problem?
2. List the errors frequently found in worksheet applications.
3. What are the five criteria that good worksheets meet?
4. How should you deal with complexity in a worksheet? What questions must you answer prior to development?
5. What is the advantage of structuring a worksheet in the same way from application to application?
6. When planning for the design of a worksheet, what is the lowest common denominator with respect to user experience with 1-2-3?
7. Describe the worksheet structure at a high level.
8. How should the Models and Data quadrant be laid out?
9. Why should a dynamic model contain only formulas and no values?
10. What is the purpose of a data area that supports each model?
11. Why lay out models and data areas in a diagonal?
12. Describe the layout of the Worksheet Identification and Development Map quadrant.
13. What is the difference between a macro name and the name description in the Macros quadrant?
14. List the seven hygiene issues that worksheet developers should consider.
15. What is the purpose of a block? How do blocks help you in maintaining worksheets?
16. Describe the different techniques that can be used to trap user errors.
17. What are the most useful @functions for detecting input errors in data?
18. What are the possible effects of failing to test models prior to their use?
19. Discuss the three types of worksheet tests.
20. What is the difference between bad cell references and poor cell addresses?
21. How do bad cell references occur?
22. Describe each of the four types of documentation and the benefits of each type.
23. How can you limit user access over sensitive areas of the worksheet?

Skill-Building Activities: Setting Up a Data and Model Area

Activity 1: Setting Up a Data Area

Let's continue developing the Harrison Electronics worksheet. Use the **F**ile **R**etrieve menu to bring up a copy of the file from Chapter 4, or start new with the data in the following table.

NOTE: To help you with this exercise, ***boldface*** *letters indicate a message from the system or the worksheet while the commands in the list tell you to make a specific entry.*

	Year 1				Year 2				Year 3				
Category	**1 Qtr**	2 Qtr	3 Qtr	4 Qtr	1 Qtr	2 Qtr	3 Qtr	4 Qtr	1 Qtr	2 Qtr	3 Qtr	4 Qtr	Avg
Repair Sales	56	77	111	98	81	103	165	139	143	179	202	164	
Appliance Sales	15	31	12	22	19	47	17	27	28	55	19	31	
Small Products	5	11	5	34	4	17	7	55	5	21	8	79	

The data area will be set up in cell A23, where A23 will be named DATA, cell A25 will contain the headings, and rows 28, 30, and 32 will contain the raw data.

Move the cell pointer to cell A23.

Use the /**R**ange **N**ame **C**reate command to create a range name called DATA in cell A23.

Move the cell pointer to cell A25 and begin entering the titles in the table above.

Enter the rest of the data, observing blank rows.

Use the /**W**orksheet **C**olumn **W**idth **C**olumn-range **S**et command to set the width to 5 for each of the columns that contain quarterly data.

Invoke WYSIWYG with either the alternate mouse button or the :.

Bold the headings and set up a light shadow for rows 25 and 26.

Your worksheet should now look similar to the one illustrated in Figure 5.11.

Activity 2: Graphing the Data

You will now graph the data to see if you can identify trends in any of the three sales categories. At first glance, the data appear to be cyclical in nature, with

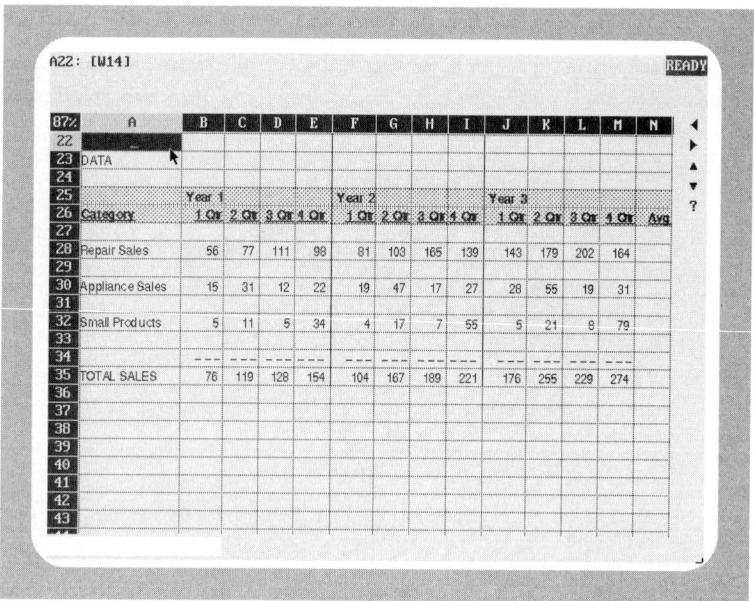
A22: [W14] READY

87%	A	B	C	D	E	F	G	H	I	J	K	L	M	N
22														
23	DATA													
24														
25		Year 1				Year 2				Year 3				
26	Category	1 Qtr	2 Qtr	3 Qtr	4 Qtr	1 Qtr	2 Qtr	3 Qtr	4 Qtr	1 Qtr	2 Qtr	3 Qtr	4 Qtr	Avg
27														
28	Repair Sales	56	77	111	98	81	103	165	139	143	179	202	164	
29														
30	Appliance Sales	15	31	12	22	19	47	17	27	28	55	19	31	
31														
32	Small Products	5	11	5	34	4	17	7	55	5	21	8	79	
33														
34		---	---	---	---	---	---	---	---	---	---	---	---	
35	TOTAL SALES	76	119	128	154	104	167	189	221	176	255	229	274	
36														
37														
38														
39														
40														
41														
42														
43														

Figure 5.11
Setting Up a Data Range

highs for repair sales in Quarter 3 of each year. Graphs are part of the data area in a worksheet and so should be placed directly under the data you are graphing.

1. Invoke the graph menu by using the /**G**raph command.
2. Set the graphing ranges:

   X: `B26..M26`
   A: `B28..M28`
   B: `B30..M30`
   C: `B32..M32`

3. To enter the legends and titles, press the (F2) key to edit the settings and select Legends & Titles.
4. Enter the following legends:

   A: `Repair Sales`
   B: `Appliance Sales`
   C: `Small Products`

5. Enter the first title: `Harrison Electronics, Inc.`
6. To place the graph on the worksheet, move the cell pointer to A38.
7. Invoke WYSIWYG with either the alternate mouse key or the :.
8. Enter the WYSIWYG command /**G**raph **A**dd **C**urrent.

9. Highlight the range A38..N55 and press the (ENTER) key to confirm.
10. To print the graph, enter the WYSIWYG command /**P**rint **R**ange **S**et and highlight the range A38..N55.
11. Select the **G**o command from the Print menu.

Your graph should look similar to the one in Figure 5.12. Notice the cyclical nature of the three sales categories and the strong growth in Repair Sales over the past three years.

Activity 3: Setting Up the Structure for a Model

In this activity you will set up a model in the Home position of the worksheet so that you can use the data area for your analysis. This will include setting up headings and creating categories.

Use the /**C**opy command to copy the headings from A25..N26 to A5.

Use the /**C**opy command to copy the categories from A27..A32 to A8.

Use the /**M**ove command to move the labels Appliance Sales and Small Products from A10..A12 to A13.

Use the /**M**ove command to move the label Small Products from A15 to A18.

Go to cell A9 and enter the label `' Change`.

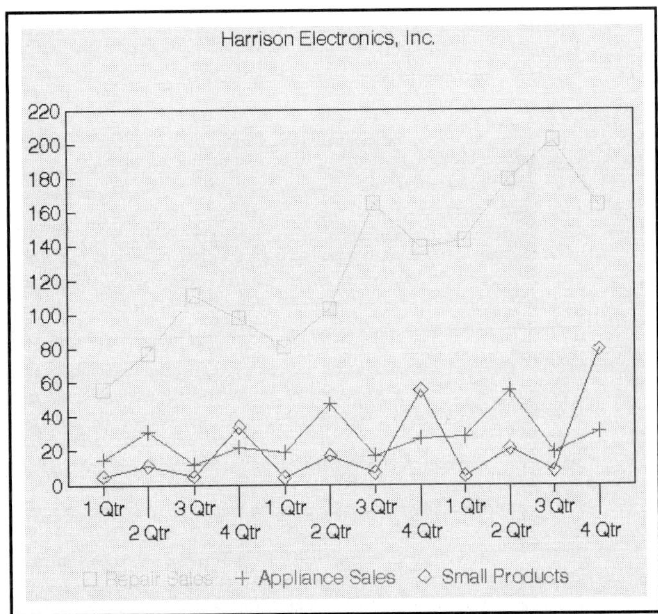

Figure 5.12
Graph for the Data Range

Go to cell A10 and enter the label `' % Change`.

Use the **/C**opy command to copy the labels in A9..A10 to A14..A15 and A19..A20.

Invoke WYSIWYG by using either the alternate mouse button or the :.

Select the **/F**ormat **B**old **S**et command to bold the main categories in cells A8, A13, and A18.

Your worksheet should now resemble the worksheet shown in Figure 5.13. Next, you will use the data in the model for your analysis.

Activity 4: Using Data in the Model for Analysis

In this activity you will calculate the changes in each of the sales categories, including the dollar change and the percentage change between each quarter. Leave the cells in column B blank, since it is the first quarter.

To calculate Change:

Position the cell pointer on cell C9.

Enter the formula `+C28-B28`.

Use the **/C**opy command to copy the formula from C9 to D9..M9.

Use the **/C**opy command to copy the formula from C9 to C14 and C19.

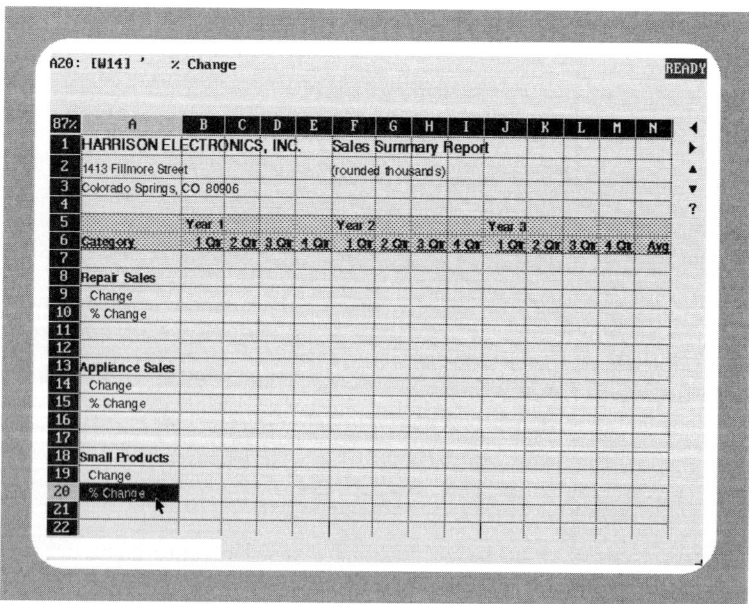

Figure 5.13
Setting Up the Structure for the Model

Position the cell pointer on cell C14.

Edit the formula with the F2 key to `+C30-B30`.

Use the **/C**opy command to copy the formula from C14 to D14..M14.

Position the cell pointer on cell C19.

Edit the formula with the F2 key to `+C32-B32`.

Use the **/C**opy command to copy the formula from C19 to D19..M19.

You have now entered the formulas in the model to calculate changes for each of the sales categories for the 12 quarters.

You are now ready to enter the formulas for the percentage change in each sales category. You will use a similar set of keystrokes for entering these formulas.

To calculate the % Change:

Position the cell pointer on cell C10.

Enter the formula `+(C28-B28)/B28`.

Use the **/C**opy command to copy the formula from C10 to D10..M10.

Use the **/C**opy command to copy the formula from C10 to C15 and C20.

Position the cell pointer on cell C15.

Edit the formula with the F2 key to `+(C30-B30)/B30`.

Use the **/C**opy command to copy the formula from C15 to D15..M15.

Position the cell pointer on cell C20.

Edit the formula with the F2 key to `+(C32-B32)/B32`.

Use the **/C**opy command to copy the formula from C20 to D20..M20.

You have now finished entering the main formulas, except for the averages, for the model. Your worksheet should resemble the one shown in Figure 5.14.

Activity 5: Calculating the Average Sales in Each Category

You are now ready to calculate the average sales in each category. The most efficient way is to enter a single formula in cell N9 and copy it to the other sales categories.

Position the cell pointer on cell N9.

Enter the formula `@AVG(C9..M9)`.

Use the **/C**opy command to copy the formula from N9 to N10.

Use the **/R**ange **F**ormat **P**ercent command to format cell N10 as a percentage with 0 decimals.

C20: {SWISS10} (P0) [W5] (C32-B32)/B32 READY

87%	A	B	C	D	E	F	G	H	I	J	K	L	M	N
1	HARRISON ELECTRONICS, INC.					Sales Summary Report								
2	1413 Fillmore Street					(rounded thousands)								
3	Colorado Springs, CO 80906													
4														
5		Year 1				Year 2				Year 3				
6	Category	1 Qtr	2 Qtr	3 Qtr	4 Qtr	1 Qtr	2 Qtr	3 Qtr	4 Qtr	1 Qtr	2 Qtr	3 Qtr	4 Qtr	Avg
7														
8	Repair Sales													
9	Change		21	34	−13	−17	22	62	−26	4	36	23	−38	
10	% Change		38%	44%	−12%	−17%	27%	60%	−16%	3%	25%	13%	−19%	
11														
12														
13	Appliance Sales													
14	Change		16	−19	10	−3	28	−30	10	1	27	−36	12	
15	% Change		107%	−61%	83%	−14%	147%	−64%	59%	4%	96%	−65%	63%	
16														
17														
18	Small Products													
19	Change		6	−6	29	−30	13	−10	48	−50	16	−13	71	
20	% Change		120%	−55%	580%	−88%	325%	−59%	686%	−91%	320%	−62%	888%	

Figure 5.14
Calculating the Percentage Change in Sales

Position the cell pointer on cell N9.

Use the /**C**opy command to copy the formulas in cells N9..N10 to N14..N15 and to N19..N20.

Before you finish developing your model, you must interpret it by examining the output. Where is the biggest change? It appears that the Small Products category yields the biggest percentage change. Yet in terms of dollars, the Repair Sales category is the largest. Let's calculate a standardized value that takes into account both the dollar change and the percentage change in sales for each sales category.

Position the cell pointer in cell N28 and average the sales categories: `@AVG(C28..M28)`.

Copy this formula to cells N30 and N32.

Position the cell pointer on cell N11.

Enter the formula `+N9*N28`.

Copy the formula from cell N11 to N16 and N21 and edit the formula to address the appropriate cells in the data area.

You now have a standardized value that shows the average growth in both dollar and percentage terms, as shown in Figure 5.15. Based on this value it appears that the Repair Sales represents the largest growth category, followed by Small Products. This value gives us a better idea of the sales category to focus on in upcoming quarters.

Before you quit the 1-2-3 program, save the file by using the /**F**ile **S**ave command. Save the new worksheet as HARRIS5.

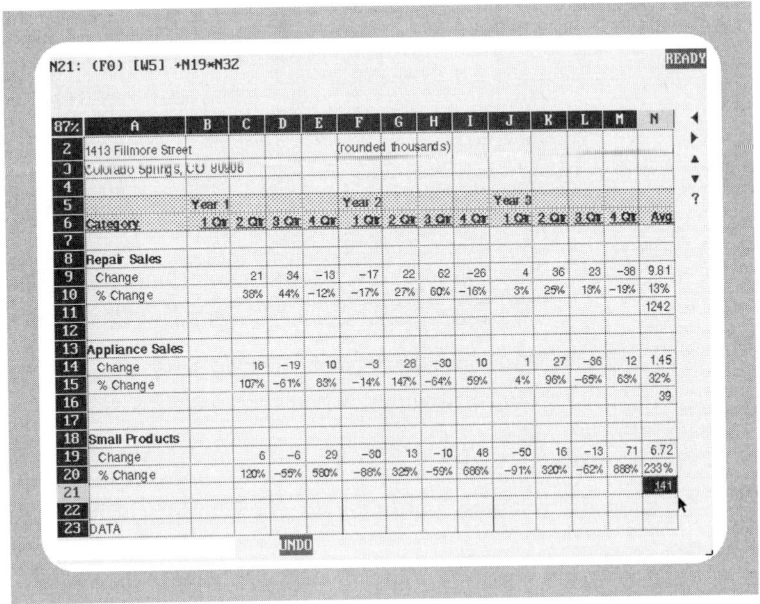

Figure 5.15
Calculating the Standardized Growth Value

Hands-On Exercises

1. Using a blank worksheet, set up a formal structure with three models and three associated data areas. Use the /**R**ange **N**ame **C**reate command and refer to the following table:

Quadrant	Description	Range Name	Cell Reference
Models and Data	Integrated model		A1
	Integrated data area	DATA	A21
	Model #1	Model1	J41
	Model #1 data area	Data1	J61
	Model #2	Model2	U81
	Model #2 data area	Data2	U101
Worksheet Identification	Identification area	ID	A121
	Worksheet map	Map	A131
	Associated files	Files	A141
	Table of range names	Table	A151

Quadrant	Description	Range Name	Cell Reference
Custom User Menus	Menu #1	Menu1	AE1
	Menu #2	Menu2	AM1
	Menu #3	Menu3	AU1
Macros	Overall macros area	Macros	AE121
	Main macro menu	\M	AF121
	Average calculations	Average	AF130

2. Within the Worksheet Identification quadrant, complete the developer identification and worksheet map descriptions.
3. Print a table of range names in cell A151 by using the **/R**ange **N**ame **T**able command. Widen columns A and/or B so that you can read both the cell references and the range descriptions or names.

Problem-Solving Projects

1. Create a worksheet for Knick-Knacks Unlimited that compares estimated inventory with actual inventory for selected items. Use a formula to calculate the difference between estimated and actual inventory counts. Use the following table to list your inventory:

Inventory Item	**Estimated Count** September 1992	**Actual Count** December 1992	Difference /2
China fan	12	23	5.5
Toy wooden cabin	6	4	-1
Snow church	5	19	7
Glass figurine	7	1	-3
Painting of Pikes Peak	10	3	-3.5

Make the formula in the first cell of the Difference column a mixed cell-referenced formula with the column absolute, but leave the row relative. For example, if the estimated count is in column B and the actual count is in column B, the following formula will achieve mixed cell referencing:

```
($B6-$B5)/2
```

Do not use your range names here, since we need mixed cell addressing. Copy the formula to the remainder of the cells in the Difference column.

2. Name the column with the estimated count "Estimated" and the column with the actual inventory count "Actual".
3. In the column to the right of the Difference column, create a title called Visual Difference. Copy the formula from the Difference column to the new Visual Difference column. Format the range as +/- to display high and low values.
4. Prepare a three-dimensional bar graph to illustrate the difference between estimated and actual inventory levels. The A range should be the estimated inventory count; the B range should be the actual inventory count.
5. To the right of the Visual Difference column, prepare a formula that checks for differences greater than 0; otherwise an ERR should be entered in the cell. Identify all inventory items whose levels have fallen below zero.
6. Create two new rows that: (1) totals Estimated Count, Actual Count, and the Difference/2 categories; (2) averages Estimated Count, Actual Count, and the Difference/2 categories.

Quality Assurance Checklist

As we conclude our discussion of spreadsheet commands, be sure you have considered the following factors that will contribute to the quality of your worksheet:

✓ Always use the same development methodology on every worksheet you develop so that you minimize worksheet errors.

✓ Always consider the degree of complexity that your worksheet must contain. Combining the three complexity factors (multiple users, frequent use, and inexperienced users) increases the complexity of the development project and the time it takes to plan for development.

✓ When the application will involve multiple users, develop the worksheet to the lowest common denominator—the users who have the least amount of experience in using 1-2-3.

✓ Use the block format for structuring a worksheet: (1) models and data, (2) worksheet identification and development map, (3) custom user menus, and (4) macros.

✓ Include graphs in the data areas adjacent to the relevant model.

✓ Place your models and their associated data in a diagonal arrangement within the Models and Data quadrant.

- ✓ If you are using separate sheets for each quadrant, they should be clearly listed in the Worksheet Identification and Development Map quadrant.
- ✓ Name each important cell of your worksheet block so that any developer can go to that area easily.
- ✓ Always use the standard range names for naming worksheet blocks.
- ✓ Remember that the macro names shown in the Name area of the Macros block do not represent the true names of the macros. The macro names are shown for documentation. The true name of a macro is the first cell.
- ✓ Use the +/- formatting in adjacent cells to illustrate the high and low values of a variable.
- ✓ Set column widths to trap values at the high end. Change column widths to reflect the data they contain rather than variable headings.
- ✓ Fit variable headings within smaller column widths by changing font sizes in WYSIWYG.
- ✓ Use the @IF function together with the @CELL function to test the validity of data input.
- ✓ Use graphs to visually detect wide variances and inconsistencies of model data.
- ✓ Always perform the three worksheet tests (cell testing, module testing, and integration testing) before putting an application into production.
- ✓ Use mixed cell addressing especially when copying a formula across both columns and rows.
- ✓ Do not use blank spaces in range names that will use absolute cell addressing.
- ✓ Do not try to use mixed cell addressing with range names.
- ✓ Be sure that you don't move or copy formulas outside the physical spreadsheet boundaries. Doing this can result in bad cell references.
- ✓ Document "pivotal" cells that contain complex formulas or that link one module to another. Use a cell noter if one is available.
- ✓ Limit control over user access by protecting cells and/or assigning a password to the worksheet.

PART

2 DDS Development Techniques

CHAPTER

6 Managing Data Areas

Broad numbers are always false.

—Samuel Johnson

Objectives

- Understand the importance of data areas in the worksheet.
- Discuss data pollution and how it contaminates the data area.
- Set up a database.
- Manage data by using sort, query, and distribution features.
- Use different types of graphic to display data.
- Learn hints for graphing that communicates clearly.

The Database in Decision Support Systems

Earlier in this text we introduced a decision support system (DSS), describing it as an interactive application that gives you easy access to decision models and data to support semistructured decision making. Figure 6.1 illustrates the structure of a DSS with three components: a database, a model base, and a user interface. Here we will delve into the database component, beginning with the issues that surround data management, and the ability of the database to interact with models. We will develop and query a database in Lotus 1-2-3. Later in this text we will discuss the other two components of the decision support system: the model base (in Chapter 7) and the user interface (in Chapter 8).

A **database** is a collection of data grouped according to logical organizational needs. Databases vary in size from a small group of data captured in small and medium-size firms, to extremely large amounts of data collected and managed for traditional applications such as accounts payable, inventory management, and payroll. Data are also collected for critical business applications

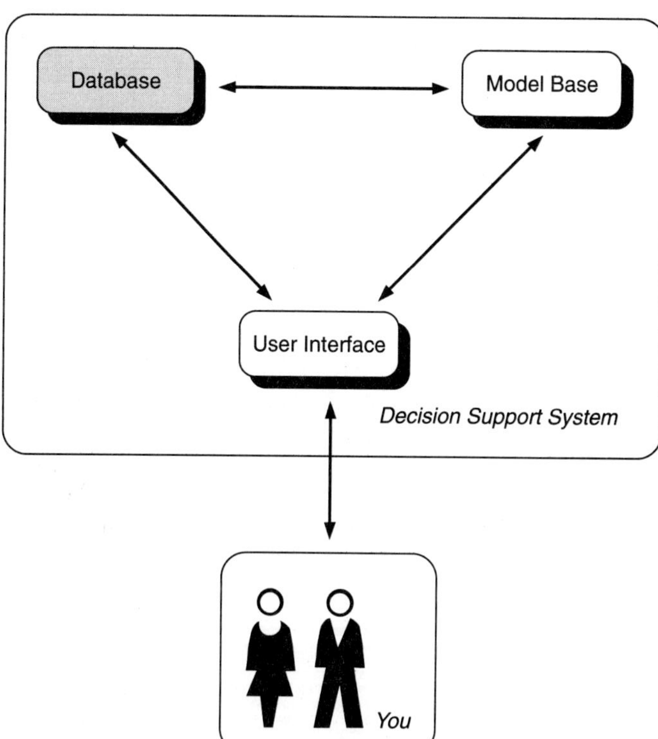

Figure 6.1
Components of a Decision Support System

such as aircraft product development, airline reservations, student information systems, and elevator repairs, etc.

Spreadsheet developers and users often shy away from data management activities, primarily because the language associated with data is difficult for them to understand without adequate training. Unfortunately, few models are built and little analysis can be conducted without one or more data areas to draw from. Lotus 1-2-3 makes the creation and management activities associated with databases quite simple compared to other programs. In association with its simplicity, the Lotus 1-2-3 database is therefore limited in its query and report generation power. However, you will find that the data management functions are useful, and that you can save a tremendous amount of time by learning how to create, sort, and query Lotus 1-2-3 databases. Since data are central to any model that supports decision making, whether a spreadsheet or some other decision support software is used, a good understanding of this material is critical. To avoid some of the jargon that often accompanies the management of data bases, this material will be introduced as concisely as possible.

Data Management Issues

Large databases are often centralized and managed by a data administrator and information systems (IS) staff. The size of these databases and the large volume of corporate data being captured dictates the need for a centralized group to manage it. The end-user computing movement of the 1980s and 1990s, fueled by microcomputers, powerful software, and micromainframe links, has created an environment in which spreadsheet developers have the capability to download data from the corporate database to their personal computers. Some spreadsheet users simply do not have the skills to use databases and so have resorted to rekeying data from reports and financial statements, keeping offline databases current while neglecting corporate data upgrades.

The result of these actions has been the decentralization of data throughout the organization. In a study of corporate data management, Amoroso, McFadden, and White (1990), *Information Resources Management Journal*, report a spreading of data pollution, especially with spreadsheet developers who do not create data areas to manage the corporate data they are using. **Data pollution** is the contamination of the information supply with incomplete, inconsistent, or incorrect information. Because data are embedded within several hundreds or sometimes thousands of formulas, the maintenance of these data becomes a horrendous task. Data pollution was found to be rampant in the study of 394 nontechnical end-users located in 21 firms. Seventy-five percent of self-reported "expert" spreadsheet developers and users claimed to have never used the /**D**ata commands in Lotus 1-2-3 or the equivalent in other spreadsheet packages. Yet 67 percent of these spreadsheet users were importing corporate data to perform some sort of analysis.

Sorting the Database

The fields, field names, and records for Harrison Electronics are shown in Figure 6.2. The figure depicts the basic file structure that you will use throughout this chapter to query and sort the data. In your database, you have five fields (variables when modeling) and eight records. The range encompassing A5..E12 constitutes the data.

Once you have set up the database, you will need to sort the database records into alphabetical or numerical order. When you **sort** a database in Lotus 1-2-3, you physically rearrange the rows of a worksheet into a certain ascending or descending order. One of the fields must act as a **primary key**, specifying the field on which the data range is sorted. Field names must, therefore, be unique in order to act as primary keys. A **secondary key** may also be specified if there is a possibility of duplicate data in the primary key. In this case, there is a duplication of data in both the Repair Rate (14, for example) and Avg Repair Time (2.1, for example) fields.

Sorting with a Primary Key

Use the **/D**ata **S**ort command to order the data. You have six options in the **/D**ata Sort menu structure:

Data-Range Primary-Key Secondary-Key Reset Go Quit

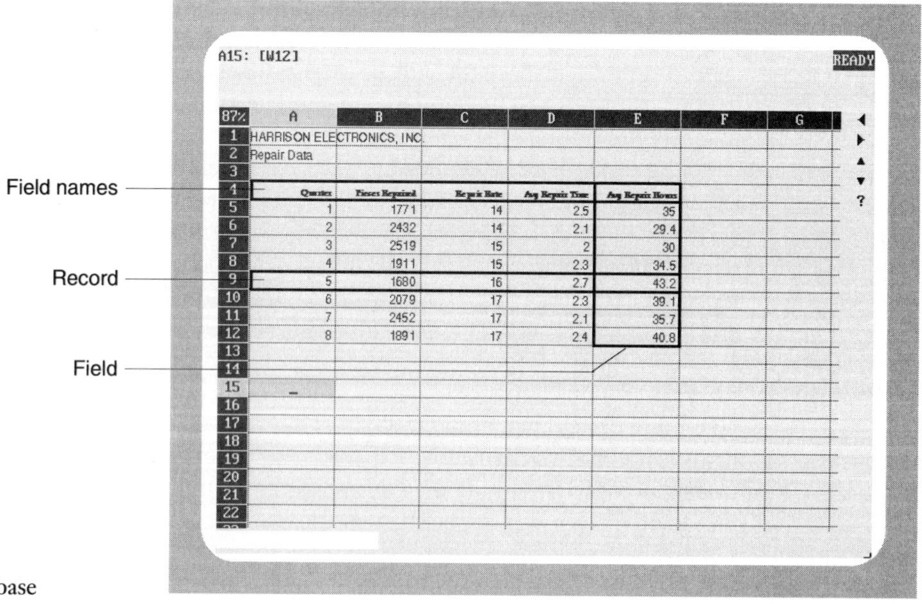

Quarter	Pieces Repaired	Repair Rate	Avg Repair Time	Avg Repair Hours
1	1771	14	2.5	35
2	2432	14	2.1	29.4
3	2519	15	2	30
4	1911	15	2.3	34.5
5	1680	16	2.7	43.2
6	2079	17	2.3	39.1
7	2452	17	2.1	35.7
8	1891	17	2.4	40.8

Figure 6.2
Repair Database

HINT: Do not include field names in the data range.

HINT: Never separate a data record or field when sorting.

You will want to conduct a simple sort on Pieces Repaired as the primary key. First, specify the entire data area as your *data range*, as shown in Figure 6.3. Be careful not to include the field names in your data range; otherwise they will get sorted into the data. The entire data set must be included in your data range, or else you will have some of the data sorted alongside unsorted data. There is one important guideline for sorting data: never separate a data record (a row of data) or field; if you do this, the data will become tainted. Always save a copy of the worksheet *prior to sorting*. Forgetting some of the data in the data range—which happens invariably—can produce disastrous results.

Second, identify the primary key. You need only point to the cell that contains the field name. Highlight the Pieces Repaired field name as the primary key on which the data will be sorted. You asked for a descending sort. Since you do not need a secondary key for this field, you must ignore this subcommand by pressing (ENTER). To start the sort, select **G**o from the menu.

Notice that in Figure 6.3 the database is sorted by Pieces Repaired in descending order. Harrison Electronics repaired more units in the 3rd and 7th quarters, followed by the 2nd and 6th quarters, indicating seasonality. In Chapter 7 you will analyze seasonality in an effort to uncover variable trends.

Sorting with Secondary Keys

HINT: Use a secondary key when there are duplicate data in the primary key field.

Now you need to find the quarters that have an unusually high average repair time and/or repair rate so that you can target those quarters. In Figure 6.4 you will have to sort by Avg Repair Time in descending order so that you can identify the quarters in which the most time is spent repairing each piece. Since this field has duplicate data, you must also specify a secondary key. The Repair Rate field will serve as your secondary key. Interestingly, by examining the Pieces Repaired field, you will find that fewer pieces are repaired when the average repair time is increased. This conclusion is not necessarily intuitive, since you might hire more

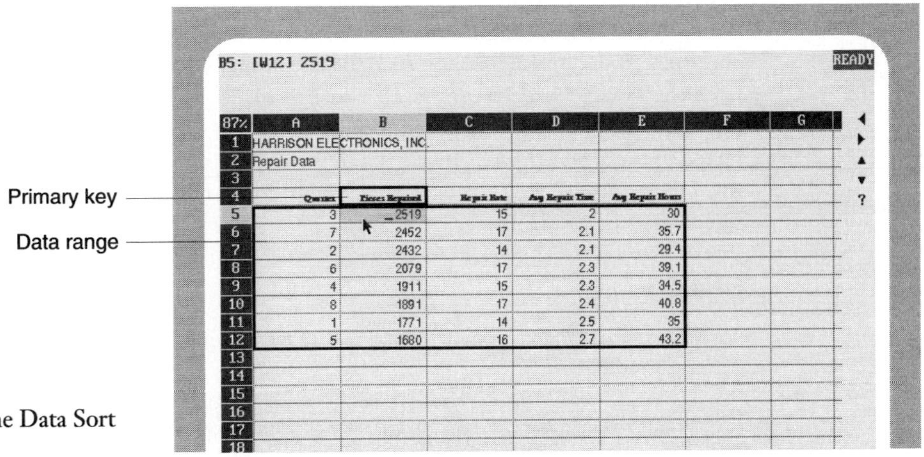

B5: [W12] 2519 READY

	A	B	C	D	E	F	G
1	HARRISON ELECTRONICS, INC.						
2	Repair Data						
3							
4	Quarter	Pieces Repaired	Repair Rate	Avg Repair Time	Avg Repair Hours		
5	3	2519	15	2	30		
6	7	2452	17	2.1	35.7		
7	2	2432	14	2.1	29.4		
8	6	2079	17	2.3	39.1		
9	4	1911	15	2.3	34.5		
10	8	1891	17	2.4	40.8		
11	1	1771	14	2.5	35		
12	5	1680	16	2.7	43.2		

Primary key

Data range

Figure 6.3
Results of the Data Sort Command

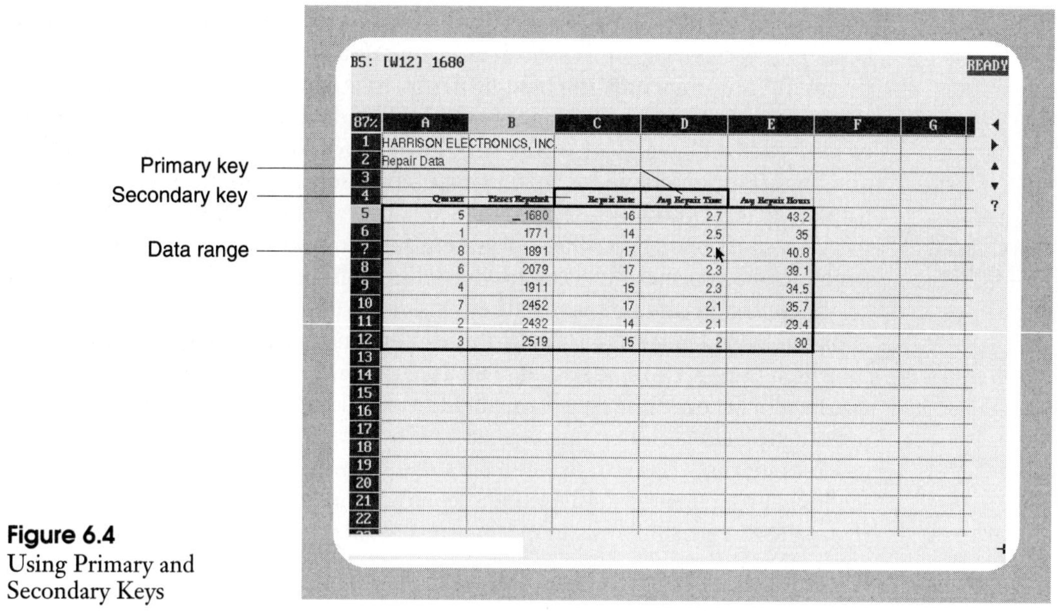

Figure 6.4
Using Primary and Secondary Keys

repairers in Quarters 3 and 7. You may wish to investigate this business issue later when developing your dynamic models.

Querying the Database

As databases get larger, they become more difficult to manage. When conducting analyses or maintaining existing records, you may not want to see the entire database, especially if it is large. It is useful then to extract a more manageable number of records in order to understand the data and make subsequent modifications. With smaller databases, you can sort the database on a number of criteria and then go down the list to search for the records you are looking for. However, with the **/D**ata **Q**uery command, you can **query** the database to find or delete records that meet specified criteria, or to create a new database containing selected records and fields. Once a database query has been established, you can use the Query ((F7)) key to repeat the last query performed without changing the Query menu selections.

Finding

To query a database, you will use the **/D**ata **Q**uery command, which has nine subcommands:

```
Input Criteria Output Find Extract Unique Delete Reset Quit
```

Two measures must be specified: an input range and a criterion range. First you must set the *input range*. Unlike the **/D**ata **S**ort command, the field names must be specified as part of the input range. The data range includes only the data that will be manipulated. You must also specify the *criteria* that will be used to isolate the records you are investigating. This task must be done outside the **/D**ata command. Notice in Figure 6.5 that the criterion range has been set up for the Average Repair Time by copying the field from cell D4 to D14. Directly under the field name, you enter the value of the record(s) you are looking for. In this case, you are looking for all records that match the criteria in which "Average Repair Time" is 2.1 hours.

The results are shown in Figure 6.5 where the cursor highlights the first record that meets the criteria. Quarter 2 is highlighted with a bar, indicating that the Average Repair Time is 2.1 hours. Also, Quarter 7 is highlighted when the ⓓ key is pressed (not shown in the figure). When the cursor stops moving and the system beeps, the program is indicating that no more records qualify.

Extracting

You can choose to extract the records to another area in the worksheet rather than highlight them with the cell pointer. Extracting is a more powerful query technique for printing records of interest. Also, it allows you to save a new database file that does not contain the full data set but contains the records that are important for a specific analysis.

To extract records, follow the same guidelines that were just discussed for finding records, with one exception: you must identify an output range, as shown in Figure 6.6. Notice that the field names have been copied to the output area

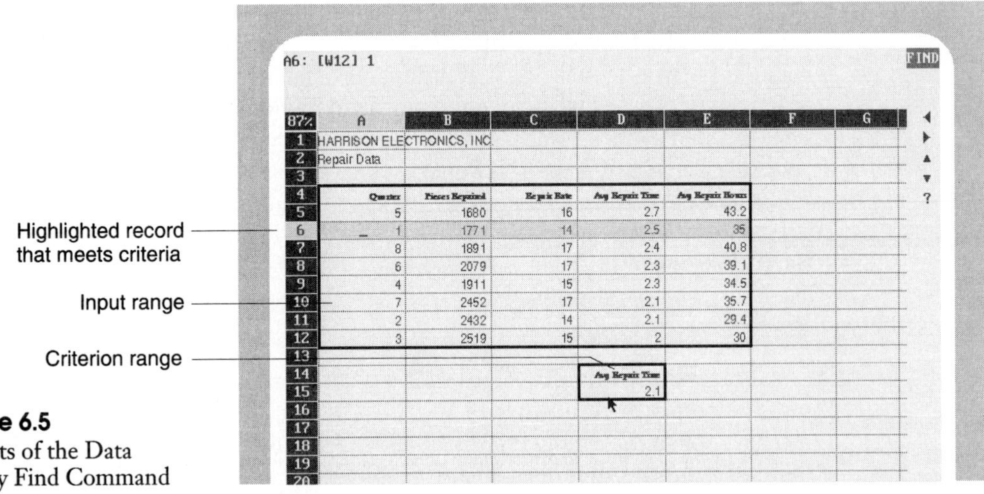

Figure 6.5
Results of the Data Query Find Command

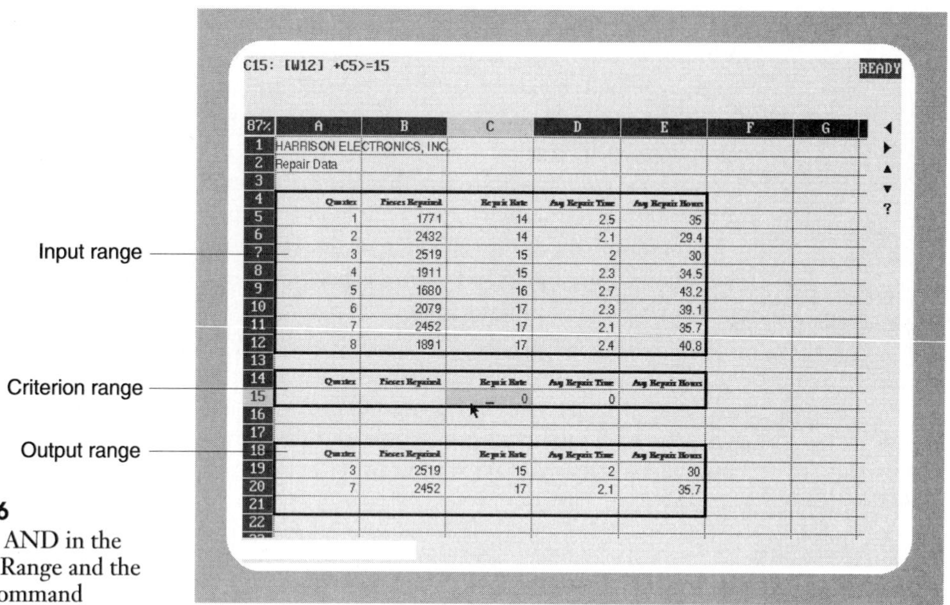

	A	B	C	D	E
1	HARRISON ELECTRONICS, INC.				
2	Repair Data				
5	1	1771	14	2.5	35
6	2	2432	14	2.1	29.4
7	3	2519	15	2	30
8	4	1911	15	2.3	34.5
9	5	1680	16	2.7	43.2
10	6	2079	17	2.3	39.1
11	7	2452	17	2.1	35.7
12	8	1891	17	2.4	40.8
15			0	0	
19	3	2519	15	2	30
20	7	2452	17	2.1	35.7

Figure 6.6
Using the AND in the Criterion Range and the Extract Command

prior to executing the **/D**ata command. The field names must be included in your output area.

HINT: Specify between 40-60% of the total data area for the output range.

How should you effectively manage your workspace, considering good spreadsheet hygiene? Normally, the number of rows made available for data extraction should be in the range of between 40 percent to 60 percent of the total data area. In this case, there are eight data items, so to be safe we set up six rows in the output area. If there is an unlimited number of rows available for the output area, then you do not need to worry about this issue. The program will warn you if there are too many records for the specified output area.

It is possible to utilize the AND and OR logical connectors when formulating queries. In Figure 6.6 the full set of field names has been copied into the criteria area so as to make each of the fields available for query. Be sure to respecify your criterion range to include the new field names, as shown in Figure 6.6. We have decided to create an AND query in which both criteria have to be met. To specify a criterion for an AND query, place both formulas in the same row.The question is, Which records have an Average Repair Time of less than or equal to 2.1 *and* have a Repair Rate of 15 or greater? The formula that would address this question is this:

```
+C5>=15 #AND# D5<=2.1
```

Only two records met these criteria—Quarters 3 and 7, which were extracted into the output area in Rows 19 and 20. The business issue here is whether you can keep down the average repair time by hiring more repairers and yet charge a higher repair rate, and if so, what time of year would be the most appropriate to try out this scheme? Quarter 3 would also have met the criteria if you were searching for an average repair time *less than* 2.1 hours.

The OR connector is illustrated in Figure 6.7. By using more than one row for the criteria area, it is possible to combine both the AND and the OR logical connectors to formulate a query. Suppose you wanted to answer the question by also considering the quarters in which 2,000 or more pieces were repaired. The formula would now read:

```
+B5>2000 #OR# C5>=15 #AND# D5<2.1
```

With this formula structure set in the criterion range, four records are pulled from the database. For clarity, we have asked for an "Average Repair Time" of less than 2.1. Quarter 3 alone met the criterion before the OR portion of the statement. Three records were extracted that met the criteria following the OR portion of the statement. This arrangement with respect to querying the database gives you a great deal of flexibility.

You can write criteria that match label or value entries in a database by using different characters. As in DOS, the asterisk (*) can be used to match labels with the same characters. For example, TO* matches TOM, TOMMY, TOR, and TOP. The tilde (~) matches all labels except the one you specify. ~TOM matches all records (TOMMY, TOR, and TOP) in the range except TOM. The logical operators (< >) can be used to match labels that precede or follow alphabetically the string you specify. For example, >TOM matches the labels that follow TOM alphabetically (TOMMY, TOR, and TOP).

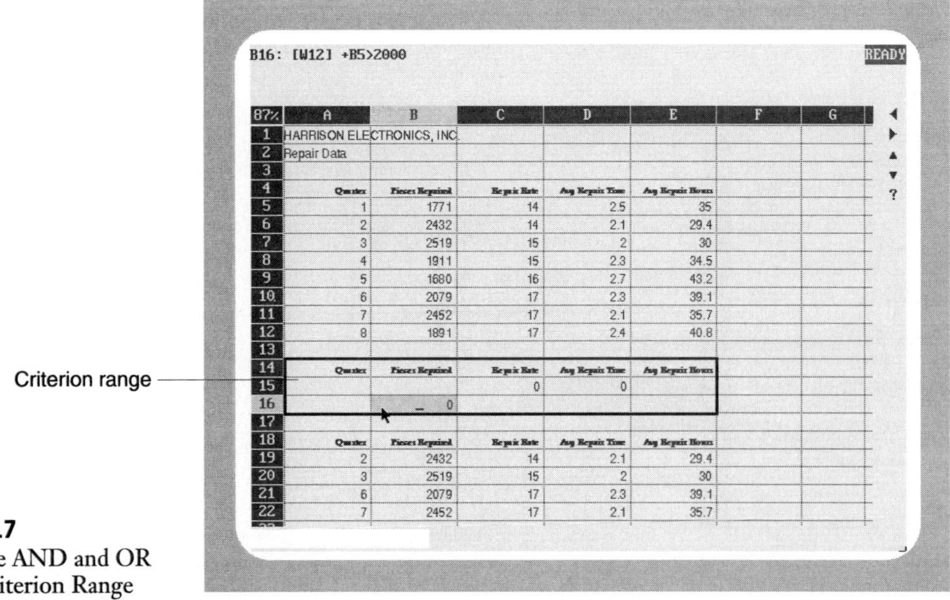
B16: [W12] +B5>2000 READY

	A	B	C	D	E
1	HARRISON ELECTRONICS, INC.				
2	Repair Data				
3					
4	Quarter	Pieces Repaired	Repair Rate	Avg Repair Time	Avg Repair Hours
5	1	1771	14	2.5	35
6	2	2432	14	2.1	29.4
7	3	2519	15	2	30
8	4	1911	15	2.3	34.5
9	5	1680	16	2.7	43.2
10	6	2079	17	2.3	39.1
11	7	2452	17	2.1	35.7
12	8	1891	17	2.4	40.8
13					
14	Quarter	Pieces Repaired	Repair Rate	Avg Repair Time	Avg Repair Hours
15			0	0	
16		0			
17					
18	Quarter	Pieces Repaired	Repair Rate	Avg Repair Time	Avg Repair Hours
19	2	2432	14	2.1	29.4
20	3	2519	15	2	30
21	6	2079	17	2.3	39.1
22	7	2452	17	2.1	35.7

Criterion range

Figure 6.7
Using the AND and OR in the Criterion Range

Creating a Frequency Distribution

HINT: The range to the right of the bin range must be empty.

HINT: Read the results of the frequency distribution as equal to the interval up to the value of the next interval.

Frequency distributions are especially useful in determining the number of records that fall into predefined and regular intervals. The /**D**ata **D**istribution command counts the number of values in the range, called the *bin range*. Although you do not have to specify regular numeric intervals, it is strongly suggested that you do so in order to present results that are more easily interpreted by the decision maker. You must decide on the *bin range* before entering the /**D**ata command. Two ranges must be allocated for the data-distribution function. The first range is the *bin range*. The program places the counts (*output range*) in the column directly to the right of the *bin range*. Figure 6.8 displays the *values range* required with the use of the /**D**ata **D**istribution command.

The *values range* includes only the data within a single field. The *bin range* in Figure 6.9, previously specified in the worksheet, evenly divides the values in the field you are exploring. We read the results of the frequency distribution as equal to the interval up to the value of the next interval. For example, only one record is equal to 2.0 and less than 2.1 hours—Quarter 3. Two records are equal to 2.1 and less than 2.2 hours—Quarters 2 and 7. One record is greater than 2.5—Quarter 5—in which the average repair time is 2.7 hours.

You could set up a different interval scheme for the bin range—say, one that increases by an interval of .25, as illustrated in Figure 6.9. Of course, you do not want to mislead the decision maker into believing that four quarters had an average

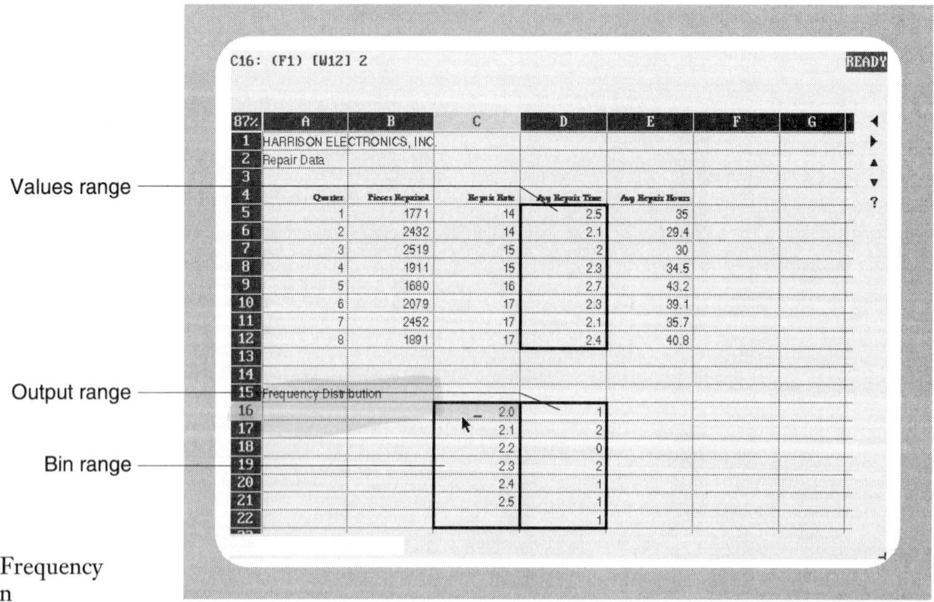

Figure 6.8
Creating a Frequency Distribution

C16: (F2) [W12] 2 READY

87%	A	B	C	D	E	F	G
1	HARRISON ELECTRONICS, INC.						
2	Repair Data						
3							
4	Quarter	Pieces Repaired	Repair Rate	Avg Repair Time	Avg Repair Hours		
5	1	1771	14	2.5	35		
6	2	2432	14	2.1	29.4		
7	3	2519	15	2	30		
8	4	1911	15	2.3	34.5		
9	5	1680	16	2.7	43.2		
10	6	2079	17	2.3	39.1		
11	7	2452	17	2.1	35.7		
12	8	1891	17	2.4	40.8		
13							
14							
15	Frequency Distribution						
16			2.00	1			
17			2.25	2			
18			2.50	4			
19			2.75	1			
20				0			
21							
22							

Figure 6.9
Using a Different Bin Range

repair time of 2.50 hours. Rather, the frequency distribution tells us that four records had average repair times greater than 2.25 and less than or equal to 2.50 hours.

Graphics As a Way of Communicating Information

The frequency distribution can be illustrated with a bar graph. Before you graph the frequency distribution for Average Repair Time, we will highlight the different graph types. Our discussion of data areas in Lotus 1-2-3 would not be complete without considering the presentation of the output. Graphics allow decision makers to view data by using a visual medium. Lotus 1-2-3 can convert numbers residing in records and decision variables to pictures that illustrate relationships and changes over time.

Lotus 1-2-3 can produce seven types of graphs:

1. line
2. XY
3. bar
4. stacked-bar
5. pie
6. HLCO (high-low-close-open)
7. mixed

You invoke the graph menu by using the /**G**raph command:

```
Type X A B C D E F Reset View Save Options Name Group Quit
```

To select one of the seven graph types, use the **T**ype command. Each of the graph types has a specified use as summarized in the following table. There is a "best" time in which to use a pie chart versus a line graph, and so forth.

Graph Type	Best Suited For
Line	Showing data over time
Bar/Stacked-Bar	Showing differences among data items
XY	Showing relationships among data variables
Pie	Comparing parts of one variable
HLCO	Tracking high and low fluctuations in one variable over time
Mixed	Combining the effects of line and bar graphs

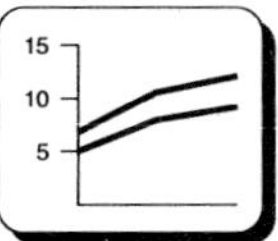

The **line graph** displays as a continuous line the values from a row or column in a worksheet. Each graph has an X (horizontal) and Y (vertical) axis. Six sets of data can be represented on a line chart. The best use of line graphs is to illustrate changes or trends over time. Time is normally used as the X variable. Although other variables can be used as X variables, it is recommended that you use the bar graph for X variables other than time. Examples include sales over time, cash-flow statements, and other predictions.

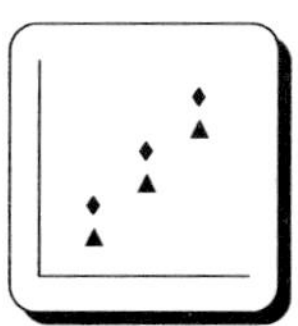

The **XY graph** pairs independent variables, showing their correlation in a line format. It answers the question of how related is variable A to variable B. The X value determines how far left or right a point is on the graph, while the Y value controls the vertical placement of a point. The XY graph should be used primarily to show relationship between two variables, keeping in mind the positive and negative correlations. Examples include the relationship between advertising to sales or the number of sales reps to total new sales for the month.

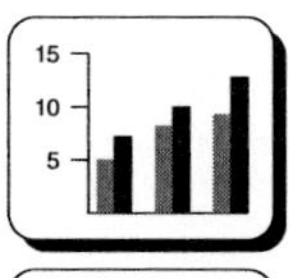

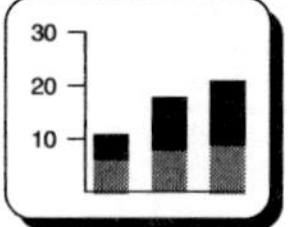

The **bar graph** represents a set of data as vertical bars. Each bar reflects a specific data value stored in the worksheet. You can distinguish each set of data by using different colors and/or shadings. The **stacked-bar graph** places multiple sets of data on top of each other rather than next to each other. Different colors and shadings, coupled with labels, are used to distinguish each variable. The primary visual advantage of bar graphs and stacked-bar graphs is to distinguish between different data items. Time probably will not be in the running for the choice of X variables. Examples include comparing four divisions in a firm and six products.

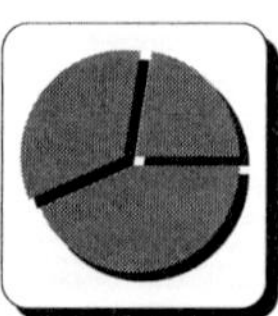

The **pie chart** divides one set of data into pie slices, with each slice representing a cell value. For accent, Lotus 1-2-3 allows the user to explode one or more slices of the pie. Pie charts should be used only to compare parts to a whole with one decision variable. Often, pie charts are used inappropriately. The most common misuse is to take, for example, sales over five years, with each year occupying a slice of the pie. Since years do not logically add up to a whole, using pie charts in this way misleads the reader.

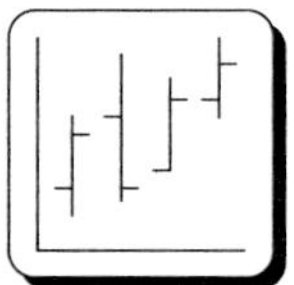

The **HLCO** chart tracks fluctuations in data over a specific period of time. This type of chart is used most frequently to plot the high, low, closing, and opening of stock prices. The X range is used to set the X-axis labels, while the A through F ranges should represent high, low, closing, and opening values respectively. The **mixed graph** integrates the characteristics of line and bar graphs to record trends in different data items, usually over time.

Creating a Basic Graph

You will now develop a bar graph with the frequency distribution for the Average Repair Time data in Figure 6.9. Before you begin creating the graph with the /**G**raph command, you must set up a new area in the worksheet for the X range that accurately reflects the meaning of the frequency intervals. Remember that the intervals are continuous and do not reflect exact values. A mistake developers often make is to use the bin range as the X range in their bar graphs. The bin range is misleading because it indicates that two records had an average repair time of 2.25 hours, for example. This would be a problem because the values did not precisely fall on those interval values. Figure 6.10 shows the graph settings menu.

Viewing a Graph

You can view a graph in two ways. The first is to use the /**G**raph **V**iew command or press the (F10) (graph) key from any mode. The graph with which you have

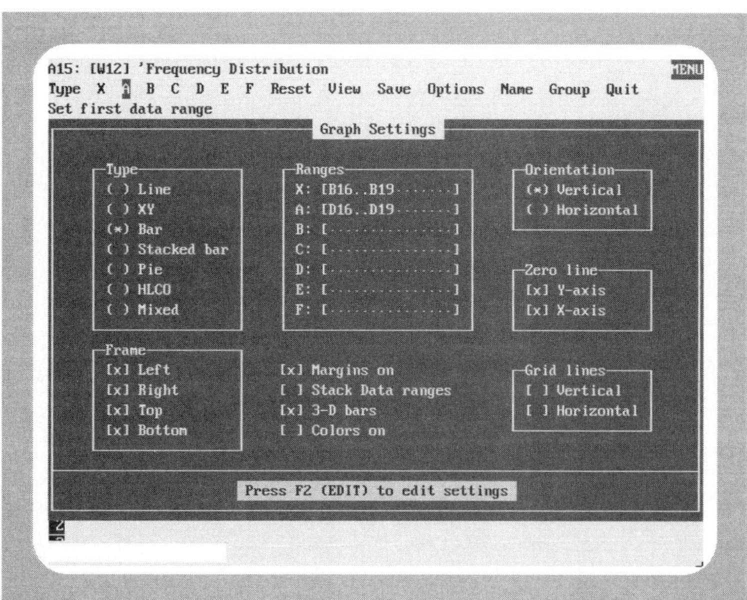

Figure 6.10
Graph Settings Menu

most recently worked will be displayed. The second way to view a graph is to use the WYSIWYG:**G**raph command once the graph has been saved to a .PIC file.

We used the /**G**raph **V**iew command to view the graph that was just created for Harrison Electronics in Figure 6.11. If you want to develop more than one graph, you must *name* the graph. Then you can view any number of graphs that reside within your worksheet. To name a graph, use the /**G**raph **N**ame **C**reate command. You can also get a table of named graphs similar to the table of range names that were shown earlier. To view a previously named graph, use the /**G**raph **N**ame **U**se command and select from the list of graph names.

HINT: You *must* name each graph.

You may also want to view a graph that has been saved as a .PIC file. Naming and saving graphs are fundamentally different activities. When you name a graph, the graph is stored within the worksheet but not to a file. When you save a graph, it is not necessarily stored in the worksheet (unless you have named it), but it is stored in a .PIC file. WYSIWYG can include named graphs for inclusion in your worksheet, so it is not necessary to *save* your graphs to files. You can print your graph right from your worksheet using WYSIWYG. .PIC files are not updated when changes are made to the worksheet.

Including Graphs in a Worksheet

To include a graph, invoke WYSIWYG either by using the mouse or by typing the colon (:). Select the :**G**raph **A**dd command and then choose the name of the graph you are adding. You should select **N**amed and then choose the graph you want to add. You must then specify the entire range in which you want to place

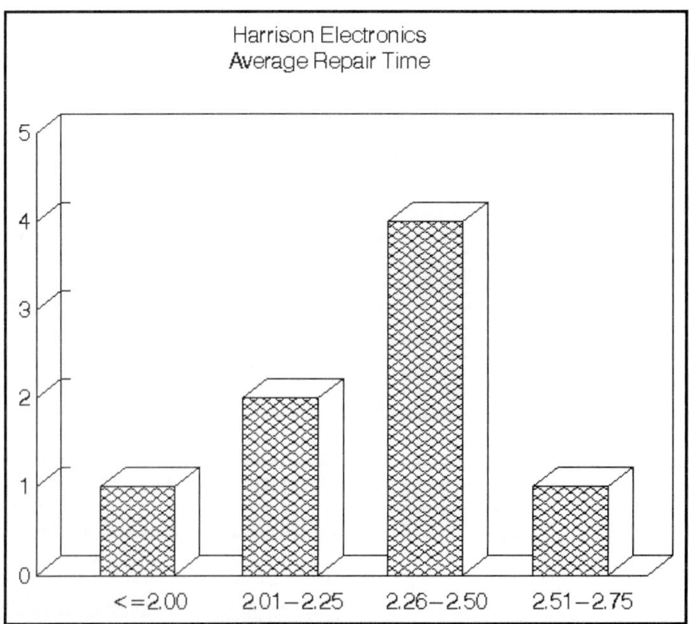

Figure 6.11
Bar Graph for Average Repair Time

the graph. Notice that the graph in Figure 6.12 occupies the range E16..G22. You can see in the control panel that the cell contents displays:

```
{Graph REPAIR}
```

The graph that was named earlier called REPAIR was then added into the worksheet. You can now print the worksheet that contains the graph. Invoking WYSIWYG and the :**P**rint command, you must first set the print range to include the worksheet and the graph that you added. Set A1..G22 as the range to be printed. Then select **G**o to print the worksheet.

With included graphs, you can change worksheet data and immediately observe changes to your graph. Try changing one of the values in the A range, such as the value of 2 in cell D17, to 3. Note that the bar showing the frequency distribution for average repair times between 2.01 and 2.25 reflects the changed data.

Working with Graph Options

It is important to add titles, legends, and data labels to your graph as necessary. The reader needs to know what the axes mean and how to distinguish between the different types of data being graphed.

You can add headings and axis titles to your graph in two ways. Both methods require that you first select the /**G**raph **S**ettings command. Then you can either type the name of the title or type a backslash (\) followed by the cell address or name of the cell that contains the title text.

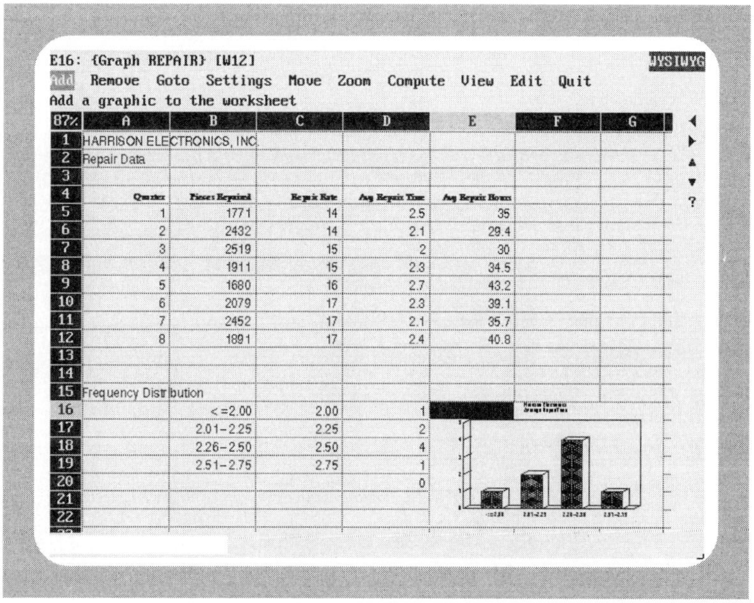

E16: {Graph REPAIR} [W12]
Add Remove Goto Settings Move Zoom Compute View Edit Quit
Add a graphic to the worksheet

87%	A	B	C	D	E	F	G
1	HARRISON ELECTRONICS, INC.						
2	Repair Data						
3							
4	Quarter	Pieces Repaired	Repair Rate	Avg Repair Time	Avg Repair Hours		
5	1	1771	14	2.5	35		
6	2	2432	14	2.1	29.4		
7	3	2519	15	2	30		
8	4	1911	15	2.3	34.5		
9	5	1680	16	2.7	43.2		
10	6	2079	17	2.3	39.1		
11	7	2452	17	2.1	35.7		
12	8	1891	17	2.4	40.8		
13							
14							
15	Frequency Distribution						
16		<=2.00	2.00	1			
17		2.01-2.25	2.25	2			
18		2.26-2.50	2.50	4			
19		2.51-2.75	2.75	1			
20				0			
21							
22							

Figure 6.12
Using WYSIWYG to Add a Graph to the Worksheet

To add legends that describe the data in the A-through-F graph ranges, you can either type the legend name or use the backslash (\) followed by the cell address or cell name. You can set data labels in the same way by editing the data labels from the Settings box. You can also select the placement of the data label in relation to points on a graph.

Creating a Quick Graph

If the data that you want to graph is located in a self-defined range consisting of consecutive columns or rows, you can use the /**G**raph **G**roup command to create the graph. You must specify whether you want 1-2-3 to group the data columnwise or rowwise. If the labels are located in the uppermost row to describe a field, as you would normally set up your database, then you would select *rowwise.* This would place the field names on the X axis. If you want to place the data in the first field on the X axis, such as Quarter in the example, then you would select *columnwise*. Figure 6.13 illustrates a graph organized by row, using Quarters for the X axis.

Hints for Effective Graphing

Graphs are especially powerful in that they communicate information in a different way from tables of data. You have heard it said that a picture is worth a thousand words. It is easy to see that graphs provide an effective way to communicate important business information. Because they are so effective, care must be taken not to

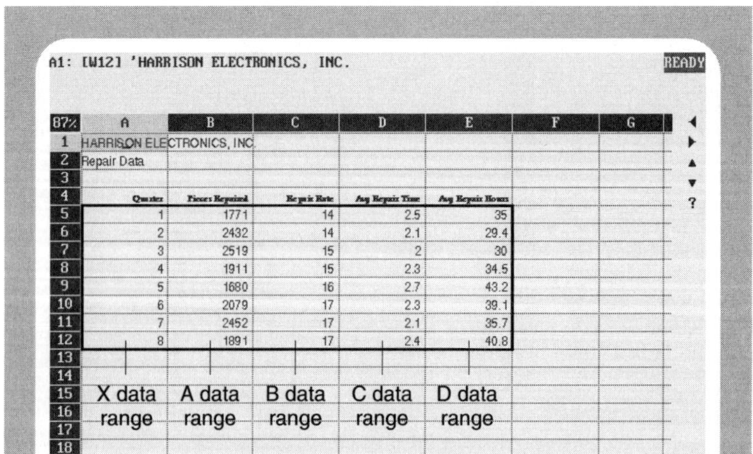

Figure 6.13
Using the Group Command to Create a Graph

mislead the reader with inaccurate graphs. For example, the line graph, useful for showing trends and changes, can be used to misdirect or even deceive readers.

HINT: Avoid graphs that mislead the reader into making false conclusions.

Figure 6.14 seems clear enough. The average repair hours at Harrison Electronics generally increased in the past eight quarters. Increased how much? On the average of about .8 of an hour per quarter. Figure 6.15 displays the average increase, which appears to be quite desirable for most business owners. Now let's chop off the bottom end of the scale, since we are not using it anyway.

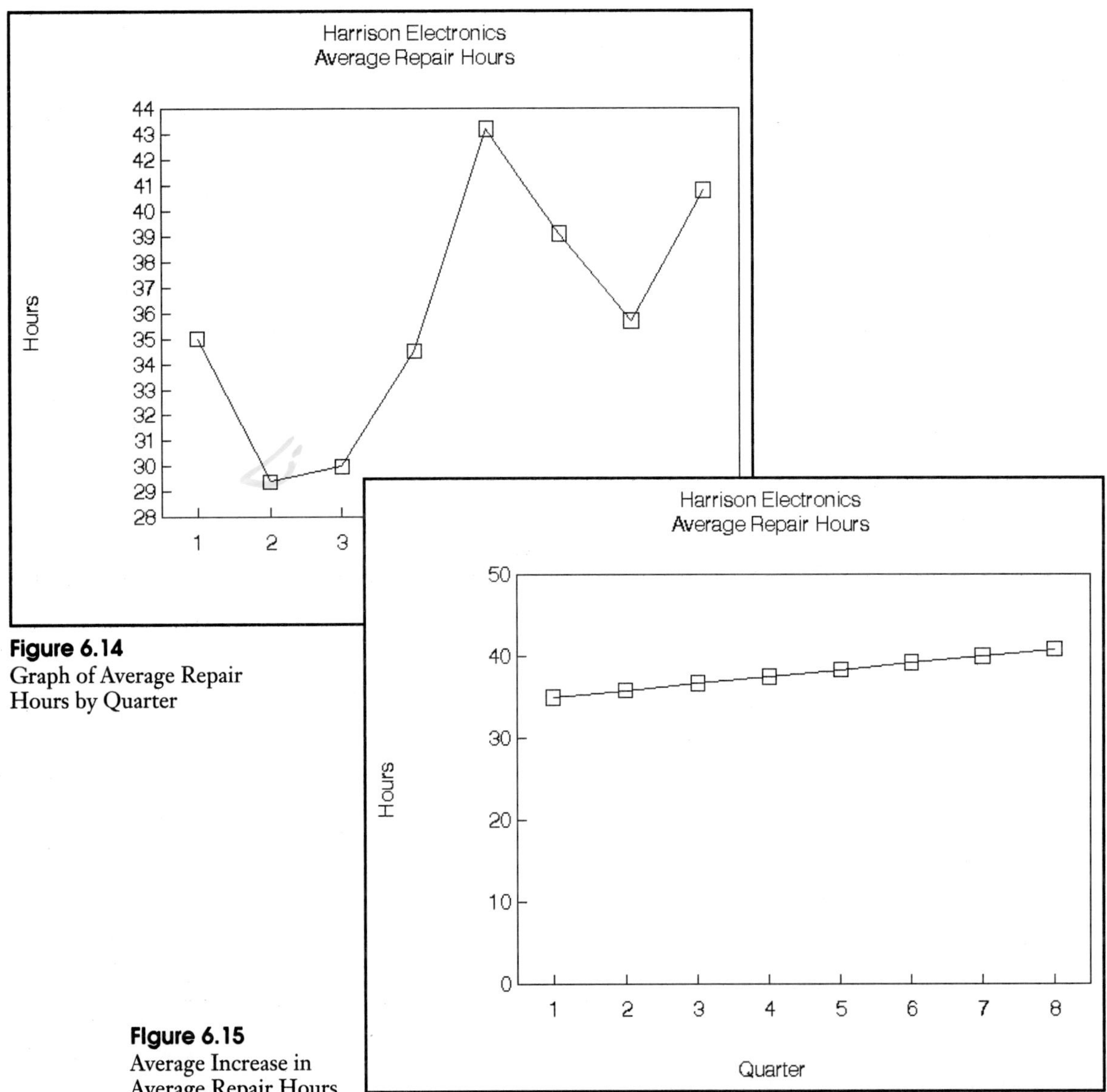

Figure 6.14
Graph of Average Repair Hours by Quarter

Figure 6.15
Average Increase in Average Repair Hours

Figure 6.16 shows the same figures and therefore the same line. However, notice now that the slope of this line is steeper and even more impressive than in Figure 6.15. This new line gives the reader the impression of an increase of about 100% from the eighth quarter over the first quarter. The analyst hasn't falsified the data—only given a different impression.

Considering this example, let's discuss five techniques for developing more effective graphs. First, include an empty cell at both ends of the data range or ranges to be graphed. This moves the data away from the edges of the graph, providing a less cluttered illustration. Second, to prevent the X-range graph labels from running into each other, try using the /Graph **O**ptions **S**cale **S**kip command to skip every other label, or every three labels. Third, use empty cells in the data range(s) to reduce the width of the bars in a bar graph or stacked-bar graph. Smaller bar widths provide a more visual display. Fourth, instead of typing graph titles for the /**G**raph **O**ptions **T**itles command, type a backslash (\) followed by the cell containing the cell address or, better yet, the range names. Lotus 1-2-3 has a limitation of thirty characters for titles; however, using range names overcomes this drawback. Fifth, and most important, always set the Y-axis scales manually when creating graphs to avoid misrepresentation by using the /**G**raph **O**ptions **S**cale command. Lotus 1-2-3 automatically adjusts the Y axis unless you set the lower and upper limits.

You have now developed the data area of your decision support system. Based on this data area, you are now ready to build the model base needed to conduct what-if analyses.

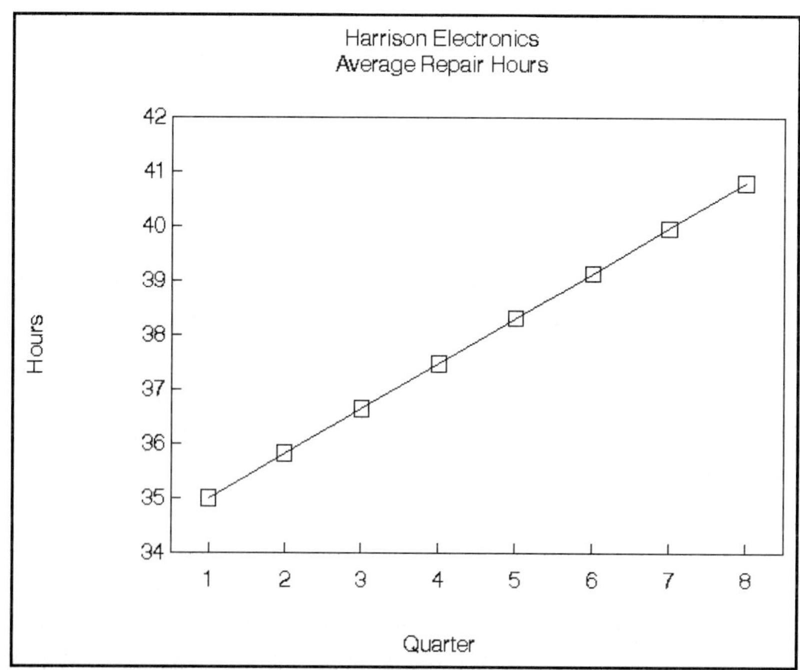

Figure 6.16
Average Increase in Average Repair Hours

Review Questions

1. Describe the characteristics of a database.
2. Why have spreadsheet developers shied away from using /**D**ata commands in Lotus 1-2-3?
3. How are large, centralized databases managed in organizations?
4. What is data pollution?
5. What is the difference between a field, a field name, and a record, and how are these laid out in a Lotus worksheet?
6. How is parsing accomplished? List the steps.
7. Why must you always parse the data and field names separately?
8. What is the difference between primary and secondary keys?
9. When setting the output range for a data extraction, how much of the total data should be specified?
10. How can the #OR# or #AND# connector be used to enhance the criteria statement?
11. Describe the layout of the criterion range that has multiple ANDs and ORs.
12. Why must the range to the right of the bin range be empty?
13. How should you read the results of the frequency distribution?
14. Each type of graph has a different purpose. Describe each graph type and the type of activity that each is best suited for.
15. How do you name a graph?
16. List the steps necessary to include a graph in the worksheet.
17. How can you use a graph to mislead the reader into making false conclusions?

Skill-Building Activities: Creating Databases and Graphs

Activity 1: Retrieving a Worksheet

Use the /File **R**etrieve command to bring up the Harrison worksheet from Chapter 3 called HARRIS2. At this point, the worksheet should look similar to the one you left at the end of Chapter 3 as shown in Figure 6.17.

C15: READY

87%	A	B	C	D	E	F	G	H
1	HARRISON ELECTRONICS, INC.					Sales Summary Report		
2	1413 Fillmore Street					(rounded thousands)		
3	Colorado Springs, CO	80906						
4								
5								
6	Category	Code		1 Qtr	2 Qtr	3 Qtr	4 Qtr	Total
7								
8	Repair Sales	1000		143	179	202	164	688
9								
10	Appliance Sales	2000		28	55	19	31	133
11								
12	Small Products	3000		5	21	8	79	113
13								
14				---	---	---	---	---
15	TOTAL SALES			176	255	229	274	934
16								
17								
18								

Figure 6.17
The Harrison Electronics Worksheet

NOTE: To help you with this exercise, ***boldface*** *letters indicate a message from the system or the worksheet while the commands in the list tell you to make a specific entry.*

Activity 2: Cleaning up the Worksheet

You will need to do a bit of work to clean up your worksheet before manipulating your database. You will also need to delete unnecessary rows and to position your field names. First, you will delete row 7 so that your data lie directly under the field names.

Position the cell pointer anywhere in row 7.

Select the /**W**orksheet **D**elete **R**ow command, press (ENTER).

Position the cell pointer anywhere in row 8, press (ENTER).

Select the /**W**orksheet **D**elete **R**ow command.

Position the cell pointer anywhere in row 9, press (ENTER).

Select the /**W**orksheet **D**elete **R**ow command.

You now have a small database in which to sort, conduct queries, and generate a frequency distribution.

Activity 3: Sorting the Database

You are ready to sort your database. The major contribution to total sales is the Repair Sales field. There is no further work to do to the data area, so you can invoke the /**D**ata command now.

Select the **/D**ata **S**ort command.

Select the **D**ata-Range subcommand.

Move the cell pointer to A7, press the period key (.), and then move the cell pointer to H9 and press (ENTER) to confirm your data range.

Select the **P**rimary Key subcommand.

Move the cell pointer to cell H6 and press (ENTER) to confirm your primary key.

Enter `A` to sort in ascending order and press (ENTER).

Select **G**o from the menu to sort your data range.

Your worksheet should be sorted in ascending order on the Total field (see Figure 6.18). You are now ready to create a frequency distribution to count the number of responses on a field.

Activity 4: Creating a Frequency Distribution

Let's say you would like a count of the number of records that fall into a set of intervals, which you will define, for Total Sales. You will use the **/D**ata **F**ill command to create the intervals:

Move the cursor to cell G14.

Invoke the frequency distribution by selecting the **/D**ata **F**ill command.

Anchor the cell pointer by typing a period (.).

Move the cursor down to cell G17 and press the (ENTER) key.

Enter `100` for the Start prompt and press the (ENTER) key.

Enter `200` for the Step prompt and press the (ENTER) key.

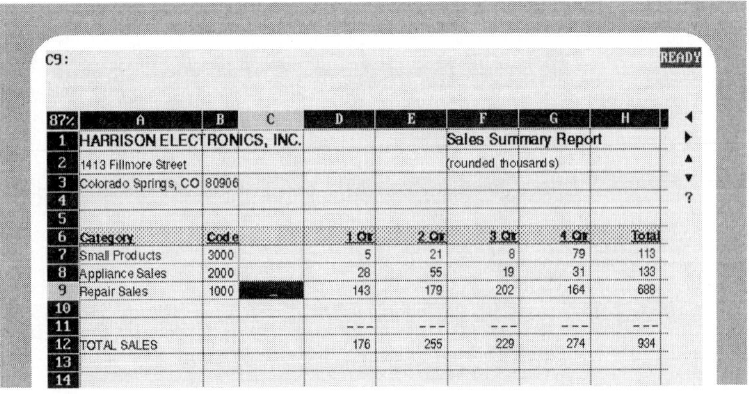

Figure 6.18
Sorting the Worksheet on the Total Field

Ignore the Stop prompt and press the (ENTER) key to confirm.

Now you are ready to create the frequency distribution:

Select the /**D**ata **D**istribution command.

For the values range, move the cursor to cell H7.

Anchor the range by typing a period (.).

Move the cursor down to cell H9 and press the (ENTER) key.

For the bin range, move the cursor to G14.

Anchor the range by typing a period (.).

Move the cursor down to G17 and press the (ENTER) key.

The frequency distribution values should now appear in column H alongside the bin range, as shown in Figure 6.19. You will have an opportunity to graph the frequency distribution later.

Activity 5: Querying the Database with the Find Command

Before you can query your worksheet, you need to set up a criterion area. To do this, copy the field names below the database:

Position the cell pointer on cell A6.

Select the command /**C**opy.

Anchor the cell pointer and then move the cell pointer to cell H6 for the FROM range and press (ENTER).

G14: [W10] 100 READY

87%	A	B	C	D	E	F	G	H
1	HARRISON ELECTRONICS, INC.					Sales Summary Report		
2	1413 Fillmore Street					(rounded thousands)		
3	Colorado Springs, CO	80906						
4								
5								
6	Category	Code		1 Qtr	2 Qtr	3 Qtr	4 Qtr	Total
7	Small Products	3000		5	21	8	79	113
8	Appliance Sales	2000		28	55	19	31	133
9	Repair Sales	1000		143	179	202	164	688
10								
11				---	---	---	---	---
12	TOTAL SALES			176	255	229	274	934
13								
14							100	0
15							300	2
16							500	0
17							700	1
18								0

Figure 6.19
Frequency Distribution for Total Sales

Move the cell pointer to cell A20 for the TO range and press (ENTER) to confirm.

Position the cell pointer anywhere in row 4.

Select the /**W**orksheet **D**elete **R**ow command.

Next, identify the sales categories (highlight the records) in which Total Sales are greater than $500,000.

Move the cell pointer to cell H20.

Enter the formula `+H6>500`. A zero (0) should appear in the cell.

Format the formula by using the /**R**ange **F**ormat **T**ext command to show the formula.

Now use the /**D**ata **F**ind command to highlight the records that meet the criterion:

Select the /**D**ata **Q**uery command.

For the **I**nput-Range, highlight the area A5.H8, and press the (ENTER) key.

For the **C**riterion Range, highlight the area A19.H21 and press the (ENTER) key.

Select **F**ind from the menu.

One record, Repair Sales, should be highlighted, as shown in Figure 6.20. Finally, you will use the same criterion to extract that same record from the database.

A8: [W17] 'Repair Sales FIND

87%	A	B	C	D	E	F	G	H
1	HARRISON ELECTRONICS, INC.					Sales Summary Report		
2	1413 Fillmore Street					(rounded thousands)		
3	Colorado Springs, CO	80906						
4								
5	Category	Code		1 Qtr	2 Qtr	3 Qtr	4 Qtr	Total
6	Small Products	3000		5	21	8	79	113
7	Appliance Sales	2000		28	55	19	31	133
8	Repair Sales	1000		143	179	202	164	688
9								
10				---	---	---	---	---
11	TOTAL SALES			176	255	229	274	934
12								
13							100	0
14							300	2
15							500	0
16							700	1
17								0
18								
19	Category	Code		1 Qtr	2 Qtr	3 Qtr	4 Qtr	Total
20							+H6>500	
21								
22								

Figure 6.20
Using the Find Subcommand to Locate Matching Records

Activity 6: Querying the Database with the Extract Command

Before you set up your query and invoke the /**D**ata **Q**uery command, you need to quit the Data menus in order to copy your field names into an output area:

Select **Q**uit to exit from the Data menus.

Position the cell pointer anywhere on row 9.

To delete row 9, select the /**W**orksheet **D**elete **R**ow command.

Position the cell pointer on cell A5.

Select /**C**opy to copy the labels to the new output area.

Move the cell pointer to cell H5 to complete the FROM range and press (ENTER).

Move the cell pointer to cell A22 and press (ENTER).

To invoke the /**D**ata **Q**uery command, select /**D**ata **Q**uery **O**utput.

Move the cell pointer to cell A22.

Anchor the output range by typing a period (`.`).

Move the cell pointer to cell H25 and press (ENTER) to confirm.

Now you are ready to begin your query for extracting the records that meet the criterion for Total Sales greater than $500,000.

Select **E**xtract from the /**D**ata submenu.

You should see one record extracted (the same one that you found).

Select **Q**uit from the menu to abandon the menu.

You have now extracted a single record that meets the simple criterion. Now place a multiple query into the criterion range. Remember that an AND condition belongs on the same row, while you use a different row for an OR condition. What if you asked the business question, Which product sales dropped below $10,000 for any quarter? In this case, you have to check each of the quarters on a separate line indicating the OR condition.

Move the cell pointer to cell H19.

Select the command /**R**ange **E**rase and press the (ENTER) key.

While on row 19, select /**W**orksheet **I**nsert **R**ow command and insert 3 rows. The output area of field names should now reside in row 25.

Go to cell D19, enter the formula `+D6<=10`, and press (ENTER).

Go to cell E20, enter the formula `+E6<=10`, and press (ENTER).

Go to cell F21, enter the formula `+F6<=10`, and press (ENTER).

Go to cell G22, enter the formula `+G6<=10`, and press (ENTER).

Format the criterion range, D19..G22, as text by using the /**R**ange **F**ormat **T**ext command.

Invoke the command /**D**ata **Q**uery **E**xtract.

Select the **Q**uit option to exit the /**D**ata menu.

Notice in Figure 6.21 that each formula resides in a separate row. Only one record met the criterion—Small Products, in which less than $10,000 in sales was found in Quarters 1 and 3.

Activity 7: Graphing a Frequency Distribution

You will now graph the frequency distribution for the Total Sales count. Since you do not want to mislead the decision makers at Harrison Electronics, you need to create X-axis labels that depict the intervals you have developed.

Position the cell pointer in cell F12 and type the label `'<=100`.

Move to cell F13 and type the label `'100-300`.

Move to cell F14 and type the label `'300-500`.

Move to cell F15 and type the label `'500-700`.

G22: (T) [W10] +G6<=10 READY

87%	A	B	C	D	E	F	G	H
5	Category	Code		1 Qtr	2 Qtr	3 Qtr	4 Qtr	Total
6	Small Products	3000		5	21	8	79	113
7	Appliance Sales	2000		28	55	19	31	133
8	Repair Sales	1000		143	179	202	164	688
9				---	---	---	---	---
10	TOTAL SALES			176	255	229	274	934
11								
12							100	0
13							300	2
14							500	0
15							700	1
16								0
17								
18	Category	Code		1 Qtr	2 Qtr	3 Qtr	4 Qtr	Total
19				+D6<=10				
20					+E6<=10			
21						+F6<=10		
22							+G6<=10	
23								
24								
25	Category	Code		1 Qtr	2 Qtr	3 Qtr	4 Qtr	Total
26	Small Products	3000		5	21	8	79	113

Figure 6.21
Using the Extract Subcommand to Locate Matching Records

Next, you will select a graph type and enter your graph ranges. Use the bar graph for your Total Sales frequency distribution.

Invoke the /**G**raph menu.

Select the **T**ype command and then **B**ar.

Select X to set the X range, and move the cell pointer to cell F12.

Anchor the cell pointer with the period (.), and then move to cell F15 and press the ENTER key.

Select A to set the A range, and move the cell pointer to cell H12.

Anchor the cell pointer with the period (.), and then move to cell H15 and press the ENTER key.

To view the graph, select the **V**iew option.

Figure 6.22 illustrates the X range. Obviously, you have quite a bit more work to do on the graph to enhance it and to label the axes.

Activity 8: "Spicing Up" the Graph

It is time to add some important features to your graph, such as titles, legends, and data labels. Without a title for Figure 6.22, no one knows what the figure illustrates. You must first adjust the bar graph features to include a 3-D effect. The bar graph that seems to show depth is more pleasing to look at.

Select the **T**ype and **F**eature subcommands.

To make the bar graph 3-dimensional, select **3**-D Effect.

F16: [W10] READY

87%	A	B	C	D	E	F	G	H
5	Category	Code		1 Qtr	2 Qtr	3 Qtr	4 Qtr	Total
6	Small Products	3000		5	21	8	79	113
7	Appliance Sales	2000		28	55	19	31	133
8	Repair Sales	1000		143	179	202	164	688
9				---	---	---	---	---
10	TOTAL SALES			176	255	229	274	934
11								
12						<=100	100	0
13						100 – 300	300	2
14						300 – 500	500	0
15						500 – 700	700	1
16								0
17								
18	Category	Code		1 Qtr	2 Qtr	3 Qtr	4 Qtr	Total
19				+D6<=10				
20					+E6<=10			
21						+F6<=10		
22							+G6<=10	
23								
24								
25	Category	Code		1 Qtr	2 Qtr	3 Qtr	4 Qtr	Total
26	Small Products	3000		5	21	8	79	113

Figure 6.22
Setting Up the X-Range Labels for a Graph

Select **O**ptions **T**itles **F**irst from the menu, and enter `Harrison Electronics.`

Choose the **T**itles **S**econd from the menu, and enter `Total Sales.`

Select **G**rid **H**orizontal to turn on a grid.

To view the graph, select **V**iew.

You will now enhance your graph by using WYSIWYG.

Before you add your new graph to your worksheet, you need to name it. Call it TOTAL SALES. Then add the graph to your worksheet and print it by using WYSIWYG:

Select **N**ame **C**reate from the menu.

Type `Total Sales` and press (ENTER).

Quit the /**G**raph menus.

Move the cell pointer to cell A30.

Invoke WYSIWYG with the colon (:).

Select **G**raph **A**dd **N**amed from the menu, and then select Total Sales.

To enter the graphic display range, anchor the cell pointer with the period (.).

Move the cell pointer to cell H43 and press the (ENTER) key.

Your worksheet should look similar to the one in Figure 6.23 with the new graph added in the specified range.

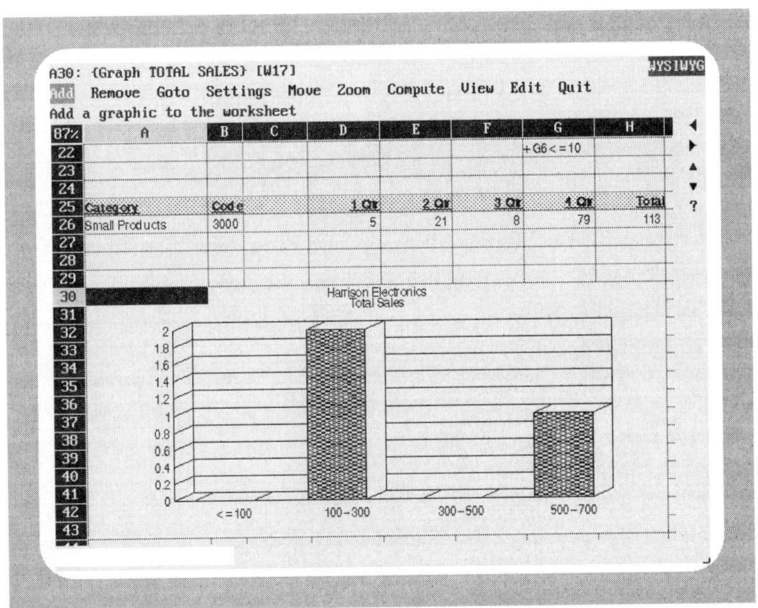

Figure 6.23
Displaying the Graph with WYSIWYG

Congratulations! You have set up a data area, sorted and queried it, extracted matching records, created a frequency distribution, and created a graph. Before you quit, save your worksheet as HARRIS6.WK1.

Hands-On Exercises

1. Create a worksheet that contains the following data area for Mopar Commercial AutoSupplier, Inc.:

Auto Year	Engines Installed	Price per Job	Total Income
1975–1976	25	2,000	50,000
1977–1979	43	2,200	99,000
1980–1984	22	2,350	51,700
1985–1989	18	2,500	45,000
1990–1992	4	2,625	10,500

2. Sort the database by using Total Income as the primary key in descending order. Print a copy of your new worksheet.
3. Query the database to find all records in which Total Income equals or exceeds $50,000.
4. Set up an output area for 5 records. Develop a criteria statement that extracts all records in which engines installed exceeded 20 per auto year.
5. Extract the records that meet one of the following conditions:
   a. Engines installed are greater than 20, or
   b. Price per job exceeds $2,200 *and* total income exceeds $50,000, or
   c. Total income is greater than or equal to $51,000.
6. Create and interpret a frequency distribution for total income by using the following intervals:

   10,000

   30,000

   50,000

   70,000

   90,000

   110,000

7. Generate a basic bar graph for the frequency distribution. Include and print the graph in the worksheet.
8. Add the following options to the bar graph:

   Titles

   Y and X titles

   Legends

   Grid lines

Problem-Solving Projects

1. Create the following database for Freemont Office Printer Rentals in Lotus 1-2-3. Format the Price and Cost as currency with 2 decimal places, Ordered and Sold as comma with 0 decimal places, and the Last Date as DD-MMM-YY. Note that there is no row between the field names and the records. Your worksheet should look like the one illustrated below. Use WYSIWYG to print a copy of your file.

Code	Description	Price	Cost	Ordered	Sold	Last Date	Person
DX104	IMwriter ribbon	$5.50	$3.75	3,625	3,522	12/21/91	Lonnie
DX500	IMwriter, 4 color	$19.00	$16.50	500	496	11/24/91	Frank
VR502	K.Itoh 8510 ribbon	$9.25	$4.50	550	400	12/04/91	Lonnie
ML799	Oki 193 ribbon	$8.49	$7.25	300	250	11/16/91	Susan
DX524	Maxon EX800 ribbon	$12.75	$11.00	1,350	1,250	12/05/91	Susan
DX045	Maxon FX80 ribbon	$4.40	$4.00	200	155	12/01/91	Frank
DX250	Disento II multistrike	$5.09	$4.25	600	450	11/28/91	Debra
DX460	Galaxy NL10 ribbon	$15.55	$12.75	1,200	1,455	11/30/91	Susan
DX205	Mann Tally 1000 ribbon	$6.95	$6.75	2,350	950	12/14/91	Sam
DX750	Spirit 7 multistrike	$14.00	$12.00	900	775	11/22/91	Sam
DX300	NIC P-565 ribbon	$9.25	$6.00	1,755	224	11/16/91	Lonnie
DX119	SAM 1300 multistrike	$12.50	$12.25	4,000	3,689	12/05/91	Susan
ML347	Oki 192 ribbon	$7.99	$6.95	250	245	11/30/91	Frank
VR660	HP Deskjet ink well	$21.00	$17.25	2,400	2,250	11/16/91	Frank

Code	Description	Price	Cost	Ordered	Sold	Last Date	Person
AM430	IBM Proprinter ribbon	$11.50	$9.50	600	600	11/23/91	Lonnie
PE106	HP Laserjet III toner	$17.50	$16.25	4,565	4,234	12/13/91	Susan
DX589	NCR multistrike	$15.95	$11.50	1,600	487	12/09/91	Debra
DX555	NEC D-774, 4 color	$23.50	$17.95	600	455	12/22/91	Sam

All figures in this database table reflect the quantities ordered by the store and purchased by the customer in the last two months of 1991. The last date of the purchase is indicated as well as the salesperson responsible for the Code Account.

Check your data after you have saved it, to be sure you have entered all your data correctly. Incorrect data will yield unexpected results when you query your database.

2. Sort the database with item Code as the primary key in ascending order. Be sure to include all your data in the data range, but not the field names.
3. Add a new field called Profit Ratio in column 1 of the worksheet. Create a modifiable formula, using mixed cell addresses, that divides the Price by the Cost and then subtracts 1 from that difference, as shown:

```
(Price / Cost) - 1
```

4. Format the new field as Percent with 1 decimal place.
5. Print a copy of the enhanced database by using WYSIWYG and by turning on the automatic Compression feature so that the entire worksheet fits onto a single page.
6. Query the database by using the /**D**ata **Q**uery **E**xtract command to answer the following business questions. Show a copy of each query worksheet, and briefly answer each question. You will need to set up (1) the input range, which now includes the field names, (2) a criterion range where you will copy all the field names to an area a few rows below the worksheet, and (3) an output range that will consist of 12 rows. You must copy all the field names again to this new area and include them in your output range.
   a. Which ribbons showed a profit ratio greater than or equal to 17%?
   b. Which salespersons were responsible for accounts that had a profit ratio greater than 20% and that had sales greater than 1,000?
   c. Which ribbons had profit ratios greater than 17% and sold at a price greater than or equal to $10.00, or which ribbons had profit ratios greater than 17% and had orders greater than 900 over the two months?
7. Create a frequency distribution for profit ratio by using the following intervals, and print a hard copy of the entire worksheet including the frequency distribution:

Bin Range	Intervals
10%	< 10%
15%	10%–14.9%
20%	15%–19.9%
25%	20%–24.9%
30%	25%–29.9%
	> 29.9%

8. Graph the frequency distribution you just created. To do this, you must set up a separate X range that depicts the intervals listed in item 7.
9. Save the worksheet as FREEMONT.

Quality Assurance Checklist

As we conclude our discussion of data management techniques, be sure you have considered the following factors that will contribute to the quality of your worksheet:

- ✓ Use the data parse technique when importing data to your worksheet. Parsing is the activity that separates data labels into contiguous columns of values.
- ✓ Remember that a database in Lotus 1-2-3 cannot contain a blank row between the field names and records.
- ✓ When parsing field names in the database, edit the format line to be sure that appropriate blank spaces are removed.
- ✓ Always parse the data and field names separately.
- ✓ When sorting your data, do not include field names in the data range.
- ✓ Never separate a data record or field when sorting.
- ✓ Whenever you think you have duplicates in your primary key, use a secondary key to assure unique records.
- ✓ When entering criteria for extracting or finding matching records, place AND conditions on the same row and OR conditions on separate rows.
- ✓ Specify between 40 to 60 percent of the total data area for the output range.
- ✓ Be sure that the range to the right of the bin range in a frequency distribution is empty.

- ✓ Always read the results of the frequency distribution as equal to the interval up to the value of the next interval.
- ✓ It is more effective to both name and save your graph and then use WYSIWYG to add the graph to the worksheet and print it from there (rather than use the PrintGraph program).
- ✓ Always use the graph options to set titles, legends, and data labels to make your graph more readable.
- ✓ Avoid creating graphs that mislead the reader into making false conclusions; use the scale options to reformat the Y scale so that it more appropriately reflects the scenario you are graphing.
- ✓ To prevent X-range labels from running into each other, use the /Graph Option Scale Skip command to skip every other label.

CHAPTER

7 Building Dynamic Models

When asked what single event was most helpful in developing the theory of relativity, Albert Einstein is reported to have answered, "Figuring out how to think about the problem."

Objectives

- Understand models and their relevance as a tool to solving business problems.
- Understand the types of activities used in dynamic modeling.
- Use the two-stage approach to uncover relationships between and within worksheet columns.
- Conduct what-if analysis to investigate different scenarios.
- Perform goal-seeking and sensitivity analysis.

The Dynamic Model

Often, translating the problem we are solving into a model in which to conduct analysis is a difficult if not arduous task. We may start by immediately firing up the spreadsheet program and entering values and formulas into cells. This reaction to dealing with solutions to problems parallels that of novice programmers who, instead of mapping out the problem structure, immediately create a block of low-level code. Decision makers do not formally and explicitly march through the steps inherent for building good models. Figure 7.1 illustrates the components of a decision support system (DSS). We will concentrate on developing the model base in this chapter.

A **model** is a simplified representation of reality. There is a variety of models developed to represent reality, such as models that physically resemble a system or analog models that behave like the phenomenon you are studying. However complex they may be, business-oriented problems lend themselves most to representations by **mathematical models**, those models that are executed numerically with the aid of formulas. Lotus 1-2-3 is a good modeling tool, as it naturally operates with formulas.

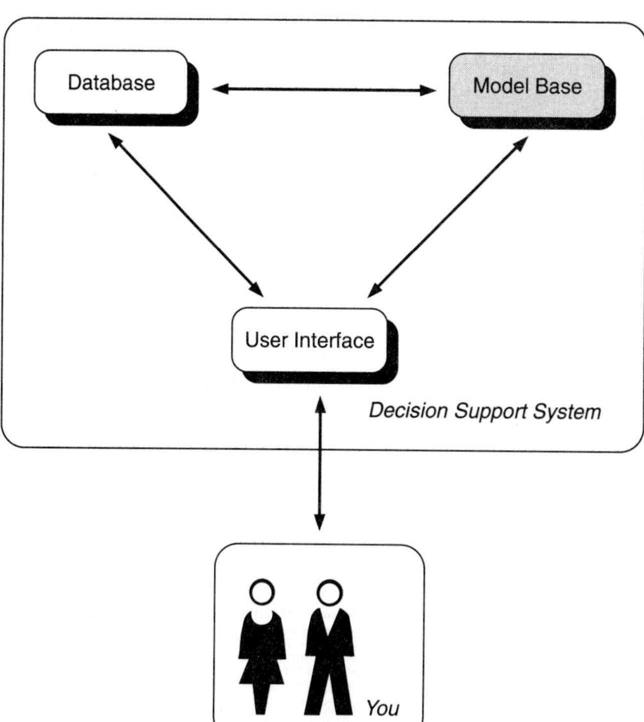

Figure 7.1
The Components of a Decision Support System

A **dynamic model** is a mathematical model that can adapt to a change in scenarios as initiated by the Lotus 1-2-3 user, yielding new information critical to the analysis at hand. The dynamic model must be interactive. It must allow for interchanges and queries by the decision maker. The Lotus 1-2-3 user must feel in control of a variety of scenarios that can be used to gather evidence in favor of a specific decision. The dynamic model, therefore, will allow for flexibility as defined by the model user.

The Two-Stage Analysis Approach

Up to this point, you have just begun to build your decision support system. You have entered the data in a data area to be used in support of your decisions. You may have multiple data areas which support a single model or many different models. Before you develop a model area from which you will conduct your analyses, you must first conduct an analysis on your data area to uncover variable relationships. You will build your dynamic model based upon the relationships you discover. Then you will perform a variety of analyses on the newly created model in order to generate different scenarios. This is called a **two-stage analysis approach**. In the second stage, you will conduct the what-if, goal-seeking, and sensitivity analyses to gain a better understanding of the impacts of different variables on the decision environment. The two distinct stages of analysis in developing dynamic models is shown in Figure 7.2.

Making Sense of the Data

Managers have revealed that a major problem that creates havoc in their professional lives is their inability to make sense of large volumes of data they receive regularly. Making sense of the data is what modeling is all about. It underlies the reasons we produce models to simulate real-world situations. If we are not careful, we will join other managers who are unable to understand how to evaluate model output or able to derive implications from the context of a problem situation.

Building a Common Platform for Analysis

The alternative to developing a dynamic model that can be tweaked when conducting subsequent analyses and creating a common platform from which to compare analysis results is to conduct analysis by trial and error or to develop a series of noninteractive models. Trial-and-error analysis costs time and increases the potential for errors. As the corporate environment continues to change, and change rapidly, existing models will need to be updated and new models will need to be developed on a constant basis. Creating models that do not allow us to change

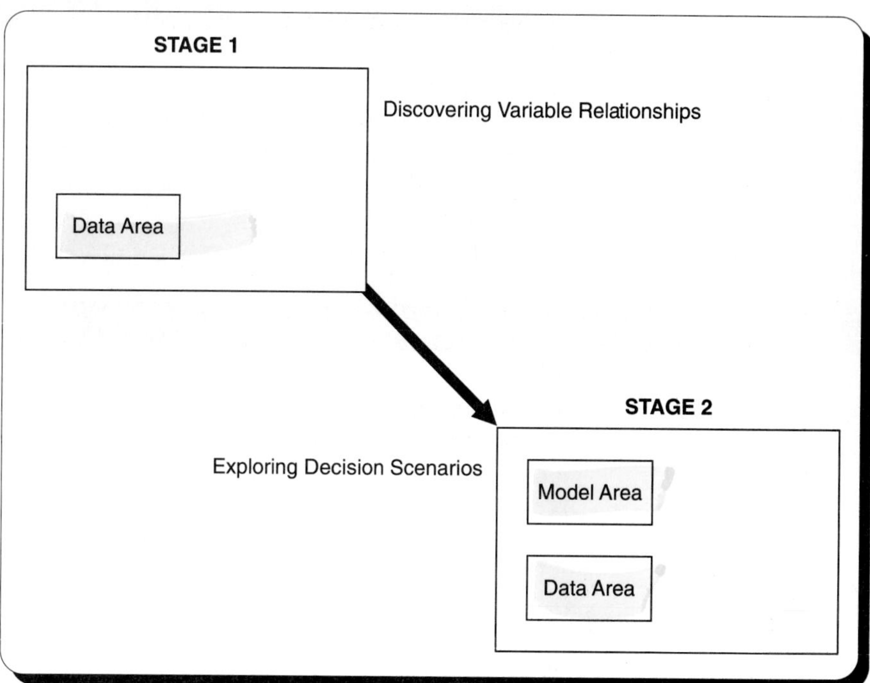

Figure 7.2
The Two-Stage Analysis Approach to Developing Dynamic Models

key decision variables inevitably results in the rekeying and reconceptualization of model components. This kind of activity is not productive.

Modeling Activities You Will Conduct

You will use Lotus 1-2-3 to help you conduct all model building activities, as follows:

Activity 1. You will conduct stage 1 modeling activities by using all of the techniques available to discover relationships between and within worksheet columns. The between-column techniques you will use include: (1) simple percent forecasting, (2) moving average, (3) exponential smoothing, and (4) linear regression; the within-column techniques are: (1) ratio analysis and (2) correlation analysis. It is important that you understand how to use all of the techniques to make sense of the data.

Activity 2. You will select the best technique to model each variable in Lotus 1-2-3. After identifying the best technique, you will create an area in the worksheet that contains your modeling statements. Then you will build your dynamic model using these modeling statements.

Activity 3. After your dynamic model is built, you will query the model using: (1) what-if analysis, (2) goal-seeking analysis, and (3) sensitivity analysis. To do this, you will change one or more values in the modeling statement area you just set up. You will also use data tables to conduct many what-if analyses at one time. Based on these analyses, you can make recommendations to the managers at Harrison Electronics.

Now let's concentrate our attention on the first stage: discovering model relationships. It is important to understand that you cannot develop a dynamic model unless you have a clear understanding of variable relationships. You will discover variable relationships by looking at (1) trends with the *same* variable across different columns in a worksheet and (2) relationships between *different* variables within the same column. With the former, you are looking for changes or trends of a variable, usually across time—for example, Total Sales increases at about 5 percent per quarter on average. With the latter, you are looking for a different type of relationship, in which one variable is associated with another variable, such as how the cost of goods sold is about 60 percent of the total sales.

Stage 1: Techniques for Uncovering Between-Column Trends

There is nothing more frustrating than staring at a financial statement or at another table of historical corporate data, and thinking, *What do I do with the data now? What does it all mean? How do I build a dynamic model from the data?* These are commonly asked questions. Remembering that a worksheet is essentially nothing more than a matrix of columns and rows can make your analysis a bit easier. You can look either horizontally or vertically for changes and relationships. In looking at past data for trends, you can try to find patterns that you can use to predict future sales. In this discussion, we will use the following four techniques to discover a trend between columns:

1. simple percent forecasting
2. moving average
3. exponential smoothing
4. linear regression

Although there are other techniques, these four are the ones most often used by managers and analysts seeking to solve a problem using historical data.

Simple Percent Forecasting

The least complex of the four techniques, **simple percent forecasting**, computes the average change in a decision or performance variable—often a variable such as sales over a certain period of time. You will build a dynamic model for the

Harrison Electronics case. You have now collected more data on the expenses for the firm. In Figure 7.3 you see a rather simple income statement for the last eight-quarter period. Notice that three expense categories have been added to the worksheet: (1) Operating Expenses, (2) Wages, and (3) Supplies and Parts. Your objective now is to discover what trends and relationships exist within the data presented at Harrison Electronics. Only after you use all of the modeling techniques and compare their results will you be able to build a dynamic model for Harrison Electronics.

In the example of Harrison Electronics, sales and expense data has been added for eight contiguous time periods. The first step in your analysis is to examine the change in sales by calculating the changes in each of the sales-line items.

Calculating a simple percent with historical data and making projections requires three steps. First, you must compute the percentage of change for each pair of quarters. Second, you must calculate the average percentage of change. Third, you must make your projections by multiplying the previous value by the average percentage of change.

Step 1. You use the simple formula `+D8-C8` to calculate change, and then divide the result by the first number to calculate the percentage of change. The formula in cell D9, then, is `+(D8-C8)/C8`. You must copy this formula to each of the remaining quarters and to the other sales categories.

Figure 7.3
Simple Income Statement

HARRISON ELECTRONICS, INC.
1413 Fillmore Street
Colorado Springs, CO 80906

Income Statement
(rounded thousands)

Category	Code	1 Qtr	2 Qtr	3 Qtr	4 Qtr	5 Qtr	6 Qtr	7 Qtr	8 Qtr	Total
Repair Sales	1000	143	179	202	164	166	197	221	183	1,455
Appliance Sales	2000	28	55	19	31	44	60	23	46	306
Small Products Sales	3000	5	21	8	79	8	30	12	80	243
TOTAL SALES		176	255	229	274	218	287	256	309	2,004
Operating Expenses	9100	45	54	44	67	50	67	62	75	464
Wages	9200	19	28	21	31	21	29	26	36	211
Supplies & Parts	9300	98	122	129	116	120	137	147	125	1,004
TOTAL EXPENSES		162	204	204	214	191	233	235	236	1,679
GROSS INCOME		14.0	51.0	25.0	60.0	27.0	54.0	21.0	73.0	325.0
Taxes	9300	5.6	20.4	10.0	24.0	10.8	21.6	8.4	29.2	130.0
NET INCOME		8.4	30.6	15.0	36.0	16.2	32.4	12.6	43.8	195.0

Step 2. The average percentage of change is calculated by averaging the seven change percentages. Figure 7.4 displays the percentage of change for the repair sales category over the eight periods.

Let's examine the results of the analysis at this point. Notice first how misleading the straight percentages are to a casual reader. Although Repair Sales captures the largest sales dollars, it represents the smallest average increase in sales by percentage. In fact, only 4.9 percent was averaged, due to seasonal fluctuations. The same seasonal fluctuations affect Small Products Sales as well. Apparently, much of the sales for small products occurs around the winter holidays (Harrison Electronics is on a January-to-December fiscal year), thereby accounting for the large jump in the fourth and eighth quarters.

HINT: To compute the simple average, multiply the previous value by the average change.

Step 3. You will now want to use the average change to estimate the growth in each of the sales categories for the next four periods. To illustrate this, you can use the growth rate for Repair Sales to predict the next four quarter periods. Figure 7.4 shows the original sales values and the predicted values for quarters 1 through 12. Notice the use of absolute cell addressing when referencing the Avg % Chg. value in cell O10.

The formula we are using to estimate historical sales data and to make projections is obtained by multiplying the previous projected sales value by the average change of 4.9 percent to compute the sample average. We needed a starting value for the trend line. There are two ways to come up with this value. The first

D11: (F0) [W5] +C11*(1+$O$10) READY

HARRISON ELECTRONICS, INC. Income Statement
1413 Fillmore Street (rounded thousands)
Colorado Springs, CO 80906

Category	1 Qtr	2 Qtr	3 Qtr	4 Qtr	5 Qtr	6 Qtr	7 Qtr	8 Qtr	9 Qtr	10 Qtr	11 Qtr	12 Qtr	Total
Repair Sales	143	179	202	164	166	197	221	183					1,455
Change (%)		25%	13%	−19%	1%	19%	12%	−17%					
Avg % Chg.													4.9%
Projected	155	163	170	179	187	197	206	216	227	238	249	262	

UNDO

Figure 7.4
Simple Average Projection for Repair Sales

is to use the starting value in cell C8, in this case 143. However, should seasonality be present, we should determine where the repetition occurs in the data and use the average of that cycle. In our example, we notice a repetition in the sales data every four quarters. The second way to derive a starting value, then, is to take the average of the two starting quarters. In this example, we averaged the values of 143 (in cell C8) and 166 (in cell G8) for quarters 1 and 5, respectively, to yield a starting value of 155.

HINT: The larger the average change, the greater the bias in the line.

Using an average to make projections on historical data creates a problem. Simple average forecasting, using average increases, yields a curvilinear line rather than a linear projection. Notice in Figure 7.5 the slightly curved line biasing our projection. A rule of thumb here is that the larger the average change, the larger the curve, and therefore the greater the bias. Other techniques may prove more useful given large average changes, such as the moving average or linear regression.

Moving Average

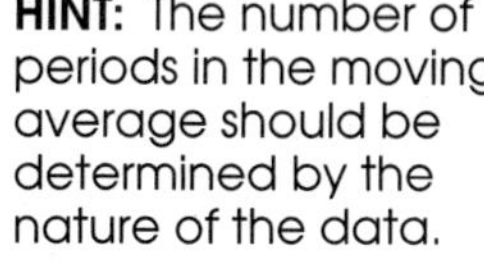

HINT: The number of periods in the moving average should be determined by the nature of the data.

The **moving average** method takes, as the projected value in the period under investigation, the average value of the decision variable over a number of periods. The number of periods to be included in the moving average should be determined by the nature of the data. In this case, the data suggests a four-period average due to the cyclical nature of sales. Once again, use the Repair Sales data

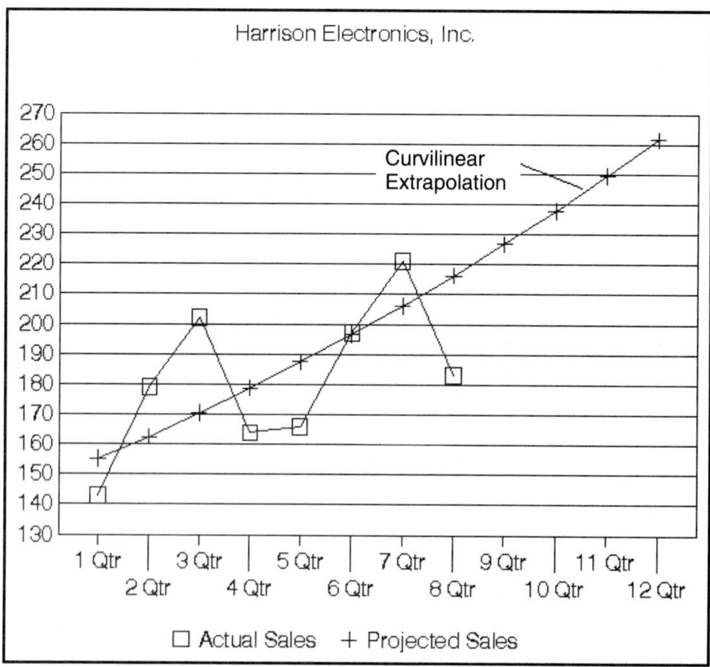

Figure 7.5
Simple Average Projection for Repair Sales

to conduct the moving average so that you can compare the results with your simple average forecast.

Calculating a moving average with historical data and making projections requires three steps. First, you must produce the moving average formula. Second, you must calculate the actual change (not percentage) of each moving average value. Third, you must make your projections with the most recent moving average value, providing there is some stability in the change figures, or use the average change value.

Step 1. The main formula used to compute the moving average is quite simple: for Quarter 3 you must enter the formula `@AVG(C8..F8)`. Notice that we are averaging a four-quarter period, but placing the value in Quarter 3 (cell E13) so that we capture two quarters of sales before and one quarter of sales after Quarter 3. You must then copy the formula through Quarter 7. Figure 7.6 shows the worksheet for the moving average to project the Repair Sales data.

Step 2. You must calculate the actual change (not percentage) of each moving average value by subtracting the current period from the previous one. Place the change data in the row directly below the moving average formula, starting in cell F14.

HINT: If there is stability in the change figure use the most recent value; otherwise, use the average.

Step 3. You must make your projections with the most recent moving average value, provided there is some stability in the change figures. If there is not stability, as is true in most cases, you must use the average change value in cell O14 to project from the moving average. In this case, you will use the average change value, an increase of 4.94, to project into the remaining five quarters. Carry down the last moving average value for Quarter 7 in cell I13 to cell I15 to start the projection. The formula used to make your predictions in cell J15 is `+I15+$O$14`. When you copy the formula through Quarter 12, you should see the formula

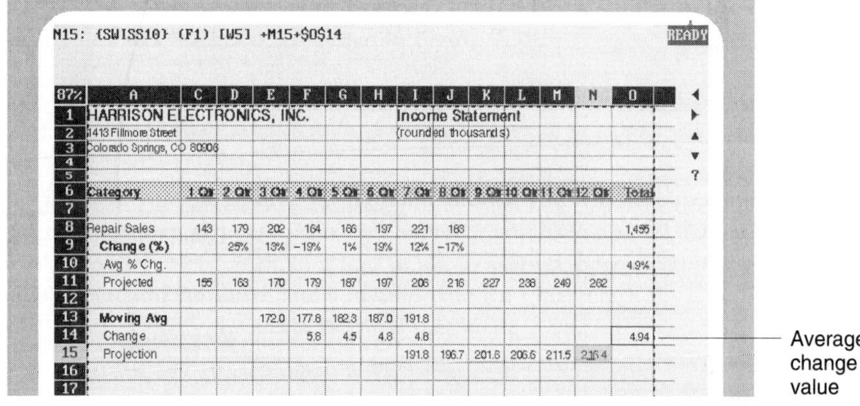

N15: {SWISS10} (F1) [W5] +M15+$O$14 READY

87%	A	C	D	E	F	G	H	I	J	K	L	M	N	O
1	HARRISON ELECTRONICS, INC.							Income Statement						
2	1413 Fillmore Street							(rounded thousands)						
3	Colorado Springs, CO 80906													
4														
5														
6	Category	1 Qtr	2 Qtr	3 Qtr	4 Qtr	5 Qtr	6 Qtr	7 Qtr	8 Qtr	9 Qtr	10 Qtr	11 Qtr	12 Qtr	Total
7														
8	Repair Sales	143	179	202	164	166	197	221	183					1,455
9	Change (%)		25%	13%	−19%	1%	19%	12%	−17%					
10	Avg % Chg.													4.9%
11	Projected	155	163	170	179	187	197	206	216	227	238	249	262	
12														
13	Moving Avg			172.0	177.8	182.3	187.0	191.8						
14	Change				5.8	4.5	4.8	4.8						4.94
15	Projection							191.8	196.7	201.6	206.6	211.5	216.4	
16														
17														

Figure 7.6
Moving Average Projection for Repair Sales

+M15+$O$14, as shown in Figure 7.6. To make projections, you are using the previous moving average value, adding it to the 4.94 change value. Figure 7.7 shows the graph for the moving average projection.

Notice that, since you are using a moving average value based upon the unit in question (dollars in this case), you see more of a straight line than a curved line. This is not always true, especially when the data reflect great ups and downs. In those cases, the moving average line tends to follow the data to a greater extent than shown here with the Harrison Electronics data. Keep in mind that the line that results from using the moving average technique is usually smoother when more periods are averaged into the formula. As a result of this more linear line, the Quarter 12 prediction of Repair Sales is $216,400 rather than the previous value of $262,000, obtained when using simple average forecasting.

HINT: The greater the number of periods in the moving average, the smoother the resulting line.

Exponential Smoothing

Exponential smoothing is a technique that gives greater weight to the most recent period of time while adjusting for sharp upward or downward swings with a smoothing constant (represented by the symbol alpha, *a*). The **smoothing constant** is a value that adjusts or "smooths" a line, generally in the range of .2 to .8. The smoothing constant depends upon the degree to which you want to smooth out swings in the data. The smaller the smoothing constant, the less variance in the line and the smoother the resulting trend line.

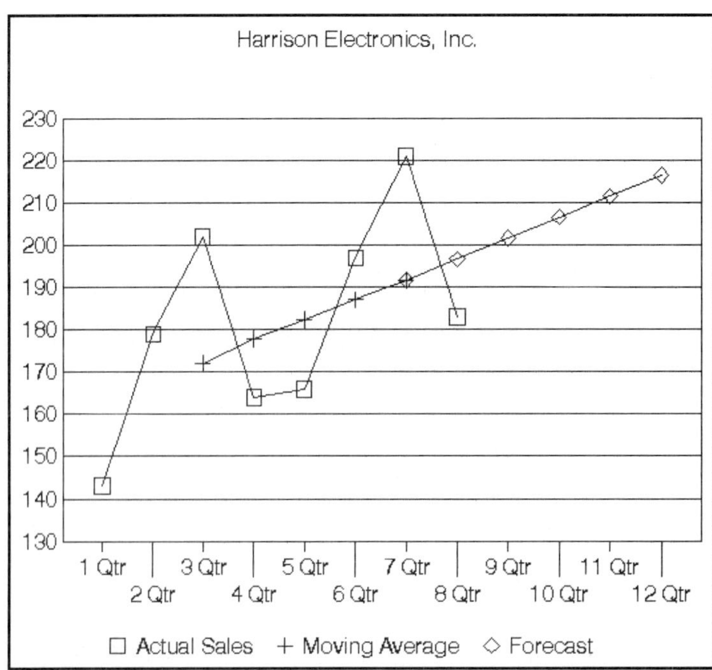

Figure 7.7
Moving Average Projection for Repair Sales

Projecting sales with the exponential smoothing technique requires four steps. First, you will initially set the smoothing constant at .2. Second, you must enter the formula that gives you the exponential smoothing estimates of historical sales for repairs. Third, you will compute the change in forecasted sales for projecting. Fourth, you will bring down the last projected value and compute the forecasted sales using the same approach as you did for the moving average technique.

Step 1. You must enter the value of .2 in the cell designated for the smoothing constant, O18. Also, bring down the Quarter 1 sales figure of 143 into cell C18 as a starting value. Figure 7.8 shows the worksheet for projecting Repair Sales with the exponential smoothing technique.

Step 2. You must enter the formula that gives us the exponential smoothing estimates of historical sales for repairs. The generic formula is as follows:

Prior Period Forecast + (Smoothing Constant * (Current Period Actual Sales – Prior Period Forecast))

In cell D18 of Figure 7.8, you will enter the exponential smoothing formula. The reference to cell O18 is absolute so that we can copy it to the remaining cells for which you have historical sales data. The formula must be copied through Quarter 8 in cell J18.

Step 3. You will compute the change in forecasted sales for projection purposes, placing the change values in the row directly below the exponential smoothing

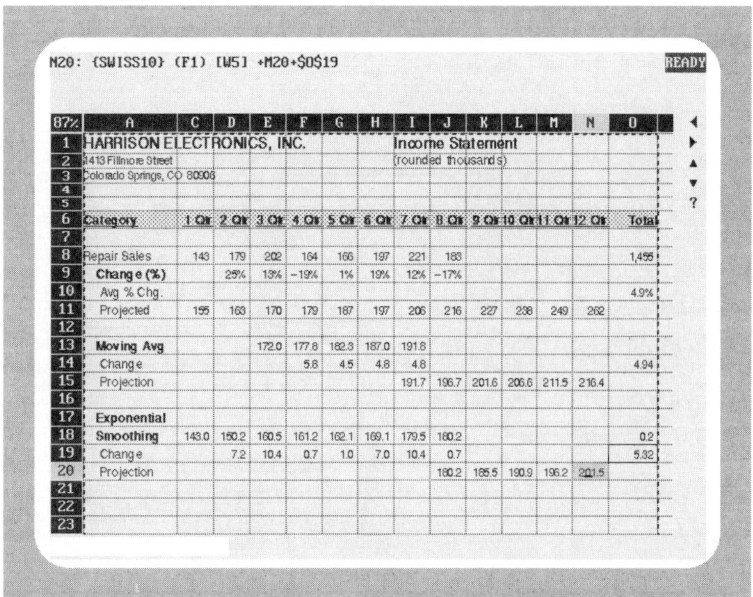

N20: {SWISS10} (F1) [W5] +M20+$O$19 READY

87%	A	C	D	E	F	G	H	I	J	K	L	M	N	O
1	HARRISON ELECTRONICS, INC.							Income Statement						
2	1413 Fillmore Street							(rounded thousands)						
3	Colorado Springs, CO 80906													
4														
5														
6	Category	1 Qtr	2 Qtr	3 Qtr	4 Qtr	5 Qtr	6 Qtr	7 Qtr	8 Qtr	9 Qtr	10 Qtr	11 Qtr	12 Qtr	Total
7														
8	Repair Sales	143	179	202	164	166	197	221	183					1,455
9	**Change (%)**		25%	13%	−19%	1%	19%	12%	−17%					
10	Avg % Chg.													4.9%
11	Projected	155	163	170	179	187	197	206	216	227	238	249	262	
12														
13	**Moving Avg**			172.0	177.8	182.3	187.0	191.8						
14	Change				5.8	4.5	4.8	4.8						4.94
15	Projection							191.7	196.7	201.6	206.6	211.5	216.4	
16														
17	**Exponential**													
18	**Smoothing**	143.0	150.2	160.5	161.2	162.1	169.1	179.5	180.2					0.2
19	Change		7.2	10.4	0.7	1.0	7.0	10.4	0.7					5.32
20	Projection								180.2	185.5	190.9	196.2	201.5	
21														
22														
23														

Figure 7.8
Exponential Smoothing Projection for Repair Sales with a=.2

formula starting in cell D19. After calculating the change values, you must compute the average change in cell O19 using the @AVG function.

Step 4. Bring down the last projected value of 180.2 from cell J18 to cell J20 for consistency of formula development. Using the change created by the exponential formula coupled with the smoothing constant, you can project into Quarter 12 by copying the formula. Since the change is not stable, you will use the average change value in cell O19, adding the forecast value in the previous quarter. The formula used to make your predictions in cell J20 is `+I20+$O$19`. When you copy the formula through Quarter 12, you should see the formula `+M20+$O$19`, as shown in Figure 7.8. Figure 7.9 illustrates a graph of the actual data and the projected data. The line does not appear to represent the actual data.

Changing the smoothing constant to .4, as shown in Figures 7.10 and 7.11, changes the twelfth quarter sales projection from $201,500 to $218,600. Notice that the projected line is more closely aligned with the actual Repair Sales data. Finally, when you change the smoothing constant to .8, you find a slight drop in Quarter 12 sales and an even tighter fit of the projected data with the actual data although not as useful for prediction.

HINT: The smaller the smoothing constant, the less variance in the line and smoother the line.

Linear Regression

The final technique for discovering relationships between columns and identifying trends involves the use of linear regression. Probably the most sophisticated

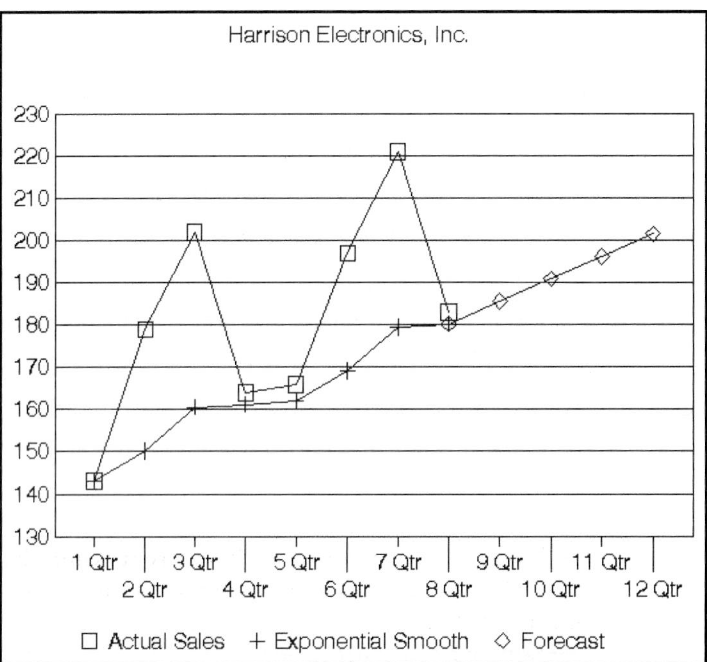

Figure 7.9
Exponential Smoothing Projection for Repair Sales with a=.2

Figure 7.10
Exponential Smoothing Projection for Repair Sales with a=.4

O18: {SWISS10} [W7] 0.4 READY

87%	A	C	D	E	F	G	H	I	J	K	L	M	N	O
1	HARRISON ELECTRONICS, INC.							Income Statement						
2	1413 Fillmore Street							(rounded thousands)						
3	Colorado Springs, CO 80906													
4														
5														
6	Category	1 Qtr	2 Qtr	3 Qtr	4 Qtr	5 Qtr	6 Qtr	7 Qtr	8 Qtr	9 Qtr	10 Qtr	11 Qtr	12 Qtr	Total
7														
8	Repair Sales	143	179	202	164	166	197	221	183					1,455
9	**Change (%)**		25%	13%	−19%	1%	19%	12%	−17%					
10	Avg % Chg.													4.9%
11	Projected	155	163	170	179	187	197	206	216	227	238	249	262	
12														
13	**Moving Avg**			172.0	177.8	182.3	187.0	191.8						
14	Change				5.8	4.5	4.8	4.8						4.94
15	Projection							191.7	196.7	201.6	206.6	211.5	216.4	
16														
17	**Exponential**													
18	**Smoothing**	143.0	157.4	175.2	170.7	168.8	180.1	196.4	191.0					0.4
19	Change		14.4	17.8	−4.5	−1.9	11.3	16.4	−5.4					6.87
20	Projection								191.1	197.9	204.8	211.7	218.6	
21														

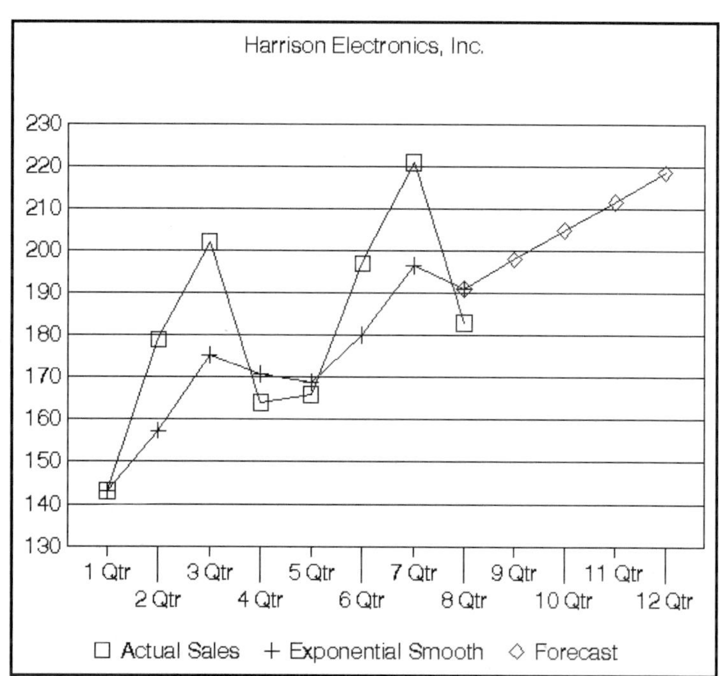

Figure 7.11
Exponential Smoothing Projection for Repair Sales with a=.4

of the forecasting techniques, **linear regression** fits a straight, or linear, line through historical data in order to project future values with the least amount of unexplained variance. Lotus 1-2-3 has a built-in linear regression function for developing a linear regression line.

The linear regression technique fits a linear line with predicted values based on actual historical data. The least-squares approach determines the slope of the line such that, in total, as much of the variance is explained as possible, as measured by the R^2 statistic. This statistic tells the analyst how well two variables are related. Lotus 1-2-3 allows up to six independent variables to be entered, in contiguous columns, as predictors that explain the dependent variable being studied. In the case in which you are projecting sales for repairs, Quarters will be your independent variable and Repair Sales will serve as your dependent variable. It is important to have as many data points as possible when running a regression analysis—20 to 30 data points are preferable. However, you can use linear regression as a comparison with the other forecasting techniques, even without a large number of data points.

HINT: It is important to have as many data points as possible when running a regression.

Projecting sales with linear regression requires three steps. First, you must set up the regression area with columns for the independent variable values, dependent variable values, and predicted values. Second, invoke the **/D**ata **R**egression command identifying the X, Y, and output ranges, and run the regression. Third, you must place the linear regression formula in the Predicted Sales range.

Step 1. Set up the regression area where you will place the data and results. In Figure 7.12, you should type in labels for the Quarter (X range), Actual (Y range), and Predicted Sales starting in cell P6. Type in the Quarter and Actual data. Since you are predicting Repair Sales through Quarter 12, be sure to include Quarters 1 through 12 in cells P9 through P20. The Predicted Sales range, cells R9 through R20, will be blank until you run the regression.

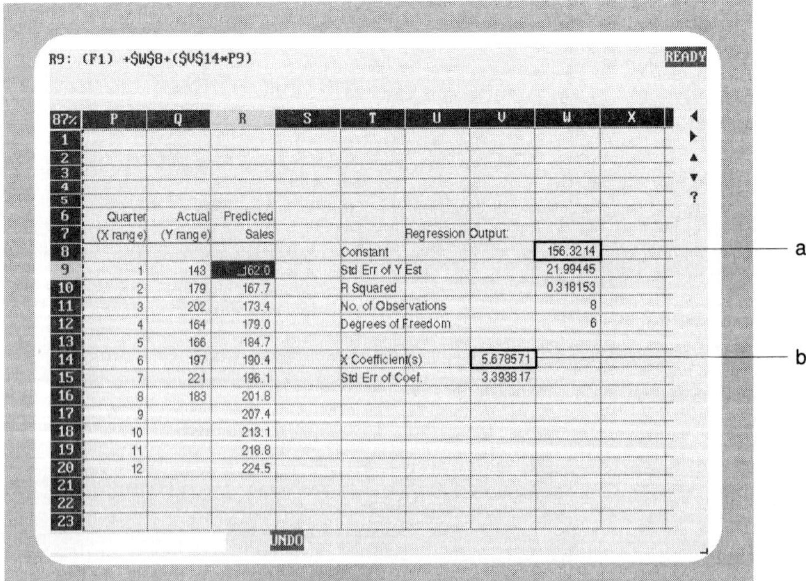

Figure 7.12 Multiple Regression Projection for Repair Sales

HINT: Don't include the forecast cells in the X range.

Step 2. To use the linear regression function within Lotus 1-2-3, you must invoke the /**D**ata **R**egression command. You have to identify the X, Y, and output ranges before Lotus 1-2-3 will run the regression. The X value, then, is the independent variable located in column P, specifically cells P9 through P16. Be certain not to include cells for Quarters 9 through 12 in the range that you will later predict. The actual sales data, the dependent variable, resides in column Q, in cells Q9 through Q16. Set the Output Range starting at cell T7; you need not specify the entire range. You must then select **G**o to run the regression.

Step 3. Now you have to enter the regression formula in the area you've designated for Predicted Sales (column R). Notice that in Figure 7.12 the regression output is printed in the range starting in cell T7 as you specified. You need to extract two values from the regression output in order to calculate Predicted Sales. The formula you will need to enter and copy into column R is as follows:

Regression algorithm: y = a + bx
Lotus 1-2-3 formula: `+$W$8 + ($V$14 * P9)`

In the regression algorithm, *a* is the constant and *b* is the X coefficient. So in cell R9 you must enter the copyable formula that accesses both the constant and the X coefficient. Be careful to make the cells referencing the constant and X coefficient values absolute so that the formula can be copied to the rest of the cells in column R. Figure 7.13 depicts the actual and predicted data for the Repair

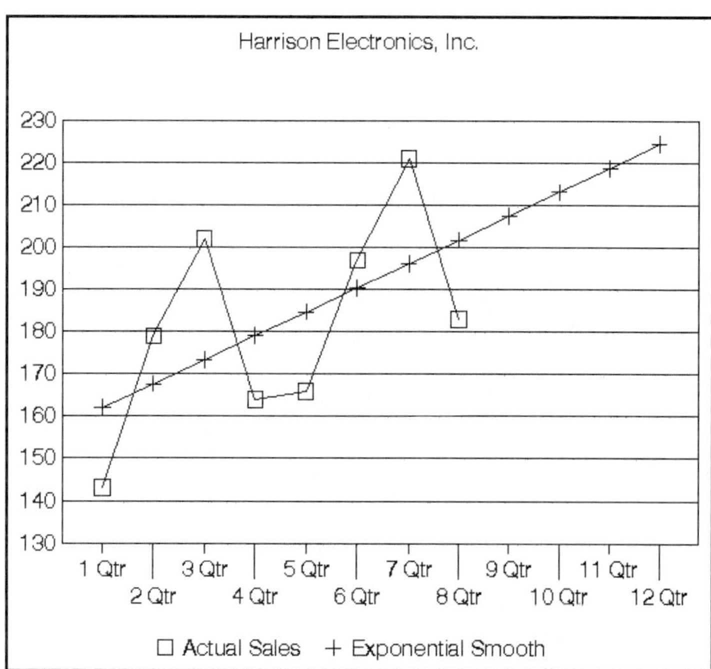

Figure 7.13
Multiple Regression Projection for Repair Sales

Sales. Notice that the predicted value for Quarter 12 is $224,500, similar to the amount indicated when a smoothing constant of .4 was used in the exponential smoothing technique.

Comparison of Between-Column Techniques

All four of the techniques we have discussed in this chapter are useful for uncovering trends between columns. It is important that you apply all of the techniques to your data so that you can make comparisons. Try not to use only the one technique you feel most comfortable using, since it may not fit the data as well as another technique. Figure 7.14 compares the techniques and the results gathered from them. The projected Quarter 12 repair sales for Harrison Electronics ranged from a low of $201,500 (exponential smoothing with *a*=.2) to a high of $262,000 (simple average). The spread is significant, especially when you are trying to convince a loan manager to invest in your business.

The larger sales figure was expected from the simple average technique, which yields an exponential distribution. Wouldn't we all want to project our sales to grow in this fashion? The moving average, however, yielded a more conservative projection. The differences in the exponential smoothing technique based on the smoothing constant are especially important. The smoothing constant should not be set too high, because the smoothing effect will be lost. Linear regression, as expected, projected a line in the middle, between the highest and lowest projections.

Figure 7.14
Comparison of Between-Column Techniques for Repair Sales

Techniques	Characteristics	Smooth Constant	Forecast Error	Qtr8	Qtr12
Simple average	Simple to use; results in a curvilinear line; should not be used for large percentage rates, appropriate for small sample sizes.		3,268	216,000	262,000
Moving average	Use three- to six-period average to calculate trend depending on nature of data; produces smooth (not linear) line; appropriate for smaller sample sizes.		2,496	201,600	216,400
Exponential smoothing	Adjusts or smooths line based on smoothing constant; easy to conduct what-if analyses with trend line.	a=.2 a=.4 a=.8	4,242 1,722 191	180,200 191,100 189,400	201,500 218,600 215,900
Linear regression	Suitable for larger numbers of data points; fits linear line, minimizing error and setting the slope.		2,462	202,000	224,000

Assessing the Accuracy of the Forecasts

Which forecast is the most accurate? To answer this question, you must measure the accuracy of the line resulting from the use of each technique. You will use a three-step process. First, calculate the difference between the forecast and the historical data. Second, square the differences to eliminate the negative values and emphasize the large differences. Third, total the differences for each forecast and compare the differences, selecting the forecast with the smallest value.

Step 1. For each forecast, subtract the actual value from the projected value. You must do this for each of the quarters that you have data for all of the forecasts. Since you have only six periods (Quarters 3–8) with overlapping actual and projected data for all of the forecasting techniques, you must use only the six periods when calculating the forecast error. This will ensure comparability between the error results. Starting with the average percentage in Figure 7.15, enter the formula `+E11-E$8` in cell E12 and copy it through cell J12. Copy the formula to the other three forecasts in the worksheet.

Step 2. You must now square the difference to eliminate the effect of negative values and emphasize the large differences. In cell E13, enter the formula `+E12*E12` and copy it through J13 and to the other three forecasts.

Step 3. Now sum the squared differences to complete the error calculations using the @SUM function. Cell O13 contains the sum of the squared differences for the percentage change forecast.

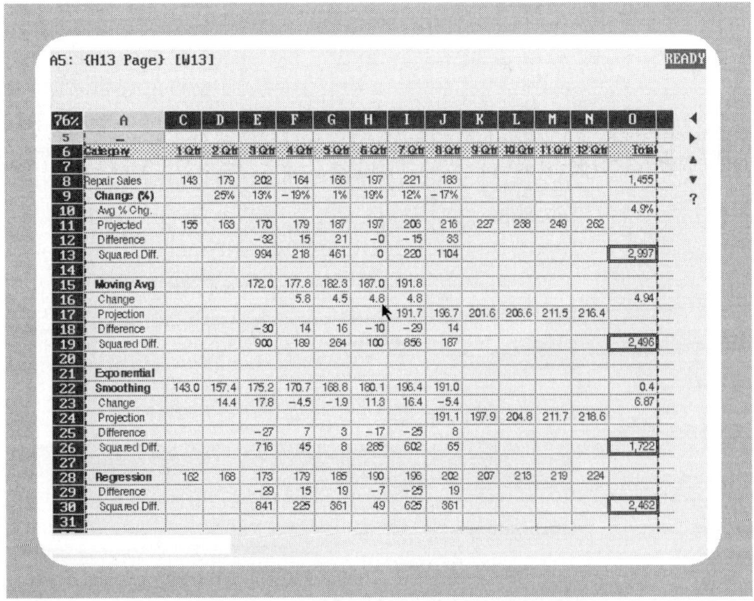

A5: {H13 Page} [W13]   READY

76%	A	C	D	E	F	G	H	I	J	K	L	M	N	O
5	—													
6	Category	1 Qtr	2 Qtr	3 Qtr	4 Qtr	5 Qtr	6 Qtr	7 Qtr	8 Qtr	9 Qtr	10 Qtr	11 Qtr	12 Qtr	Total
7														
8	Repair Sales	143	179	202	164	166	197	221	183					1,455
9	**Change (%)**		25%	13%	−19%	1%	19%	12%	−17%					
10	Avg % Chg.													4.9%
11	Projected	155	163	170	179	187	197	206	216	227	238	249	262	
12	Difference			−32	15	21	−0	−15	33					
13	Squared Diff.			994	218	461	0	220	1104					2,997
14														
15	**Moving Avg**			172.0	177.8	182.3	187.0	191.8						
16	Change				5.8	4.5	4.8	4.8						4.94
17	Projection							191.7	196.7	201.6	206.6	211.5	216.4	
18	Difference			−30	14	16	−10	−29	14					
19	Squared Diff.			900	189	264	100	856	187					2,496
20														
21	**Exponential**													
22	**Smoothing**	143.0	157.4	175.2	170.7	168.8	180.1	196.4	191.0					0.4
23	Change		14.4	17.8	−4.5	−1.9	11.3	16.4	−5.4					6.87
24	Projection								191.1	197.9	204.8	211.7	218.6	
25	Difference			−27	7	3	−17	−25	8					
26	Squared Diff.			716	45	8	285	602	65					1,722
27														
28	**Regression**	162	168	173	179	185	190	196	202	207	213	219	224	
29	Difference			−29	15	19	−7	−25	19					
30	Squared Diff.			841	225	361	49	625	361					2,462
31														

Figure 7.15
Comparison of Between-Column Techniques

Choosing the Best Forecast

HINT: Select the technique that best fits the data and that possesses the lowest forecast error.

You are now ready to select the best forecast for Repair Sales. We want to select the forecast that has the lowest sum of the squared differences, or forecast error. The simple average technique did not appear to be very accurate with Harrison Electronics. The main reason for this is the compound percentage rate of 4.9 percent. The next-highest total forecast error (2,496) lies with the moving average forecast, while the lowest forecast error (1,722) resides with the exponential smoothing forecast (smoothing constant = .4). Be careful when you interpret exponential smoothing forecasts. The greater the smoothing constant, the closer the forecast is to the actual line and the lower the forecast error. A forecast that mirrors the actual data is not useful for predictions, however. A smoothing constant that is too low will create a very high forecast error. Always try to use a smoothing constant of between .1 and .6 to compare the accuracy of this technique with that of the others.

Based on these results, you will select the exponential smoothing forecast for Repair Sales. You must also use the four forecasting techniques for Appliance Sales and Small Products Sales to determine which of the forecasting techniques yields the best forecast. One last note: It is not recommended that you make long-range projections without adequate historical data to support your analysis. A rule of thumb is to project only as many periods as are represented by the historical data.

Stage 1: Techniques for Uncovering Within-Column Relationships

Once you understand between-column techniques, uncovering within-column relationships is a natural extension. Most of the accounts reported on financial statements are tied directly to sales or production levels. Also, current levels of assets are often optimal for a current sales level. The procedure for uncovering within-column relationships involves two distinct steps. First, isolate the items that vary directly with sales. Second, examine other data items to determine whether they are related to other decision variables. If a relationship cannot be found between the item under investigation and either sales or another decision variable, then it is recommended that you apply one of the techniques described previously for between-column analysis. Two techniques are available for exploring within-column relationships: ratio analysis and correlation analysis.

Ratio Analysis

HINT: Ratios relate one variable to another—do not expect a "correct" value.

Ratio analysis is a technique that relates one variable to another and is widely used by managers, investors, and other analysts interested in the health of an organization. Ratios are critical when variables have unique relationships with other variables in the firm. A **ratio** is simply the number resulting from the division of one number by another. There is no "correct" value when you are calculating a ratio.

Ratio analysis is the comparison of a ratio (indicating a relationship within a column) with another ratio within another column, so that the analyst can find clues. Ratios can be used in a trend analysis after patterns within the data have become more recognizable. Accounting and financial analysts use a variety of ratios to make sense of income statements and balance sheets. Some of these include:

- current ratio: $\frac{\text{current assets}}{\text{current liabilities}}$
- acid-test ratio: $\frac{\text{current assets} - \text{inventories}}{\text{current liabilities}}$
- inventory turnover: $\frac{\text{sales}}{\text{inventory}}$
- average collection period: $\frac{\text{receivables}}{\text{average sales per day}}$
- fixed-asset turnover: $\frac{\text{sales}}{\text{net fixed assets}}$
- total-asset turnover: $\frac{\text{sales}}{\text{total assets}}$
- total debt to total assets: $\frac{\text{total debt}}{\text{total assets}}$
- times interest earned: $\frac{\text{earnings before interest and taxes}}{\text{interest charges}}$
- basic earning power: $\frac{\text{earnings before interest and taxes}}{\text{total assets}}$
- return on total assets: $\frac{\text{net income available to common stockholders}}{\text{total assets}}$
- return on equity: $\frac{\text{net income}}{\text{equity}}$
- price/earnings ratio: $\frac{\text{price per share}}{\text{earnings per share}}$
- market/book ratio: $\frac{\text{common equity}}{\text{shares outstanding}}$

HINT: Ratios can be misleading when seasonality is present.

Because seasonal factors can distort ratio analysis, ratios can be misleading. Some firms operate in a variety of industries from which ratios cannot adequately capture the correct information relative to specific products or net incomes. Accounting statements (income statements, balance sheets, or cash-flow statements) often do not break out the data as needed to conduct a good ratio analysis. Therefore, you must learn to be a detective when analyzing corporate data. Figure 7.16 shows the summary data for Harrison Electronics for the three sales categories, three expense categories, and the impact of taxes on net income.

There are two steps required for using ratio analysis to explore the relationship between two variables. First, compute the ratios for the two variables for each period and compute the average ratio value for all periods. Second, compute the difference between the ratio in a period and the average ratio and compare the results.

Step 1. Examine Operating Expenses to see if they're related to Repair Sales or to Total Sales. Since Repair Sales constitutes the bulk of sales for Harrison Electronics, Operating Expenses may be more related to Repair Sales than to other sales categories. You will need to set up six rows in the worksheet, as shown in Figure 7.17. The first row is for the ratios, the second for the average, and the third for the difference. To compute the ratio of Operating Expenses to Repair Sales,

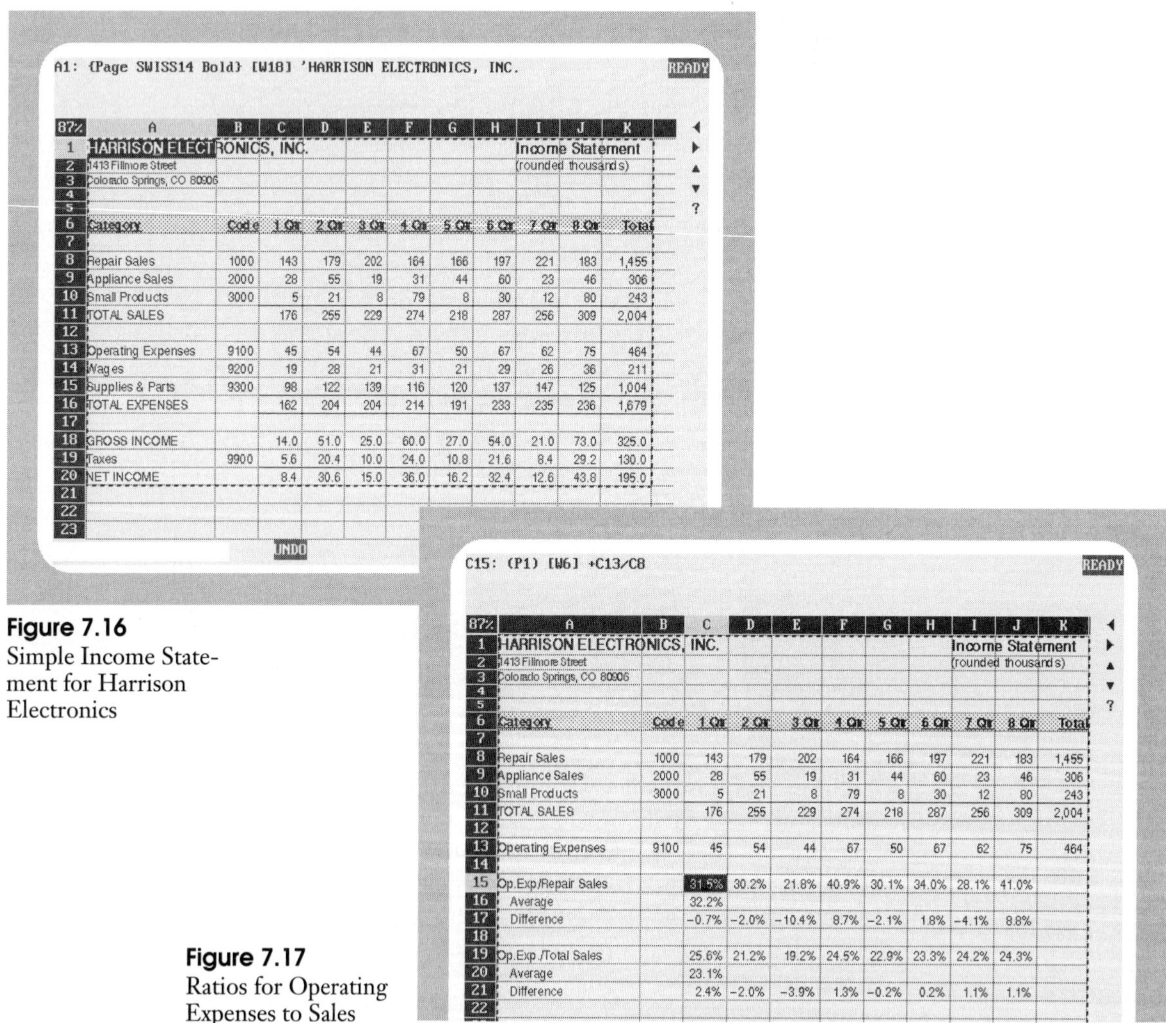

A1: {Page SWISS14 Bold} [W18] 'HARRISON ELECTRONICS, INC. READY

HARRISON ELECTRONICS, INC. — Income Statement (rounded thousands)
1413 Fillmore Street
Colorado Springs, CO 80906

Category	Code	1 Qtr	2 Qtr	3 Qtr	4 Qtr	5 Qtr	6 Qtr	7 Qtr	8 Qtr	Total
Repair Sales	1000	143	179	202	164	166	197	221	183	1,455
Appliance Sales	2000	28	55	19	31	44	60	23	46	306
Small Products	3000	5	21	8	79	8	30	12	80	243
TOTAL SALES		176	255	229	274	218	287	256	309	2,004
Operating Expenses	9100	45	54	44	67	50	67	62	75	464
Wages	9200	19	28	21	31	21	29	26	36	211
Supplies & Parts	9300	98	122	139	116	120	137	147	125	1,004
TOTAL EXPENSES		162	204	204	214	191	233	235	236	1,679
GROSS INCOME		14.0	51.0	25.0	60.0	27.0	54.0	21.0	73.0	325.0
Taxes	9900	5.6	20.4	10.0	24.0	10.8	21.6	8.4	29.2	130.0
NET INCOME		8.4	30.6	15.0	36.0	16.2	32.4	12.6	43.8	195.0

Figure 7.16
Simple Income Statement for Harrison Electronics

C15: (P1) [W6] +C13/C8 READY

HARRISON ELECTRONICS, INC. — Income Statement (rounded thousands)
1413 Fillmore Street
Colorado Springs, CO 80906

Category	Code	1 Qtr	2 Qtr	3 Qtr	4 Qtr	5 Qtr	6 Qtr	7 Qtr	8 Qtr	Total
Repair Sales	1000	143	179	202	164	166	197	221	183	1,455
Appliance Sales	2000	28	55	19	31	44	60	23	46	306
Small Products	3000	5	21	8	79	8	30	12	80	243
TOTAL SALES		176	255	229	274	218	287	256	309	2,004
Operating Expenses	9100	45	54	44	67	50	67	62	75	464
Op.Exp/Repair Sales		31.5%	30.2%	21.8%	40.9%	30.1%	34.0%	28.1%	41.0%	
Average		32.2%								
Difference		-0.7%	-2.0%	-10.4%	8.7%	-2.1%	1.8%	-4.1%	8.8%	
Op.Exp./Total Sales		25.6%	21.2%	19.2%	24.5%	22.9%	23.3%	24.2%	24.3%	
Average		23.1%								
Difference		2.4%	-2.0%	-3.9%	1.3%	-0.2%	0.2%	1.1%	1.1%	

Figure 7.17
Ratios for Operating Expenses to Sales

enter the ratio formula +C$13/C8 in cell C15 and copy through cells J15. You must also enter a formula that calculates the ratio of Operating Expenses to Total Sales in row 19. You must average the ratios in cell C15 for each of the ratio categories.

Step 2. You are now ready to enter the formula +C15-C16 in cell C17, which computes the difference between the ratio of Operating Expenses to Repair Sales and the average of the ratios. You must copy that formula across the row through cell J17 and for Operating Expenses to Total Sales in row 21. Let's examine the high and low values of the ratio differences for each ratio category. For Repair Sales, the ratio difference varies from a low of 10 percent in Quarter 3 to a high of 8.8 percent in Quarter 8. Although there are no rules to follow when evaluating ratios, it appears that the spread of 19 percent is so great that we would have a difficult time making a definitive statement about the true relationship between these two variables. The total difference is 0 percent when summing up the positive and negative differences.

The results of comparing Operating Expenses to Total Sales appears to be more promising. Notice that the differences range from –4 percent to 2 percent, with four of the eight observations in the 0 percent or 1 percent range. Comparing the difference of actual ratios of Operating Expenses to Repair Sales and Total Sales, as illustrated in Figure 7.18, we are directed to consider Operating Expenses as being related to Total Sales because the differences are significantly smaller. When Operating Expenses is related to Repair Sales, the range of variance from specific ratios to the average ratio is significantly larger than when

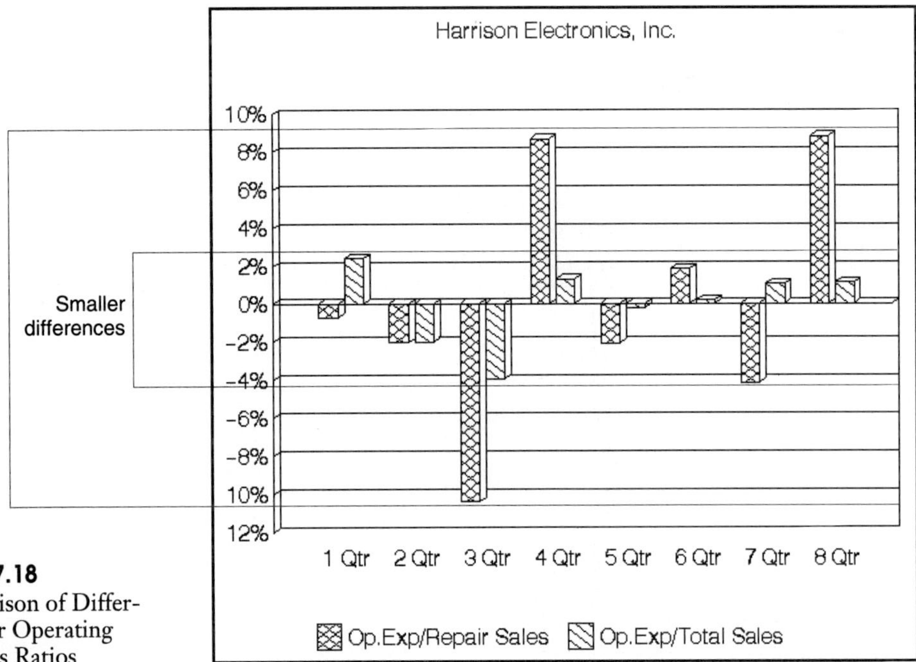

Figure 7.18
Comparison of Differences for Operating Expenses Ratios

Operating Expenses is related to Total Sales. You will therefore use the following general formula when you put together your dynamic model:

Operating Expenses = Total Sales * 23.1%

We also calculated the ratios for Wages to Repair Sales and Total Sales in Figure 7.19 and for Supplies & Parts to Repair Sales and Total Sales in Figure 7.20. As we might have expected, Wages is strongly related to Total Sales, with all of the observations falling into the 0 percent to 1 percent difference range.

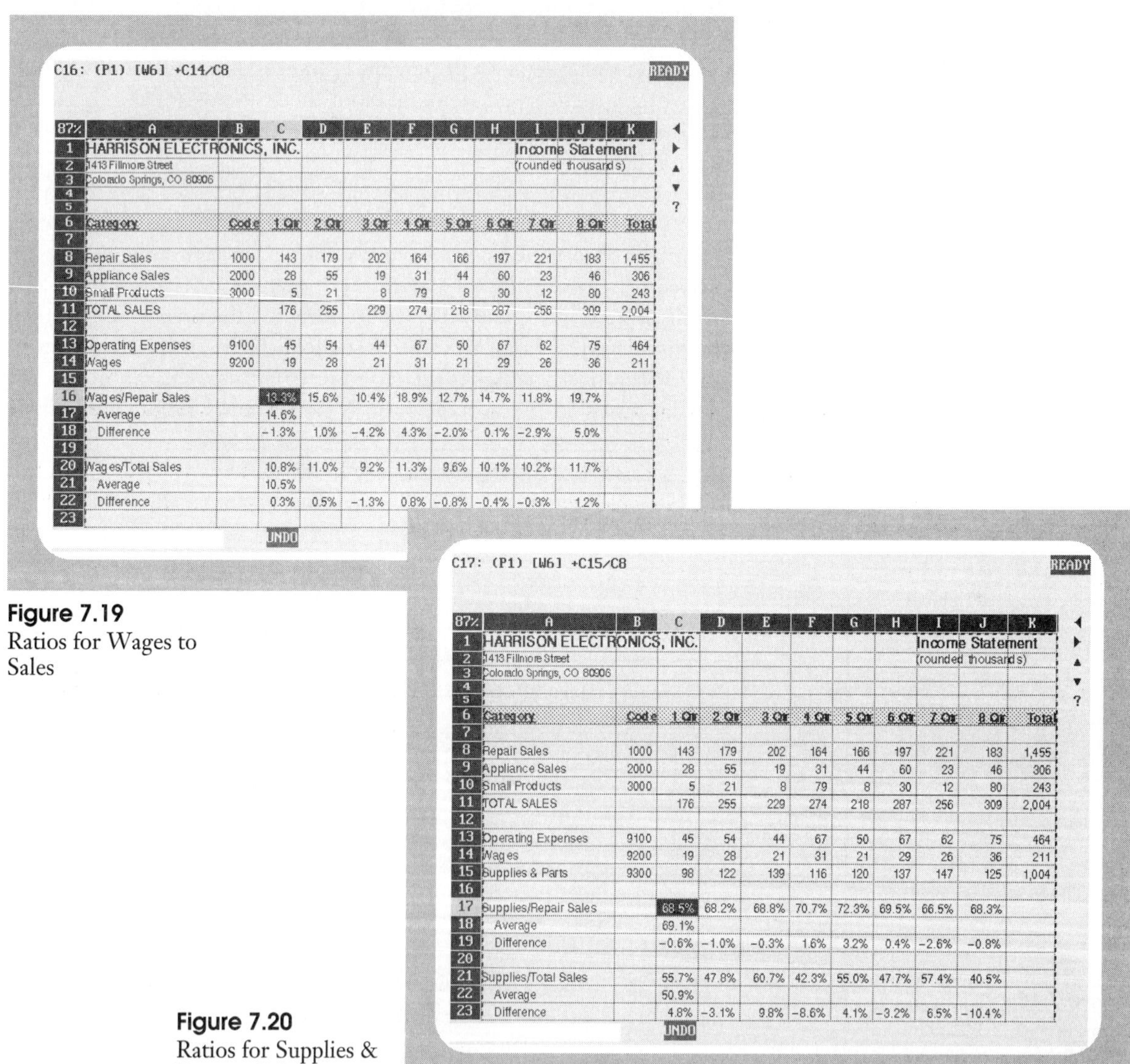

C16: (P1) [W6] +C14/C8 READY

87%	A	B	C	D	E	F	G	H	I	J	K
1	HARRISON ELECTRONICS, INC.								Income Statement		
2	1413 Fillmore Street								(rounded thousands)		
3	Colorado Springs, CO 80906										
4											
5											
6	Category	Code	1 Qtr	2 Qtr	3 Qtr	4 Qtr	5 Qtr	6 Qtr	7 Qtr	8 Qtr	Total
7											
8	Repair Sales	1000	143	179	202	164	166	197	221	183	1,455
9	Appliance Sales	2000	28	55	19	31	44	60	23	46	306
10	Small Products	3000	5	21	8	79	8	30	12	80	243
11	TOTAL SALES		176	255	229	274	218	287	256	309	2,004
12											
13	Operating Expenses	9100	45	54	44	67	50	67	62	75	464
14	Wages	9200	19	28	21	31	21	29	26	36	211
15											
16	Wages/Repair Sales		13.3%	15.6%	10.4%	18.9%	12.7%	14.7%	11.8%	19.7%	
17	Average		14.6%								
18	Difference		-1.3%	1.0%	-4.2%	4.3%	-2.0%	0.1%	-2.9%	5.0%	
19											
20	Wages/Total Sales		10.8%	11.0%	9.2%	11.3%	9.6%	10.1%	10.2%	11.7%	
21	Average		10.5%								
22	Difference		0.3%	0.5%	-1.3%	0.8%	-0.8%	-0.4%	-0.3%	1.2%	
23											

UNDO

Figure 7.19
Ratios for Wages to Sales

C17: (P1) [W6] +C15/C8 READY

87%	A	B	C	D	E	F	G	H	I	J	K
1	HARRISON ELECTRONICS, INC.								Income Statement		
2	1413 Fillmore Street								(rounded thousands)		
3	Colorado Springs, CO 80906										
4											
5											
6	Category	Code	1 Qtr	2 Qtr	3 Qtr	4 Qtr	5 Qtr	6 Qtr	7 Qtr	8 Qtr	Total
7											
8	Repair Sales	1000	143	179	202	164	166	197	221	183	1,455
9	Appliance Sales	2000	28	55	19	31	44	60	23	46	306
10	Small Products	3000	5	21	8	79	8	30	12	80	243
11	TOTAL SALES		176	255	229	274	218	287	256	309	2,004
12											
13	Operating Expenses	9100	45	54	44	67	50	67	62	75	464
14	Wages	9200	19	28	21	31	21	29	26	36	211
15	Supplies & Parts	9300	98	122	139	116	120	137	147	125	1,004
16											
17	Supplies/Repair Sales		68.5%	68.2%	68.8%	70.7%	72.3%	69.5%	66.5%	68.3%	
18	Average		69.1%								
19	Difference		-0.6%	-1.0%	-0.3%	1.6%	3.2%	0.4%	-2.6%	-0.8%	
20											
21	Supplies/Total Sales		55.7%	47.8%	60.7%	42.3%	55.0%	47.7%	57.4%	40.5%	
22	Average		50.9%								
23	Difference		4.8%	-3.1%	9.8%	-8.6%	4.1%	-3.2%	6.5%	-10.4%	

UNDO

Figure 7.20
Ratios for Supplies & Parts to Sales

To model the Wages variable, we will use the following general formula for our dynamic model:

Wages = Total Sales * 10.5%

It appears, however, that the Supplies & Parts variable is more related to Repair Sales, where five observations fell in the 0 percent or 1 percent range, than to Total Sales, with differences found between –3 percent and 3 percent. This is an intuitive conclusion, since we are purchasing supplies and parts primarily to support our repairs, and hence the sales that result from this activity. Therefore, we will use the following formula:

Supplies = Repair Sales * 69.1%.

HINT: Always run at least two different types of analyses for each variable.

The ratio analysis appears to have been somewhat successful. Often, we do not yield clear results when running our ratios as we have with our Harrison Electronics case. Continue the within-column exploration by using the correlation analysis technique. Always run at least two types of analyses for each variable so that you have confidence in the formula that you will use in your dynamic model.

Correlation Analysis

HINT: Use XY plots in conjunction with correlation analysis.

Correlation analysis is a form of linear regression that concentrates on the correlation coefficient. Usually this use of linear regression is referred to as *simple linear regression* because you are using only one independent variable and one dependent variable in your model. Another aspect of correlation analysis that is useful in determining relationships is the scatterplot, or XY plot, in Lotus 1-2-3. An **XY plot** shows the movement of variable A with that of variable B. We obtain additional information when conducting a correlation analysis that we did not acquire with ratio analysis, such as the direction of the relationship (positive or negative). Certain variables that move in an opposite direction (for example, as operating expenses increase, net income decreases) indicate a negative relationship.

There are two steps to using correlation analysis. First, set up a regression area with columns for the X and Y values, similar to the linear regression technique you used earlier. Second, invoke the **/D**ata **R**egression command, identifying the X, Y, and output ranges, and run the regression.

Step 1. Set up the regression area for Total Sales (column P) and Operating Expenses (column Q). Figure 7.21 shows the basic layout for the correlation analysis. Notice that you have essentially the same worksheet screen that you had when you conducted linear regression, except that now you do not need the Predicted Data column. Because of this you are dealing only with those periods for which we have historical data.

Step 2. You will use the /**D**ata **R**egression command in Lotus 1-2-3 to conduct the correlation analysis. Since you are correlating only two variables, you need not be concerned with which variable is in the X range and which is in the Y range. First you will correlate Operating Expenses to Total Sales, as shown in Figure 7.21. Since you found earlier that Operating Expenses is more related to Total Sales, you can expect to find the correlation coefficient (R^2) higher for Total Sales than Repair Sales. Then you will confirm your findings when using ratio analysis.

You will use the R^2 statistic to assess the degree of relationship between the two variables. Figure 7.22 illustrates an XY plot for the two variables. When

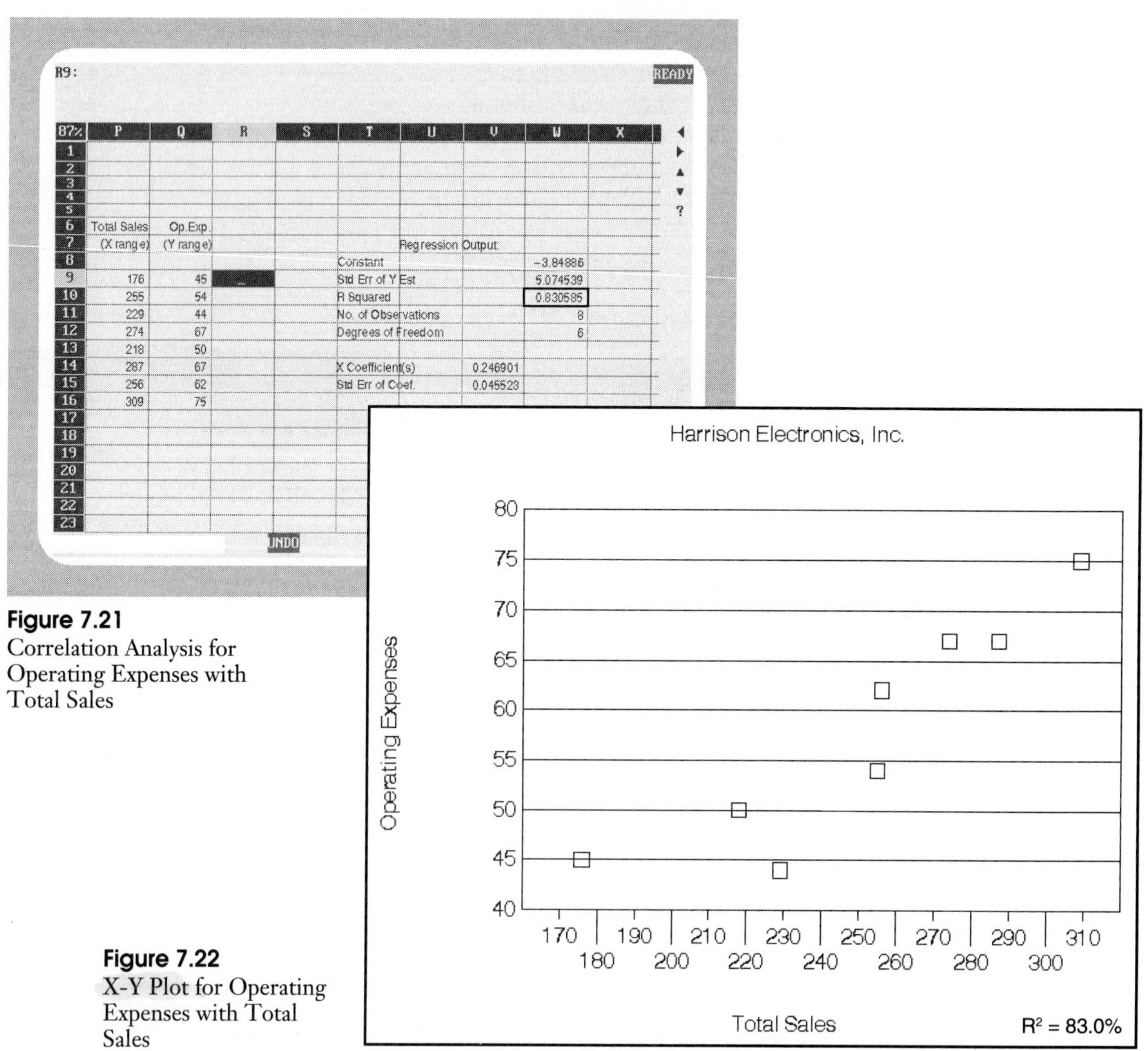

Figure 7.21
Correlation Analysis for Operating Expenses with Total Sales

Figure 7.22
X-Y Plot for Operating Expenses with Total Sales

HINT: When setting up an XY plot, set the graph X range to the regression X range and the graph A range to the regression Y range.

setting up an XY plot, set the graph X range to the regression X range and the graph A range to the regression Y range. The two variables appear to be highly related to each other, following a positive upward pattern.

As with ratio analysis, there is no definite rule for what is an acceptable level of correlation. You will want to use the correlation coefficient derived from this analysis with other relationships that you may want to examine. So, to make a comparison, substitute Repair Sales, since they tend to comprise a large component of the total sales. You will note the significant drop in the correlation coefficient from 83.0 percent to 6.8 percent. Comparatively, we must conclude that Operating Expenses is much less correlated to Repair Sales than it is to Total Sales. The XY plot in Figure 7.23 does not show any recognizable pattern. These variables (Operating Expenses and Repair Sales) are not related.

HINT: You do not need to reset the regression ranges when performing subsequent regression runs.

Once you have set up your worksheet for correlation, you need only substitute the new values for either the X or the Y range. You do not need to reset the regression ranges; simply issue the /**D**ata **R**egression **G**o command. You will now want to correlate the other two expense variables with each of the sales variables. Note in Figure 7.24 that Wages tends to be strongly related to Total Sales, showing a correlation coefficient of 88.7 percent. The XY plot shows a very strong correlation. In Figure 7.25, the Supplies & Parts variable is highly correlated with Repair Sales, at 96.9 percent. The XY plot for this variable, looks almost linear, since the R^2 value is so close to 1.00.

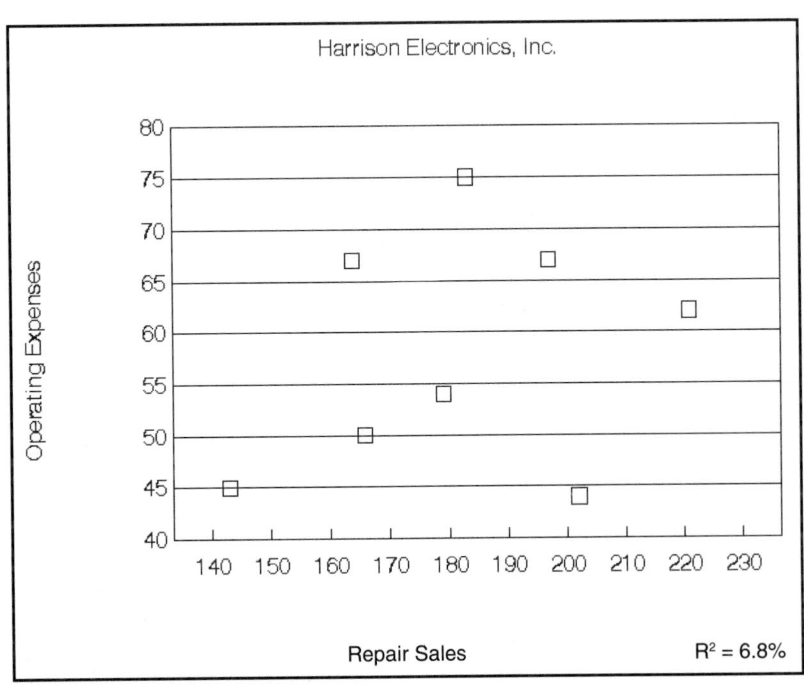

Figure 7.23
X-Y Plot for Operating Expenses with Repair Sales

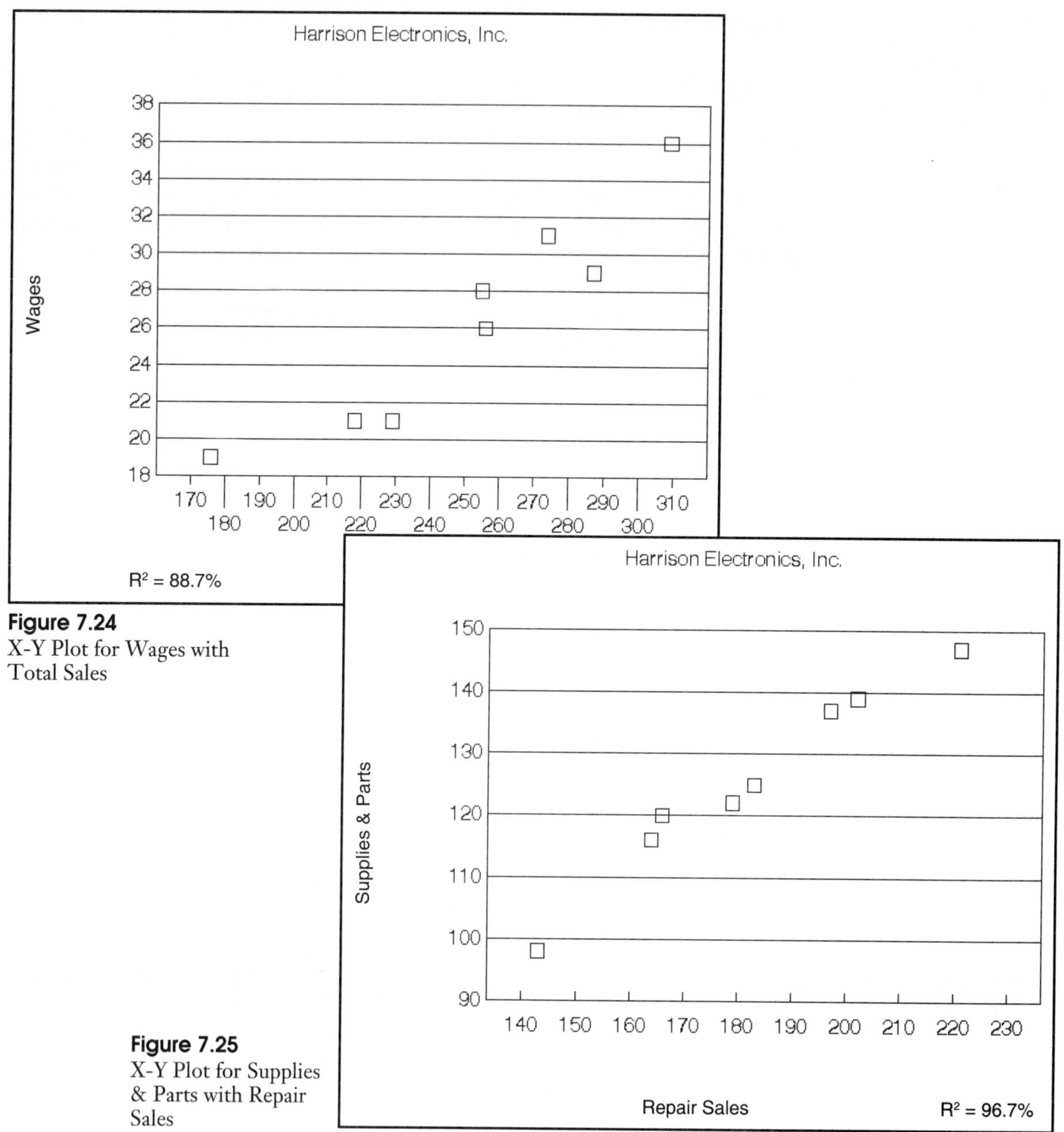

Figure 7.24
X-Y Plot for Wages with Total Sales

Figure 7.25
X-Y Plot for Supplies & Parts with Repair Sales

Comparison of Within-Column Techniques

Both ratio analysis and correlation analysis allow you to explore the relationships embedded within a financial statement or marketing research report. In fact, both of these within-column techniques can be used with any table of data that has been

HINT: Analysis should be performed to correlate all variables.

compiled to impart information to decision makers. Figure 7.26 shows the differences in characteristics and results between the two techniques. You need not be limited to examining the relationships of expense information—for example, with sales. Certain expenses are highly correlated with other expenses. Therefore, the possibilities for analyses on even the smallest amount of data are endless.

Technique	Decision Characteristics	Repair Variable	Total Sales	Sales
Ratio analysis	Simple ratio for one variable with another; uses average ratio and differences to determine acceptable ratio ranges.	Op. Expenses Wages Supplies & Parts	–10% to 9% –4% to 4% –3% to 3%	–4% to 2% –1% to 1% –10% to 7%
Correlation	Simple linear regression and XY plots used to measure the correlation between two variables; R^2 statistic measures strength of relationship.	Op. Expenses Wages Supplies & Parts	R^2 = 6.8% R^2 = 4.5% R^2 = 96.7%	R^2 = 83.0% R^2 = 88.7% R^2 = 23.5%

Figure 7.26
Comparison of Within-Column Techniques

It seems that for Harrison Electronics both the ratio analysis and correlation analysis yielded clear choices as to variable relationships. Notice the differences between the Wages variable and Repair Sales (4.5 percent) and between Wages and Total Sales (88.7 percent). Based on the comparison, Wages, for example, is clearly more aligned with Total Sales than with Repair Sales. We can agree intuitively with this finding and conclude that the firm needs to staff the store for all types of sales. Had we conducted further correlational studies, we might have found a strong relationship with Appliance Sales or Small Products Sales.

Putting It All Together: The Dynamic Model

Now it is time for you to put together all of the formulas you have discovered based upon your between-column and within-column analyses. Starting with sales and working through the income statement, you will use the results you found in your analysis. We noted earlier that different results were yielded depending on which between-column technique was used. So that you use an approach that leads to balanced results, you will build your formulas for each of the sales categories by using the exponential smoothing formulas. The growth rate in the modeling statement comes directly from the average change value of 6.87 in Figure 7.10. Likewise, you will model each of the expenses categories by using ratio analysis and confirming them with the correlation coefficient. Figure 7.27 illustrates each of the modeling statements you will use in developing your dynamic model in Lotus 1-2-3.

There are three steps to developing the dynamic model. First, set up a modeling statement area in the data area to hold the starting values, growth rates, and related variables. Second, you must set up the model area and copy starting values from the data area. Third, enter your modeling statements into the model area.

Step 1. To set up the modeling statements area, as shown in Figure 7.28, you will use four columns for your information, labeled as follows: Decision Variable, From Data, What-if, and To Model. In essence, the modeling statements area acts as a bridge from the data area to the dynamic model. When setting up the modeling statements area, use formulas in the form of cell references in the From Data column to extract starting values, growth rates, and ratio percentages. These values come from the Stage 1 analysis you have just completed. Initially the what-if column, where the worksheet changes will be entered, are set to 100 percent. In the To Model column, you must multiply From Data values by the What-if percentages. The values in the To Model column will be extracted in the dynmaic model.

HINT: Formulas for the first period in the dynamic model pull values out ot the data area.

Step 2. Now you must set up the dynamic model. Figure 7.29 shows the dynamic model area which was created by inserting blank rows at the top of the worksheet, pushing down the data area to lower-level rows. You have to copy the headings, titles, and codes from the data area. Enter your starting values by extracting the data from the data area. For example, enter the formula `+B30` in cell C8, and so forth. Copy the formulas that will not change from the data area for Total Sales, Total Expenses, Gross Income, and Net Income.

Decision Variable	Starting Value	Generic Dynamic Modeling Statements	Sample Modeling Statements in Lotus
Repair Sales	143	Previous + 6.87	(D8) `+C8 + $F31`
Appliance Sales	28	Previous + 1.77	(D9) `+C9 + $F34`
Small Products	5	Previous + 5.68	(D10) `+C10 + $F37`
TOTAL SALES		@SUM(sales)	(D11) `@SUM(D8..D10)`
Operating Expenses		Total Sales * 23.1%	(D13) `+C11 * $F39`
Wages		Total Sales * 10.5%	(D14) `+C11 * $F40`
Supplies & Wages		Repair Sales * 69.1%	(D15) `+C8 * $F41`
TOTAL EXPENSES		@SUM(expenses)	(D16) `@SUM(D13..D15)`
GROSS INCOME		Total Sales - Total Expenses	(D18) `+D11 - D16`
Taxes		Gross Income * 40%	(D19) `+D18 * $F43`
NET INCOME		Gross Income - Taxes	(D20) `+D18 - D19`

Figure 7.27
Modeling Statements for Harrison Electronics

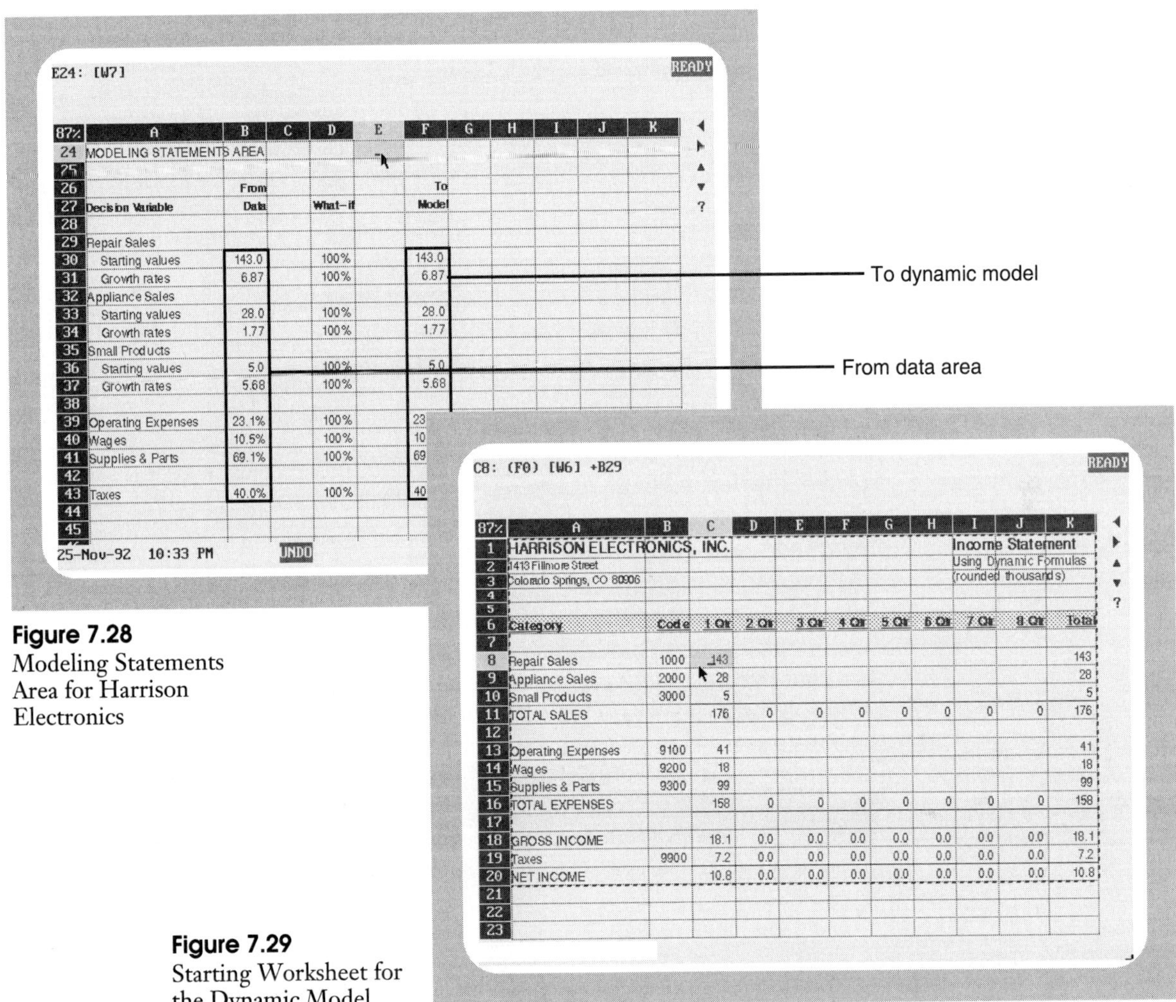

	A	B	C	D	E	F
24	MODELING STATEMENTS AREA					
25						
26		From				To
27	Decision Variable	Data		What-if		Model
28						
29	Repair Sales					
30	Starting values	143.0		100%		143.0
31	Growth rates	6.87		100%		6.87
32	Appliance Sales					
33	Starting values	28.0		100%		28.0
34	Growth rates	1.77		100%		1.77
35	Small Products					
36	Starting values	5.0		100%		5.0
37	Growth rates	5.68		100%		5.68
38						
39	Operating Expenses	23.1%		100%		23
40	Wages	10.5%		100%		10
41	Supplies & Parts	69.1%		100%		69
42						
43	Taxes	40.0%		100%		40
44						
45						

	A	B	C	D	E	F	G	H	I	J	K
1	HARRISON ELECTRONICS, INC.								Income Statement		
2	1413 Fillmore Street								Using Dynamic Formulas		
3	Colorado Springs, CO 80906								(rounded thousands)		
4											
5											
6	Category	Code	1 Qtr	2 Qtr	3 Qtr	4 Qtr	5 Qtr	6 Qtr	7 Qtr	8 Qtr	Total
7											
8	Repair Sales	1000	143								143
9	Appliance Sales	2000	28								28
10	Small Products	3000	5								5
11	TOTAL SALES		176	0	0	0	0	0	0	0	176
12											
13	Operating Expenses	9100	41								41
14	Wages	9200	18								18
15	Supplies & Parts	9300	99								99
16	TOTAL EXPENSES		158	0	0	0	0	0	0	0	158
17											
18	GROSS INCOME		18.1	0.0	0.0	0.0	0.0	0.0	0.0	0.0	18.1
19	Taxes	9900	7.2	0.0	0.0	0.0	0.0	0.0	0.0	0.0	7.2
20	NET INCOME		10.8	0.0	0.0	0.0	0.0	0.0	0.0	0.0	10.8
21											
22											
23											

Figure 7.28
Modeling Statements Area for Harrison Electronics

Figure 7.29
Starting Worksheet for the Dynamic Model

Step 3. You are now ready to enter your modeling statements in the dynamic model. Remember, your objective in building a dynamic model is to rid it of all values, incorporating only formulas into the model area of the worksheet based on the results of your Stage 1 analysis. With formulas, you can change specific values, percentages, and so on, while observing changes in the worksheet. We have identified seven variables by using either between- or within-column analysis techniques. You can now begin entering your formulas into either the C or D column, as appropriate, and later copy them across the row, as shown in Figure 7.30. Extract your values from cells in column F in the modeling statements area. When entering formulas that reference a growth rate, be careful to make any reference to a cell in the data area mixed or absolute. If necessary, you could project this information four or six quarters into the future by copying the formulas across the rows.

HINT: Make references to growth rates in the data area mixed or absolute.

A1: {Page SWISS14 Bold} [W19] 'HARRISON ELECTRONICS, INC. READY

	A	B	C	D	E	F	G	H	I	J	K
1	HARRISON ELECTRONICS, INC.								Income Statement		
2	1413 Fillmore Street								Using Dynamic Formulas		
3	Colorado Springs, CO 80906								(rounded thousands)		
4											
5											
6	Category	Code	1 Qr	2 Qr	3 Qr	4 Qr	5 Qr	6 Qr	7 Qr	8 Qr	Total
7											
8	Repair Sales	1000	143	150	157	164	170	177	184	191	1,336
9	Appliance Sales	2000	28	30	32	33	35	37	39	40	274
10	Small Products	3000	5	11	16	22	28	33	39	45	199
11	TOTAL SALES		176	190	205	219	233	248	262	276	1,809
12											
13	Operating Expenses	9100	41	44	47	51	54	57	61	64	418
14	Wages	9200	18	20	21	23	24	26	28	29	190
15	Supplies & Parts	9300	99	104	108	113	118	123	127	132	923
16	TOTAL EXPENSES		158	168	177	187	196	206	215	225	1,531
17											
18	GROSS INCOME		18.1	22.8	27.6	32.3	37.1	41.9	46.6	51.4	277.7
19	Taxes	9900	7.2	9.1	11.0	12.9	14.8	16.7	18.6	20.6	111.1
20	NET INCOME		10.8	13.7	16.5	19.4	22.3	25.1	28.0	30.8	166.6
21											
22											
23											

UNDO

Figure 7.30
Income Statement Using Dynamic Formulas

Your dynamic model is now complete. You have completed Stage 1 of your analysis by applying a variety of techniques for analyzing data in order to build a dynamic model. You were able essentially to use the power of the spreadsheet to make some sense of the data. A dynamic model allows you to query it, to test underlying assumptions, and to deal with risk issues. You will now conduct what-if, goal-seeking, and sensitivity analysis on the dynamic model to create new scenarios, and you will test the viability of each.

Conducting Stage 2 Analysis

The most exciting part of developing a dynamic model is the opportunity to query it, change it, and observe the results. Model query takes the form of what-if analysis, goal-seeking analysis, and/or sensitivity analysis. **What-if analysis** calculates the effects of a change in one variable on other variables or the entire worksheet. You might ask: *If you manipulate one decision variable and all other variables remain stable, what are the effects on the other important variables?*

Goal seeking, in essence, is the reverse of what-if analysis. Here you set an objective variable, such as market share or net sales, and then ask, for example, *What change do I need in sales volume to generate this?* **Sensitivity analysis** is the process of examining the assumptions and parameters of the model and scrutinizing the range of the results to those assumptions. As an analyst, you ask the question, *How sensitive are one or more of the decision variables to changes that would lead* *me to another alternative or to make another decision?* You want to detect the range of change in this case. You might also ask, *What are the low and high values of one or more decision variables?*

Other opportunities to use dynamic models for deriving information about the problem you are studying include simulation and optimization. Both simulation and optimization involve using the spreadsheet language to iterate a number of scenarios. **Simulation** is a process in which a distribution of individual scenarios is created so that the behavior of the model can be examined. Usually a random-number generator is used to run the experiment. **Optimization** is a machine-intensive operation that runs a number of scenarios to select the best one, based on the value of the objective variable you have chosen. Optimization is often combined with simulation to generate probability distributions.

Stage 2: Conducting What-If Analysis on the Dynamic Model

Once you have created a base model, you need to build in the flexibility to query a variety of variables so that you can investigate different scenarios. Model querying can be used to effect changes in different phases of the model-building process. New information resulting from a model query can change the way that you conceptualize a problem. You may redefine your decision variables, objectives, or consequences. You may make these changes to your variable ratings or to the algorithm that describes the variable in question. Most commonly you will query a dynamic model to help generate alternatives or to evaluate potential solutions.

Within the broad framework of model building and querying, we will explore three categories of analysis: what-if, goal-seeking, and sensitivity analysis. If you want to make changes temporarily to a variable in the dynamic model to observe the effects of those changes on other important variables, you would be performing what-if analysis. You may wish to challenge the assumptions on which the variable algorithms are built. Changes based on this analysis may be reflected in the model variables that are related to the decision variable under investigation.

Using Data Table 1

HINT: You can use the /**D**ata **T**able command to conduct what-if analysis on one or two variables.

Lotus 1-2-3 provides a technique for generating many simultaneous what-if scenarios, in addition to substituting new values for direct use or for inclusion into formulas. Using the **/D**ata **T**able command, you can process either one or two what-if variables. A **data table** is a set of closely related data organized into rows and columns, as are all spreadsheet data areas and models. A five-by-five, two-variable data table contains twenty-five what-if results that, if calculated by Lotus 1-2-3, will save you tremendous time. Without the data table, you would have to change the model statements one-by-one, observing changes in your dynamic model twenty-five times before you could compare the results. We will use the model statements area (Figure 7.28) for the Harrison Electronics case from which we will conduct our what-if analysis.

There are three steps to conducting what-if analysis using one-way data tables in Lotus 1-2-3. First, set up the data table area using the /**D**ata **F**ill command. Second, enter the formula that extracts values from the dynamic model. Third, identify the table range, and input cell, and fill the table.

HINT: Use the /**D**ata **F**ill command to place values in a data table.

Step 1. To set up our single-variable data table for our analysis, you should enter your labels for the variable you are changing and the variable you want to observe the impact on. Figure 7.31 illustrates the data table area with Operating Expenses in column H and Gross Profit in column I. You can use the /**D**ata **F**ill command to place a range of values in column H under the Op.Exp. % field in our data table. Having invoked the /**D**ata **F**ill command, you are asked to supply a data range to fill; H29..H37 is the range you want to fill with values. Then you must furnish the *starting value* of .15 and the *step value* of .02. The *stop value* is unimportant because the range you have provided will limit the number of values that will be filled. The area now has values of 15% through 31%. The range had to be formatted as a percentage. Each percentage reflects a different what-if scenario.

HINT: The upper-left cell in the data table 1 must be left blank.

Step 2. You must create a formula that calculates the impact on Gross Profit given different percentages of Operating Expenses with Total Sales for the eighth quarter, `+J18`. The formula, which extracts a value from the dynamic model, is key to the operation of your data table and must be entered above the data that will be calculated, in cell I28. The formula is formatted using the /**R**ange **F**ormat **T**ext command to show its reference. It is usually nothing more than a direct reference to another cell containing the formula, although we might have placed the formula that resides in cell J18 here rather than referencing it. The upper-left cell in the data table 1 (cell G28) must be left blank.

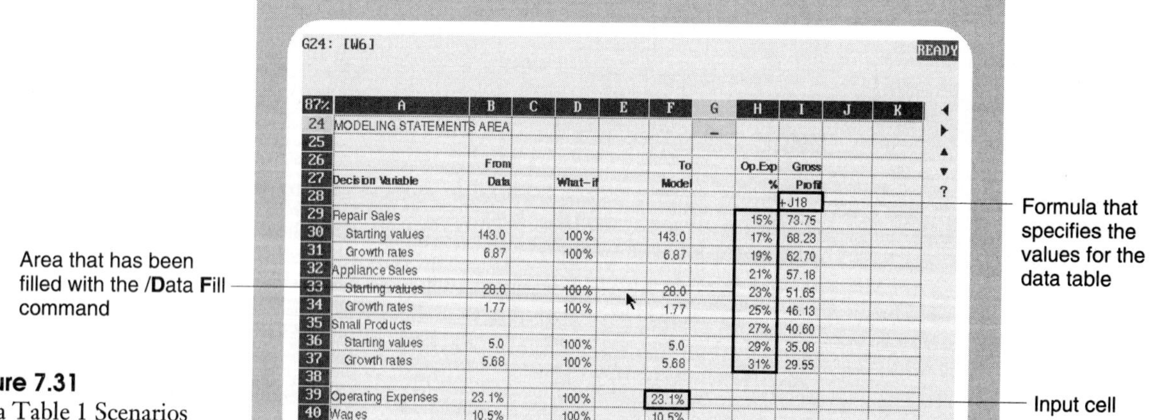

Figure 7.31
Data Table 1 Scenarios

Step 3. Now you are ready to invoke the **/D**ata **T**able **1** command. You will be asked to provide two things: the data table range and the input cell. The *table range* for the one-variable data table in Figure 7.31 must have two contiguous columns. The first must contain the values of the variable that will be changed in our formula, and the second must contain the blank cells directly to the right, where the results will be placed. The top left cell of the table range must be blank, and the top right cell must contain the formula that will be used to calculate the results that will be entered into each of the cells below. The *input cell*, shown in Figure 7.31, is the cell (F39) where the values in column H will be substituted into the formula.

The set of values provided by the data table gives you a wide spectrum of information that can help you understand the simple relationships of the dynamic model. Obviously, we expected to find a Gross Income figure around $51,000 when the Operating Expenses percentage is close to 23 percent, as shown from the Stage 1 analysis. Figure 7.32 illustrates the XY plot showing the inverse relationship between Operating Expenses percentage and Gross Income. Instead of setting up a data table, you could have produced the same results by simply substituting nine different values into cell F39. However, you would have had to save each of the results somewhere in the worksheet in order to produce a range for graphing. The data table saved you time and also laid out all of the variables and relationships in the worksheet for later audit and closer examination.

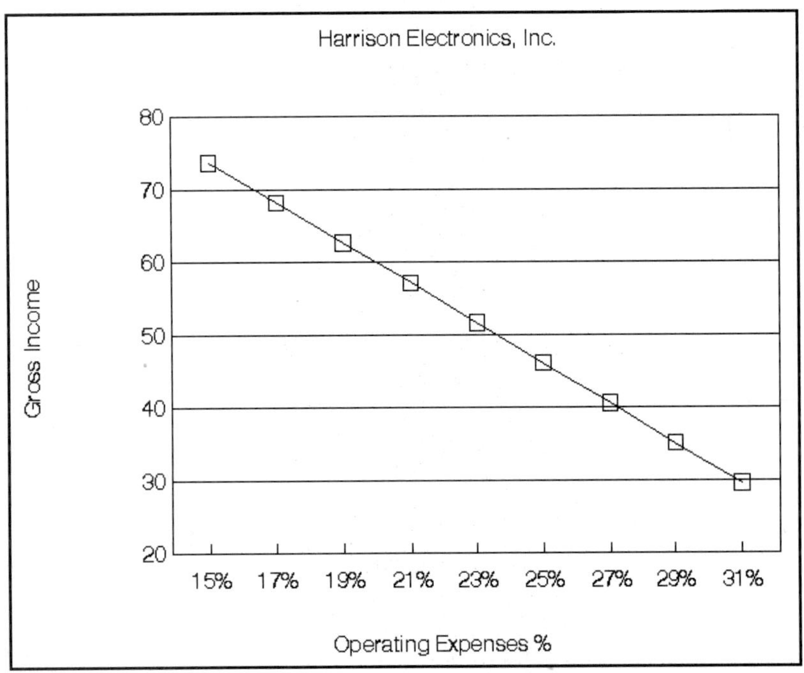

Figure 7.32
Data Table 1 Scenarios

Using Data Table 2

You may want to apply a more sophisticated version of the what-if analysis on data tables, in which you can manipulate two variables simultaneously to produce results. Some situations make it easy for you to evaluate the impact of two variables simultaneously. The **/D**ata **T**able **2** command allows you to do this. Using our original question of the impact of the percentage of Operating Expenses with Total Sales on Gross Income for Harrison Electronics, it would be useful to also know the simultaneous impact of the Repair Sales Growth Rate. The business question you are investigating is, *How will gross income be affected by the manipulation of both variables simultaneously?* Here you are looking at both the income and expense sides of the income statement.

HINT: The driving formula that calculates values in the two-way table must be placed in the intersection of the two variables.

As with the one-variable data table, you need to set up the table format before invoking the **/D**ata **T**able **2** command. Although the table format for two-way variable manipulation in Lotus 1-2-3 is different from the one-way table, the steps are the same. In Figure 7.33 the data table area has been reformatted to make room for the Repair Sales Growth Rate on the screen. The second variable needs to be added across the columns in row 28. The **/D**ata **F**ill command has been used again to place these values in the row. The critical formula that calculates the values in the data table is now placed in the intersection cell of the two variables for the dual-variable data table (cell H28).

Now you will invoke the **/D**ata **T**able **2** command to set the table range and input cells. Notice that the table range in Figure 7.33 includes the driving formula in the upper-left cell and the data values in the table, cells H28 through M37. The program now requests information for two input cells—one for the Operating Expenses percentage (F39) and one for Repair Sales Growth Rate (F30). Input cell 1 represents the leftmost data in the two-way table—in this case Operating Expenses.

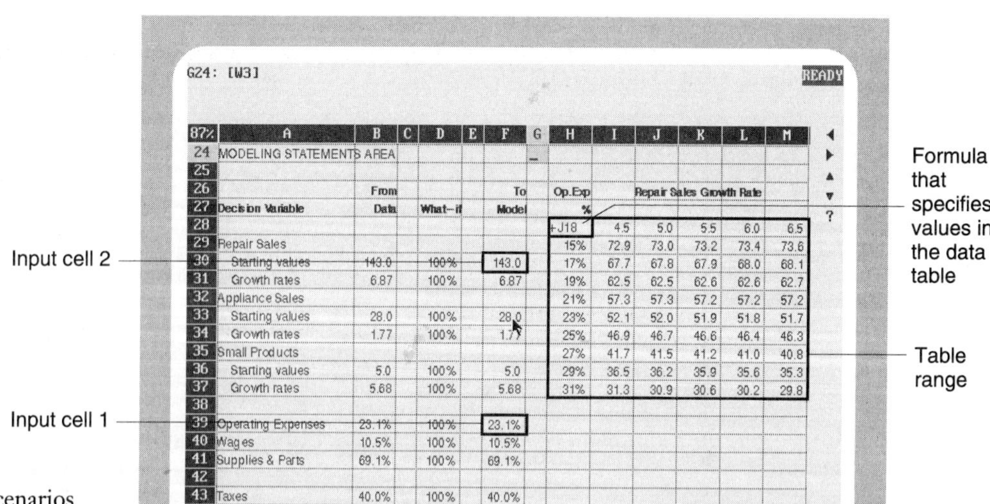

87%	A	B	C	D	E	F	G	H	I	J	K	L	M
24	MODELING STATEMENTS AREA												
25													
26		From				To		Op.Exp		Repair Sales Growth Rate			
27	Decision Variable	Data		What-if		Model		%					
28								+J18	4.5	5.0	5.5	6.0	6.5
29	Repair Sales							15%	72.9	73.0	73.2	73.4	73.6
30	Starting values	143.0		100%		143.0		17%	67.7	67.8	67.9	68.0	68.1
31	Growth rates	6.87		100%		6.87		19%	62.5	62.5	62.6	62.6	62.7
32	Appliance Sales							21%	57.3	57.3	57.2	57.2	57.2
33	Starting values	28.0		100%		28.0		23%	52.1	52.0	51.9	51.8	51.7
34	Growth rates	1.77		100%		1.77		25%	46.9	46.7	46.6	46.4	46.3
35	Small Products							27%	41.7	41.5	41.2	41.0	40.8
36	Starting values	5.0		100%		5.0		29%	36.5	36.2	35.9	35.6	35.3
37	Growth rates	5.68		100%		5.68		31%	31.3	30.9	30.6	30.2	29.8
38													
39	Operating Expenses	23.1%		100%		23.1%							
40	Wages	10.5%		100%		10.5%							
41	Supplies & Parts	69.1%		100%		69.1%							
42													
43	Taxes	40.0%		100%		40.0%							

Figure 7.33
Data Table 2 Scenarios

The results in the data table are interesting. If Repair Sales Operating Expenses are at 15 percent of Total Sales (cell H29), then the Gross Income continues to grow slightly from $72,900 to $73,600. However, at 21 percent, Gross Income remains relatively steady, and at 31 percent, it drops with each increase in Repair Sales Growth Rate. Overall, the increase and/or decrease in Gross Income is so slight that we are led to conclude that the growth rate in repair sales alone does do not significantly impact Gross Income. Rather, Operating Expenses must be controlled to alleviate substantial decreases in Gross Income.

Stage 2: Conducting Goal Seeking on the Dynamic Model

Goal seeking is a reverse model query technique that specifies the bottom-line value of an objective variable and then asks what the value of a decision variable or set of variables should be. Like what-if analysis, goal seeking can be used to discover the performance of a bottom-line variable at a single point in time or over a time horizon. When using the goal-seeking technique for one point in time, you might ask the question, *To attain a net income of $100,000 in 1995, what should be the level of sales?* Here you are dealing with a change in a value for one performance variable at one point in time. A change in an algorithm usually involves multiple time periods. Using the same example, you might ask, *To attain a net income of $100,000 in 1995 with a 12 percent increase each year thereafter, what should the sales volume be in 1995 and each successive year?*

Conducting goal seeking with Lotus 1-2-3 is a bit tricky. As a rule, formulas are entered in a unidirectional mode to avoid circular formulas. You can solve a goal-seeking exercise in Lotus 1-2-3 in one of two ways. The first utilizes circular formula references. A **circular formula** in Lotus 1-2-3 is a formula that eventually refers to its own cell reference.

Circular formulas are displayed in the status indicator in the lower-right portion of the screen. However, circular formulas can prove valuable when you are attempting to solve goal-seeking problems. There is no absolute answer in manipulating Lotus 1-2-3 to solve these problems. Sometimes circular formulas do provide the model variables with enough interaction to work backward and to solve for performance goals.

The second way to solve a goal-seeking problem is to set up another model in reverse format, in which you copy formulas and appropriate references. This might be time-consuming, but it is effective. Unfortunately, Lotus 1-2-3 is not designed to solve goal-seeking analyses without the help of an add-in package. However, goal seeking is discussed here because it is a major type of analysis used by a variety of decision support systems. Newer versions of spreadsheet packages are being equipped with "backsolver" programs, such as Lotus 1-2-3 Version 1.1 for Windows. The Backsolver add-in will allow you to solve for one objective variable while manipulating one decision variable.

Stage 2: Conducting Sensitivity Analysis on the Dynamic Model

The more powerful of the three analysis types described in this chapter is **sensitivity analysis**. Like what-if analysis, sensitivity analysis allows you to test the amount of change required in a decision variable to lead you to make a different decision. Sensitivity is a form of what-if analysis that is especially useful when you are uncertain about the assumptions that are made about a specific variable. Sensitivity analysis is the most useful when you are evaluating the relevance of the alternative, the decision, or the final choice. Sensitivity analysis can provide you with important information, especially when two or more decision variables can be independently tested. You can then compare the results and further investigate the variables that are extremely sensitive (which may lead you to another alternative or decision). Variables that are too sensitive introduce vulnerabilities into your model. Once you have identified the sensitive variables, you need to consider one of the following courses of action:

1. Revise your model to eliminate large sensitivities.
2. Add details about sensitive variables or scenarios.
3. Obtain better estimates of sensitive external variables.
4. Alter the real-world system to reduce actual sensitivities.
5. Live with real-world uncertainties, monitoring actual results closely.

HINT: Use the same percentage increase or decrease to compare results when conducting sensitivity analysis.

Let's change three of the variables independently in the Harrison Electronics worksheet to observe the resultant change in net income. To compare results and determine which variable is the most sensitive, you will increase three cost variables by 25 percent. It is important to use the same percentage increase in expenses and/or decrease in income in order for the results to be comparable. In our example, the variable that yields net income results farthest from the base line is the most sensitive.

First, you will modify the growth rate for Operating Expenses (in cell D39), increasing it by 25 percent, as shown in Figure 7.34. Change the What-if percentage from 100 percent to 125 percent. Second, you will observe the change to your worksheet, as shown in Figure 7.35. Notice that Quarter 8 net income has changed from the original value of $30,800 to $21,300, a significant drop.

HINT: Use the /**R**ange **V**alues command to convert formulas to values for graphing.

Third, you should save each of the independent modifications in a separate area for graphing. In Figure 7.36, a graphic area has been set up and the net income formula has been copied from the dynamic model. This was done by using a simple cell reference. The formula `+C20` was placed in cell AD6 (Operating Expenses for Quarter 1) so that the net income values move over. Then the formula was copied to the remaining quarters. So that you can make changes in your variables, you must change the formulas in your graph area values. You can use the /**R**ange **V**alues command to convert your formulas to values.

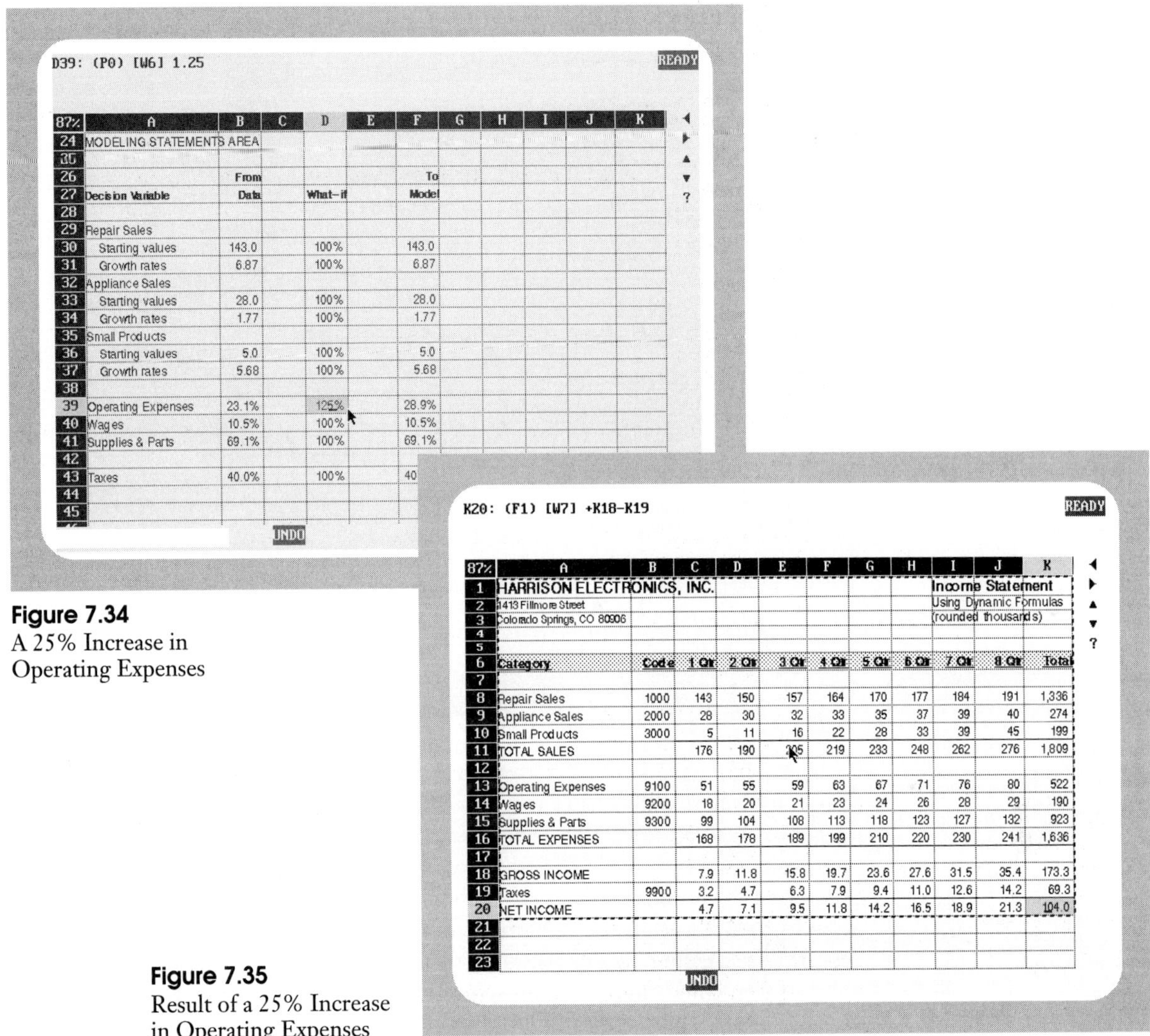

D39: (P0) [W6] 1.25

	A	B	C	D	E	F
24	MODELING STATEMENTS AREA					
25						
26		From				To
27	Decision Variable	Data		What-if		Model
28						
29	Repair Sales					
30	Starting values	143.0		100%		143.0
31	Growth rates	6.87		100%		6.87
32	Appliance Sales					
33	Starting values	28.0		100%		28.0
34	Growth rates	1.77		100%		1.77
35	Small Products					
36	Starting values	5.0		100%		5.0
37	Growth rates	5.68		100%		5.68
38						
39	Operating Expenses	23.1%		125%		28.9%
40	Wages	10.5%		100%		10.5%
41	Supplies & Parts	69.1%		100%		69.1%
42						
43	Taxes	40.0%		100%		40
44						
45						

Figure 7.34
A 25% Increase in Operating Expenses

K20: (F1) [W7] +K18-K19

	A	B	C	D	E	F	G	H	I	J	K
1	HARRISON ELECTRONICS, INC.								Income Statement		
2	1413 Fillmore Street								Using Dynamic Formulas		
3	Colorado Springs, CO 80906								(rounded thousands)		
4											
5											
6	Category	Code	1 Qtr	2 Qtr	3 Qtr	4 Qtr	5 Qtr	6 Qtr	7 Qtr	8 Qtr	Total
7											
8	Repair Sales	1000	143	150	157	164	170	177	184	191	1,336
9	Appliance Sales	2000	28	30	32	33	35	37	39	40	274
10	Small Products	3000	5	11	16	22	28	33	39	45	199
11	TOTAL SALES		176	190	205	219	233	248	262	276	1,809
12											
13	Operating Expenses	9100	51	55	59	63	67	71	76	80	522
14	Wages	9200	18	20	21	23	24	26	28	29	190
15	Supplies & Parts	9300	99	104	108	113	118	123	127	132	923
16	TOTAL EXPENSES		168	178	189	199	210	220	230	241	1,636
17											
18	GROSS INCOME		7.9	11.8	15.8	19.7	23.6	27.6	31.5	35.4	173.3
19	Taxes	9900	3.2	4.7	6.3	7.9	9.4	11.0	12.6	14.2	69.3
20	NET INCOME		4.7	7.1	9.5	11.8	14.2	16.5	18.9	21.3	104.0
21											
22											
23											

Figure 7.35
Result of a 25% Increase in Operating Expenses

As we go back to the modeling statements area, you must change the what-if variable back to its original value and then change another variable. Continue to adjust the variables until you have three or four scenarios to observe.

Which variable is the most sensitive? Although all of the expense variables in your worksheet were increased by 25 percent, the graph in Figure 7.36 shows that by increasing Operating Expenses you will yield a greater negative impact on Net Income. By testing the sensitivity of three expense variables, you can infer that managing Operating Expenses is critical for the success of Harrison Electronics.

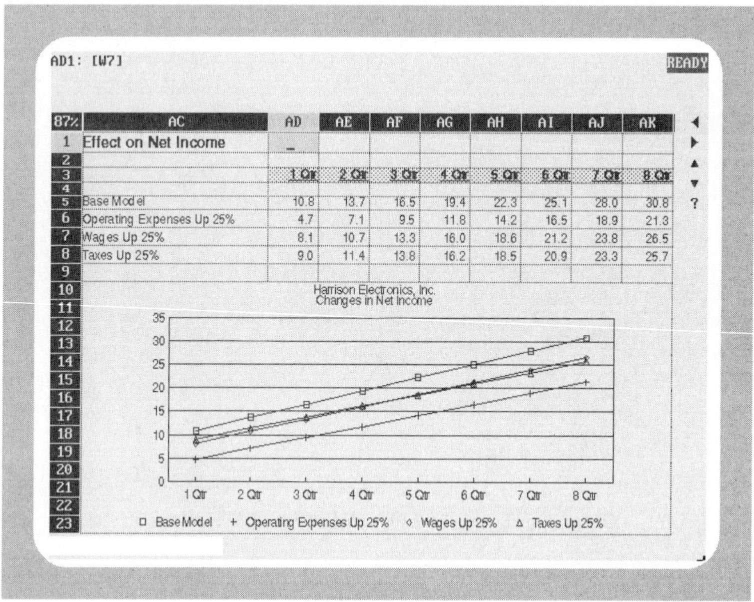

AD1: [W7] READY

Effect on Net Income	1 Qtr	2 Qtr	3 Qtr	4 Qtr	5 Qtr	6 Qtr	7 Qtr	8 Qtr
Base Model	10.8	13.7	16.5	19.4	22.3	25.1	28.0	30.8
Operating Expenses Up 25%	4.7	7.1	9.5	11.8	14.2	16.5	18.9	21.3
Wages Up 25%	8.1	10.7	13.3	16.0	18.6	21.2	23.8	26.5
Taxes Up 25%	9.0	11.4	13.8	16.2	18.5	20.9	23.3	25.7

Figure 7.36
Comparison of Three Scenarios

Deriving Implications from the Analysis

Now that you have an idea of the types of analyses that can be conducted with trends and relationships that you can discover, let's once again address a basic question: *How can we take a block of data, usually presented in tabular format, and figure out what is going on?* Often there may be so much data available that you hardly know where to begin your analysis. Even though it may appear confusing at times, analysis can be equally challenging, posing untold opportunities for uncovering interesting, often unknown relationships between organizational variables. If you could figure out how to improve performance by managing these variables, then your model-building efforts will have been successful.

Before you can make recommendations, you must build your analysis on a firm foundation. Visualize for a minute an oil rig in the middle of the North Sea, as illustrated in Figure 7.37. Notice that the rig is composed of case facts and that the recommendations are hanging over the water by the implications. The purpose of the oil rig is to find and bring in oil. Likewise, you must find and bring in a recommendation that contributes to a quality decision. Too often, analysts make recommendations without having conducted substantial analysis. In other words, they are hanging out over open water without the support of implications drawn from an analysis of the case facts. The oil rig scenario tells you that you must build your analysis on a clear understanding of the case facts. Only when you have conducted an extensive analysis can you answer the question, *What does it all mean?* In other words, you must develop implications from the results of your

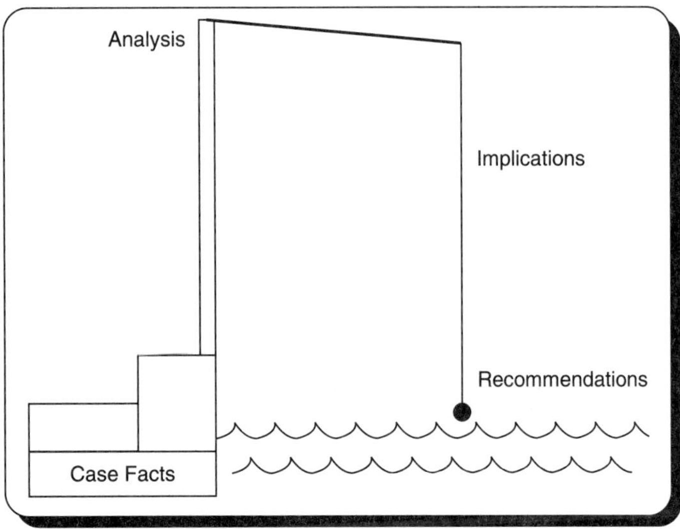

Figure 7.37
"Oil Rig" Approach to Developing Recommendations

analysis prior to making recommendations. Only when the implications are clearly outlined can you dare to put forth your recommendations.

Your recommendations should shed some light on improving bottom-line performance. Ask yourself the question, *What are the performance measures I should concentrate on when developing recommendations?* The bottom-line performance measures that we will discuss can be subdivided into two components: quantitative and qualitative. Both types of performance measures can be built into the models you are developing with Lotus 1-2-3.

Some of the quantitative measures you should consider using in your models include gains in profit, net income, market share, return on equity, or earnings per share. You may want to show impacts on net income, for example, by manipulating such decision variables as sales or operating expenses, or by providing a variety of scenarios to identify sensitive variables. Developing quality programs as a result of information learned through modeling may yield important results, such as lowering overhead or direct costs or reducing lead times for custom product orders.

While qualitative measures are not as easily measurable, they should be analyzed and included in your dynamic models in order to provide added information value to products, show gains in competitive positioning within the industry, or improve business cycles that are susceptible to seasonality. Internal alignment of organizational structure to changing markets may be another area that you can target with dynamic models developed with spreadsheets. You may focus your efforts on objectives such as protecting the firm's assets (which may include information) or the impact of not making critical corporate investments.

The importance of considering bottom-line measures in your analysis, implications, and recommendations cannot be understated in business. The future is uncertain. Ultimately, firms need to perform on bottom-line measures or they will not be in business in future years. You certainly do not want to condense all business decisions to quantitative or monetary terms. You should understand the value of "gut feel" and its relative importance in decision making. Yet many managers have a difficult time making sense of data. Many do not even know where to start; others feel inadequate in interpreting model results. Understanding the costs of doing business is critical to success. Decision models can be used to discover an enterprise's leverage points. Organizational managers can use information generated by decision models to better manage their resources.

Review Questions

1. What is the natural action that managers often take when faced with a business problem?
2. Describe a model. How does a model represent reality?
3. What is the difference between a dynamic model and a mathematical model?
4. Discuss the differences between what-if analysis, goal-seeking analysis, and sensitivity analysis.
5. What are the components of the dynamic model?
6. Describe the two-stage analysis approach to developing a dynamic model. How do the stages differ?
7. What are the advantages and disadvantages of using the simple forecasting techniques to uncover between-column trends?
8. How does the moving average method work?
9. Describe the steps you would go through to use the exponential smoothing technique.
10. What is the importance of the smoothing constant?
11. How does the linear regression technique differ from the other three techniques you may use to uncover between-column trends?
12. Why should you not include the forecast values in the X range when developing a regression?
13. What does the correlation coefficient tell you?
14. How do you determine which forecasting technique is the most accurate in predicting between-column trends?

15. In what way does ratio analysis relate one variable to another in the same column?
16. What additional information does correlational analysis yield over ratio analysis?
17. When you develop your dynamic model, in which cells do you place formulas, and in which cells do you place values?
18. Describe the difference between changes in relationships versus changes in trends.
19. How can a data table be used to conduct what-if analysis?
20. Where must you place the driving formula that calculates values in a two-way table?
21. What is a circular formula, and how can it be effective in conducting Stage 2 analysis?
22. Discuss the different courses of action available when conducting sensitivity analysis.
23. Describe the "oil rig" approach to presenting your analysis results to management.

Skill-Building Activities: Creating the Dynamic Model

Activity 1: Retrieving the Worksheet and Enhancing the Data Area

Use the /**F**ile **R**etrieve command to bring up the Harrison worksheet called HARRIS6. At this point, your worksheet should look similar to the one you left at the end of Chapter 6, as shown in Figure 7.38.

NOTE: To help you with this exercise, boldface letters indicate a message from the system or the worksheet while the commands in the list tell you to make a specific entry.

Before you can build your dynamic model, you will have to conduct Stage 1 analysis on your data area. From Chapter 6 you have a small data area for three categories of sales—four quarters in all. You must now delete the query areas, delete and add columns, and add sales data for Quarters 5–8.

Position the cell pointer on cell A12.

Select the /**W**orksheet **D**elete **R**ow command.

D1: [W10] READY

	A	B	C	D	E	F	G	H
1	HARRISON ELECTRONICS, INC.					Sales Summary Report		
2	1413 Fillmore Street					(rounded thousands)		
3	Colorado Springs, CO 80906							
4								
5	Category	Code		1 Qtr	2 Qtr	3 Qtr	4 Qtr	Total
6	Small Products	3000		5	21	8	79	113
7	Appliance Sales	2000		28	55	19	31	133
8	Repair Sales	1000		143	179	202	164	688
9				---	---	---	---	---
10	TOTAL SALES			176	255	229	274	934
11								
12						<=100	100	0
13						100-300	300	2
14						300-500	500	0
15						500-700	700	1
16								0
17								
18	Category	Code		1 Qtr	2 Qtr	3 Qtr	4 Qtr	Total
19				+D6<=10				
20					+E6<=10			
21						+F6<=10		
22							+G6<=10	

Figure 7.38
Harrison Electronics Worksheet

Move the cell pointer to row 44, and press (ENTER) to confirm.

Move the cell pointer to column C, and delete it (/**W**orksheet **D**elete **C**olumn).

Move the cell pointer to column G (you should be on the Total column).

Select the /**W**orksheet **I**nsert **C**olumn command, and insert four columns.

Add new cell labels in row 5: `"5 Qtr`, `"6 Qtr`, `"7 Qtr`, `"8 Qtr`.

Sort the sales categories using the /**D**ata **S**ort command.

Now it is time to add new sales data for Quarters 5–8. Examine Figure 7.39 and enter the data you see. You must copy your cell underlines and @SUM formula from F10 to the new quarters.

Move the cell pointer to cell F9.

Select the /**C**opy command, and copy the cell underlines and @SUM in cells F9..F10 to cells G9..J10.

Press (ENTER) to confirm the copy.

Finally, you need to add 4 rows under each of the sales categories so that you can conduct Stage 1 analysis and build your forecasts into the worksheet.

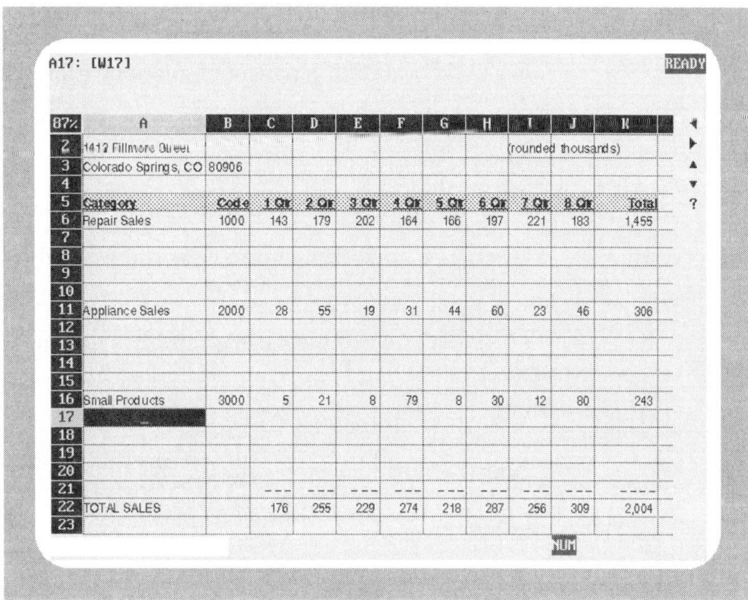

A17: [W17] READY

87%	A	B	C	D	E	F	G	H	I	J	K
2	1412 Fillmore Street								(rounded thousands)		
3	Colorado Springs, CO	80906									
4											
5	Category	Code	1 Qr	2 Qr	3 Qr	4 Qr	5 Qr	6 Qr	7 Qr	8 Qr	Total
6	Repair Sales	1000	143	179	202	164	166	197	221	183	1,455
7											
8											
9											
10											
11	Appliance Sales	2000	28	55	19	31	44	60	23	46	306
12											
13											
14											
15											
16	Small Products	3000	5	21	8	79	8	30	12	80	243
17											
18											
19											
20											
21			---	---	---	---	---	---	---	---	----
22	TOTAL SALES		176	255	229	274	218	287	256	309	2,004
23											

NUM

Figure 7.39
Data Area After Enhancements

Move the cell pointer to row 7.

Use the /**W**orksheet **R**ow **I**nsert command to insert four rows, and press (ENTER).

Move the cell pointer to row 12.

Use the /**W**orksheet **R**ow **I**nsert command to insert four rows, and press (ENTER).

Move the cell pointer to row 17.

Use the /**W**orksheet **R**ow **I**nsert command to insert four rows, and press (ENTER).

Activity 2: Conducting Stage 1 Analysis

Although you can use four different forecasting techniques to analyze between-column trends, you will use the exponential smoothing technique in this activity. To do this, you create a formula that you will use to estimate the data. You will want to use all of the techniques and compare them when you discover variable relationships. You are now ready to conduct your first exponential smoothing formula for Repair Sales. You will place the results of your analysis in row 7.

Move the cell pointer to cell F2, and insert the value `.4` for the smoothing constant.

In cell C7 place the starting value: `+C6`.

In cell D7 place the exponential smoothing formula: `+C7+($F$2*(D6-C7))`.

Format the range D7..J7 by using the /**R**ange **F**ormat **F**ixed with 0 decimal places.

Use the /**C**opy command to copy the formula from D7 to E7..J7.

Use the /**C**opy command to copy the @SUM formula in cell K6 to K7.

You must now copy the exponential smoothing formula in row 7 to rows 12 and 17 so that you can forecast Appliance Sales and Small Products for the eight quarters.

Move the cell pointer to cell C7.

Copy the formula from cells C7..K7 to cell C12 with the /**C**opy command.

Likewise, copy the formula from cells C7..K7 to cell C17.

Now you need to calculate the forecast error for the exponential smoothing forecast. First you will calculate the difference.

Move the cell pointer to cell C8, and enter the formula `+C7-C6`.

Copy the formula from C8 to cells D8..J8 with the /**C**opy command.

Format row 8 with the /**R**ange **F**ormat **F**ixed **0** command.

Now you need to square the difference and sum the squared differences.

Move the cell pointer to cell C9, and enter the formula `+C8^2`.

Copy the formula from cell C9 to D9..J9 with the /**C**opy command.

Format the range C9..J9 with the /**R**ange **F**ormat **F**ixed **0** command.

To sum the differences and squared differences, move the cell pointer to cell K9 and enter the formula `@SUM(C9..J9)`.

Now you need to copy the differences and squared differences to the other two sales categories. To do this, go to cell C8. Use the /**C**opy command to copy range C8..K9 to cell C13.

Likewise, use the /**C**opy command to copy range C8..K9 to cell C18.

At this point, TOTAL SALES makes no sense, since it totals all values in the range 1QTR, and so on. You also need to format the Total column (K) so that the values include a comma.

Move the cell pointer to cell C22, and enter the new formula: `+C6+C11+C16`.

Use the /**C**opy command to copy the new formula from C22 to the range D22..K22.

Move the cell pointer to cell K6.

Use the /**R**ange **F**ormat **F**ixed **0** command to format the range K6..K22.

Your worksheet should look similar to Figure 7.40.

At this point, you have finished entering your formulas with the exponential smoothing technique and have computed the forecast error. In the example, you would expect to find the greatest amount of forecast error in the Repair Sales category, since it has the greater percentage of sales. However, the sharp increases and decreases in sales have provided a large forecast error.

Now you will graph the actual and forecast sales for each sales category. Your line graph will allow for six graph ranges, so you will use the line graph to illustrate the data.

Invoke the graph menu, and set the graph type (/**G**raph **T**ype **L**ine).

Set the X range to C5..J5, the A range to C6..J6, the B range to C7..J7, the C range to C16..J16, and the D range to C17..J17.

View the graph with the **V**iew command.

You may now want to change the smoothing constant to .2 for a smoother line before you examine the changes. Figure 7.41 illustrates the Repair Sales and Small Products.

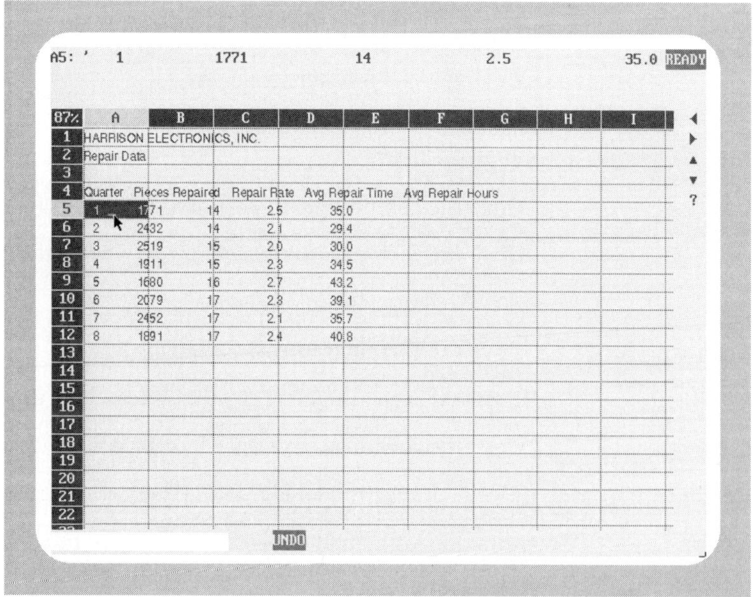

	A	B	C	D	E
1	HARRISON ELECTRONICS, INC.				
2	Repair Data				
3					
4	Quarter	Pieces Repaired	Repair Rate	Avg Repair Time	Avg Repair Hours
5	1	1771	14	2.5	35.0
6	2	2432	14	2.1	29.4
7	3	2519	15	2.0	30.0
8	4	1911	15	2.3	34.5
9	5	1680	16	2.7	43.2
10	6	2079	17	2.3	39.1
11	7	2452	17	2.1	35.7
12	8	1891	17	2.4	40.8

Figure 7.40
Forecast Error Calculations Exponential Smoothing Formula

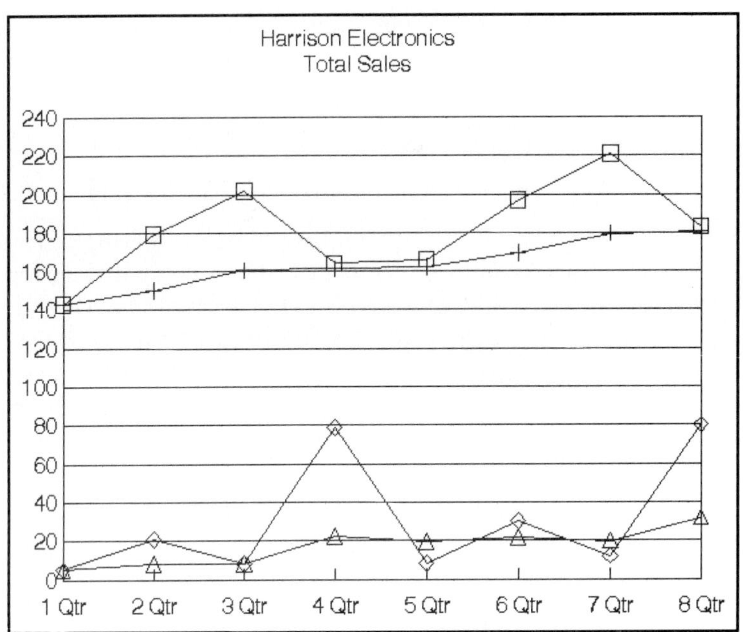

Figure 7.41
Graph of Repair Sales and Small Products a=.2

Activity 3: Building the Dynamic Model

Now you are ready to assemble the dynamic model. To do this, you must first insert some blank rows at the top of the data area. Then you must move the formula-driven rows to the dynamic model area.

Move the cell pointer to cell A4.

Use the /**W**orksheet **I**nsert **R**ow command to insert fifteen blank rows in range A4..A19.

Move the cell pointer to A21, and copy the labels from row 21 to row 5.

Move the formulas in row 23 to row 7 with the /**M**ove command.

In cell A7 type the label `Repair Sales`.

Move the formulas in row 28 to row 8.

In cell A8, type the label `Appliance Sales`.

Move the formulas in row 33 to row 9.

In cell A9 type the label `Small Products Sales`.

To complete your small dynamic model, you must add a new Total row.

In cell A11 type `TOTAL`.

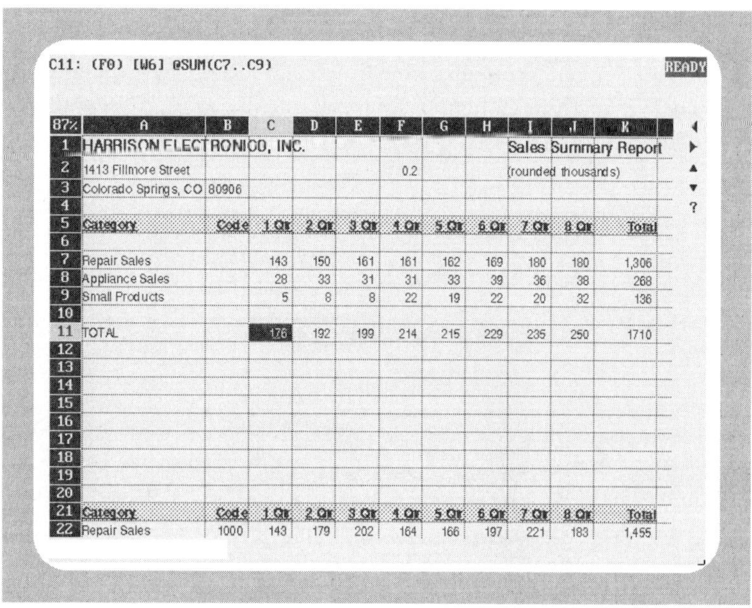

C11: (F0) [W6] @SUM(C7..C9) READY

87%	A	B	C	D	E	F	G	H	I	J	K
1	HARRISON ELECTRONICCO, INC.								Sales Summary Report		
2	1413 Fillmore Street					0.2			(rounded thousands)		
3	Colorado Springs, CO	80906									
4											
5	Category	Code	1 Qr	2 Qr	3 Qr	4 Qr	5 Qr	6 Qr	7 Qr	8 Qr	Total
6											
7	Repair Sales		143	150	161	161	162	169	180	180	1,306
8	Appliance Sales		28	33	31	31	33	39	36	38	268
9	Small Products		5	8	8	22	19	22	20	32	136
10											
11	TOTAL		176	192	199	214	215	229	235	250	1710
12											
13											
14											
15											
16											
17											
18											
19											
20											
21	Category	Code	1 Qr	2 Qr	3 Qr	4 Qr	5 Qr	6 Qr	7 Qr	8 Qr	Total
22	Repair Sales	1000	143	179	202	164	166	197	221	183	1,455

Figure 7.42
Building the Dynamic Model

In cell C11 enter the formula `@SUM(C7..C9)`.

Use the /**C**opy command to copy the formula across the row.

To format the row, use /**R**ange **F**ormat **F**ixed **0**.

Your worksheet should now resemble the one illustrated in Figure 7.42.

Activity 4: Conducting Stage 2 Analysis

In this activity, you will use the data table to conduct what-if analysis on the data, varying the smoothing constant to observe the change in Total Sales. First you must fill the data range that will contain the smoothing constant variable changes.

Use the /**D**ata **F**ill command to fill the range E14..E19 with smoothing-constant values.

Enter `.2` for the start value and `.1` for the step value.

Go to cell F13, and enter the formula `+K11`.

Format the formula cell with the /**R**ange **F**ormat **T**ext command.

Now you are ready to conduct your what-if analysis on the data.

Invoke the data table command (/**D**ata **T**able **1**).

Set the table range as E13..F19 and the input cell as K11.

Format the range F14..F19 with the /**R**ange **F**ormat **F**ixed **0** command.

You have now finished building your dynamic model. Figure 7.43 illustrates the completed model. Compare your results against this model, and save it as HARRIS7.WK1.

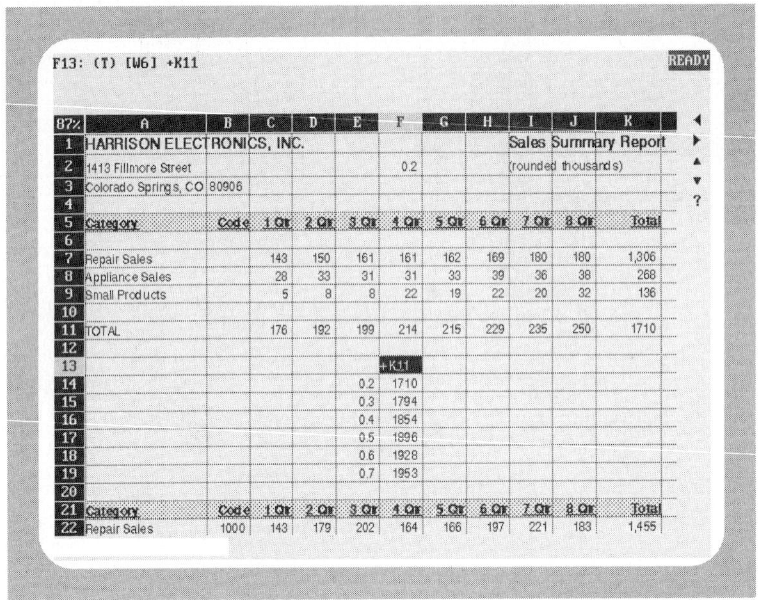

Figure 7.43
Creating a Data Table

Hands-On Exercises

1. Enter the following data into two columns of cells, starting in cell A21:

1	1200	7	1800
2	1400	8	2000
3	1600	9	2100
4	1700	10	2400
5	1850	11	2450
6	1900	12	2600

2. Create a line graph, using the values 1–12 as the X range and the data entered in exercise 1 as the A range.

3. Use column C to calculate the percentage change in the data.

4. Average the average percentage change, and use it to predict the data from period 1 through period 16. Use column D for your forecast and a starting value of 1200 in period 1.
5. Add the average percentage change forecast to the graph as the B range. Label your legend.
6. Develop the exponential smoothing formula (column E), starting in period 2 and carrying it down to period 12. Use a starting value of 1200 in period 1 and the following formula:

   Prior period forecast + (smoothing constant * (current period value – prior period forecast))

7. Calculate the change (not the percentage change) in the exponential smoothing constant in column F.
8. Average the change values in column F from period 2 through period 12. Use the average to forecast the data for periods 13–16.
9. Add the exponential smoothing line to your graph as the C range. Label your legend.
10. Run a linear regression model, using the values 1–12 as the X range and the data as the Y range. Place the regression output in cell A41.
11. Use the regression formula `y=mx+b` to create "predicted values" for periods 1–16.
12. Add the linear regression line to your graph as the D range. Label your legend.

Problem-Solving Projects

1. Create a data area, starting in cell A41, for Stillwater Bottling that captures the following data:

Year	Gross Income	Expenses
1978	342,000	242,000
1979	344,000	237,000
1980	351,000	253,000
1981	349,000	251,000
1982	382,000	263,000
1983	385,000	279,000

Year	Gross Income	Expenses
1984	387,000	278,000
1985	401,000	281,000
1986	404,000	279,000
1987	417,000	296,000
1988	413,000	297,000
1989	423,000	294,000
1990	430,000	301,000
1991	433,000	307,000
1992	445,000	309,000

Place the Year in column A, the Gross Income in column B, and the Expenses in column C.

2. Calculate the average percentage change in Gross Income for 1978–1992. Use column D to calculate the percentage change. Average the percentage change and use the percentage to calculate the forecast for years 1978–1996. Use $342,000 in 1978. Place the forecast in column E.
3. Calculate the three-year moving average in Gross Income for 1978–1992. Use column F to calculate the moving average. Compute the change (not the percentage) and place it in column G. Average the change and use the average to project the Gross Income for 1994–1996.
4. Calculate the exponential smoothing formula in Gross Income for 1978–1992 with a smoothing constant of .4. Use column H to calculate the exponential smoothing formula. Use $342,000 in 1978. Calculate the change (not the average) for each year and place it in column I. Average the change, and use the average to project the Gross Income for 1993–1996.
5. Calculate the linear regression equation in Gross Income for 1978–1992. Use column A for the X coefficient and column B for the Y coefficient, and place the predicted Y value for 1978–1996 in column J.
6. Develop a single-line graph for the actual Gross Income and for each of the four modeling techniques. Be sure to label your axes and each line as legends.
7. Insert two columns between each of the forecasting techniques. Use the columns to calculate the difference between the forecast and the actual data, and the squared differences. Sum the squared differences for each technique.
8. Which technique produces the best line?

9. Calculate the ratio of expenses to gross income for each year. Use column S to show your ratios. Can you detect a trend? What are the lower and upper ranges of the ratios?
10. Use correlation analysis to analyze the ratios. What is the R^2 value? Is it acceptable? Does it corroborate the ratio analysis?
11. Build the modeling statements area for your worksheet.
12. Develop a dynamic model (starting in cell A1), using your best forecast and the average of the ratios (expenses/gross income). Add another variable to your dynamic model:

    `Net Sales = Gross Sales - Expenses.`
13. Conduct a Stage 2 analysis for the Stillwater Bottling data. Consider the following independent questions:

    What if the expenses (percent of Gross Sales) rose by 10 percent?

    What if Gross Income (starting value in 1978) declined by 10 percent?
14. Conduct Stage 2 what-if analysis on your dynamic model, addressing the same questions. To do this, set up a two-way what-if data table (in cell A81) to assess the simultaneous impact of a decrease in Gross Income and an increase in Expenses on Net Sales.

    Decision variables:

    Gross Income (Input Cell #1) - 95%, 90%, 85%, 80%, 75%
    Expenses (Input Cell #2) - 105%, 110%, 115%, 120%, 125%

    Objective variable:

    Net Sales (Table will calculate automatically.)
15. Print out a copy of (1) the dynamic model, (2) the raw data area, (3) the new data area containing relationships, and (4) the two-way data table.

Quality-Assurance Checklist

As we conclude our discussion of modeling techniques, be sure you have considered the following factors that contribute to the quality of your worksheet:

✓ When building the dynamic model, use a two-stage analysis approach. The first stage of analysis enables you to discover model relationships, and the second stage gives you a better understanding of the impact of the variables on the bottom line.

- ✓ To compute the simple average, multiply the previous value by the average change.
- ✓ Remember that the larger the average change in a variable, the greater the bias in the forecast line.
- ✓ Determine the number of periods in the moving average by the nature of the data.
- ✓ If there is stability in the change figure when using the moving average or exponential smoothing technique, use the most recent value; otherwise use the average.
- ✓ Remember that the greater the number of periods in the moving average, the smoother the resulting moving average line.
- ✓ Remember that the smaller the smoothing constant, the less variance in the line and the smoother the forecast.
- ✓ Be sure to have as many data points as possible when running a regression; otherwise you can use the technique in a confirmatory manner.
- ✓ Remember to not include the forecast area in the X range when setting up linear regression ranges.
- ✓ Use more than one between-column technique so that you can compare the results and choose the most appropriate one.
- ✓ Always calculate forecast error to check the validity of each between-column technique.
- ✓ Select the technique that best fits the data and that contains the lowest forecast error.
- ✓ Because ratios relate one variable to another, do not expect a "correct" value; instead, compare the changes in a ratio across time.
- ✓ Remember that ratios can be misleading when seasonality is present.
- ✓ Use correlation analysis to confirm ratio findings.
- ✓ Use XY plots in conjunction with correlation analysis to analyze the strength of the relationship between two variables.
- ✓ Remember that formulas for the first period in the dynamic model pull values directly out of the data area.
- ✓ Make references to growth rates in the data area mixed or absolute so that they do not change when you copy them to subsequent periods.
- ✓ Be sure that you understand the difference between changes in relationships versus changes in trends.

✓ As an option, use the /**D**ata **T**able command to conduct what-if analysis on one or two variables.

✓ Leave blank the upper-left cell of the one-way data table.

✓ Be sure that the driving formula that calculates values in the two-way table is placed in the intersection of the two variables.

✓ When saving the results of different what-if scenarios for graphing, use the /**R**ange **V**alues command to convert formulas to values.

CHAPTER

8 Developing the User Interface with Macros

Some things have to be seen to be believed.

—S. Harward

Some things have to be believed to be seen.

—Roalf Hodgson

Objectives

- Understand the role of the user interface in decision support systems.
- Understand macros and the development process.
- Use macros to save keystrokes and to develop the user interface.
- Customize menus to enhance the worksheet.
- Use advanced macro commands to filter out complexity.
- Branch and loop with macros.

The User Interface in Decision Support Systems

In previous chapters we have discussed two of the three components that a decision support system must contain: the database and the model base. We will now explore the third component: the user interface, illustrated in Figure 8.1. The **user interface** is the component responsible for all interaction and communication between the application and the decision maker.

One primary goal of the user interface is to make the technical and complex attributes of the spreadsheet understandable to the decision maker. The user interface presents the DSS output, controls the DSS operation by allowing you to select from a custom menu, and adds flexibility to your input so that you can create a variety of scenarios. The user interface provides the coordination between the Lotus 1-2-3 program, the database, and the model base. In this chapter we will talk about building the user interface by using macros. You will use advanced macro commands to provide a custom menu and other commands so that the decision makers who use your spreadsheets do not need to understand the complexities of using Lotus 1-2-3.

Until now, you have created decision support systems by building dynamic models and setting up data areas without using macros to customize your

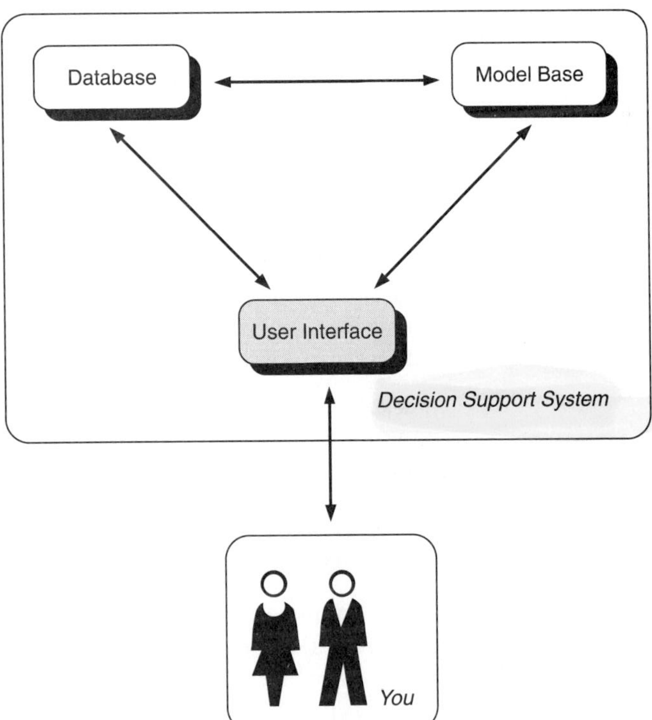

Figure 8.1
Components of a Decision Support System

worksheets. One reason for this is that you developed the applications for your own use. You have relied on your own knowledge of the Lotus 1-2-3 program to operate the model and conduct your analyses. Development of the same dynamic models becomes more difficult, however, when you are developing them for use by someone else.

The user interface makes the application more accessible to other users. The worksheet development effort becomes even more complex when you know in advance that the application will have multiple users—all of them having different degrees of competency with Lotus 1-2-3. In that case, you must build into the user interface not only a structure of nested menus but also shortcuts for more sophisticated users.

Several issues must be addressed before you develop the user interface:

HINT: Always develop your data area and dynamic model before you develop the user interface.

- When faced with a new business problem, always design the dynamic models before even considering the user interface. Developing the macros and the dynamic models simultaneously is one of the mistakes that developers make most often. Be sure that both the database and model base are working before you consider macro development. Define the data areas and then conduct both stages of the two-stage analysis to be sure your model works effectively.
- Design screens and menus that allow decision makers to make choices. Then, based on their choice, you will be moved to another menu or area of the worksheet, or a variable will be calculated based upon input.
- Try each menu selection or entry in order to completely test the effectiveness of the user interface. The rule here is to expect the unexpected.
- Consider providing decision diagrams within the user interface. Decision trees are good examples of screens that you can provide from the custom menu. Decision trees lay out the structure of the problem, or of a piece of the problem, that you are trying to solve. When developing the user interface in Lotus 1-2-3, you will find it helpful to think of screens as program modules.

HINT: Use the same user interface when developing different applications.

- When developing several related or different applications, use the same user interface dialogs, menu structures, and screens. In addition to having menus and screens, the decision maker should be able to print a number of reports that are either extracted directly from screens that he or she is viewing or that are put together in an area of the worksheet that the user does not see.
- Graphic illustrations should be available for any data set the decision maker needs to see. Graphs can include any range in any dynamic model in the worksheet. Good graphs are critical to the decision support system, since many managers state they are "visually oriented."

Graph options can be incorporated into any menu and then executed with a macro, all behind the scenes.

- The decision maker must be allowed to change critical data which will affect potential solutions and which will contribute to an overall understanding of the problem under investigation. When we develop our worksheet, we should be careful to protect areas of the dynamic model that must not be altered. The **/R**ange **P**rotect command is useful in sheltering areas that contain sensitive formulas and data.

Macros

A **macro** is a set of commands that instructs Lotus 1-2-3 to execute a series of keystrokes or perform a specific task. The tilde (~) is used to represent the ENTER key. The following list of Lotus 1-2-3 keystrokes can be simulated with macro commands:

Lotus Keystroke	Macro Equivalent	Lotus Keystroke	Macro Equivalent
ENTER	~	F1	{HELP}
→ ←	{RIGHT} {LEFT}	F2	{EDIT}
↑ ↓	{UP} {DOWN}	F3	{NAME}
PGDN	{PGDN}	F4	{ABS}
PGUP	{PGUP}	F5	{GOTO}
BACKSPACE	{BS}	F6	{WINDOW}
ESC	{ESC}	F7	{QUERY}
HOME	{HOME}	F8	{TABLE}
END	{END}	F9	{CALC}
INS	{INS}	F10	{GRAPH}
DELETE	{DEL}	ALT F6	{ZOOM}*
CTRL ←	{BIGLEFT}	ALT F7	{APP1}
CTRL →	{BIGRIGHT}	ALT F8	{APP2}
First File	{FF}	ALT F9	{APP3}
Last File	{LF}*	ALT F10	{ADD-IN}
Prev Sheet	{PS}*	File (CTRL END)	{FILE}*
Next Sheet	{NS}*		
First Cell	{FC}*		
Last Cell	{LC}*		

*available in Version 3.1 and 1.1 for Windows

There is a prescribed area in every worksheet for macros, as we identified in Chapter 5. The southeast quadrant of each worksheet is reserved for macros. Macros occupy three adjacent columns and are separated by blank cells to indicate the end of one macro and the beginning of another. The first column identifies the macro name, the second lists the macro commands, and the third describes the macro. Macros are written, stored, and executed vertically within a single column. In conjunction with macros, menus are positioned in the northeast quadrant of the worksheet. Menus differ from macros in that they are developed horizontally in a series of rows. Every individual macro and menu must be named.

Like all programs, macros must be developed using sound logic. Program development usually follows the **systems development life cycle**, which contains four steps: 1) planning, 2) design, 3) implementation, and 4) testing. Macro development is no different. The user interface needs careful planning—the phase most often overlooked. We all go through each of the development steps whether we realize it or not. It is better to explicitly plan for and effectively execute each activity. We will use the Harrison Electronics database in Figure 8.2 to sort Pieces Repaired in descending order from highest to lowest. We will develop our macros using the activities in the systems development life cycle.

Development Phase	Activity
Planning	1. Identify the task to be accomplished. 2. Outline the keystrokes or macro commands needed to carry out the task. 3. Map out the macro module, from start to finish.
Design	1. Enter the keystrokes and/or macro commands. 2. Divide logical keystrokes or macro commands into separate cells. 3. Name each macro. 4. Document each macro command in the module.
Implementation	1. Save the worksheet. 2. Run the macro using the appropriate (ALT) command.
Testing	1. Test the functioning of each macro individually. 2. Debug the macro if necessary.

Macro Development: Planning Phase

HINT: Good planning of the user interface saves time.

The planning phase is very important to effective development and when properly conducted will save time in the phases that follow. It is here that productivity of the worksheet can be exponentially increased. First, the task that must be accomplished should be carefully outlined. Too often, we take on multiple tasks rather than a single, simple task. This creates a problem because then we have a difficult time conceptualizing the types of macro commands that will accomplish the tasks. Second, the Lotus keystrokes or macro commands need to be outlined prior to their entry. All recent versions of Lotus 1-2-3 have a Learn facility which is useful for recording keystrokes. The **LEARN mode** can be switched on by using the ALT-F5 key combination, which acts as a toggle. When the LEARN mode is on, the mode indicator displays the message "LEARN" on the bottom line of the screen. Use the /**W**orksheet **L**earn **R**ange command to specify the range which will be used to record the keystrokes. There are four steps to using the LEARN function in Lotus, as follows:

1. Specify the learn range.
2. Turn on the LEARN mode by pressing the ALT-F5 keys.
3. Record the keystrokes.
4. Turn off the LEARN mode by pressing the ALT-F5 keys.

HINT: Remember to turn off the LEARN function to stop recording your keystrokes.

Consider working through the planning activities on paper rather than going directly to the computer. Often preliminary ideas and thoughts can be worked through most effectively on a yellow pad before proceeding to the computer, although the LEARN function can be useful in replaying the keystrokes that need to be captured within a specific macro. If you record more keystrokes than you intended, you can edit the macro with the F2 key.

Macro Development: Design Phase

The design phase acts on the results of the planning phase. The first activity of the design phase is to enter the Lotus keystrokes and/or macro commands into the macro area of the worksheet. Laying out complex macro blocks can be accomplished more effectively with a structure chart. **Structure charts** are diagrams which hierarchically display program modules, showing links between modules as data or control flows. Structure charts are an integral part of every system designer's toolkit. When we have more than one macro block, structure charts are useful for illustrating complex interrelationships. It is very important to lay out how all of the blocks will fit together before attempting to code the macro blocks. A **block or module** is a set of macro code which carries out related activities and is located in the same area. Remember that we can execute one macro command after another until we reach a blank cell. The group of macro commands between the blank cells is a block or module.

HINT: A blank cell marks the end of the macro.

The structure chart has only a few components: the rectangular box depicts a macro module, and an arrow with a tail indicates a data flow. The data flow should be named so as to indicate what data a module needs in order to do its processing. We will use structure charts later in this chapter. A structure chart illustrates a program hierarchy similar to the organizational chart.

Once Lotus 1-2-3 keystrokes, macro commands, and the interactions between macro modules are identified, the developer can begin entering the macros into the macro area. Here are some guidelines to entering macros. Macros are entered as labels in consecutive cells within a single column. The only exception to these guidelines is the macro menu, which requires up to seven columns, one for each menu command. Since many of the macros that are entered involve

HINT: Enter labels in consecutive cells within a single column.

HINT: Macros that begin with a /, \, or numeric symbol must begin with a '.

the slash (/) key, from which the Lotus command menu is invoked, the macros must be built as labels. We must use a label prefix (') when the macro in question begins with a slash (/), backslash (\), or numeric symbol.

In general, we want to divide logical keystrokes or macro commands into different cells for easier reading and debugging. A macro command that is enclosed in braces { } must be placed in the same cell. Macros can be typed in either upper- or lowercase. Macros continue to execute until they reach a blank cell or a cell value (nonlabel), or until the {QUIT} command is used. Blank cells are the most common way to terminate a macro.

HINT: Name the first cell only of the macro block.

Before we can run our macros, we must name the first cell of our macro block. Macro names, like all other range names, can contain up to 15 characters. Be careful not to duplicate any other range names. There are 26 special macro names which should be reserved for macros that you want to execute directly from the keyboard with the (ALT) key. These special macros names consist of a backslash (\) followed by a single letter A through Z. Macro names that incorporate two words, such as ACCT_REC, must be connected with an underscore symbol (_). All macro blocks, whether part of the main macro or a subroutine which was called, must be named.

Macro Development: Implementation Phase

HINT: Save your macro before running it.

At this point, you will be ready to run your macro. Before you do however, you should save your worksheet so that you do not experience significant difficulties. This routine of saving before running macros must become second nature. Otherwise you may find that the macro will change your worksheet, damaging it in some way. The risks you will encounter when the worksheet is damaged could be catastrophic, and you may not be able to recover all of your recent work.

You can now run your worksheet macros in one of two ways. If you have named the macro with the backslash key (\) and one letter, you could invoke it using the (ALT) key followed by the letter. Second, the RUN function key combination, (ALT)-(F3), coupled with the NAME function key, (F3), displays a listing of all range names in the worksheet, allowing the user to execute any macro regardless of its name. (CTRL)-(BREAK) can be used to cancel a macro while it is running. After interrupting a macro, press (ESC) or (ENTER) to clear the error message and return to the 1-2-3 READY mode. One word of caution here: if you interrupt your macro, you will be in the middle of accomplishing some task in your worksheet. Depending on the task, you must reset counters and variables, such as a counter for an @IF function.

Macro Development: Testing Phase

HINT: If you use (CTRL)-(BREAK) to interrupt a macro, check your worksheet to reset all counters and variables.

Before you put a macro into production, you must test its functioning under a variety of conditions. You should input a diversity of data, testing both the high and low extremes. This is one area that developers sometimes neglect, thereby putting their worksheet at risk. Should an error be found in the macro, you will want to debug it. **Debugging** is a systems term which means to find and eliminate program errors. There are two ways to debug macros. The first is to use the

HINT: When debugging a macro using (ALT)-(F2), the word STEP appears in the status indicator area.

debug feature in Lotus 1-2-3, which can be invoked using the (ALT)-(F2) keys. When the debug feature is invoked, the word **STEP** appears in the status indicator area. The space bar is used to "step" through each line of the macro. To stop stepping through the macro once an error is found, use the (CTRL)-(BREAK) keys to terminate the debugging procedure.

The use of the (ALT)-(F2) keys for debugging can be tedious and time consuming when macros are large or complex. Alternatively, consider inserting a blank row at various points in the macro to force its termination and evaluate whether the shortened macro runs correctly or is halted with an error. You want to start close to the beginning of the macro and work down until you are satisfied that the macro works correctly. Blank cells may get at the problem more efficiently than stepping through a large macro in its entirety.

HINT: Too many or missing tildes are the most common macro error.

One of the most common errors includes missing tildes (simulating the (ENTER) key) or including too many tildes in the macro command. This type of problem creates situations that can be the most difficult to problem solve. The program expects an (ENTER) keystroke at the end of a sequence and instead receives another instruction. Other errors that occur frequently include incorrect cell references, which were discussed in the material on formula building (Chapter 4), insertion of extra spaces where they are not needed, branches to other macro subroutines, and failure to name one or more macros. Since each macro should be developed and tested independently, module links should be the final tests to be conducted to ensure integration.

There are four useful keys that support each of the development phases. The (ALT) key combined with (F2) through (F5) allows us to accomplish several tasks, as shown below. Each of these keys and associated tasks will be discussed as we work through the Harrison Electronics case.

Key	Purpose	Phase Supported	Description
(ALT)-(F2)	STEP	Testing	Allows you to debug the macro.
(ALT)-(F3)	RUN	Implementation	Runs the macro; can be used in conjunction with the (F3) (Name) key to select the macro you wish to run.
(ALT)-(F4)	UNDO	Implementation	Used to reverse the running of a macro.
(ALT)-(F5)	LEARN	Design	Creates a macro by recording keystrokes in a LEARN range in the worksheet.

Working with a Simple Macro

There are two reasons why we use macros: 1) to store command keystrokes so that they can be retrieved later, and 2) to develop the user interface. Storing command keystrokes is useful when the decision maker has to rekey 1-2-3 commands that are repetitive. This type of macro is extremely useful when entering functions such as printing or formatting or creating a range. Macros that store keystrokes provide the measure of *efficiency* from Lotus 1-2-3 by speeding up worksheet development and operations. The second type of macro, however, adds an extra level of *effectiveness* by enhancing the worksheet, in essence, making it possible to do things we could not do before with the Lotus menus. We will discuss both types of macros which are valuable for the development of the user interface.

The first type of macro consists of those commands that include Lotus 1-2-3 keystrokes, that is, those commands that start with a slash (/) or colon (:) for WYSIWYG commands and are followed by the first letter of the menu item. For Harrison Electronics, we will develop a macro that will name and sort a range. The database is illustrated in Figure 8.2. Repair Rate is average repair rate charged for the quarter; Avg Repair Time indicates the average amount of time it took to repair an applicance; while Avg Repair Hours is a field calculated by multiplying Repair Rate by Repair Hours, in essence yielding average total dollars per piece of equipment repaired. Remember that when using the **/D**ata **S**ort command, you must set at least two parameters: the data range and the primary key. A secondary key may be needed when there is repeating data in the data area of the primary key field. For future use, we will use the **/R**ange **N**ame command to set up the data area and then we will sort it by Pieces Repaired. The Lotus keystrokes that we will need to sort the database include:

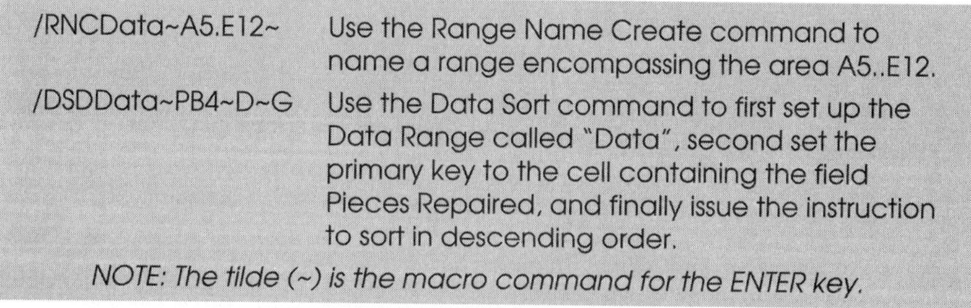

/RNCData~A5.E12~	Use the Range Name Create command to name a range encompassing the area A5..E12.
/DSDData~PB4~D~G	Use the Data Sort command to first set up the Data Range called "Data", second set the primary key to the cell containing the field Pieces Repaired, and finally issue the instruction to sort in descending order.

NOTE: The tilde (~) is the macro command for the ENTER key.

Name the upper left cell in the macro area MACROS. Remember, we are naming the first cell of the macro command column. In Figure 8.3 the first column

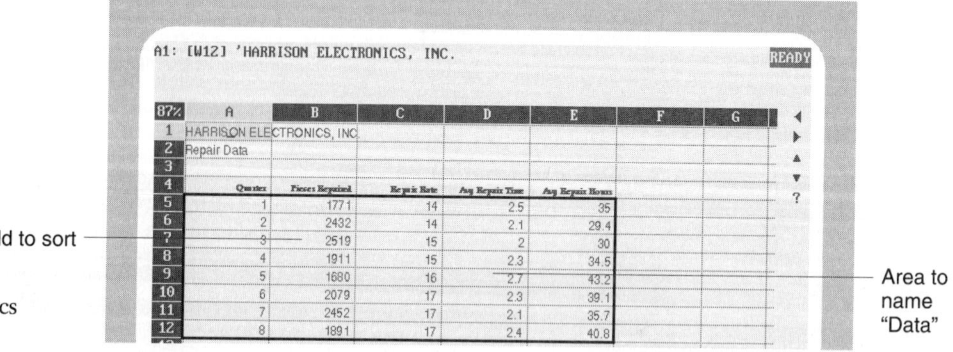

A1: [W12] 'HARRISON ELECTRONICS, INC. READY

87%	A	B	C	D	E	F	G
1	HARRISON ELECTRONICS, INC						
2	Repair Data						
3							
4	Quarter	Pieces Repaired	Repair Rate	Avg Repair Time	Avg Repair Hours		
5	1	1771	14	2.5	35		
6	2	2432	14	2.1	29.4		
7	3	2519	15	2	30		
8	4	1911	15	2.3	34.5		
9	5	1680	16	2.7	43.2		
10	6	2079	17	2.3	39.1		
11	7	2452	17	2.1	35.7		
12	8	1891	17	2.4	40.8		

Figure 8.2
Harrison Electronics Repair Data

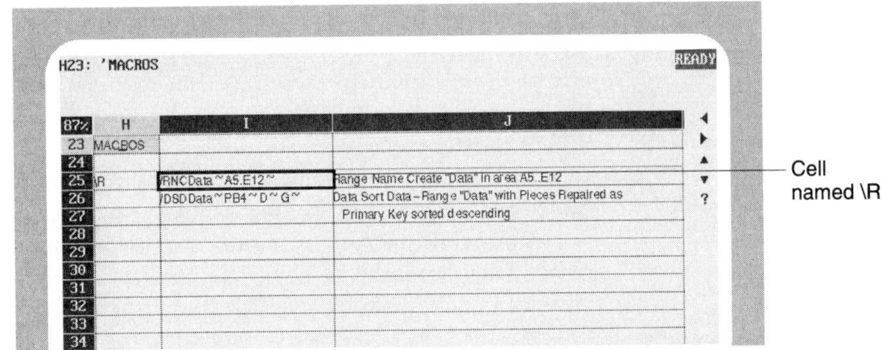

Figure 8.3
Keystroke Macros to Name and Sort Data Range

displays the range name (\R) for the macro, yet this cell is not named; rather, cell I25 is named \R. Be sure to document the macro's range name and macro commands. This is done in the third column, next to the macro commands. The column containing macro commands should be quite wide so that the macros can easily be seen. But do not worry about cutting off the macro commands from the worksheet view. In our example, we named our macro \R, so we can invoke our macro by using the ALT-R keys. Or we can use the ALT-F3 key combination and select \R from the menu of available macros. The results of our macro, displayed in Figure 8.4, show the records reorganized in descending order by Pieces Repaired.

HINT: Always name the upper left cell of your macro area MACROS.

Developing Custom Menus

Custom menus provide the overall packaging for the user interface. Although not critical for the effective operation of the worksheet, **custom menus** make the Lotus commands and procedures transparent to the user by replacing traditional Lotus 1-2-3 menus. Custom menus also limit the choices a user can make, moving

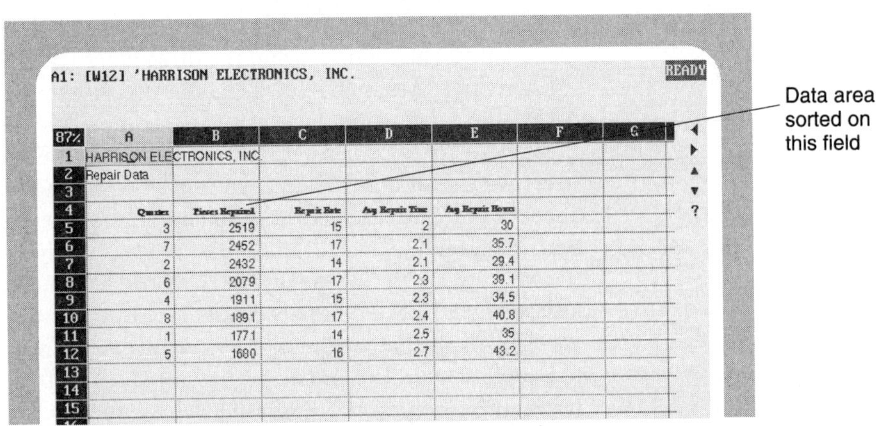

Quarter	Pieces Repaired	Repair Rate	Avg Repair Time	Avg Repair Hours
3	2519	15	2	30
7	2452	17	2.1	35.7
2	2432	14	2.1	29.4
6	2079	17	2.3	39.1
4	1911	15	2.3	34.5
8	1891	17	2.4	40.8
1	1771	14	2.5	35
5	1680	16	2.7	43.2

Figure 8.4
Results of the Name and Sort Macros

away from some of the keyboard errors we just talked about earlier in this chapter. Macro menus work in the same way in which the standard 1-2-3 menus operate, using the top lines of the spreadsheet screen. Up to eight menu items can be made available to worksheet users. Menu selections should each begin with a different letter so the user can either move the cursor to the appropriate item or type the first letter of the menu item. Descriptions of the menu item will appear under each selection so the user will know its function.

HINT: Advanced macros must be placed in braces with arguments separated by commas.

Advanced macro commands are instructions that perform built-in functions. They are indicated by a macro keyword enclosed within braces { }. All advanced macro commands must contain braces around the command, a space between the keyword and first argument, and a comma following each argument (except the final one). Advanced macro commands must begin and end in the same cell. Each cell can hold up to 240 characters and may hold more than one advanced macro command.

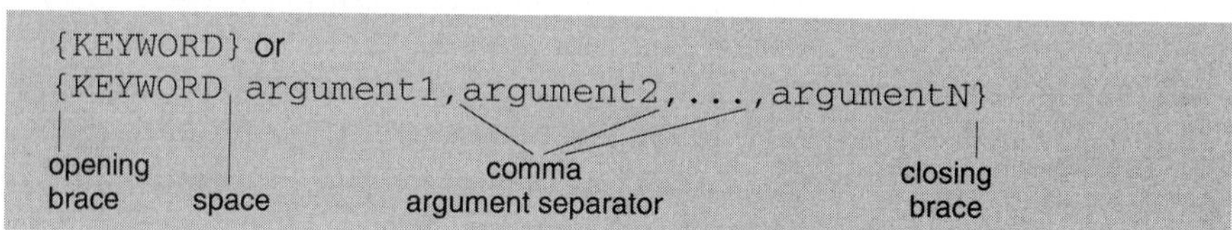

There are two advanced macro commands which can be used to set up custom Lotus menus: {MENUBRANCH} and {MENUCALL}. The {MENUBRANCH} keyword displays a custom menu in the control panel, waits for the user to select a menu item, and then branches to the macro instructions associated with the selected menu item. In contrast the {MENUCALL} keyword performs a subroutine call to the macro instructions and then executes the next instruction upon returning from the subroutine call.

Creating a Simple Custom Menu

Addressing the same task we had earlier, we will create a custom menu to allow the user to choose which of the three fields he or she wants to format. Figure 8.5 illustrates the menu macro and the three macro modules which actually carry out the activities. Alternatively, we could use either the {GET LABEL} or {GET NUMBER} command, however these commands are not as effective.

There are four menu items: Rate, Time, Hours, and Quit. Each menu item starts with a different letter. Do not be concerned that the menu descriptions appear to run into each other. Remember, each cell can contain up to 240 characters. At the end of each of the FOR_ macros in Figure 8.5, control is returned to the main menu with the {BRANCH \M} statement. Without this feature, the user may get lost in the main Lotus 1-2-3 program.

We invoked the menu by pressing ALT-M. The custom menu appears on the top of the screen. We should pause a moment to discuss the importance of always using \M to name the highest-level menu in a hierarchy. If the novice user

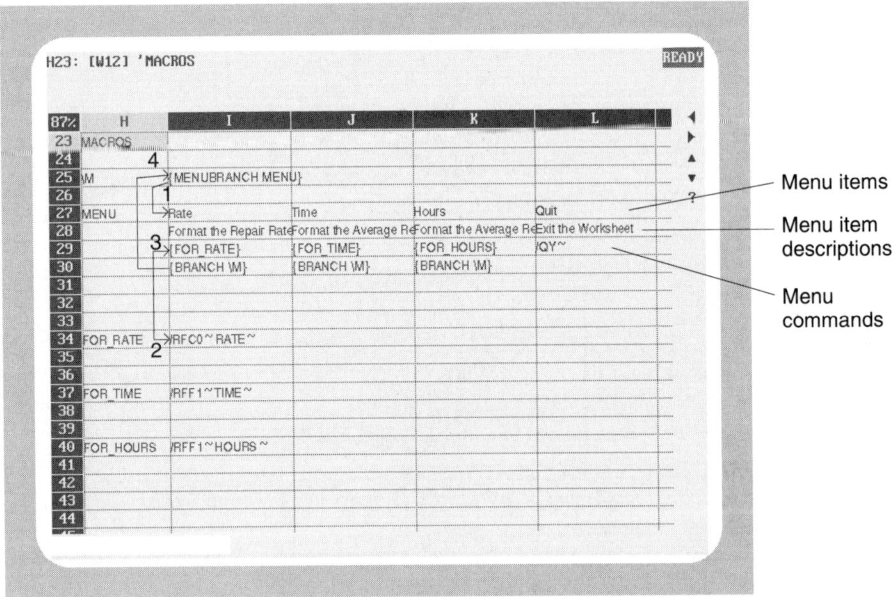

Figure 8.5
Simple Custom Menu for Formatting a Range

HINT: (ALT)-(M) is the user's SOS in case s(he) gets lost.

accidentally presses the (ESC) key or if the macro has an error, for some reason, the user will be left in the Lotus program. This must be avoided at all costs. The (ALT)-(M) keys are considered to be the user's SOS. Whenever the user gets "lost" in the Lotus 1-2-3 program, (ALT)-(M) provides the life-saving measures needed to return to the custom menus. The command {BRANCH \M} at the end of each menu item macro instructs the macro to bring back the custom menu.

Let us examine the execution of the menu macro statements. First, by pressing (ALT)-(M), we are given the custom menu in Figure 8.6. Assuming we select "Rate", the program then executes the {FOR_RATE} module. The program then formats the range named "rate" as currency with 0 decimal places. Upon completion,

Custom menu

A1: [W12] 'HARRISON ELECTRONICS, INC.

MENU

Rate Time Hours Quit
Format the Repair Rate

HARRISON ELECTRONICS, INC
Repair Data

Quarter	Pieces Repaired	Repair Rate	Avg Repair Time	Avg Repair Hours
3	2519	$15	2.0	30.0
7	2452	$17	2.1	35.7
2	2432	$14	2.1	29.4
6	2079	$17	2.3	39.1
4	1911	$15	2.3	34.5
8	1891	$17	2.4	40.8
1	1771	$14	2.5	35.0
5	1680	$16	2.7	43.2

Figure 8.6
Execution of Custom Menu

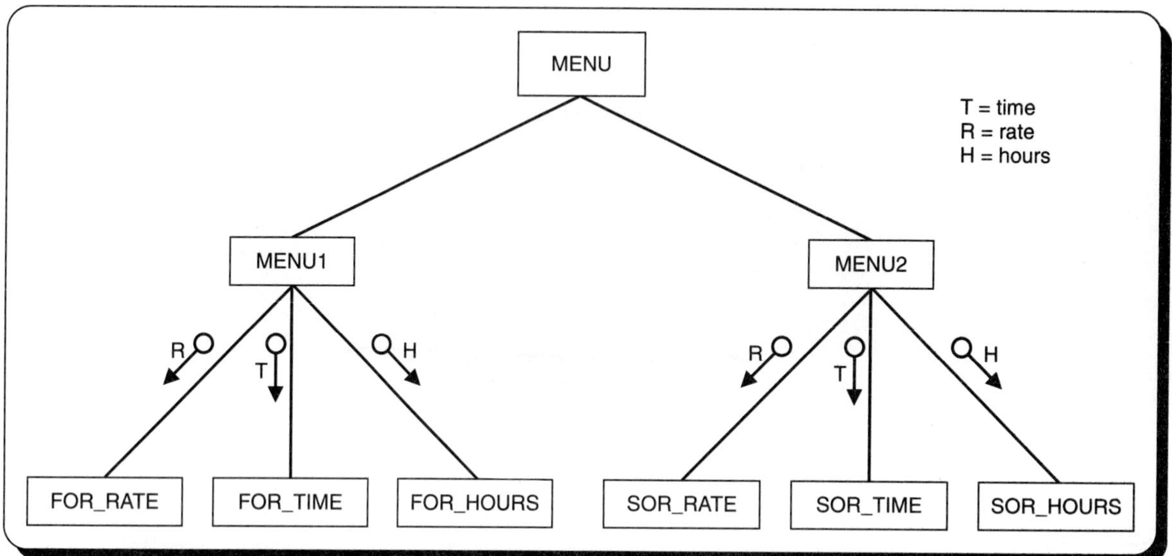

Figure 8.7 Structure Chart for Multilevel Custom Menu

the macro returns to cell I30 from which it was launched and then executes the next command, {BRANCH \M}, which brings up the custom menu again.

Creating a Multilevel Custom Menu

We can use the third line of the menu macro to branch to another menu, thereby creating multiple levels of menus similar to the standard 1-2-3 menus. Suppose we wanted to give the user the capability to format and sort the three ranges we have been using. We want to add functionality to our original menu by enhancing the structure. Figure 8.7 illustrates the structure chart for this problem.

From our main menu we have three menu items, two of which are primary: Format and Sort. Selecting the Format option, the macro branches to another menu which gives the user the option of formatting the Rate, Time, or Hours. The Sort submenu also allows for the selection of the same three options. Upon selecting any of these options, the menu macro branches to the appropriate macro for execution in Figure 8.8. The last statement in each of these lower-level menu macros is a BRANCH statement back to the top-level menu.

Using Advanced Macros to Filter Out Complexity

Now you will begin developing worksheets by using advanced macro commands, which can tremendously improve the quality of your user interface. Advanced macro commands can be categorized in three program structures: (1) sequence, (2) iteration,

H23: [W12] 'MACROS   MENU
Format Sort Quit
Rate Time Hours

80%	H	I	J	K	L
23	MACROS				
24					
25	\M	{MENUBRANCH MENU}			
26					
27	MENU	Format	Sort	Quit	
28		Rate Time Hours	Rate Time Hours	Exit the Worksheet	
29		{MENUBRANCH MENU1}	{MENUBRANCH MENU2}	/QY~	
30					
31	MENU1	Rate	Time	Hours	
32		Format the Repair Rate	Format the Avg Repair Time	Format the Avg Repair Hours	
33		{FOR_RATE}	{FOR_TIME}	{FOR_HOURS}	
34		{BRANCH \M}	{BRANCH \M}	{BRANCH \M}	
35					
36	MENU2	Rate	Time	Hours	
37		Sort the Repair Rate	Sort the Avg Repair Time	Sort the Avg Repair Hours	
38		{SOR_RATE}	{SOR_TIME}	{SOR_HOURS}	
39		{BRANCH \M}	{BRANCH \M}	{BRANCH \M}	
40					
41	FOR_RATE	/RFC0~RATE~			
42					
43	FOR_TIME	/RFF1~TIME~			
44					
45	FOR_HOURS	/RFF1~HOURS~			
46					
47	SOR_RATE	/DSDData~PC4~D~G~			
48					
49	SOR_TIME	/DSDData~PD4~D~G~			
50					
51	SOR_HOURS	/DSDData~PE4~D~G~			

CMD

Figure 8.8
Multilevel Custom Menu for Formatting and Sorting

and (3) selection. We will discuss each of these macro command categories as well as commands that have other purposes, such as to control parts of the screen display or to work with files. Figure 8.9 illustrates the three types of program structures. Program structures are most often developed in a nested fashion, combining macro commands to achieve a goal or to accomplish a specific task.

Macro Commands That Support Sequence

Sequence structures provide a basis for executing computer instructions in the order in which they are listed in the macro. The sequential order is changed only

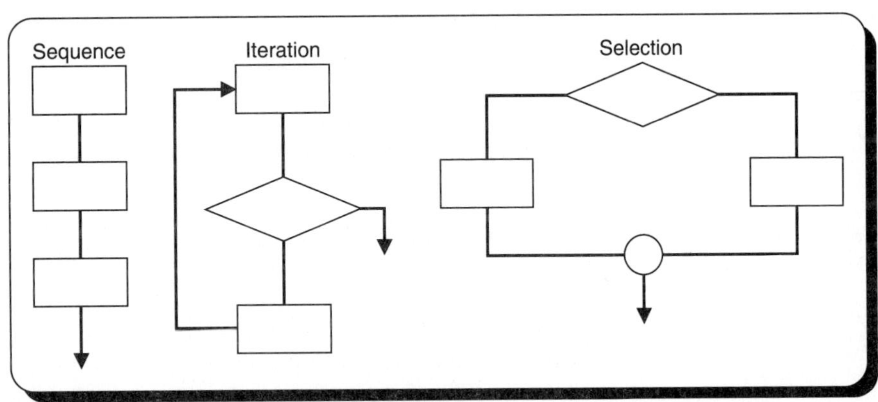

Figure 8.9
Program Structures

when one of the other program structures is encountered. Macro commands that support the sequence structure include {LET}, {RECALC}, {PUT}, {CONTENTS}, and {BLANK}.

The {LET} Command. The {LET} command creates a number or label entry in a specified cell. The {LET} command always left-aligns label entries regardless of the global label-prefix setting. This command can include a formula or reference, but it recalculates the results of the formula and enters it as a fixed value in the target cell. Figures 8.10 and 8.11 compare the {LET} macro command with the {GOTO} equivalent.

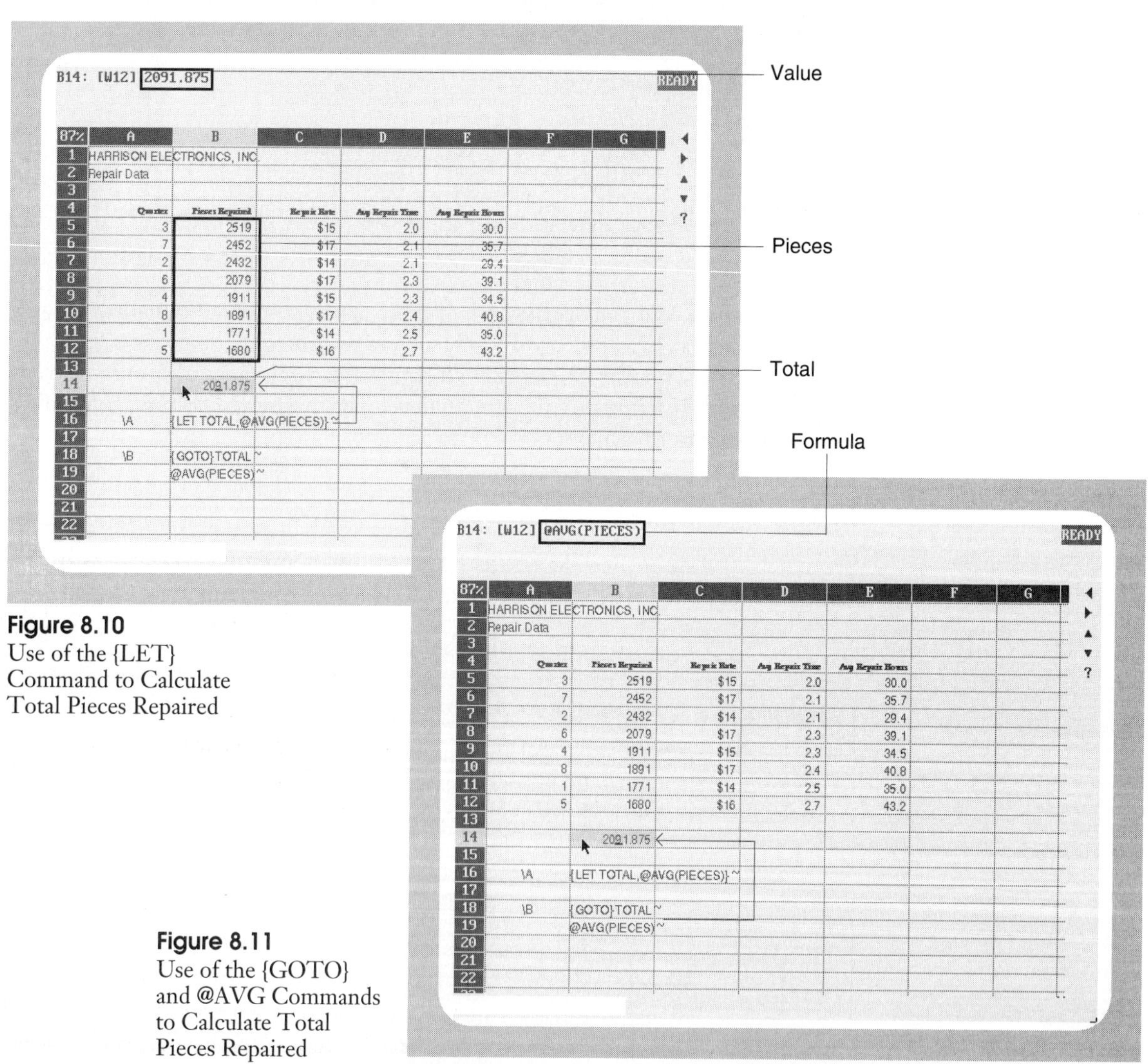

Figure 8.10
Use of the {LET} Command to Calculate Total Pieces Repaired

Figure 8.11
Use of the {GOTO} and @AVG Commands to Calculate Total Pieces Repaired

The format of the {LET} statement is as follows:

{LET *location,entry*}

In Figure 8.10 the Pieces range and the Total cell were previously named. After the \A macro has been executed, the Total cell contains the value 2091.875, which is the average of the Pieces Repaired data. After the \B macro has been executed (see Figure 8.11), the Total cell also *displays* the value 2091.875 but instead *contains* the formula @AVG(PIECES). The difference in how the {LET} formula executes in Lotus 1-2-3 is important for you to know because you may need a formula in a designated cell rather than its calculated value. The {LET} command is more efficient because it takes only one line to execute.

HINT: The {LET} command is more efficient than {GOTO} because the {LET} command places a value rather than a formula in the cell.

The tilde (~) is optional with the {LET} statement. Using the tilde will cause Lotus 1-2-3 to automatically recalculate the worksheet. You may not want this to happen, however, because if there are many {LET} commands, recalculation slows down the operation of the entire worksheet.

The {RECALC} Command. {LET} commands without tildes require that you later use the {RECALC} command, which recalculates those cells on which the {LET} command depends on. The {RECALC} command saves you valuable worksheet execution time by avoiding the recalculation of the entire worksheet, which is required when executing the {CALC} command. The format of the {RECALC} command is as follows:

HINT: Using the tilde with the {LET} command recalculates the worksheet.

{RECALC *location,(condition),(iterations)*}

The brackets indicate that the argument is optional. The *location* can consist of any cell or range. The *condition* argument (which is optional) tells Lotus 1-2-3 to repeat the recalculation until a condition becomes true, while the *iterations* argument (which is also optional) repeats the recalculation over a specified number of passes. The *iterations* argument cannot be used without specifying a condition and can contain a number or cell reference. A companion command, {RECALCCOL}, recalculates a range one column at a time.

The {PUT} Command. The {PUT} command, which is similar to the {LET} command, stores a number or a string in a specified location within a range. The difference between the two commands is that {PUT} requires a specific column and row location while {LET} requires a cell reference. Column and row numbers start at zero. You will find the {PUT} command useful for changing entries in a database when you know the relative position in the database but not the specific cell address. The format of the {PUT} command is as follows:

{PUT *address, column number, row number, value or string*}

In Figure 8.12 a new range named Average has been created to include all of the cells from B14 through E14. Calculate the average for the Average Repair

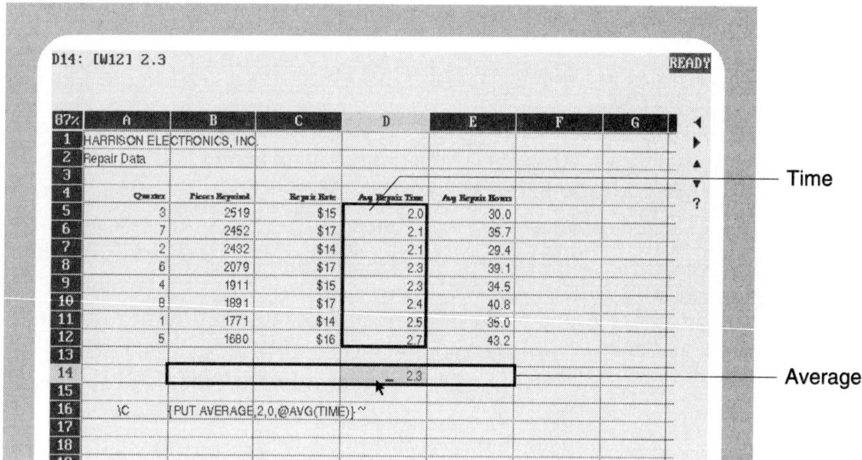

Figure 8.12
Use of the {PUT} Command to Calculate Average for the Average Repair Time

Time data in cell D14. Notice that when you use the {PUT} command, it is similar to {LET} in that the entry contains a value of 2.3 rather than a formula.

The {CONTENTS} Command. The {CONTENTS} macro command converts a number to a label that uses any of the formats in Lotus 1-2-3. This command is similar to {LET} except that it stores only a left-aligned label. You can use the {CONTENTS} command to convert a value to a label so that the value can be used in a string formula. The format of the {CONTENTS} command is as follows:

{CONTENTS *target location,(source location),(width),(cell format)*}

The width number and cell format number arguments are optional. The width argument can be a value, a formula, or a reference to a cell that contains a value or formula. The cell format argument can include one of the code numbers from the following list of code formats:

Code: 0 to 15	Fixed, 0 to 15 decimal places
Code: 16 to 31	Scientific, 0 to 15 decimal places
Code: 32 to 47	Currency, 0 to 15 decimal places
Code: 48 to 63	Percent, 0 to 15 decimal places
Code: 64 to 79	Comma, 0 to 15 decimal places
Code: 112	+/-
Code: 113	General
Code: 114	Date 1 (DD-MMM-YY)
Code: 115	Date 2 (DD-MMM)
Code: 116	Date 3 (MMM-YY)
Code: 117	Text
Code: 118	Hidden
Code: 119 to 124	Time formats
Code: 125	Worksheet's global cell format

HINT: The {CONTENTS} command places a left-aligned label in the cell.

Figure 8.13 illustrates the use of the {CONTENTS} command. Cell B14, which is named TOTAL, has been instructed to contain the formula in E16, @SUM(PIECES), with a width of 10 and a cell format of 3 (fixed with 3 decimal places). Notice that cell B14 now has the left-aligned label 16735.000. It is important to note that this cell entry is not a value, as we found with the {LET} and {PUT} commands.

Macro Commands That Support Selection

Selection structures test a condition. If the condition is met, a specific macro is executed; if the condition is not met, a different macro is performed. These commands are critical when you want to tap into the power of the programming logic that resides in Lotus 1-2-3. These macro commands include {IF}, coupled with {BRANCH}, and {DISPATCH}.

The {IF} and {BRANCH} Commands. The {IF} command is considered by some worksheet developers to be one of the most important commands in Lotus 1-2-3 for building an effective user interface. The {IF} command can test for user input, check the status of a counter (to keep track of the number of times to execute a macro), or decide to loop in conjunction with the {BRANCH} or {subroutine} command. The {IF} macro command behaves much the same as its function counterpart, @IF. The general format of the {IF} command is as follows:

```
{IF condition}
```

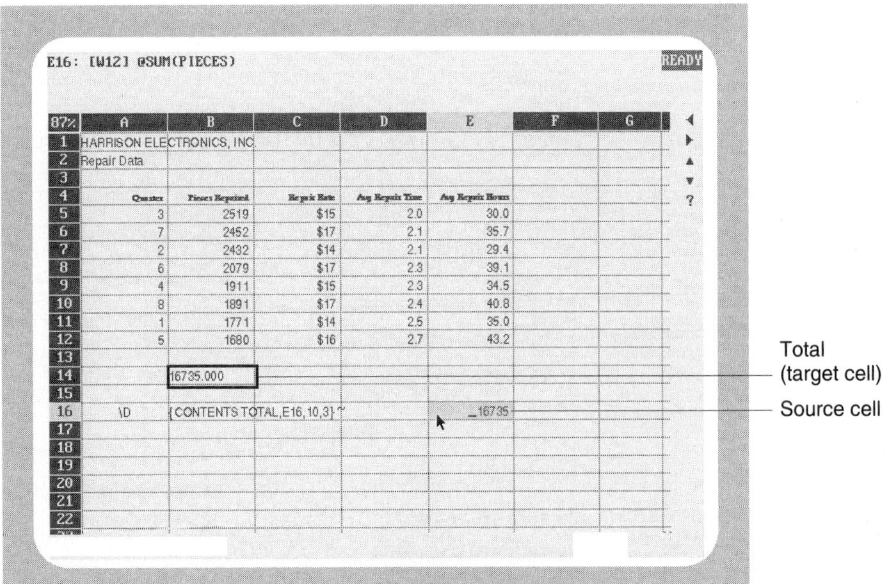

Figure 8.13
Use of the {CONTENTS} Command to Place Cell Contents

HINT: If the {IF} condition is true, Lotus executes the next command in the same cell.

HINT: Use the {BRANCH} command sparingly.

If the condition is true, then the next command in the *same cell* is executed. Otherwise, the program drops down to the next cell and begins executing any macro command it finds there. Using the {IF} command in conjunction with the {BRANCH} command enables you to control the processing or execution of macros. The {BRANCH} command transfers macro control from the current macro to a macro in another location and should therefore be used cautiously. The {BRANCH} macro, when coupled with the {IF} command, creates a selection or loop, providing you with a powerful tool for developing your user interface. The format of the {BRANCH} command is as follows:

{BRANCH *location*}

The {subroutine} macro executes a specified subroutine and then returns control to the original macro. The {RETURN} command should be used with {BRANCH} to return control to the calling macro.

Figure 8.14 illustrates a structure chart for calculating the set of summary statistics for each repair category in the Harrison Electronics case. The user has been prompted for a label that indicates the range in which to calculate statistics, including (1) the average, (2) the sum, (3) the standard deviation, or (4) the entire set of statistics.

Three rows with labels in column A have been set up to indicate what the statistics represent. The user has been asked to enter one of four values to indicate preference:

A for Average
S for Sum
D for Standard Deviation
L for All Statistics

In setting up your macros, you need to divide the problem into three levels as shown in Figure 8.14. The first level asks for user input and directs subsequent processing with the {IF} command. The second level performs the main

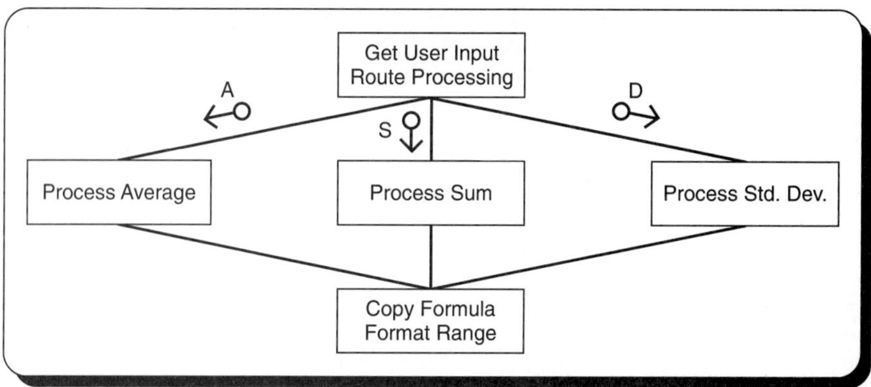

Figure 8.14
Structure Chart for Statistical Calculations

computations, while the third level copies the appropriate formula to the remainder of the Total range and then formats the range. If you had not divided the Format activities into a separate module, you would have had to duplicate those activities in each of the level-two computational modules.

Figure 8.15 illustrates the macros that carry out this task. The five macro blocks match the hierarchy shown in the structure chart. Although not needed for this example, the {subroutine} macro command ({AVG}, {SUM} and {STD}) has been used to branch to the appropriate computational macro. All computational macros use the FORMAT macro, which copies the formula and formats the Total range. Notice that the {GET LABEL} command is used here to elicit user input rather than custom menus.

The tricky part of this task is to calculate all three statistics at once if the decision maker requests it. The {subroutine} command can help you do this. If the user inputs an L, the program will execute the AVG and FORMAT macros, return to the {IF} statement line, drop down one cell using the {DOWN} command, execute the SUM and FORMAT macros, and so on. This example illustrates the use of the {IF} statement coupled with the {subroutine} and {BRANCH} commands to make a selection based on user input. In Figure 8.16 the user has entered an L to calculate all of the statistics.

The {DISPATCH} Command. The {DISPATCH} command lets you transfer macro control to the cell whose name or address is entered within the location argument. The {DISPATCH} command avoids the use of multiple {BRANCH}

I32: [W17] '1 READY

87%	H	I	J	K	L
23	MACROS				
24					
25	\A	{GETLABEL "Enter: (A) Average, (S) Sum, (D) Standard Deviation, (L) All: ",LABEL}			
26		{GOTO}TOTAL~			
27		{IF LABEL="A"}{AVG}			
28		{IF LABEL="S"}{DOWN}{SUM}			
29		{IF LABEL="D"}{DOWN 2}{STD}			
30		{IF LABEL="L"}{AVG}{DOWN}{SUM}{DOWN}{STD}			
31					
32	LABEL	l			
33					
34	AVG	@AVG(PIECES)~{BRANCH FORMAT}			
35					
36	SUM	@SUM(PIECES)~{BRANCH FORMAT}			
37					
38	STD	@STD(PIECES)~{BRANCH FORMAT}			
39					
40	FORMAT	/C~{RIGHT}.{RIGHT 2}~			
41		/RFF1~.{RIGHT 3}~			
42					
43					
44					

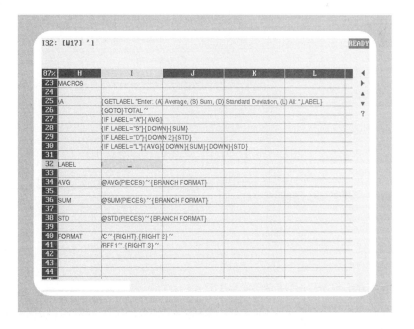

Figure 8.15
Macro Commands for Statistical Calculations

B16: (F1) [W12] @STD(PIECES) READY

87%	A	B	C	D	E	F	G
1	HARRISON ELECTRONICS, INC.						
2	Repair Data						
3							
4	Quarter	Pieces Repaired	Repair Rate	Avg Repair Time	Avg Repair Hours		
5	3	2519	$15	2.0	30.0		
6	7	2452	$17	2.1	35.7		
7	2	2432	$14	2.1	29.4		
8	6	2079	$17	2.3	39.1		
9	4	1911	$15	2.3	34.5		
10	8	1891	$17	2.4	40.8		
11	1	1771	$14	2.5	35.0		
12	5	1680	$16	2.7	43.2		
13							
14	Average	2091.9	15.6	2.3	36.0		
15	Sum	16735.0	125.0	18.4	287.7		
16	Std. Dev.	311.0	1.2	0.2	4.6		
17							

Figure 8.16
Results of the Statistical Calculations

and {subroutine} statements, which slow overall worksheet operation. The location argument must contain a single cell. The format for the {DISPATCH} command is as follows:

{DISPATCH *location*}

In Figure 8.17 the {DISPATCH} command is used to accomplish the same task you have just worked through with the {IF} and {subroutine} commands. Another cell was named to hold the label from which you will dispatch—cell

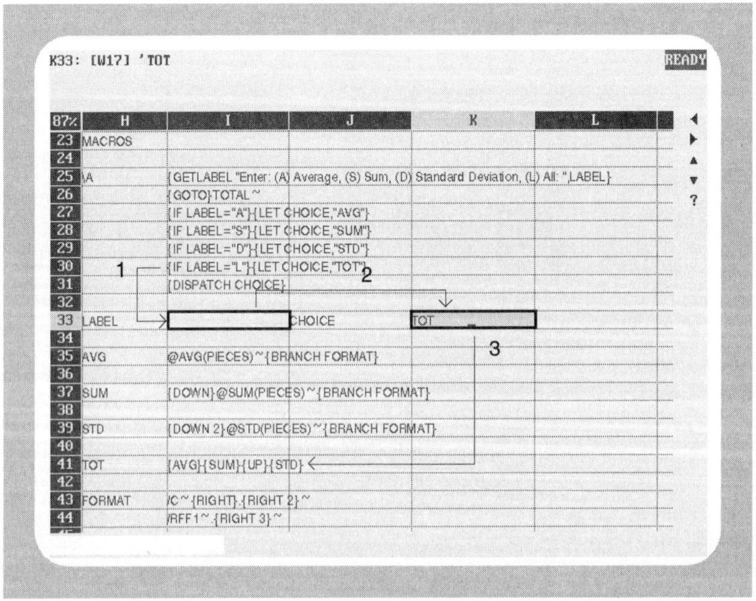

Figure 8.17
Use of the {DISPATCH} Command for Statistical Calculations

K33, named Choice. Based on the results of this Label cell, which you test by using the {IF} statement, you will branch to the Choice cell. Then you will use the {LET} command to enter a label into the Choice cell, indicating which macro to subsequently branch to. The {DISPATCH} command then instructs the program to branch to the macro based on the label in this cell.

Once again, calculating the full range of statistics poses a challenge. Since the starting point for each calculation is the Total cell, B14 (which you go to at the beginning of the control macro), you must move down one cell to calculate the sum statistic and down two cells to calculate the standard deviations. However, when computing all statistics, you want to move down only one cell (not two) after calculating the sum statistic. So you must insert the {UP} statement before calling the STD subroutine.

Macro Commands That Support Iteration

HINT: Looping with the {IF} command means looping back to the main macro.

HINT: Iteration macros involve setting up and managing a counter.

The iteration structure is characterized by macros that control the flow of the Lotus 1-2-3 program. They manage the movement and positioning within the macro subarea of the worksheet. These commands include {IF} statements, coupled with branches and subroutine calls, and the {FOR} command. Rather than branching to a macro and continuing the processing, you may loop back to a place *within* the main macro. Looping with the {IF} command means setting up a macro within a macro for execution.

Both the {IF} and {FOR} commands usually require you to set up and manage a counter that tells the macro how many times to iterate, or loop. The purpose of the counter then is to tell the iterating macro the number of times to loop. A counter must be initialized at the beginning of each macro run and can be tied directly to a range count. During execution, a counter must be increased or decreased by some value. You can use the {LET} statement to accomplish this task.

The {FOR} Command. The {FOR} command repeatedly executes a macro or subroutine the number of times indicated by its built-in counter. (This command is the equivalent of the DO loop in COBOL.) The counter keeps track of the number of times a macro has been executed. The counter argument indicates which cell will be used as a counter. Three arguments regulate the built-in counter: start, stop, and step. The {FOR} command is similar to the **/D**ata **F**ill command in that the start number is the initial value to be placed in the counter, and the stop number is the value at which the macro stops executing. When the macro stops, the control is returned to the macro statement that follows the {FOR} statement. The step number tells the {FOR} counter how much to increment each time the macro is invoked. {FOR} counters increment rather than decrement. If logic dictates that a counter should decrement, you might consider using the {IF} and {BRANCH} commands. The general structure of the {FOR} command is as follows:

{FOR *counter,start number,stop number,step number,macro*}

HINT: Use the @COUNT function to set up a flexible counter.

Your task in the Harrison Electronics case is to name each cell in the Pieces Repaired column. Therefore, you will want to start at cell B5 in Figure 8.18 and move down until you reach the end of the data, in cell B12. Since you know the number of entries in the range (called Pieces), you could insert an 8 for the stop-number argument. But if you change your worksheet and insert additional rows, you will want to create a macro that is flexible enough to accommodate changes. To ensure this flexibility, you can use the @COUNT function to count the number of entries in your range for the stop argument. When you invoke \A in Figure 8.18, you have named cell B21 Count, which you initialize with a 1 and stop with a value that counts the number of entries in the Pieces range. In Figure 8.18 the macro has already been executed; therefore the counter has a value of 9, which equals the starting value of 1 plus the number of entries in the range, 8.

The macro you are executing 8 times is \B, which names the current cell and prompts the user to enter the range name at the user prompt ({?}). The cursor then moves down one cell, and the macro is executed until it reaches the stop value set in the {FOR} command. You have just created 8 range names—one for each cell in the Pieces range.

HINT: With the {IF} command, you loop only when (rather than while) a condition is satisfied.

The {IF} and {Branch} Commands. The {IF} and {BRANCH} commands, which were introduced in our discussion of selection, are also useful in setting up program loops. The thinking is different from the logic inherent in the {FOR} command. When using the {FOR} command, you continue looping *while* a

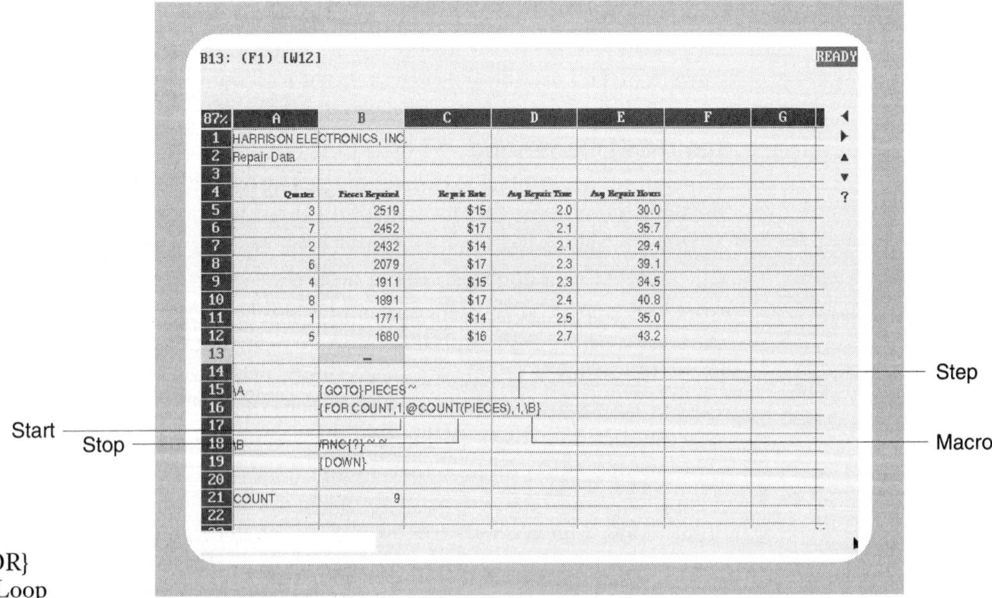

Figure 8.18
Using the {FOR} Statement to Loop

condition exists. With the {IF} and {BRANCH} commands, you loop only *when* a condition is satisfied.

You can address the problem we just solved with the {FOR} command by using the {IF} and {BRANCH} commands, as shown in Figure 8.19. There are still two macros, only they now are nested within each other: \B is nested within \A. There are two {LET} commands—one to set up the counter and the other to decrement the counter by one each time through the macro. {IF} and {BRANCH} looping macros show you each of the activities required for looping through the macro.

There must be two {LET} counter statements with {IF} and {BRANCH} looping macros. The {IF} statement, used to test the counter status, can be placed either as the last statement of the control macro, as shown in Figure 8.19, or as the first statement of the nested macro coupled with a {BRANCH} command. The {IF} statement in the latter case must take into account that you have not yet entered the macro loop shown in Figure 8.20. Notice that you are asking the reverse question, {IF COUNT<1}, to branch out of the looping macro, rather than {IF COUNT>0} to continue looping.

Fine-Tuning the User Interface

Several other issues must be considered when you want to develop an effective user interface: autoexecution, screen design and control, and macro block initialization.

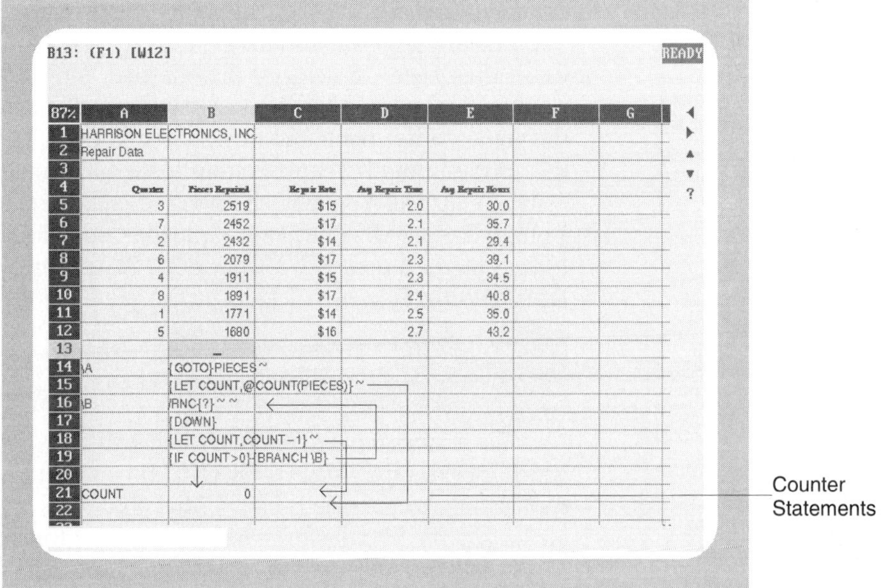

Figure 8.19
Using the {LET} Statement to Loop (Posttest)

B13: (F1) [W12] READY

	A	B	C	D	E	F	G
1	HARRISON ELECTRONICS, INC.						
2	Repair Data						
3							
4	Quarter	Pieces Repaired	Repair Rate	Avg Repair Time	Avg Repair Hours		
5	3	2519	$15	2.0	30.0		
6	7	2452	$17	2.1	35.7		
7	2	2432	$14	2.1	29.4		
8	6	2079	$17	2.3	39.1		
9	4	1911	$15	2.3	34.5		
10	8	1891	$17	2.4	40.8		
11	1	1771	$14	2.5	35.0		
12	5	1680	$16	2.7	43.2		
13							
14	\A	{GOTO}PIECES~					
15		{LET COUNT,@COUNT(PIECES)}~					
16	\B	{IF COUNT<1}{QUIT}					
17		/RNC{?}~~					
18		{DOWN}					
19		{LET COUNT,COUNT-1}~					
20		{BRANCH \B}					
21							
22	COUNT	0					

Figure 8.20
Using the {LET} Statement to Loop (Pretest)

Autoexecution

To further customize your user interface, you will want the worksheet and associated macros to load automatically when Lotus 1-2-3 is invoked. By following just two steps, you will save the novice user the trouble of using the /**F**ile **R**etrieve command and the \M keystrokes to bring up the custom menus.

The first step is to use the /**W**orksheet **G**lobal **D**efault **D**irectory command to set the default directory—the one that is read each time the /**F**ile **R**etrieve command is invoked. Remember to update the default settings file before exiting the menus. Then name the worksheet AUTO123.WK1 or AUTO123.WK3 so that as the Lotus 1-2-3 program is loaded into memory, the worksheet is automatically loaded. You may also want to create a batch file in DOS, which loads Lotus 1-2-3 as well. The name of the file resembles the application that is characterized by the Lotus 1-2-3 worksheet. An example of such a batch file, named REPAIRS.BAT, might include:

HINT: Remember to update the default settings prior to exiting the /**W**orksheet **G**lobal **D**efault **D**irectory menu.

```
cd \LOTUS
123
```

The second step is to assign the name \0 to the first cell of the macro quadrant, which includes the {MENUBRANCH} command, usually named \M. \0 is the special autoexecute macro name. After the Lotus 1-2-3 program and the add-ins are loaded, the \0 name tells the program to automatically load the custom menu. Macro cells can have more than one name, and the top-level user menu cell should also include the \0 name so that it can be called up without user intervention.

HINT: Using the AUTO123 filename and \0 enables autoexecution.

Screen Control

You can also use several screen-control commands such as {PANELOFF}, {WINDOWSOFF}, {BORDERSOFF}, and {INDICATE}. The {PANELOFF} command freezes the control panel and status line until Lotus 1-2-3 encounters either the end of a macro or a {PANELON} command. As a macro is executing Lotus 1-2-3 keystrokes (/ commands), the panel that usually shows the fast-moving command execution is frozen so that the "busy" effect is reduced.

The {WINDOWSOFF} command freezes the screen display during macro execution until {WINDOWSON} restores the normal setting. Worksheet operation will be faster since every cursor movement will not need to be displayed. Normally, the {WINDOWSOFF} and {WINDOWSON} commands are used to help the decision maker position the cursor on the chosen screen. This position is determined by the selected custom menu item so that he or she will see only the changes. The benefits of the {PANELOFF} and {WINDOWSOFF} command can be seen only during macro execution.

The {BORDERSOFF} command turns off the display of the worksheet frame so that the column letters and row numbers do not distract the decision maker. When the macro ends or the {BORDERSON} command is encountered, the frame is returned to its normal display.

The {INDICATE} command changes the mode indicator to the string you specify. You must specify either a string or a cell:

```
{INDICATE string or cell}
```

The mode indicator continues to display the string until another {INDICATE} command is issued or used with an empty string. Figure 8.21 shows the use of the four screen-control commands; Figure 8.22 shows the results.

The {BEEP} command activates the computer bell. Four different bell tones can be invoked with a number from 1 to 4. The general format of the {BEEP} command is:

```
{BEEP number}
```

Each of these commands that control screen display can be used many times within a macro block to turn the desired attribute on or off.

Initializing a Macro Block

One of the most often overlooked and important activities in developing the user interface is the initialization of a macro block. Two of the activities that you must consider when initializing a macro block are setting up a counter and naming ranges. Earlier in this chapter we discussed the importance of setting up a counter. Range name initialization can be complex if a cell name must be used more than once in a macro—for example, a cell that drops down in a range to calculate a value. A range name must be deleted and recreated each time it is reused. Developers often erroneously assume that a macro will be executed only once. The types of macro commands you must include when initializing a macro block include:

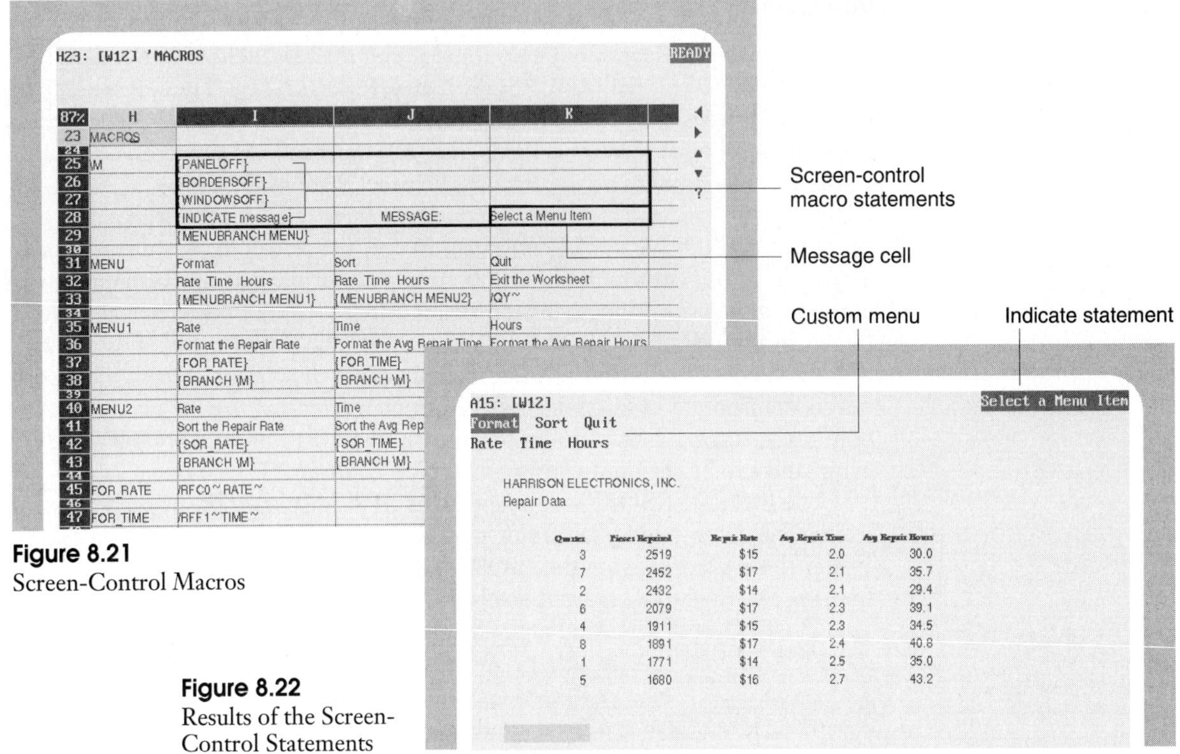

Figure 8.21
Screen-Control Macros

Figure 8.22
Results of the Screen-Control Statements

- {PANELOFF} {BORDERSOFF} and other screen control commands
- {GOTO} cell~ statements
- /RNDcellname~/RNCcellname~~
- {LET count,@count(range)}~
- main statements
- {GOTO} cell~ coupled with /RNDcellname~{DOWN}/RNCcellname~~
- {LET count,count–1}~
- {IF count>0}{BRANCH loop}

There are usually two {GOTO} statements. The first moves the cellpointer to the upper-left cell of the part of the worksheet you want to see (to set the screen) and the second {GOTO} statement goes to the first cell on which you will perform an operation. You then need to delete and then recreate range names to set up your macro to work properly. The {LET} statement sets your counter based on the number of values in some key range. You will have some main macro statements that you must now enter. After the main macro statements, you have to delete and recreate your range names again. Don't forget to decrement (or increment) your counter and test its value, looping back to the main statements if appropriate.

Some Afterthoughts

As you have seen, creating the user interface for your worksheet can take a good bit of time. The logic involved in developing the user interface is quite different from the logic used in building the dynamic model or in managing a data area. You must know the organizational decision makers well enough to determine the level of complexity that must be filtered out. Too often, developers build user interfaces that he or she will personally use rather than user interfaces that serve as tools for the decision makers to effectively work with the application.

It is important to understand, however, that without the user interface you would have a difficult time making the dynamic model understandable to the Lotus 1-2-3 user. The more complex the worksheet, the more complex the knowledge needed to successfully operate the worksheet and to make a decision.

The user interface is a powerful tool which links together the database and model base in a decision support system. It effectively enables the smooth functioning of the decision support system and encourages what-if analyses. This can only lead to better decisions by managers and that is the reason we build decision support systems.

Review Questions

1. What is the user interface? Why should you develop the user interface?
2. What are the six issues you must consider before developing the user interface?
3. Define a macro.
4. What are the benefits of using macros to design the user interface?
5. How should a macro be documented?
6. What is the general structure of a macro? What should be included in a macro?
7. Where should a macro be located in a worksheet?
8. Describe the phases that should be carefully observed when developing macros.
9. Planning for a macro should include what three activities?
10. How are macros invoked? What keystrokes are needed?
11. What name must be given to the autoexecution macro?
12. How do you debug a macro?
13. Describe the macros area and naming conventions. How many columns should be used? How should macros be documented?

14. List some common errors made when developing macros.
15. Why would you include an error-checking statement in your macros?
16. When does a macro stop its execution?
17. What commands should be used to create custom menus in Lotus 1-2-3?
18. Can one custom macro menu call another menu?
19. Name the macro commands that support the sequence program structure.
20. What is the operational difference between using the {LET} statement and using the {GOTO} statement to place the result of a formula in a cell? Describe the results of both statements and the difference in speed.
21. Describe an alternative to using the tilde (~) to recalculate a number of {LET} statements.
22. How does the {RECALC} command differ from the {CALC} command?
23. When would you want to use the {PUT} command rather than the {LET} command?
24. Which macro commands support the selection program structure?
25. How does the {IF} command operate to control the execution of the macro?
26. Do the {BRANCH} and {GOTO} commands perform the same task? Why or why not?
27. Describe the difference in the ways the {BRANCH} and {subroutine} commands execute a macro block.
28. How does the {DISPATCH} command execute a macro block based on user input?
29. What do the {FOR} and {IF} {BRANCH} commands have in common?
30. To customize the user interface after it has been built, how do you build in autoexecution?
31. Describe the functioning of each of the four screen-control commands.
32. What tasks must you perform when initializing a macro block?

Skill-Building Activities: Using Macros to Build the User Interface

Activity 1: Retrieving and Modifying Your Worksheet

Use the /File Retrieve command to bring up from Chapter 7 the Harrison worksheet called HARRIS7. At this point, your worksheet should look similar to the one you left at the end of Chapter 7, as shown in Figure 8.23.

F13: (T) [W6] +K11 READY

87%	A	B	C	D	E	F	G	H	I	J	K
1	HARRISON ELECTRONICS, INC.								Sales Summary Report		
2	1110 Fillmore Street					0.2			(rounded thousands)		
3	Colorado Springs, CO	80906									
4											
5	Category	Code	1 Qtr	2 Qtr	3 Qtr	4 Qtr	5 Qtr	6 Qtr	7 Qtr	8 Qtr	Total
6											
7	Repair Sales		143	150	161	161	162	169	180	180	1,306
8	Appliance Sales		28	33	31	31	33	39	36	38	268
9	Small Products		5	8	8	22	19	22	20	32	136
10											
11	TOTAL		176	192	199	214	215	229	235	250	1710
12											
13						+K11					
14					0.2	1710					
15					0.3	1794					
16					0.4	1854					
17					0.5	1896					
18					0.6	1928					
19					0.7	1953					
20											
21	Category	Code	1 Qtr	2 Qtr	3 Qtr	4 Qtr	5 Qtr	6 Qtr	7 Qtr	8 Qtr	Total
22	Repair Sales	1000	143	179	202	164	166	197	221	183	1,455

Figure 8.23
Harrison Electronics Worksheet

NOTE: To help you with this exercise, ***boldface*** *letters indicate a message from the system or the worksheet while the commands in the list tell you to make a specific entry.*

You must now get your worksheet ready for your macros. To do this, you need to delete several rows so that your worksheet is more compact. Also, you need to name several ranges for use by your macros.

Move the cell pointer to row 23 and use the /**W**orksheet **D**elete **R**ow command to delete rows 23 through 26.

Likewise, move the cell pointer to row 24 and delete rows 24 through 27.

Then, move the cell pointer to row 25 and delete rows 25 through 28.

Name the following ranges by using the /**R**ange **N**ame **C**reate command:

C7..J7	`Repair`
C8..J8	`Appliance`
C9..J9	`Small`
F2	`Smoothing`
F13	`Results`

At this point, your worksheet should look similar to the one in Figure 8.24. The **D**isplay **Z**oom **M**anual command in WYSIWYG has been used to set the worksheet to 75% so that you can see it all on one screen.

C24: [W6] 5 READY

75%	A	B	C	D	E	F	G	H	I	J	K	L	M
1	HARRISON ELECTRONICS, INC.								Sales Summary Report				
2	1413 Fillmore Street					0.2			(rounded thousands)				
3	Colorado Springs, CO	80906											
4													
5	Category	Code	1 Qtr	2 Qtr	3 Qtr	4 Qtr	5 Qtr	6 Qtr	7 Qtr	8 Qtr	Total		
6													
7	Repair Sales		143	150	161	161	162	169	180	180	1,306		
8	Appliance Sales		28	33	31	31	33	39	36	38	268		
9	Small Products		5	8	8	22	19	22	20	32	136		
10													
11	TOTAL		176	192	199	214	215	229	235	250	1710		
12													
13						+K11							
14					0.2	1710							
15					0.3	1794							
16					0.4	1854							
17					0.5	1896							
18					0.6	1928							
19					0.7	1953							
20													
21	Category	Code	1 Qtr	2 Qtr	3 Qtr	4 Qtr	5 Qtr	6 Qtr	7 Qtr	8 Qtr	Total		
22	Repair Sales	1000	143	179	202	164	166	197	221	183	1,455		
23	Appliance Sales	2000	28	55	19	31	44	60	23	46	306		
24	Small Products	3000	5	21	8	79	8	30	12	80	243		
25			---	---	---	---	---	---	---	---	----		
26	TOTAL SALES		176	255	229	274	218	287	256	309	2,004		

Figure 8.24
Modified Worksheet for Harrison Electronics

Activity 2: Using the {MENUBRANCH} Macro to Create a Menu

You are now ready to develop a custom menu by using the {MENUBRANCH} command. You will enter your macros beginning in cell M41. First, you must name the macro area Macros.

Move the cell pointer to cell M41 and name it Macros by using the /**R**ange **N**ame **C**reate command.

In cell M41 type the label `"\M`.

In cell N41 enter the macro command `{MENUBRANCH MENU}`.

Go to cell M43 and type the label `'MENU`.

You are now ready to type the menu commands, descriptions, and macro commands. Use the following structure for your macros:

Cell	*Label*
N43	Change smoothing constant
O43	Change what-if result
N44	Change smoothing constant from `.2` through `.8`
O44	Change what-if result from total sales to a sales category
N45	`{MENUBRANCH MENU1}`
O45	`{MENUBRANCH MENU2}`
N46	`{BRANCH \M}`
O46	`{BRANCH \M}`

You are now ready to build your second level of menus, which will be called from the main menu and will allow the user to change either the input (smoothing constant) or the output (result).

Move to cell M48 and type the label `'MENU1`.

Move to cell M53 and type the label `'MENU2`.

You must set up the menu structure for your second level with the {MENUBRANCH} command. Use the following structure to enter your macros:

Cell	*Label*
N48	`'0.2` (be sure to enter this as a left-justified label)
O48	`'0.4`
P48	`'0.6`
Q48	`'0.8`
N49	Change smoothing constant to `0.2`
O49	Change smoothing constant to `0.4`
O49	Change smoothing constant to `0.6`
Q49	Change smoothing constant to `0.8`
N50	`{.2}`
O50	`{.4}`
P50	`{.6}`
Q50	`{.8}`
N51	`{BRANCH \M}`
O51	`{BRANCH \M}`
P51	`{BRANCH \M}`
Q51	`{BRANCH \M}`

Now you can set up the macro commands for MENU2:

You must set up the menu structure for your second level with the {MENUBRANCH} command. Use the following structure to enter your macros:

Cell	*Label*
N53	`Total Sales`
O53	`Repair Sales`
P53	`Appliance Sales`
Q53	`Small Products`
N54	Change what-if results to `TOTAL SALES`
O54	Change what-if results to `REPAIR SALES`
P54	Change what-if results to `APPLIANCE SALES`
Q54	Change what-if results to `SMALL PRODUCTS`
N55	`{total sales}`
O55	`{repair sales}`
P55	`{appliance sales}`

```
Q55  {small products}
N51  {BRANCH \M}
O51  {BRANCH \M}
P51  {BRANCH \M}
Q51  {BRANCH \M}
```

You have now finished building your multilevel menus. Your worksheet should look similar to the one in Figure 8.25. Your next step is to add functionality to your menus.

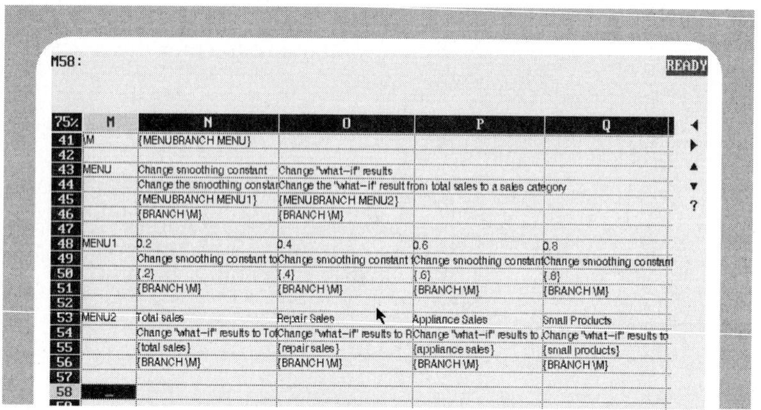

M58:

READY

75%	M	N	O	P	Q
41	\M	{MENUBRANCH MENU}			
42					
43	MENU	Change smoothing constant	Change "what-if" results		
44		Change the smoothing constar	Change the "what-if" result from total sales to a sales category		
45		{MENUBRANCH MENU1}	{MENUBRANCH MENU2}		
46		{BRANCH \M}	{BRANCH \M}		
47					
48	MENU1	0.2	0.4	0.6	0.8
49		Change smoothing constant to	Change smoothing constant t	Change smoothing constant	Change smoothing constant
50		{.2}	{.4}	{.6}	{.8}
51		{BRANCH \M}	{BRANCH \M}	{BRANCH \M}	{BRANCH \M}
52					
53	MENU2	Total sales	Repair Sales	Appliance Sales	Small Products
54		Change "what-if" results to To	Change "what-if" results to R	Change "what-if" results to	Change "what-if" results to
55		{total sales}	{repair sales}	{appliance sales}	{small products}
56		{BRANCH \M}	{BRANCH \M}	{BRANCH \M}	{BRANCH \M}
57					
58					

Figure 8.25
Second-level Menus

Activity 3: Adding Functionality to MENU1

You will now create the macros that are being called from the menus. You will begin by working with the MENU1 subroutine calls. Copy the formulas from cell N58 through N64 editing the cells to make the appropriate changes.

Enter the following labels as macro names and commands:

Cell	*Label*
M58	`.2` (be sure to enter this as a label)
M60	`.4`
M62	`.6`
M64	`.8`
N58	`{GOTO}A1~{LET SMOOTHING,.2}~`
N60	`{GOTO}A1~{LET SMOOTHING,.4}~`
N62	`{GOTO}A1~{LET SMOOTHING,.6}~`
N64	`{GOTO}A1~{LET SMOOTHING,.8}~`

Adding functionality to MENU1 resulted in four simple, one-line macros. After the execution of each of these macros, you will return to the main menu. Your worksheet should look similar to the one in Figure 8.26.

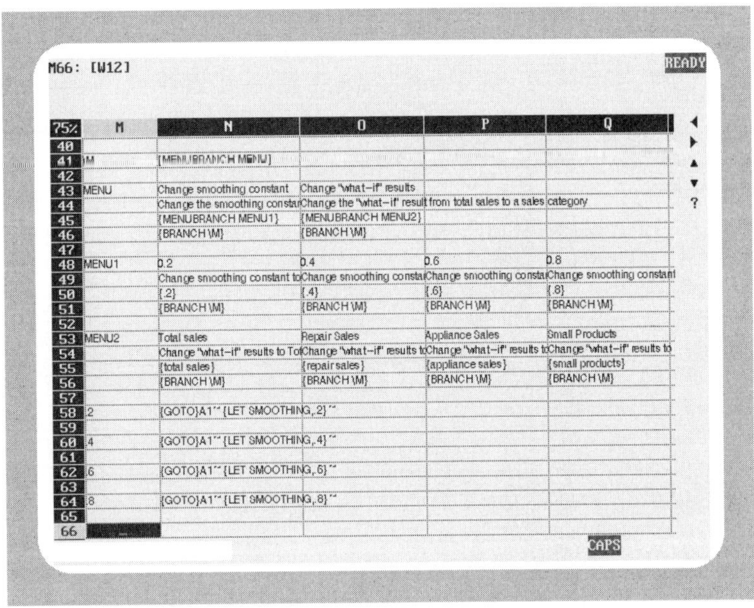

Figure 8.26
Adding Functionality to MENU1

Activity 4: Adding Functionality to MENU2

Let's now look at MENU2, in which you will change the results range in the data table to match the user's request. In this set of macros, you must enter a new formula in the formula-driven cell of the data table, called Results. Then you must recalculate the data table by using the /**D**ata **T**able command. Notice that you can copy most of your macro formulas for MENU2 and then edit each cell, changing one value.

Enter the following labels as macro names and commands:

Cell	*Label*
M66	`total sales`
M69	`repair sales`
M72	`appliance sales`
M75	`small products`
N66	`{GOTO}A1~{GOTO} RESULTS~+K11~`
N69	`{GOTO}A1~{GOTO} RESULTS~+K7~`
N72	`{GOTO}A1~{GOTO} RESULTS~+K8~`
N75	`{GOTO}A1~{GOTO} RESULTS~+K9~`
N67	`/DT1e13..f19~f2~`
N70	`/DT1e13..f19~f2~`
N73	`/DT1e13..f19~f2~`
N76	`/DT1e13..f19~f2~`

You have now finished adding functionality to your MENU2 menu items. Your worksheet should now resemble the one in Figure 8.27.

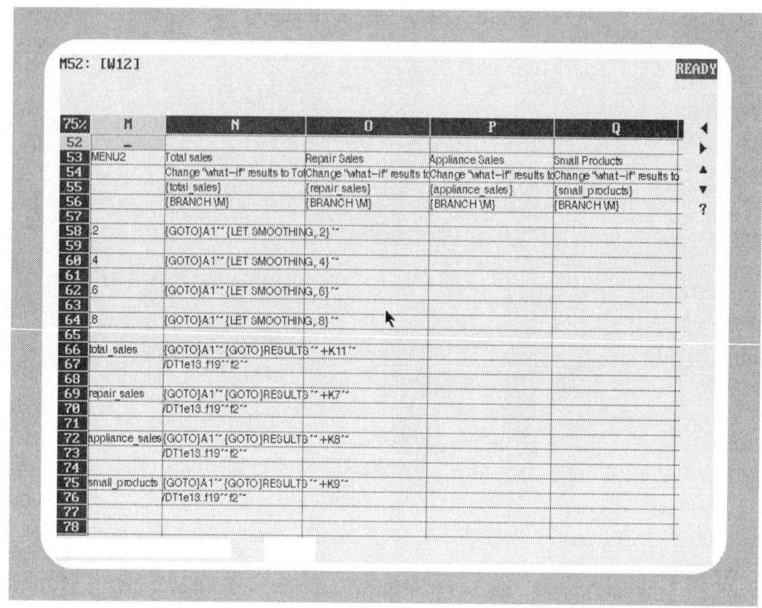

Figure 8.27
Adding Functionality to MENU2

Activity 5: Naming and Executing Your Macros

The last thing you must do before running your macros is to name them:

Move the cell pointer to M41 and use the /**R**ange **N**ame **L**abels **R**ight command to name all your macros at one time.

Move the cell pointer to M75 and press (ENTER).

Now that you have your macros, you can execute them by pressing (ALT)-(M). Figure 8.28 illustrates the worksheet and the macros in execution. Compare your model against Figure 8.28 and save your worksheet as HARRIS8.WK1.

Hands-On Exercises

1. Draw a structure chart to illustrate the following tasks:

   You have a checkbook system for a small business. The main part of the menu goes to one of three areas, depending on selection by the user: withdrawal, credit, or hold.

2. Write an interactive macro that performs certain tasks after the program has taken the user to a specific area of the checkbook program. The macro (1) solicits a dollar amount for withdrawal, credit, or hold using the {?} command; (2) places the amount in the current cell; and then (3) returns to

A1: {SWISS14 Bold} [W17] 'HARRISON ELECTRONICS, INC. MENU

Change smoothing constant Change "what-if" results

Change the smoothing constant value from .2 through .8

75%	A	B	C	D	E	F	G	H	I	J	K	L	M
1	HARRISON ELECTRONICS, INC.								Sales Summary Report				
2	1413 Fillmore Street					0.6			(rounded thousands)				
3	Colorado Springs, CO 80906												
4													
5	Category	Code	1 Qtr	2 Qtr	3 Qtr	4 Qtr	5 Qtr	6 Qtr	7 Qtr	8 Qtr	Total		
6													
7	Repair Sales		143	165	187	173	169	186	207	193	1,422		
8	Appliance Sales		28	44	29	30	38	51	34	41	297		
9	Small Products		5	15	11	52	25	28	18	55	209		
10													
11	TOTAL		176	223	227	255	233	265	260	289	1928		
12													
13						+K11							
14					0.2	1710							
15					0.3	1794							
16					0.4	1854							
17					0.5	1896							
18					0.6	1928							
19					0.7	1953							
20													
21	Category	Code	1 Qtr	2 Qtr	3 Qtr	4 Qtr	5 Qtr	6 Qtr	7 Qtr	8 Qtr	Total		
22	Repair Sales	1000	143	179	202	164	166	197	221	183	1,455		
23	Appliance Sales	2000	28	55	19	31	44	60	23	46	306		
24	Small Products	3000	5	21	8	79	8	30	12	80	243		
25			---	---	---	---	---	---	---	---	----		
26	TOTAL SALES		176	255	229	274	218	287	256	309	2,004		

CMD CAPS

Figure 8.28
Execution of the Macro Menus and Blocks

the main menu. Use the {GET LABEL} command and {IF} command. Name the macro \C.

3. Using the Learn mode, create a macro that names a group of macros by using the /**R**ange **N**ame **L**abels **R**ight command of macro cells, starting at the first menu, named \M. To do this, you must first go to the cell named \M, execute the command, and then insert the {DOWN 20} 20 cells within the command. First, you must name a cell \M so that a valid range can be assessed. Second, name this macro \R.

4. Create a custom macro menu that allows the user to choose from the following menu items:

   Withdrawal
   Credit
   Hold
   Print report
   Save worksheet
   Quit

5. Start a new worksheet and draw a structure chart that handles the following multilevel custom menu for a pet store customer sale. For simplicity, each receipt has three items:
   a. Code for sales category:
      Bird - 1
      Fish - 2
      Small mammal - 3

b. Code for each item sold
c. Price for each item

The sales category is already printed on each receipt after the user selects the appropriate menu item. Here is the menu structure for this problem:

High-level menu:	Bird	Fish	Small mammal	Save	Quit
Bird menu:	Bird	Supplies	Exit		
Fish menu:	Fish	Supplies	Exit		
Small mammal menu:		Small mammal	Supplies	Exit	

These are the additional macros needed:

Sales receipt
Save

6. Create a set of multilevel custom menus that accomplish the task in Exercise 5. You need not make the lower level menus active.

7. Using the problem and structure chart in Exercise 5, write a set of macros that accomplish the same thing without menus. You will need to use the {GETNUMBER} command to request the 1, 2, or 3 for bird, fish, or small mammal. Name the macro \S.

8. Develop an additional macro called Test that tests to be sure the user enters a 1, 2, or 3. If the result is negative, take the user back to the macro with the {GETNUMBER} command. Which technique—menu or prompt—is more effective for catching user errors?

9. Place in A13 a formula that totals the following values: Use the {LET} command to place in cell A15 the results of the formula in cell A13. Call the macro \T.

A10:	451	B10:	233
A11:	103	B11:	201
A12:	179	B12:	355

10. Name the range that encompasses A10..B12 (Total). Place in B13 a formula which averages the values in A10..B12. Use the {PUT} command to place into cell B15 the value of the formula in cell B13. Call the macro \V.

11. Use the {CONTENTS} command in cell B21 to convert the value in A13 to a label with a width of 10 and as currency with 2 decimal places (code=34). The target location is cell B15. Be sure to name the macro \C.

12. Experiment with the screen-control commands. Use all of them one by one in your macro to turn off the panel, windows, and borders.

Problem-Solving Projects

1. Recreate the data for Stillwater Bottling from Chapter 7. In Chapter 7 you built a dynamic model from the following data table by using a number of techniques to conduct analyses. Bring up your worksheet if you saved it. If not, enter the following data (and labels), starting in cell A31. You will develop a user interface for user interaction with the data area, although you may find it helpful to interact with both the data and the model areas if you have time.

Year	Gross Income	Expenses
1978	342,000	242,000
1979	344,000	237,000
1980	351,000	253,000
1981	349,000	251,000
1982	382,000	263,000
1983	385,000	279,000
1984	387,000	278,000
1985	401,000	281,000
1986	404,000	279,000
1987	417,000	296,000
1988	413,000	297,000
1989	423,000	294,000
1990	430,000	301,000
1991	433,000	307,000
1992	445,000	309,000

2. You will start your development of the user interface with custom menus. Draw a structure chart that lays out the logic for the problem. You will need to accomplish three tasks: (1) format the two ranges (Gross Income and Expenses) as currency with 2 decimal places, (2) calculate a Net Sales range, (3) allow the user to change any of the values in the Gross Income or Expenses ranges. You will therefore have 4 macro blocks—the first for the custom menu and one for each menu item.

3. Before you begin, create the following range names that can be used in your macros:

Range Name	Range
Year	A32..A46
Gross Income	B32..B46
Expenses	C32..C46
Net Sales	D32..D46
Gross	B42
Exp	C42
Net	D42
Macros	H61
Data	A31
Count	J59

   Also, add the label Net Sales to cell D31.

4. Enter your macros in cell H61. Enter the `{MENUBRANCH MENU}` command in cell I61 and name the macro \M. For the remainder of the problems, leave a blank cell between macros.

5. Name your next macro Menu, and enter the menu items in columns I through K respectively. Do not worry about labels running into each other, since each cell can hold 240 characters.

   I63: Format Ranges
   J63: Calculate Net Sales
   K63: Make Changes

   Write a suitable description for each menu item in the second row of the menu macro.

6. In the third row of the menu macro, use a subroutine macro command to branch to the following macros:

   I65: `{format}`
   J65: `{calculate}`
   K65: `{changes}`

7. In the fourth row of each menu item, add the macro command `{BRANCH \M}`, which brings up the main menu.

8. Label the {format} macro Format in cell H68. Format the two existing ranges of data, Gross Income and Expenses, as currency with 2 decimal places. This will result in a single-line macro.

9. Label the {calculate} macro Calculate in cell H70. For this macro, you must have an initialization macro that sets your counter. You must name the ranges again in case you want to run the macro more than once, then set the counter, go to the main macro statement, rename your ranges, check the counter, loop if appropriate, and at the end return to the main menu. To do all of this, enter the following macro statements:

```
{GOTO}GROSS INCOME~/RNDGROSS~/RNCGROSS~~
{GOTO}EXPENSES~/RNDEXP~/RNCEXP~~
{GOTO}NET SALES~/RNDNET~/RNCNET~~
{LET COUNT,@COUNT(YEAR)}~
{LET NET,GROSS-EXP}~/RFC2~~
{GOTO}GROSS~/RNDGROSS~{DOWN}/RNCGROSS~~
{GOTO}EXP~/RNDEXP~{DOWN}/RNCEXP~~
{GOTO}NET~/RNDNET~{DOWN}/RNCNET~~
{LET COUNT,COUNT-1}~
{IF COUNT >0}{BRANCH LOOP}
```

   Place the loop label in H74 next to the {LET NET,GROSS-EXP}~ macro statement.

10. Label the {changes} macro Changes in cell H81. For this macro, take the user to the data area first with the {GOTO}data~ command and then go to the Gross Income range. You need two {GOTO} statements to do this. Remember that, after you have run your macro, you have left the range names for Gross, Exp, and Net in the last cell of the large ranges. Then you will need a {?} command, which allows the user to move around in the data area and change a value; when the user presses ENTER, the macro will terminate.

11. The last step is to name all of your macros by using the /**R**ange **N**ame **L**abels **R**ight command.

12. After naming your macros, run the macro menu and macro blocks by invoking the \M command. If you need to debug your macros, press ALT-F2. Test each macro in the menu.

Quality-Assurance Checklist

As we conclude our discussion of modeling techniques, be sure you have considered the following factors that contribute to the quality of your worksheet:

✓ Know the decision maker and his or her skill level in operating the program.

- ✓ Always design the same user interface when developing different applications so that you and others can become familiar with it.
- ✓ Reduce the decision maker's need to memorize by providing for selection rather than keyboard entry, using range names rather than cell references, and providing access to help screens.
- ✓ Anticipate mistakes with range checks, and designing effective error messages.
- ✓ Provide a program action for every possible type of user input.
- ✓ Minimize the need for the decision maker to learn about the program by installing an "escape" function, such as ALT-M, to get back into the custom menus.
- ✓ For knowledgeable decision makers, provide program shortcuts—ways to bypass levels of menus.
- ✓ Allow the decision maker to express the same message in a number of ways—with various keystroke entries as well as menu-item selections.
- ✓ Be sure the application responds consistently and clearly.
- ✓ Adapt wording to the needs of the decision maker.
- ✓ On each selection item, provide an immediate message that tells the user what the application is doing.
- ✓ Allow the user to control the system.
- ✓ Always enclose your macro Lotus keystroke commands in quotation marks.
- ✓ Remember that a blank cell marks the end of the macro.
- ✓ Carefully move through the complete systems development life-cycle, step by step, including planning and testing, when developing your macros.
- ✓ Name only the first cell of your macro block.
- ✓ Always save your worksheet before running a macro.
- ✓ When you interrupt the running of a macro with the CTRL-BREAK command, check your worksheet to reset all counters and variables.
- ✓ Watch out for omitted tildes or too many tildes, the most common macro error.
- ✓ Use the /**R**ange **N**ame **L**abels **R**ight command to name all of your macros at one time.
- ✓ Begin each menu item with a different letter of the alphabet.
- ✓ Always use \M to name your highest-level menu.

- ✓ Remember that the {LET} command is more efficient than the {GOTO} command; however, it places the result of a formula (value) in a cell rather than the formula itself.
- ✓ Use the tilde (~) with the {LET} command to recalculate the cells that are affected in the worksheet.
- ✓ Use the {CONTENTS} command as an alternative to the {LET} command when you are working with labels rather than values and you need special formatting features.
- ✓ Use the {BRANCH} command sparingly because it represents an unconditional GOTO and control is not returned to the calling module.
- ✓ Use the {IF} command to loop back to a cell within your main macro. This command is especially useful when you want to execute only a piece of your main macro and you do not want to duplicate parts of the main macro.
- ✓ To set up a flexible counter for use with the {IF} command, use the @COUNT function to count the number of entries in the range you are working with.
- ✓ Use the AUTO123 filename and \0 to instruct Lotus 1-2-3 to automatically bring up your worksheet and execute your macros, respectively.

Appendices

APPENDIX

Function Keys, Modes, and Status Indicators

Function Keys

Key	Name	Description
F1	HELP	Displays a help screen related to the task you are performing, explains an error message, and/or provides a cross-related Help index.
F2	EDIT	Allows you to edit the entry in the current cell; also switches between LABEL and VALUE mode so you can edit an entry as you type it.
F3	NAME	Displays a list of named ranges related to the command you selected or the formula you are creating.
F4	ABS	Adjusts a cell or reference between relative, absolute, and mixed reference.
F5	GOTO	Moves the cell pointer to a specific cell or named range, another worksheet in the same file, or another active file (Versions 3.1+ and 1.1 for Windows).
F6	WINDOW	Moves the cell pointer between windows you create with /Worksheet Window Horizontal or Vertical.
F7	QUERY	Repeats the most recent /Data Query Extract or Find command.
F8	TABLE	Repeats the most recent /Data Table operation.
F9	CALC	Updates all formulas in all active files except formulas that refer to data in files on disk. Also converts a formula to its current value in the VALUE or EDIT modes.
F10	GRAPH	Displays the current graph, or creates an automatic graph using the data around the cell pointer.
ALT-F1	COMPOSE	Creates characters in 1-2-3 when used in conjunction with alphanumeric keys. Creates international characters and other characters you cannot enter directly from your keyboard.
ALT-F2	STEP	Turns on the STEP mode, which executes macros one step at a time for debugging. Press ALT-F2 again to turn off the STEP mode.
ALT-F3	RUN	Displays a list of range names so you can select the name of the macro you want to run.
ALT-F4	UNDO	Cancels any changes made to the worksheet since 1-2-3 was last in the READY mode. Press ALT-F4 again to restore changes.
ALT-F5	LEARN	Turns on the Learn feature and records subsequent keystrokes in the learn range. Press ALT-F5 again to turn off the Learn feature.

Function Keys *(cont.)*

Key	Name	Description
ALT-F7	APP1	Activates the add-in program assigned to this key, if any.
ALT-F8	APP2	Activates the add-in program assigned to this key, if any.
ALT-F9	APP3	Activates the add-in program assigned to this key, if any.
ALT-F10	ADD-IN	If no add-in program is assigned to this key, ALT-F10 displays the Add-In menu; otherwise ALT-F10 activates the add-in assigned to it.

Mode Indicators

Mode	Description
COLOR	You selected :Graph Edit Color Background or :Graph Edit Color Inside in WYSIWYG.
CYCLE	You selected :Graph Edit Select Cycle in WYSIWYG.
DRAG	You selected :Graph Edit Add Rectangle or :Graph Edit Add Ellipse or :Graph Edit View in WYSIWYG.
EDIT	You pressed F2 (EDIT) to edit an entry or you entered a formula incorrectly.
ERROR	1-2-3 is displaying an error message. Press F1 (HELP) to display the error message.
FILES	1-2-3 is displaying a menu of file names in the control panel. Press F3 (NAME) to display a full-screen menu of file names.
FIND	You selected /Data Query Find or pressed F7 (QUERY) to repeat the last query.
FRMT	You selected /Data Parse Format-Line Edit to edit a format line.
HELP	You pressed F1 (HELP) and 1-2-3 is displaying a help screen.
LABEL	You are entering a label.
MENU	You pressed / (slash) or < (less than) and 1-2-3 is displaying a menu of commands.
NAMES	1-2-3 is displaying a menu of range names, graph names, or attached add-in names.
PAN	You selected :Graph Edit View Pan.
POINT	1-2-3 is prompting you to specify a range, or you are creating a formula by highlighting a range, or you selected a WYSIWYG :Graph Edit command.
READY	1-2-3 is ready for you to enter data or select a command.
SELECT	You selected :Format Font [1-8] Replace Other, :Print Config Printer, or :Graph Edit, then pressed F2 (EDIT) to select text to edit.
SETTINGS	You activated a dialog box.
SIZE	You selected :Graph Edit Transform.
STAT	You selected /Worksheet Status or /Worksheet Global Default Status and 1-2-3 is displaying the corresponding status screen.
TEXT	You selected :Text Edit.

Mode Indicators (*cont.*)

Mode	Description
VALUE	You are entering a value (a number or formula).
WAIT	1-2-3 is completing a command or process.
WYSIWYG	You pressed : (colon) and 1-2-3 is displaying a WYSIWYG menu.

Status Indicators

Status	Description
CALC	Formulas in the worksheet need to be recalculated by pressing F9.
CAPS	The CAPS LOCK key is on.
CIRC	The worksheet contains a formula that refers to itself.
CMD	1-2-3 is running a macro.
END	You are using the END key.
LEARN	You pressed the ALT-F5 key to turn on the Learn feature and 1-2-3 is recording your keystrokes.
MEM	The amount of computer memory available for entering new data is low.
NUM	The NUM LOCK key is on.
OVR	The INS key has been pressed; you are in the overstrike mode.
RO	The worksheet has read-only status, and you cannot save any changes at this point.
SCROLL	The SCROLL LOCK key is on.
SST	A macro being executed in single-step mode is waiting for user input.
STEP	The single-step mode has been turned on; macros are processed one step at a time.
UNDO	The undo feature is on, canceling the last changes.

APPENDIX

B Lotus 1-2-3 Commands

Command	Description	Subcommands
/Add-In	Lets you use 1-2-3 programs to extend the features of 1-2-3.	Attach; Clear; Detach; Invoke
/Copy	Copies a range of data, including all cell formats and the protection status, to another range.	
/Data Distribution	Creates a frequency distribution of the values in a range by counting how many of the values in a range fall within specified numeric intervals.	
/Data Fill	Enters a sequence of values in a specified range. You can enter a sequence of numbers, dates, times, or percentages.	
/Data Matrix	Inverts or multiplies data matrices or solves simultaneous equations.	Invert; Multiply
/Data Query	Locates selected records in a database table.	Criteria; Delete; Extract; Find; Input; Output; Reset; Unique
/Data Parse	Separates and converts a single column of long labels into several columns of data of one or more types.	Format-Line; Go; Output-Range; Reset
/Data Regression	Predicts a value for a dependent variable based on the values for one or more independent variables.	Go; Intercept; Output-Range; Reset; X-Range; Y-Range
/Data Sort	Arranges the data in a range in the order you specify.	Data-Range; Go; Primary-Key; Reset; Secondary-Key
/Data Table	Creates tables that show how the results of formulas vary when you change the numbers used in the formulas.	1;2; 3
/File Admin	Performs file housekeeping functions such as link refreshing, shared file reservations, and tables of file information.	Link-refresh; Reservation; Seal; Table
/File Combine	Lets you incorporate data from a worksheet file on disk into the current file.	Add; Copy; Subtract
/File Directory	Changes the directory 1-2-3 uses when you save, retrieve, or list files.	
/File Erase	Erases a file on disk.	Graph; Other; Print; Worksheet

Command	Description	Subcommands
/File Import	Reads data from a text file created in another program into the current worksheet beginning at the current cell-pointer location.	Numbers; Text
/File List	Displays a list of files and subdirectories, temporarily overlaying the current worksheet.	Active; Graph; Linked; Other; Print; Worksheet
/File Retrieve	Reads a worksheet file from disk into memory.	
/File Save	Saves the worksheet data and settings in worksheet files on disk.	Backup; Cancel; Replace
/File View	Retrieves, links, and lets you scan through the contents of all 1-2-3 files and the text of any other file.	Retrieve; Link; Browse
/File Xtract	Extracts a range of data by copying the data from an active file and saving it in a worksheet file on disk.	Formulas; Values
/Graph A-F, X	Specifies the A-F data ranges, the ranges that contain the numeric data you want to graph, and the X range which places these values on the X axis.	
/Graph Group	Specifies multiple graph data ranges (X and A-F) at once, when the ranges are located in consecutive columns or rows.	Columnwise, Rowwise
/Graph Name	Lets you work with any number of graphs by retrieving graph settings whenever you want to display or change a graph.	Create; Delete; Reset; Table; Use
/Graph Options	Labels the points or bars in a graph, sets the graph display and printing to black and white or color, sets the way 1-2-3 displays lines in graphs, adds or removes grid lines in a graph, creates legends for the graph's data ranges, adds graph and axis titles, and sets the scaling options for the Y axis.	B&W; Color; Data-Labels; Format; Grid; Legend; Titles; Scale
/Graph Reset	Resets some or all of the current graph settings, returning them to the default settings.	X, A-F; Graph; Options; Ranges
/Graph Save	Saves the current graph as a .PIC file so that you can use the graph with other programs.	
/Graph Type	Sets the basic type of graph you are creating.	Bar; Features; HLCO; Line; Mixed; Pie; XY; Stacked-Bar
/Graph View	Temporarily removes the worksheet from the screen and displays the current graph on the full screen.	
/Move	Moves a range of data, including all cell formats and the protection status, to another range.	
/Print * Align	Ensures that the headers, footers, graphs, and page breaks will be in the correct spot when you print.	
	** Choose Printer, File, or Encoded (for each /Print command)*	
/Print * Clear	Resets some or all of your current printer settings.	All
/Print * Go	Sends your data to a printer or file.	

Command	Description	Subcommands
/Print * Line	Produces a line feed on a printer or in a file.	
/Print * Page	Advances the paper in the printer to the top of the next page.	
/Print * Options	Performs housekeeping tasks such as managing borders, headers, footers, margins, and page length.	Advanced; Borders; Footer; Header; Margins; Other; Pg-Length; Setup
/Print * Range	Specifies the print range, which is the data 1-2-3 prints when you select /Print Go.	
/Range Erase	Erases or clears data in a range but leaves the cell format(s) for the range intact.	
/Range Format	Sets the cell format for a range, overriding the global cell format.	, (comma); Currency; Date; Fixed; General; Hidden; Percent; +-; Reset; Sci; Text
/Range Input	Limits cell-pointer movement and data entry to unprotected cells in a range so you can enter or edit data in those cells, but no others. Works in conjunction with /Range Unprot.	
/Range Justify	Rearranges a column of labels so that the labels fit within a width you specify.	
/Range Label	Changes the alignment of labels in a range by changing their label prefix.	Left; Center; Right
/Range Name	Places a name of up to 15 characters that you can use instead of cell or range addresses in commands and formulas.	Create; Delete; Labels; Note; Reset; Table; Undefine
/Range Prot	Prevents changes to cells in a range when the worksheet(s) the range occupies are globally protected.	
/Range Search	Finds or replaces a specified string in labels and/or formulas within a range.	Both; Formulas; Labels
/Range Trans	Copies a range of data, transposing the copied data and replacing any copied formulas with their current values.	
/Range Unprot	Allows changes to a range when the worksheet containing the range is globally protected.	
/Range Value	Copies a range of data, replacing any copied formulas with their current values.	
/Worksheet Column	Sets the width of one or more columns, resets columns to the global column width, and hides and redisplays columns.	Set-width; Reset-width; Column-Range Set-Width; Hide; Display
/Worksheet Delete	Deletes one or more columns, rows, or worksheets in an active file, closing up the space left by the deletion.	Column; Row; Sheet
/Worksheet Global	Resets the default settings, column widths, cell formats, labels, recalculation, and protection.	Column-width; Default; Format; Label-Prefix; Recalculation; Protection; Zero
/Worksheet Learn	Specifies a range in which to record keystrokes to run in a macro.	Cancel; Erase; Range

Command	Description	Subcommands
/Worksheet Page	Inserts in the current worksheet a row containing a page break symbol :: which tells 1-2-3 to begin a new page when printing.	
/Worksheet Titles	Freezes rows and/or columns along the top and left edges of the current worksheet so those rows and/or columns remain in view as you scroll through the worksheet.	Both; Clear; Horizontal; Vertical
/Worksheet Windows	Splits the screen horizontally or vertically into two windows.	Clear; Horizontal; Map; Perspective; Sync; Unsync; Vertical

APPENDIX

Built-in @Functions

Statistical Functions

Function	Description
@AVG	Average of a range of values
@COUNT	Count of the number of nonblank values
@MAX	Maximum of a range of values
@MIN	Minimum of a range of values
@STD	Standard deviation of a range of values
@STDS	Sample standard deviation
@SUM	Total of a range of values
@SUMPRODUCT	Total of products of a range of values
@VAR	Variance of a range of values
@VARS	Sample variance
@DAVG	Average of fields in a database
@DCOUNT	Count of nonblank cells in a database field
@DGET	Finds a value or field in a database
@DMAX	Finds largest value in a database field
@DMIN	Finds smallest value in a database field
@DQUERY	Gives access to a function of external database
@DSTD	Standard deviation of a database field
@DSTDS	Sample standard deviation of a database field
@DSUM	Totals values in a field of a database
@DVAR	Variance in a field of a database
@DVARS	Sample variance of a database field

Date and Time Functions

Function	Description
@DATE	Serial date number of year, month, and day
@DATEVALUE	Integer portion of serial date number
@DAY	Day of the month between 1 and 31
@MONTH	Integer portion of month serial date number
@NOW	Current date and time on computer's clock
@TODAY	Current serial date number on computer's clock
@YEAR	Integer portion of year serial date number
@D360	Number of days between two serial date numbers
@HOUR	Integer portion of hour serial time number
@MINUTE	Integer portion of minute serial time number
@SECOND	Integer portion of second serial time number
@TIME	Time passed since 12:00 am
@TIMEVALUE	Converts time into serial time number

Financial Functions

Function	Description
@CTERM	Calculates the number of compounding periods
@DDB	Calculates double-declining depreciation
@FV	Calculates the future value of an annuity
@IRR	Calculates the internal rate of a return
@NPV	Calculates the net present value of cash flows
@PMT	Calculates the payments needed to pay off a loan
@PV	Calculates the present value of equal cash flows
@RATE	Calculates the interest rate to grow an investment
@SLN	Calculates straight-line depreciation
@SYD	Calculates sum-of-the-years digits depreciation
@TERM	Calculates the number of payment periods
@VDB	Calculates the double-declining balance depreciation

Mathematical Functions

Function	Description
@ABS	Yields the absolute value
@ACOS	Yields the arc cosine of an angle
@ASIN	Yields the arc sine of an angle
@ATAN	Yields the 2-quadrant arc tangent of an angle
@ATAN2	Yields the 4-quadrant arc tangent of an angle
@COS	Yields the cosine of an angle
@EXP	Yields the value *e* to the xth power
@INT	Yields the integer portion of a value
@LN	Yields the natural log of a value
@LOG	Yields the common log of a value
@MOD	Yields the remainder of a division operation
@PI	Yields the numeric value of *pi*
@RAND	Yields a random number between 0 and 1
@ROUND	Yields a value rounded to *n* places
@SIN	Yields the sine of an angle
@SQRT	Yields the positive square root of a value
@TAN	Yields the tangent of an angle

Logical Functions

Function	Description
@FALSE	Returns a logical value of 0 for a false condition
@IF	Evaluates condition and returns *x* if condition is true and *y* if condition is false
@ISAAF	Returns 1 for defined add-in @function, 0 otherwise
@ISAPP	Returns 1 for currently loaded add-in, 0 otherwise
@ISERR	Returns 1 for ERR, 0 otherwise
@ISNA	Returns 1 for NA, 0 otherwise
@ISNUMBER	Returns 1 for value or blank cell, 0 otherwise
@ISRANGE	Returns 1 for defined range name or valid range address, 0 otherwise
@ISSTRING	Returns 1 for string, text formula, or address containing either, 0 otherwise
@TRUE	Returns a logical value of 1 for a true condition

Cell Functions

Function	Description
@	Returns contents of cell location referred to
@?	Indicates unknown @function from an add-in program
@CELL	Returns data about a cell or its contents
@CELLPOINTER	Returns data about the current cell or its contents
@CHOOSE	Finds specified value or label in a list
@COLS	Counts the columns in a range
@COORD	Creates an absolute, mixed, or relative cell address from values provided as arguments
@ERR	Returns the value ERR
@HLOOKUP	Returns contents of a cell in a specified row or table
@INDEX	Returns a value in a cell located at a specified row or column
@INFO	Returns system information
@NA	Returns the value NA
@ROWS	Counts the rows in a range
@SHEETS	Counts the number of worksheets in a range
@SOLVER	Returns information about the status of Solver
@VLOOKUP	Returns the contents of a cell in a specified column of a table

String Functions

Function	Description
@CHAR	Returns the character that corresponds to LICS code (Version 2.3/2.4) or LMBCS (Version 1.1 for Windows)
@CLEAN	Removes control characters from a string
@CODE	Returns the LICS code (Version 2.3/2.4) or LMBCS (Version 1.1 for Windows) for the first character in a string
@EXACT	Returns 1 if string1 and string2 are the same, otherwise 0
@FIND	Returns the position of the first occurrence of one string inside another string
@LEFT	Returns the first *n* characters in a string
@LENGTH	Counts the number of characters in a string
@LOWER	Converts all letters in a string to lowercase
@MID	Returns the first *n* characters starting at a specified character
@N	Returns entry in the first cell of a range as a value

String Functions (*cont.*)

Function	Description
@PROPER	Converts the first letter in each word to uppercase and the remainder to lowercase
@REPEAT	Duplicates a string a specified number of times
@REPLACE	Replaces *n* characters in the original string
@RIGHT	Returns the last *n* characters in a string
@S	Returns entry in the first cell of a range as a label
@STRING	Converts a value into a label with *n* decimal places
@TRIM	Removes leading, trailing, and consecutive spaces
@UPPER	Converts all letters in a string to uppercase
@VALUE	Converts a number entered as a string to a value

Formulas for @Functions

@CTERM	$\dfrac{\ln(\textit{future value} / \textit{present value})}{\ln(1 + \textit{interest rate})}$	where: ln = natural logarithm
@DDB	$\dfrac{\textit{book value in that period} \times 2}{\textit{life of the asset}}$	
@DSTD	$\sqrt{\dfrac{\Sigma(\textit{ith value in field} - \textit{average of values in field})^2}{\textit{number of values in field}}}$	
@DSTDS	$\sqrt{\dfrac{\Sigma(\textit{ith value in field} - \textit{average of values in field})^2}{\textit{number of values in field} - 1}}$	
@DVAR	$\dfrac{\Sigma(\textit{ith value in field} - \textit{average of values in field})^2}{\textit{number of values in field}}$	
@DVARS	$\dfrac{\Sigma(\textit{ith value in field} - \textit{average of values in field})^2}{\textit{number of values in field} - 1}$	
@FV	$\textit{periodic payment} \times \dfrac{(1 + \textit{periodic interest rate})^n - 1}{\textit{periodic interest rate}}$	where: n = number of periods
@NPV	$\sum_{i=1}^{n} \dfrac{\textit{series of cash flows in range}}{(1 + \textit{periodic interest rate})^i}$	where: i = current iteration (1-n)
@PMT	$\textit{principal} \times \dfrac{\textit{periodic interest rate}}{1 - (1 + \textit{periodic interest rate})^{-n}}$	where: n = term
@PV	$\textit{periodic payment} \times \dfrac{1 - (1 + \textit{periodic interest rate})^{-n} - 1}{\textit{periodic interest rate}}$	where: n = term
@RATE	$\left(\dfrac{\textit{future value}}{\textit{present value}}\right)^{1/n} - 1$	where: n = term

Formulas for @Functions (*cont.*)

@SLN $$\frac{(\textit{cost of the asset} - \textit{salvage value of the asset})}{\textit{useful life of the asset}}$$

@STD $$\sqrt{\frac{\Sigma\,(\textit{ith item in list} - \textit{average of values in list})^2}{\textit{number of items in list}}}$$

@STDS $$\sqrt{\frac{\Sigma\,(\textit{ith item in list} - \textit{average of values in list})^2}{\textit{number of items in list} - 1}}$$

@SYD $$\frac{(\textit{cost of asset} - \textit{salvage value}) \times (\textit{useful life of asset} - \textit{depreciation period} + 1)}{(\textit{useful life of asset} \times (\textit{useful life of asset} + 1)/2)}$$

@TERM $$\frac{\ln\,(1 + (\textit{future value} \times \textit{periodic interest rate/periodic payment}))}{\ln\,(1 + \textit{periodic interest rate})}$$ where: ln = natural logarithm

@VAR $$\frac{\Sigma\,(\textit{ith item in list} - \textit{average of values in list})^2}{\textit{number of items in list}}$$

@VARS $$\frac{\Sigma\,(\textit{ith item in list} - \textit{average of values in list})^2}{\textit{number of items in list} - 1}$$

@VDB $$\frac{(\textit{book value in that period} \times \%\ \textit{of straight-line depreciation})}{\textit{useful life of asset}}$$

APPENDIX

D WYSIWYG Formatting Commands

Command	Description	Subcommands
:Format Bold	Adds or removes the boldface attribute from data in a range.	
:Format Color	Specifies up to seven colors.	
:Format Font	Specifies fonts for specified ranges.	
:Format Italics	Adds or removes the italics attributes from data in a range.	
:Format Lines	Adds or removes single, double, or wide lines, outlines, and 3-D effects in range.	All; Bottom; Clear; Double; Left; Outline; Right; Shadow; Top; Wide
:Format Reset	Removes all formatting applied to a range with the Format commands or Named-Style commands, returning font and color settings to the default set with the Display commands.	
:Format Shade	Adds light, dark, or solid shading to a range and removes shading from a range.	Clear; Dark; Light; Solid
:Format Underline	Adds single, double, or wide underlining to a range and removes underlining from a range.	Clear; Double; Single; Wide
:Graph Add	Includes a graph in the worksheet.	Blank; Current; Metafile; Named; PIC
:Graph Compute	Updates all graphics in the active spreadsheet file.	Arrow; Ellipse; Freehand; Line; Polygon; Rectangle; Text
:Display Colors	Specifies the colors 1-2-3 uses to display items on your screen when WYSIWYG is in memory.	Background; Cell-Pointer; Frame; Grid; Lines; Neg; Replace; Shadow; Text; Unprot
:Display Default	Creates a new set of default settings or replaces the current settings with the default display settings.	Replace; Updates
:Display Font-Directory	Specifies the font directory, the directory in which 1-2-3 looks for fonts it uses for both displaying and printing worksheets and graphics.	

Command	Description	Subcommands
:Display Mode	Lets you work with 1-2-3 in either graphics display mode or text display mode, and sets the worksheet display to black and white or color.	B&W; Color; Graphics; Text
:Display Options	Determines the display of grid lines and page breaks, worksheet frame and cell pointer, and specifies the degree of brightness for the screen display.	Adapter; Cell-Pointer; Frame; Grid; Intensity; Page-Breaks
:Display Rows	Specifies the number of worksheet rows 1-2-3 displays on the screen in graphics display mode.	
:Display Zoom	Lets you select from several worksheet display sizes.	Huge; Large; Manual; Normal; Small; Tiny
:Graph Edit	Specifies colors for a graphic and objects added to it; adds and removes arrowheads; edits and changes the font for the text, adds or removes grid lines; copies, deletes, restores, locks, and unlocks objects in the graphic; identifies one or more objects in the graphics editing window; changes the size and orientation of objects and the underlying graphic; enlarges and reduces areas of the graphics editing window.	Add; Color; Edit; Options; Rearrange; Select; Transform; View
:Graph Goto	Moves the cell pointer to a specified graph in the worksheet.	
:Graph Move	Moves the graphic to another range in the worksheet.	
:Graph Remove	Deletes a graphic from the worksheet.	
:Graph Settings	Moves and replaces graphics in the worksheet, turns the displays of graphics in the worksheet on or off, makes graphics in the worksheet transparent, and allows 1-2-3 to update automatically when the graphs are based on changes.	Display; Graph; Opaque; Range; Sync
:Graph View	Temporarily removes the worksheet from the screen and displays a graphic on the screen, except in Version 1.1 for Windows where a separate graphic window is opened.	
:Graph Zoom	Temporarily removes the worksheet from the screen and displays a specified graphic in the worksheet on the full screen.	
:Named-Style Define	Creates a named style for the WYSIWYG format in a specified cell. A named style is a collection of WYSIWYG formats taken from a single cell and then applied to one or more ranges in the current file.	
:Named-Style 1-8	Formats one or more ranges with one of the named styles you define with :Named-Style Define.	1-8
:Print Config	Sets up the configuration for the printer to use WYSIWYG characters.	Bin; 1st-Cart; Interface; Orientation; Printer; Resolution; 2nd-Cart

Command	Description	Subcommands
:Print File	Prints your data to an encoded file.	
:Print Go	Sends your data to a printer.	
:Print Layout	Controls the page layout or the overall positioning and appearance of the page.	Borders; Compression; Default; Library; Margins; Page-Size; Titles
:Print Preview	Temporarily removes the worksheet from the screen and displays the print range as WYSIWYG will format it for printing, page by page.	
:Print Range	Specifies or cancels the print range, which the data WYSIWYG prints when you select :Print Go or :Print File.	Set; Clear
:Print Settings	Specifies which pages of a print range and the number of copies to print; controls page numbering; specifies whether to print the worksheet frame and grid lines, and whether to pause the printer for manual paper feed.	Begin; Copies; End; Frame; Grid; Reset; Start; Wait
:Special Copy	Copies all WYSIWYG format in one range to another active range.	
:Special Export	Replaces the font set, all formats, named styles, and graphics in a WYSIWYG format file on disk with the formats, fonts, named styles, and graphs from the current file.	
:Special Import	Applies the formats, named styles, font set, and graphics from a WYSIWYG format file on disk to the current file.	
:Special Move	Transfers the format of one range to another range in an active file and causes the cells that originally contained the formats to revert to the default formats.	
:Text Align	Changes the alignment of labels within a text range by changing their label prefixes.	Clear; Even; Left; Right
:Text Clear	Clears the settings for a text range but does not erase the data contained in the range or change any of the formatting done to the data with :Text Reformat or :Text Edit.	
:Text Edit	Lets you enter and edit labels in a text range directly in the worksheet.	
:Text Reformat	Rearranges or justifies a column of labels so the labels fit within a text range similar to the /Range Justify command.	
:Text Set	Specifies a text range so you can use the Text commands with labels in the range.	
:Worksheet Column	Sets the width of one or more columns and resets columns to the 1-2-3 global column width.	Reset-Width; Set-Width

Command	Description	Subcommands
:Worksheet Page	Inserts or removes horizontal or vertical page breaks that tell 1-2-3 to begin a new page when printing with WYSIWYG commands.	Column; Delete; Row
:Worksheet Row	Sets the height of one or more rows which can be specified in points or automatically to accommodate the largest font in a row.	

APPENDIX

Lotus Macro Commands

Menu Development and Interactive Macro Commands

Command	Description
{MENUBRANCH *location*}	Displays in the control panel the macro menu that starts in the first cell of *location*. 1-2-3 waits for you to select an item from the menu and then branches to the macro instructions associated with that item. {MENUBRANCH} does not return control to the controlling macro when 1-2-3 completes the menu's macro instructions.
{MENUCALL *location*}	Displays in the control panel the macro menu in *location*. 1-2-3 waits for you to select an item from the menu and then calls the subroutine associated with that menu item.
{?}	Suspends macro execution to let you move the cell pointer or enter data.
{BREAKOFF}	Disables the CTRL-BREAK keys while a macro is running, protecting the macro from interruption.
{BREAKON}	Restores the use of CTRL-BREAK, undoing the {BREAKOFF} command.
{FORM *input-location,[call-table],* *[include-list],[exclude-list]*}	Suspends macro execution so that you can enter and edit data in a specified range. *Call-table* is an optional two-column range; *include-list* is an optional range that lists allowable keystrokes; *exclude-list* is an optional range that lists unacceptable keystrokes.
{FORMBREAK}	Ends a {FORM} command.
{GET *location*}	Suspends macro execution until you press a key, and then records that key in a cell called *location*.
{GETLABEL *prompt,location*}	Displays a prompt in the window specified by *prompt*, waits for a response, and enters the response as a label in a cell called *location*.
{GETNUMBER, *prompt,location*}	Displays a prompt in the window specified by *prompt*, waits for a response, and enters the response as a number (value) in a cell called *location*.
{LOOK *location*}	Checks the typeahead buffer for keystrokes and then records the first keystroke it contains as a label in *location*.
{WAIT *time-number*}	Suspends macro execution and displays the WAIT indicator until the time you specify by *time-number*.

Macro Commands that Support Sequence

Command	Description
{APPENDBELOW *target-location, source-location*}	Copies the contents of *source-location* to the rows immediately below the bottom row of *target-location*.
{APPENDRIGHT *target-location, source-location*}	Copies the contents of *source-location* to the columns immediately to the right of *target-location*.
{BLANK *location*}	Erases the contents of *location* {BLANK} but does not change the format of the cells in *location*.
{CONTENTS *target-location, source-location,[width],[cell-format]*}	Copies a value from *source-location* to *target-location* as a label. *Width* is an optional argument that specifies the width of the label 1-2-3 creates; *cell-format* is an optional argument that specifies the format of the label 1-2-3 creates corresponding to a code number.
{LET *location,entry*}	Enters a number or label in *location*. The *entry* can be a value, text, formula, or cell address that contains a value, text, or formula.
{PUT *location,column-offset,row-offset,entry*}	Enters a number or a label in a cell within *location*. *Column-offset* and *row-offset* are numbers that identify the column and row position of a cell within *location*. The *entry* can be a value, text, formula, or cell address that contains a value, text, or formula.
{RECALC *location,[condition],[iterations]*}	Recalculates the values in *location*, proceeding row by row. *Condition* is an optional argument that tells 1-2-3 to recalculate at once and then repeat the recalculation until *condition* is true. *Iterations* is an optional argument that tells 1-2-3 to perform the specified number of recalculation passes.
{RECALCCOL *location,[condition],[iterations]*}	Recalculates the values in *location*, proceeding column by column. *Condition* is an optional argument that tells 1-2-3 to recalculate at once and then repeat the recalculation until *condition* is true. *Iterations* is an optional argument that tells 1-2-3 to perform the specified number of recalculation passes.

Macro Commands that Support Selection

Command	Description
{*subroutine [arg1],[arg2]..[arg n]*}	Calls a subroutine and then returns control to the cell following the subroutine call. *Arg1* to *arg n* are optional arguments.
{BRANCH *location*}	Transfers macro control from the current macro instruction to *location* and does not return to the calling macro. {BRANCH} is not the same as {GOTO}; {GOTO} moves the cell pointer to another location while {BRANCH} transfers macro execution to the commands that begin in *location*.
{DEFINE *location1,location2,...location n*}	Specifies to store arguments for a {*subroutine*} command where *location n* is the last of several arguments in a list.

Macro Commands that Support Selection (*cont.*)

Command	Description
{DISPATCH *location*}	Transfers macro control to the cell whose address or name you specify in the *location* cell.
{FORBREAK}	Cancels a for-next loop created by a {FOR} command.
{IF *condition*}	Evaluates *condition* to determine if it is true or false. If *condition* is true, the macro continues with the next instruction in the same cell; if *condition* is false, the macro executes the next instruction in the cell below the {IF} command. {IF} commands can be stacked in subsequent cells in order to test multiple conditions.
{LAUNCH *application*}	In Version 1.1 for Windows, {LAUNCH} starts a Windows *application*.
{ONEERROR *branch-location*,[*message-location*]}	Transfers a macro to *branch-location* if certain 1-2-3 errors occur while a macro is running. *Message-location* is an optional argument which is the address or name of a cell or range, or a formula that returns the address or name of a cell or range where 1-2-3 is to store the error message.
{QUIT}	Ends a macro immediately, returning control to the user. No further instructions are executed.
{RESTART}	Cancels the return sequence of nested subroutines, ending the macro when the current subroutine ends.
{RETURN}	Returns macro control from a subroutine to the calling macro.
{SYSTEM *command*}	Temporarily halts the 1-2-3 session and performs the specified DOS command.

Macro Commands that Support Iteration

Command	Description
{*subroutine [arg1],[arg2]..[argn]*}	Calls a subroutine and then returns control to the cell following the subroutine call. *Arg1* to *argn* are optional arguments.
{BRANCH *location*}	Transfers macro control from the current macro instruction to *location* and does not return to the calling macro. {BRANCH} is not the same as {GOTO}; {GOTO} moves the cell pointer to another location while {BRANCH} transfers macro execution to the commands that begin in *location*.
{FOR *counter,start,stop,step,subroutine*}	Creates a for-next loop, repeatedly performing a call to *subroutine*. *Counter* is the address or name of a blank cell where 1-2-3 keeps track of the number of times it will run during the for-next loop; *start* is the initial value for *counter*; *step* is the value added to the counter each time 1-2-3 runs *subroutine*; and *stop* is the value that tells 1-2-3 when to terminate the for-next loop.

Macro Commands that Support Iteration (*cont.*)

Command	Description
{IF *condition*}	Evaluates *condition* to determine if it is true or false. If *condition* is true, the macro continues with the next instruction in the same cell; if *condition* is false, the macro executes the next instruction in the cell below the {IF} command. {IF} commands can be stacked in subsequent cells in order to test multiple conditions.
{RETURN}	Returns macro control from a subroutine to the calling macro.

Screen Control Macro Commands

Command	Description
{BEEP *tone-number*}	Sounds one of four tones to get the user's attention.
{BREAK}	Clears the control panel and returns 1-2-3 to the READY mode.
{FRAMEOFF}	Suppresses the display of the worksheet frame (column letters and row numbers).
{FRAMEON}	Redisplays the worksheet frame hidden by a {FRAMEOFF} command.
{GRAPHOFF}	Removes a graph displayed by a {GRAPHON} command and redisplays the worksheet.
{GRAPHON *named-graph*,[*nodisplay*]}	Displays a graph using the current settings or makes *named-graph* the current graph and displays it. {GRAPHON} displays a graph while the macro continues to run, unlike the {GRAPH} command. *Nodisplay* is the optional label you specify if you want to use the *named-graph* settings, but you do not want to display the graph.
{INDICATE *string*}	Replaces READY for another mode indicator with *string* as the mode indicator. The mode indicator continues to display *string* until 1-2-3 reaches another {INDICATE} command or until you retrieve another file.
{PANELOFF [*clear*]}	Freezes the status line and control panel until 1-2-3 encounters a {PANELON} command. *Clear* clears the control panel and status line before freezing them.
{PANELON}	Unfreezes and displays the status line and control panel.
{WINDOWSOFF}	Stops screen updates while a macro is running.
{WINDOWSON}	Cancels {WINDOWSOFF} and resumes normal worksheet display.

File Manipulation Macro Commands

Command	Description
{CLOSE}	Closes a text file that you opened with {OPEN} and saves any changes made to the file.
{FILESIZE *location*}	Counts the number of bytes in the open text file and stores that number in *location*.
{GETPOS *location*}	Retrieves the character offset position of the byte pointer and enters the number of characters between the beginning of the file and the byte pointer in *location*.
{OPEN *file-name,access-type*}	Makes a text file available for reading, writing, or both, depending on *access-type*. An open text file does not appear on the screen. *Access-type* is one of the four characters: r (read), w (write), m (modify), or a (append), or the address or name of a cell that contains one of those characters.
{READ *byte-count,location*}	Copies the number of characters specified in a *byte-count* from an open text file to *location*. *Byte-count* is a value, the address or name of a cell that contains a value, or a formula that returns a value from 0 to 240.
{READLN *location*}	Copies a line from an open text file and stores the characters in *location*.
{SETPOS *offset-number*}	Moves the byte pointer to the *offset-number* position in an open text file.
{WRITE *string*}	Copies *string* to the current byte pointer position in the open text file. *String* is a text, a text formula, or the address or name of a cell that contains a label or a text formula.
{WRITELN *string*}	Writes *string* at the byte pointer position in the open text file, adding a carriage return and line feed.

Index

WYSIWYG Graph Commands

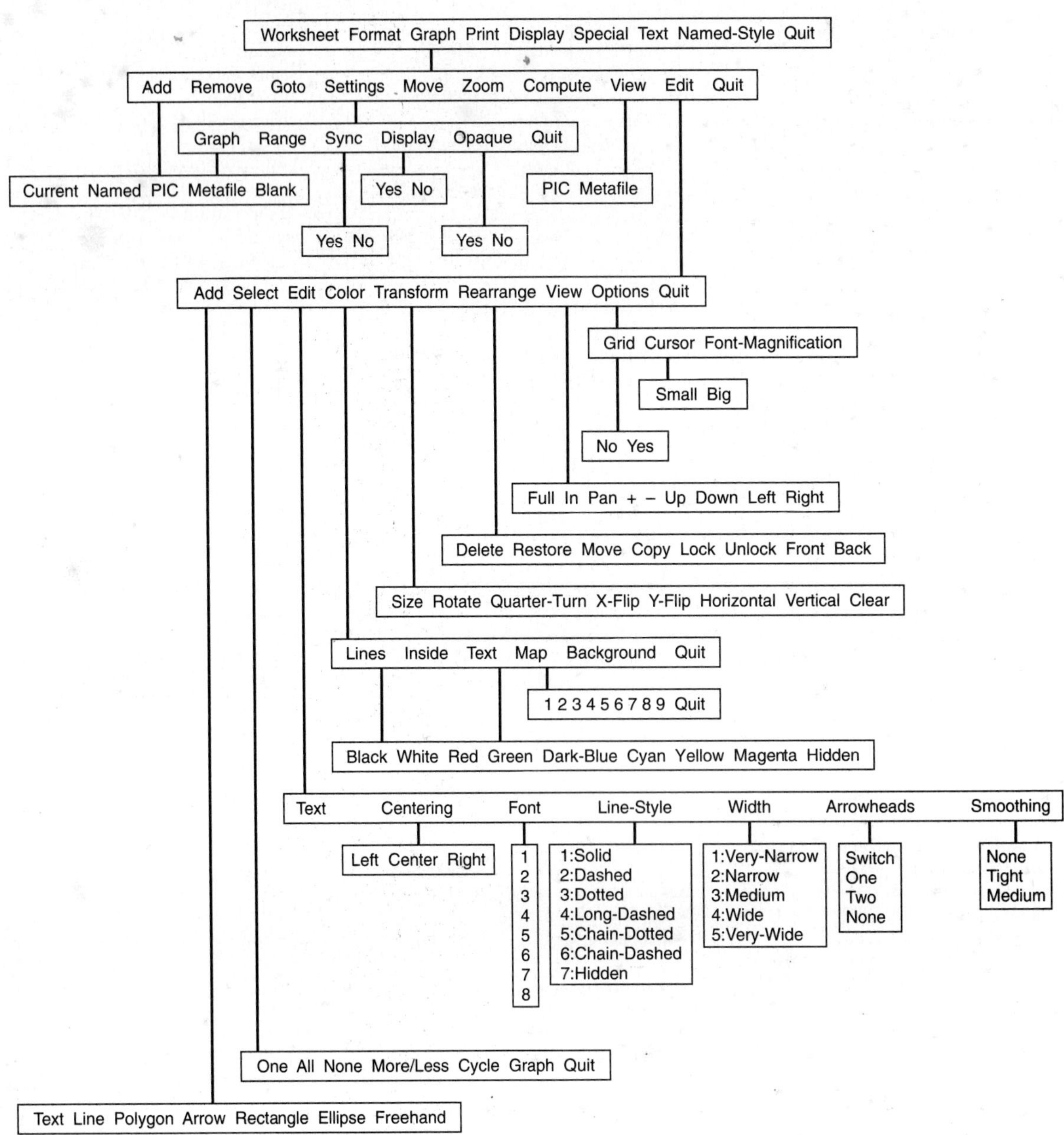